Ellangellemni...
When I Became Aware...

Eliza Cingarkaq Orr
Ben Orr
Victor Kanrilak, Jr.
Andy Charlie, Jr.

Lower Kuskokwim School District
Alaska Native Language Center

Fairbanks, Alaska
1997

Dedication

Ackiar, Theresa Hooper, was born in *Umkumiut*, a small fishcamp on *Qaluyaaq* 'Nelson Island.' The oldest child of *Nusain*, William Dull, and *Cingyukan*, Albertina Dull, she grew up in the traditional way, living in a *nep'ik*, a traditional sod dwelling, for much of the year. Her family spent falls and winters at *Negtemiut*, springs at *Umkumiut*, a small fishing and sealing camp on the Bering Sea coast, and summers at *Kaviarmiut*, a remote fishcamp on the tundra. At the age of seventeen she married *Maklak*, Edward Hooper, of *Tununeq*, and together they had and raised nine children, one of whom, *Cingarkaq*, authored this book. She was a devoted and patient mother and grand-

Ackiar, Theresa Hooper (1936-1995), of *Tununeq*. Photo by Mike Gilully, courtesy of the Edward Hooper family.

mother, a tireless worker, and a devout Catholic. For forty-two years she cared for her children and grandchildren, cut and dried the fish, butchered, stored and cooked the game, prepared the furs, sewed and made clothing, and in so many other ways tended lovingly to the needs of a large and generous family. She quietly exemplified the ideals of Yup'ik womanhood — patience, fortitude, and generosity — as well as the ideals of her Catholic faith — faith, hope, and charity. This book is dedicated to her and all *Tununermiut* who have gone before us.

Ellangellemni…
When I Became Aware…
©1997
Lower Kuskokwim School District
Alaska Native Language Center

Library of Congress Cataloging-in-Publication Data
Ellangellemni : When I became aware / [compiled by] Eliza
  Cingarkaq Orr … [et al.].
      p.   cm.
  Includes bibliographical references.
  ISBN 1-55500-061-4 (alk. paper)
  1. Yupik Eskimos—Alaska—Tununak—Folklore. 2. Yupik
mythology—Alaska—Tununak. 3. Tales—Alaska—Tununak.
4. Central Yupik language—Alaska—Tununak—Texts. I. Orr,
Eliza Cingarkaq, 1958-. II. Lower Kuskokwim School District.
III. Alaska Native Language Center.
E99.E7E45 1997   97-2509
398.2'089971—dc21   CIP

First Printing 1997   1,000 copies
Second Printing 2003   400 copies

Cover art by Xavier Lincoln; design by Rose Tomasulo and Dixon
Jones, UAF Rasmuson Library Graphics.

Lower Kuskokwim School District
P.O. Box 305
Bethel, Alaska 99559

Alaska Native Language Center
University of Alaska Fairbanks
P.O. Box 757680
Fairbanks, Alaska 99775-7680

Contents

Acknowledgments

The stories published in this book are the result of a collaborative effort involving elders of the village of *Tununeq*, the Native Village of Tununak, the Lower Kuskokwim School District, the students and staff of Paul T. Albert Memorial School, the Administration for Native Americans of the Department of Health and Human Services, the Historical Preservation Branch of the National Park Service, and various individuals in the community of Tununak. Especially deserving of our recognition and gratitude is *Iitaruaq*, Irene Reed, who has worked tirelessly with us for two years, encouraging, assisting, editing, and proofreading the *Tununeq* narratives. She has generously shared her knowledge and expertise as well as her time and substance. We owe a special debt of gratitude to the Native Village of Tununak, our collaborators and sponsors, especially Mark Charlie, John Oscar, Urban Albert, John Evan, and Teddy Angaiak, all *Tununermiut*. Gerry Kimsey, the principal of the Paul T. Albert Memorial School, and her staff welcomed us into the school and provided us with all we required to accomplish our mission. She and her staff were always kind and hospitable to our elders, making everyone connected with our project feel as though we were members of the school community. Hugh Dyment, teacher, philosopher and puppeteer, was a constant and loyal supporter whose keen interest in our work was a source of continual encouragement. We were especially fortunate to have again the illustrating talents of Xavier Lincoln and Ira Menegak, both *Tununermiuk*. Photographer and artist Andrew J. Chikoyak, *Tununermiu*, whose fine work speaks for itself, is a new contributor. We also wish to thank Irene Post, *Tununermiu*, who helped us with the logistics of having elders in the school. Finally, none of this would have been possible were it not for the elders, our teachers and mentors, who told these stories and consented to share their knowledge of the traditions and oral literature of the *Qaluyaarmiut*. In particular we wish to thank *Cuniq*, Jents Flynn; *Arnaucuaq*, Mike Angaiak; *Cakataar*, Jack Angaiak; *Uliggaq*, Susie Angaiak; *Puyangun*, Rose Charlie; and *Uyuraūrluq*, Andy Charlie, Sr. All assisted us in the translation and shared their wisdom with us.

The Lower Kuskokwim School District was, along with the Native Village of Tununak, one of our two primary supporters. Without the district's generous support and assistance none of this could have happened. We especially wish to extend our thanks to the Lower Kuskokwim Regional School Board, Superintendent Sue Hare, Administrative Assistant Susan Murphy, and Assistant Superintendent John Weise.

Throughout the project we received generous grants from the Administration of Native Americans of the Department of Health and Human Services, the Historical Preservation Grants Division of the National Park Service, and the Alaska Humanities Forum.

We obtained many of our historical photographs and photographs of *Qaluyaarmiut* people from the archives of the Anchorage Museum of History and Art, the Alaska and Polar Regions Department of the Rasmuson Library at the University of Alaska Fairbanks, and the Oregon Province Archives of the Gonzaga University Library. We particularly wish to thank Diane Brenner of the Anchorage Museum, Marge Heath of the Alaska and Polar Regions Department, and David Kingma of the Gonzaga University Library for their assistance in helping us locate photographs.

We have borrowed heavily from the ethnographic work and research of two scholars in particular: Margaret Lantis and Ann Fienup-Riordan. Through their work they have helped to clear a path for us, enabling us to better understand the meaning and significance of Yup'ik oral narrative, and for this we are deeply indebted to them.

All definitions for Yup'ik words cited in this book are from the *Yup'ik Eskimo Dictionary* (Jacobson 1984) and the *Comparative Eskimo Dictionary* (Fortescue et. al. 1994). We are also indebted to Anthony Woodbury for our method of organizing our text into a line and group format to better reflect the prosody of the original narrative performance.

At last, we wish to thank our publisher, the Alaska Native Language Center, its director Dr. Michael Krauss, and editor Tom Alton, who prepared the manuscript for publication, for their assistance in bringing all this to light.

As the compilers and translators of this present volume, we alone are responsible for all errors and inaccuracies that have come about in the production of this book.

The Authors

View of *Igvaq* along the coast of *Qaluyaaq,* Nelson Island, looking northwest from *Tununeq,* 1958. Photo by Christine Heller, courtesy of the Anchorage Museum of History and Art B91.11.406.

Ussugan, Oscar Usugan, and his *qayaq* on the sea ice, *Tununeq,* circa 1980.
Photo by Andrew J. Chikoyak.

HUNTERS AND ANIMAL HELPERS

"Lest you think I'm a person, as you go glance back at me!"
— Yup'ik saying upon encountering
and leaving an animal spirit helper

Ussugan, Oscar Usugan; *Macian,* Mathias James; and *Angakayagaq,* Andy Patrick, *Tununeq*, circa 1980. Photo by Andrew J. Chikoyak.

Food And The Social Contract

This story was narrated in the Tununak Catholic Church on March 14, 1994. It was the narrator's first time as a storyteller in this group of traditional Yup'ik elders who had been gathering every Wednesday after evening Mass to tell stories to an assembled group of elderly, middle-aged, and younger people. It is about a boy who is made blind by his grandmother, then deprived of food. After his sight is restored by a loon, he exacts vengeance on his grandmother.

It is one of the most oft-published tales of northern indigenous peoples. Another Alaskan variant was told by Anna Nelson Harry, one of the very last speakers of the Eyak language of southcentral Alaska (Krauss 1982: 85-89). Interestingly, the Eyak version and the Eastern Inuit version of the tale are quite similar. The male protagonist (a boy in Inuit, a husband in Eyak) is blind, presumably from birth; each shoots the principal big game animal of his people (a polar bear in Inuit, a moose in Eyak) guided by an immediate female relative (mother in Inuit, wife in Eyak), who then lies about his having hit the mark in order to keep all the kill for herself.

In all versions (Yup'ik, Inuit, Eyak) the offender is a primary female food provider who fails to distribute a resource which by custom must be shared. In the Eyak and Inuit versions, the motive of the female offender is stinginess; in the Yup'ik version here the narrator suggests that she acts out of laziness. In all versions, the protagonist's sight is restored by a loon diving under the water with the protagonist on its back. In the Yup'ik and Eyak versions the offenders are killed; she is eaten by killer whales in the Yup'ik version, and has her head boiled in the Eyak. In the Inuit version the offender is transformed into a whale, either a narwhal or a belukha, both food animals. In all of these stories, the consequence of hoarding is the same. The woman who fails to share food becomes food.

Uyuraũrluq draws a somewhat unique moral from his story, revealed in his commentary both at the beginning and conclusion of the tale. Although the grandmother is reprehensible for being lazy and withholding food, it is the grandson whom *Uyuraũrluq* censures because of his rash and vengeful act. As people we inevitably make mistakes, he tells his audience, but even if we are angry or upset, we must not seek revenge or recompense with evil. We must strive to ignore provocation and always try to avoid giving offense. This commandment sums up the Yup'ik law of interpersonal conduct.

On a deeper level, the descent of the loon and the restoration of the boy's sight can be interpreted as an allegory of the shaman's acquisition of what Danish ethnographer Knud Rasmussen's Iglulik informants called *qaumanɛq*, the lighting that constitutes the shaman's supernatural sight and clairvoyance. This lighting enables the shaman to penetrate the veil of ordinary reality and see and communicate with the world of spirits. As part of the Iglulik rite of initiation of shamans, the master shaman extracts the soul from the aspiring shaman's eyes, brain and entrails to entrust it to the familiar spirits. Then the master shaman procures for the neophyte an *angakua* 'his shaman,' or *qaumanɛq*. The aspiring shaman then "suddenly feels in his body, inside his head, within the brain, an inexplicable searchlight, a luminous fire, which enables him to see in the dark, both literally and metaphorically speaking, for he can now, even with closed eyes, see through darkness and perceive things and coming events which are hidden from others; thus they look into the future and into the secrets of others" (Rasmussen 1929: 112-113).

This suggests similarities with the story of the boy and the loons. In Yup'ik masks, which commonly depict the spirit world, the loon is a frequent subject. Given the loon's ability to traverse both the air and the water, it is a figure for the shaman, who is able either to descend to the infernal regions below or ascend to the celestial regions above to converse with the spirits. The boy's grandmother extracts his sight, the soul of his vision, from his eyes. His sight is restored in a symbolic enactment of death and resurrection by a spirit who has the ability to descend into the depths of the water or to ascend into the sky. When his vision is restored, it is as a type of super-vision, symbolic of shamanic clairvoyance. The notion of suffering, death, and finally resurrection of a body with supernatural elements is a common feature of shamanic initiations throughout the world (Eliade 1964).

Uyuraurluq calls his story a *quliraq*. As we shall see later on, when he narrates the story "*Tulukaruller:* The Mischievous Raven," he defines *qulirat* as 'fiction,' 'fairy tale,' or the kind of story where anything can happen.

Curiralria, Lucy Tom, from *Niugtaq,* Newtok, fishing for tomcod near *Tununeq,*
circa 1980. Photo by Andrew J. Chikoyak.

IINGILNGUQ TUNUTELLGEK-LLU

Uyuraurluq Tununermiu

***

1
Ii-i, quliramek quliritulliniata,
wiinga qulirat augkut amlleret
unimanka,
taugaam tua-i
quliramun piqapigtenrilengraan
mat'umun
wangkuta,
maa-i wangkuta umyuarteqluta,
ernerpak pilaucimta
taringvaguarcestii naugga
waten yuugurallemteni
qanirtuumalriakut
una umyuarput
maligarcesqevkenaku.

2
Cali-llu
waten yuugurallemteni
ilavut,
ciuqlirput
wall'u kinguqlirput,
umyugaa navgualuku pisqevkenaku
taugaam maligtengnaqu'urluku yuusqelluta.

***

3
Tua-llu waniwa
ayagnirlua quliramek pilliniata;
tamalkiqapigtenrilengraan ayagniqatartua taukugnek
waten tutgarrlugaquralriignek.

4
Tua-i

THE BLIND BOY AND THE TWO ARCTIC LOONS[1]

Andy Charlie of Tununak

***

1
Yes, *qulirat* have been part of our oral tradition,
but I am beginning to forget a lot of
these traditional stories;
however,
even though this doesn't exactly pertain
to this story,
[what I'm about to say is a commentary] on our
reflections:
This will enable [us] to understand about what's happening today,
for example,
that throughout our lives,
we are admonished
not to act
on impulse [but to consider things first].
2
Furthermore,
as we continue on in life,
we ought not to perturb[2]
any one among us,
whether an elder
or one of our posterity,
but to continue on in life trying to live harmoniously.

***

3
So now,
since traditional stories are being told, I shall begin;
even though it may not be given in entirety, I shall start with those two
who were grandchild and grandmother.
4
So

7

maa-i
taukuk yuullinilriik
tutgarrlugaqelriik, tauna tua-i tutgarii angutnguluni.

5
Imumek tua-i
tamaa-i miktellrani taum
maurluan
canek anglicaqcaarallinia waten maaken nunam qainganek.
Naugaqata makut nunam qaingani naunraat,
quagcit,
cat-gga tua-i egaluki pitukait, cuassaaruluki pitukait, tamakunek
    tayim' nerevkangnaqu'urluku anglicarturallinia.

6
Cali-ll' tua-i
caneg' makunek negirturluni
tengmianek—wangkuta tengmianek pitukput yaqulget.
Makut tengmiat yualuyagait,
iruita yualuyagait
yaqurrita-llu yualuyagait,
kinercirturarraarluki,
pinevqurluki,
qipiurluki,
kuvyaurciaqluni.

7
Tua-i kuvyaurciami cali
waten kiagmi
tamakutgun cali neqa'arnek
tamakut
naumrruyugaat avuliqa'aqluki
anglicarturallinikii tauna tutgarrlugani.

8
Makut maani tutgarrlugaqelriit,
waniwa-qa nunalgutaita-llu takumcuaquluki piyuitelallruit tamaani?
    Qaill' pilartat?

***

9
Tua-i-'m tauna im' tutgarii pinariani,
anglinariani, piyugngariami,
pinariani,
pingnatulliniuq maaten maaken nunamek
nuqlitevkenani.

here those two lived,
the grandchild and grandmother,
her grandchild being a boy.
5
When
he was small that
grandmother of his
struggled to raise him using whatever grew on land.
Whenever these grew on the land, that is, cloudberries,
sourdock,
whatever could be cooked, wild greens that could be cooked, with
    these she tried to nourish him and raise him.
6
Also
she constructed a net
from [the sinew] of geese—the birds that we call *tengmiat.*
Using the short strands of sinew of the geese,
the short strands of sinew from their legs
and the short strands of sinew from their wings,
after drying them,
she separated them
and twisted them
and would make them into a net.
7
So since she had made the net,
during the summer
she supplemented
his leafy diet
with some fish;
that's how she raised and nurtured her poor dear grandson.
8
These poor grandmothers and grandchildren,
didn't the people living there in the same village with them feel pity
    for them? How did they usually treat them?

***

9
And so when the time had come for that grandson of hers,
when it was time for him to be grown up, when he became able,
when it was time for him to go out hunting,
he found that he didn't have any trouble
catching game from the land.

Canek ayallra tamarmi apqiitnek pitarluni.
Ut'rinayuunani
tua-i callra tamarmi
anguluni.
10
Tua-i tayim' tuaten yuulutek kaigyugnairullutek maurlua-llu
    makugtaryugnairulluni yuilqumek waten maaken nunam
    naumrruyuinek.
Kaigyugnairullutek tukerngan tauna
pisteñi.
11
Tauna-am tua-i maurlullrii
qaillun tuaten ayuqeng'ermi umyuarteqtullinilria, umyuarteqluni-gg'
    tua-i,
caarkani amllerissiyaangata
qaillun iqlumek umyuangelliniuq tauna maurlua
taum tutgarami tungiinun.
(Maa-i tutgaraput wangkuta tua-i cakneq iluirviinaki
tangvakallemteñi tangvakput.)
12
Taugken-gguq tauna imna
tutgarrlugii
tamaani pingnaqu'urallermini
yaatmegni nanvami,
nanvak taukuk akulnguyarlutek,
tunutellgegnek tuani tangerturalliniaquq allamiaqan nancuunatek
    tekitaqamek tuanterrlainarlutek.
Taum-llu tua-i elliin
pingnatugyaurteng'ermi ilangciuryugnaunakek waten-llu
    kayangirlutek pingraagnek kayanguissaaglukek-llu piyuunakek
taugaam ayaggaarluni
waten pitaminek taquaminek-llu—
aviukar-qa nallunritarci?—waten
neqkuinermek qantaminek nanvam ceñiinun
tua-i-gguq aviukaqluni elliiqalartuq,
wall'u pitami ilarrayagaanek cali pupeskaulluni carrarmek tua-i cali
    tamaavet elliiqerluni.
Ilangciuyuunakek-llu taukuk tunutellgek;
waten aaraurangraagnek-llu mallguingermikek ilangciyuunakek.

Every time he went out, there was a *pitaq* 'a catch.'
He never returned empty-handed;
every time he went out
he caught something.
10
So they lived like that, no longer being hungry, and his grandmother
    no longer had to endure the hardship of gathering vegetation
    from the land.
They were no longer hungry now that her helper
had come of age.
11
Now that old grandmother of his
was thinking, even though she was reliant on him, she thought
that since she had so much to do [caring for the catch],
that grandmother started to harbor wicked thoughts
towards her grandson.
(In the short time we are with our grandchildren we
treat them with unconditional love.)

12
That grandson
of hers, it was said,
when he began to hunt
in an area beyond them at a certain pond,
where there was a strip of land between those two ponds,
he would see a pair of loons[3] every year in the same place, since
    every time they arrived they always went there.
And so
although he had started to hunt, he left them alone and even when
    they laid eggs he never went after their eggs;
but, on the contrary, after hunting
he would take from his catch or provisions—
do you know what '*aviukaq*' is?—he
would take a tiny piece of food from his bowl
and offer it to them by placing it on the edge of the pond,
or he would pinch a little bit off from his catch and leave it there.
He never bothered those two loons;
even if they were wailing or if he went near them, he left them alone.

***

13
Tua-i picim iliini tauna maurlua
qaillun umyuarteqluni, inerquutaqapiarmek
ukanirpak niitetukemteńek,
tauna tua tutgarami iik, qaviluku, qavaani,
kenillrem araanek,
qamellranek,
iik tua-i kevillinilukek qavaani tua-i,
iik taum tutgarami!
14
Tauna im' qavarraarluni tutgarii
tupalliniuq
tua-i qaill' kiarcesciiganani iigminek nangteqeqapiarluni.
Tua-i qaillun ca-llu man' tangerciiganaku tua-i iigminek
qakemkugnek asqialliqluni.
15
Tua-i taum maurluan tuaten iigminek assiilliqurallrani
waten
nerevkarturallermini,
kiituani qanlanglliniuq
neqkairutniluku.
Tua-i cakuinrayagarnek neqkaarainek pilangluku.
Ellii taŭgken umyuarteqaqluni,
"Aling imkurugaas-kiq pingnatukenganka
cauluteng waten cukaluteng ak'a nang'at?"
16
Neq'rugaat, kinengyagugaat, uqurugaat, ak'a nangluteng tamaa-i,
nangniluki
kainiqevkanglliniluku tamaa-i iigminek
arenqialliqurallrani.

***

17
Pivakarluni tua-i
taukug' imkuk
tunutellgek umyugaanun kanangelliniuk imkuk aviukarquratukegni.
18
Arenqiarucami tua-i waten up'nerkaq qakem' kiagluni qaillun pillrani,
aneqcaarluni-am tua ellamun pillermini

***

13

Then one day his grandmother
thought of doing him mischief, violating a very serious prohibition
which we used to hear about since time immemorial.[4]
Into her grandson's eyes, as he slept, while he was sleeping,
she placed ashes from the fire pit,
some of the ashes,
stuffing his eyes with them as he slept,
the eyes of her own grandson!

14

Having slept, that grandson
woke up
and he was unable to look around and was suffering excruciating pain.
He was unable to see anything around him and was in agony
on account of his eyes being painfully obstructed.[5]

15

While he was thus afflicted
and
as his grandmother continued to feed him,
she finally began saying
that he was running out of food.
She started giving tiny portions of food.
But he would think to himself,
"*Aling*, I wonder why all the food I've been catching
is disappearing so quickly?"

16

She said that a lot of the fish, a lot of the dried meat, a lot of the oil
      had already been consumed
and was already gone
and she made him suffer hunger
while his eyes were thus afflicted.

***

17

As time passed
the thought of those two loons
to whom he had made food offerings came to mind.

18

Since he felt restless, when spring turned to summer
and when he managed to find his way outside,

atam tua-i caqerluni niiskengaqellinikeg-am taukuk aaraurallragni
    ama-i imumi tuani pivimegni nanvami.
19
Tua-i caqerluni arenqialami
taum nanvam tungiinun
aurrurluni ayakcaaralliniuq tua tumekngalkiignun, tumekngalkiinun.

20
Tua-i
uitanrilami, tunglirnera nallunrilamiu,
tua-i tekitellinia tauna aaraurallragni. Maa-i-llu man' nanvam ceńii
    waten piurallermini maa-i tua tekilluku
nanvaucia-llu tua-i nallunrirluku; camkuk-llu cama-i, "Quaq, quaq,
    quaq," qalriaguralriik.
Qaqauraurlutek tua-i piaqlutek.
21
Atam tua-i pivakarluni
tuaten piviirluni
qanrutlinikii taum, "Aling arenqiapaa-ll' elpeni!
Tua-i anuurlurpet kat'um umyuarrliqluni tuaten elliqiiten

Caingilnguq, Allen Chikoyak, with his first *tungunquq* 'bearded seal,' *Tununeq,*
circa 1980. Photo by Andrew J. Chikoyak.

it happened that he heard those two loons when they were wailing
over there at the pond where they usually were.

19

Then once, since he couldn't sit still anymore,
the poor thing crawled despite difficulty in the direction of that pond,
in what seemed to be their direction, in what seemed to be the
direction [of the noise].

20

So

since he wasn't able to sit still and knew the direction to go,
he reached them as they were wailing. Feeling his way along,
he reached the edge of the pond
and realized where he was; those two down there were crying out,
"*Quaq, quaq, quaq.*"
They were making *quaq-quaq* noises.[6]

21

In a while
one of the loons came right up to him
and told him, "*Aling arenqiapaa*! You poor unfortunate thing!
Your grandmother down there has malevolently made you into what
you are

15

tua-i." Aũgna-ll' ava-i qanrutekluku,
"Carugarnek taipakalpet tamakut mernullni pitekluku
tua-i qaillun
tuaten anuurlurpet iigken
tuaten tua-i arallermek kevirngakek tua-i tuaten ellilriaten."

22
Alangaarlun' cakneq umyuamikun taumun maurluminun tuaten
    pianritellni umyuaqluku; ellii-llu qaillun
qanrut'laani qaillun umyuarrliqsugnaunani yuuguraami elliinun.

23
Atam tua-i piqerluni pillinia tunuminun pamavet
elavesqelluku.
Elavngan tua-i qaũraarturaqerluni anglluutelliniluku tua-i tayima
    tua-i-ll'
pugucamiu pillinia, "Tua-llu-qa tua-i qaillun kiartellren ayuqa?"
Pilliniuq tuarpiaq tang man'a tanqigmek akiugcarpiaqalria kiartellra.
Tuamte-ll' tua-i qaũraarturaqerluni tuamte-ll' tua-i anglluulluku tua
    mer'em akuliikun
tua-i ayaulluku
tuamte-ll' tua-i pugulluku.
Tuaten tua-i tallimarqunek
pillinia,
tallimarqunek anglluutaqluku uisngaluku, anglluulluku merkun
    ayautaqluku.
Tallimiitni tua-i kiarrluni tua pilliniuq tua-i tangvagluku man'a tua-i.
24
Tua-i pillinia taum quyaluku. (Aa!) Tuani ima tanem pikii, "Imumirpak
pingnatungerraanerpenek iquklunuk nerevkarpakaqevkuk
taquarpenek pitarpenek-llu
maurlurpenun iquklunuk." Tamakuquinrayagarteggun
aviukaqellmikun tua-i carugarmek cikitullinilukek taukuk
    tunutellgek.

25
Tua-i imna qaneryaraq: 'Yuuyuksuarpenga, kingyaqia!' Ayagluni
    kingyalliniuq tunutellgek unkuk imuceturraq qaũraarturalriik
    kuimaarlutek.
Tuaten tua-i ikayurluku, anirturluku.

now!" And it told him about what had happened,
"Because you had been bringing back a lot of game and she got sick
    and tired of dealing with it,
your grandmother
stuffed your eyes
with ashes and left you like that."
22
He was astonished, never having thought that his own grandmother
    could possibly have done that to him; he himself, on account
of what she taught him, had never in his life harbored evil
    thoughts towards her.
23
Then the loon told him to crouch down
on its back.
When he crouched down, it *quaq*-ed for a moment and then plunged
    under the water with him
and when it emerged, it asked him, "Well, how is your sight?"
He said it was as though he could see traces of light.
Again after *quaq*-ing for a moment, it plunged down with him into
    the midst the of water
and again it reemerged
with him.
It did that
five times,
diving with him under the water five times, taking him under water
    while he had his eyes open.
After the fifth time he could see all around him.
24
Then it thanked him. (*Aa*, I just remembered!) Before diving with
    him, the loon had said to him,
"Ever since you became able to hunt you have been including us,
    giving us food to eat
from your provisions and your catch,
including us along with your grandmother." In giving them those
    tiny portions[7]
as a food offering he was apparently giving a great amount to those
    two loons.
25
There's that saying: 'Lest you think I'm a person, as you go glance
    back at me!' As he went he looked back and saw those two
    loons swimming and *quaq*-ing as usual.[8]
That's how they helped him, saving him.

***

26
Naugg' maa-i
qaneryarautulria (qeckaq'erluku)
una-gguq kinguqliqengramteggu, ciuqliqengramteggu umyugaa
navegyaqunaku,
navgutmek-gguq imiryaqunakek ciutek.
27
Tauna-gguq tua-i tuaten pitangermi carpagtun pitauq.
Wall'u aipaakun:
Quyalingnaqu'urqiu
ciuqlin,
kinguqliqngerpeggu,
quyalingnaqu'urluku!
Tua-i taun' amllertuq!

***

28
Tua-i utercami
iterpailegmi imkut neqivitek
yurvillinii tua-i imuceturraq cakaniumaluarpegnateng neqet,
uqurugaat, kinertat, cat.
29
Tua-i nekayussiyaagami tua upluni,
tauna imna maurluni
—waten tua-i qanrumatuuq—
uyaqurrikun napirluku cangraan, pingraan,
epsugnairulluku-gg' tua pilliani tuaten pilria, tua ketmun
anguarulluku imarpigkun ayautenga'artellinia
unavet tua ketmun.
Ungungssit cali tamakut tekitelkek,
ugaani tua-i tauna pitarkain nuyurqenritem,
ungungssit tekitaarturluki
ukunun tekitaqluni, ukunun tekitaqluni, ukunun tekitaqluni!

Yuarutengqertuq. Yuarutii-llu-qa aturyugngaaqa?
30
Tua-i tamaa-i,
tamaa-i kessigilutek tamakunun tekitaanglutek.

***

26

For instance, even to this day
there is a saying (to jump ahead a bit):
whether individuals are young or old, do not break their minds
or fill their ears with anything malicious.[9]

27

Although it may be a small thing, it may in fact turn out to be huge.
To put it another way:
Endeavor to make your elder
happy,
or anyone younger than you as well,
endeavor to make them happy!
That would be enough!

***

28

So when he returned,
before going into the house he checked their food cache,
and it was just as it was before with a lot of fish, oil, dried food,
    and other things.
29

Because his feelings were so badly hurt, he made preparations
and took that grandmother of his
—it was said like this—
securing her by the neck while she fought and struggled,
taking precautions so she wouldn't suffocate, and he started towing
    her down there out into the open ocean, paddling her further
out away from the land.
And whenever they came across different species of animals,
he would go right up to these animals
on account of the fact that his prey was not skittish of him,
and he would come up to these, and he would come up to these, and
    he would come up to these!

There's a song to it. And can I sing that song?
30

And so they continued on,
getting farther away from the shore, and they started to come across
    those animals.

Tua-i taum-gguq tua-i anuurluan levaaminek tauna tuqlurturalaraa
   tamaa-i anglicaqcaarallermini, levaaminek.
Tua-i qiaūrlurluni tauna
anuurlua qiaqcaaralliniuq. Qianiaqamegteki-ll'-am makut qulirat
tua-i aturturtelluki qiavkatukait.
Atuqcaarluni pilliniuq tua aturluni:

Le-vaa-a, le-vaa, le-vaa
Le-vaa-a, le-vaa, le-vaa
Le-vaa-a, le-vaa, le-vaa-ai!
31
Canun tayim' ungungssit iliitnun tekiteqarraallemegnun
   piyaaqellinia, "Levaa, tamakunun pikia!"
Taum tua tutgarrlugiin ilangcivkenaki cenvutekluki tamakut
   kiturturluki ayallinilun' tua-i.
Tua-i imkut imarpiim unguvalriari qaqilluki, tekiteqatarqamegneki
   tamakunun pisqessaaqaqluni, kituraqluki.
Tua-i arrlugnun tekiteqataamek,
aūg'umeg-am ava-i aturluni:

20

It was said that his grandmother used to call him her *levaaq* when
    she was raising him, calling him her *levaaq*.[10]
His poor old grandmother
was crying, she was really crying. In the traditional stories when
    they say they are crying,
they indicate the crying with a song.
The poor old thing cried to him:

Le-vaa-a, le-vaa, le-vaa
Le-vaa-a, le-vaa, le-vaa
Le-vaa-a, le-vaa, le-vaa-ai![11]
31
When they came to the first animals she said to him, "*Levaa*, give
    me to those!"
That grandson of hers ignored them as if they weren't even there
    and passed them by.
They passed every living thing in the ocean; every time they were
    about to reach a group of animals, she would implore him
    to give her to them, but he would just pass them by.
Then when they were about to reach the killer whales,
she sang that song:

Agayuur, Cecelia Aluska, and *Carriralria*, Peter Aluska, with children *Tanqiar*,
Leo Aluska (front left), *Iraluq*, Godaliva, and Nellie (baby). Photo by Christine
Heller, courtesy of the Anchorage Museum of History and Art B91.11.414.

Le-vaa, le-vaa, le-vaa
Le-vaa, le-vaa, le-vaa
Le-vaa, le-vaa, le-vaa-ai!
Levaa, tamakunun piyaqun-nii!
32
Tekicamek caviggaminek nangcautaa kepluku unilluku-ll' egmian-llu
    arrluut cik'arulluku.
33
Tua-i nerluku tua-i cik'arulluku.
Tauna tua-i-am yun'erraq, tutgarrlugii, utertelliniuq
    tuavet nunaminun.
Tekicaaqelriim tua-i caarkaunani, callerkaunani,
kitumek-llu aipaunani, callerkaunani.
Qessanayuum tua-i tull'uku
angtuam cakneq.

***

34
Tua-i waten aũgna wii pitaluku, aũgna ava-i quliraquiner
    ciuqliuluku qanrutkaqa,
takluku pinrilengramku.
Taktuamek piqarraaquma elluarrlua pingaitelqa umyuaqluku.
35
Waniw'
yuilqurrunrilengraan cangnatugyaraunrilengraan
    taringcetaaruterpaungan aũgna,
qaneryararpak amlleq qemangqalriatun ayuqngaku.
Qanirtuumalriakut
ernerpak:
ak'allaurtengramta,
ak'allaurtenrilengramta,
ayagyuangramta alarcaraq una pikngamteggu.
36
Ciin-kiq?
37
Alarculartukut iliini erenrem, iliini, piciryaraunrilngurmun,
alarrluta, ukverluta allamun.
Waten-llu kinguqliput makut piarkaqenrilkeput wall'u ciuqliput
ciutait imirluki akeqnerrlugutmek.

Le-vaa, le-vaa, le-vaa
Le-vaa, le-vaa, l-evaa
Le-vaa, le-vaa, le-vaa-ai!
Levaa, don't give me to tho-o-se!
32
When they got there, he cut the line with his knife, leaving her there
    and right away the killer whales closed in on her.
33
So they closed in on her and ate her.
Then that young man, her grandson, returned to his home.
When he got there, he had nothing to do and didn't know what to
    do;
he had no companion and he didn't know what to do.
He was overcome
with great remorse.

***

34
That is the extent of that short *quliraq*, the first one I have
    told,
although I didn't make it lengthy.
If I told a long one to start off with, I think I would not have done it well.
35
Now then,
even though it's not a story about the wilderness or a way of life,
    it serves as a good example to broaden understanding
because it contains important rules and sayings.
To this very day
we are instructed thus:
although we may be old,
although we may be middle-aged,
although we may be young, we will inevitably make mistakes.[12]
36
Why, I wonder?
37
Some days we accidentally make mistakes and do something that
    isn't the right thing,
committing errors and believing otherwise.
And those who are younger than we are, whom we ought not to
    trouble, or our elders,
we fill their ears with threats.

Tuaten-gga piarkaunritlerput niiskeput amllerqunek.
Ayagyuangramta,
ayagyuanrilengramta waten,
ak'allaurtengramta
una alarcaraq pikliniamteggu.
38
Waten qanrami:
Umyuan caqapigtengraan
atuugarkaunrilngurmek
qaneryaqunak!
Wall'u umyuan caqapigtengraan
akinaurutkarpenek kiarrluten
piciunrilngurkun akinauriyaqunak!
Taũgaam manivkangnaqu'urluten yuukina!
39
Ciutegpeggun-llu yuum kia pingraaten
pellugtelluku akiakun
nallunguarturluku.
Cat-llu neplilriit
piciunrilngurmek-llu pilriit,
yuullerpet yaatiikun allakun pilriit,
ilaganrilngerpeki
cavkenani.
Waten taũgaam man'a yuuguralleq tua-i camek cimiqetaarpegnaku
    pingnaqluku
pisqaakut, pisqessaaqaakut ernerpak!
Arenqiatukut taũgaam alarcugtukut
ak'allaungramta,
ayagyuangramta,
qukaani uitangramta.
40
Man'a maa-i
survival-aamun pimanrilengraan
qanruteksuumirluku
ayuqucim mat'um ikayuutekenra umyuaqluku qanrutkeqa'arqa;
    carrauluku taũgaam piyaqliama waniw' qanertua.
Tua-i waten pitaluku piunga. Quyana!

We hear many times that we are not supposed to do this.
Although we may be young,
although we may be middle-aged,
although we may be old,
we will inevitably make mistakes.
38
Because it is said thus:
Even though you are very angry and upset,
don't say anything
rash or ill-considered!
Or even if you are very angry and upset,
don't seek revenge;
don't recompense with evil!
But live authentically![13]
39
Even if someone offends you,
let it go in one ear and out the other,
pretending it never happened.
As for those who are disputatious
and who are doing what is wrong,
whose way of life is distinct
and apart from yours,[14]
it is better to avoid them.
However, as they try to tell us nowadays,
try to live a good straight life without being hypocritical.[15]
But, unfortunately, we tend to make mistakes,
although we may be old,
although we may be young,
although we may be somewhere in the middle.

40
Although
this isn't related to survival,
I wanted to speak about it
since I think it will contribute to our way of life; however, since it's
    my first time, I'm not saying too much.
This is all I have to say. Thank you!

Tununermiut hunters with a catch of seals. *Nanugaq*, Simon Billy, is on the left. *Tununeq*, circa 1980. Photo by Andrew J. Chikoyak.

Hunting And The Power Of The Spirits

There was only one true vocation for a man, that of the *nukalpiaq* 'good hunter.' True, there were men who excelled in crafts, in dancing, in song-making, in storytelling, or in trading, and there were the *angalkut* 'sha-mans,' but none of these stood in the stead of the occupation of hunter. As Lantis remarks, success in hunting was the real source of wealth and the principal avenue to personal prestige (Lantis 1946: 247). Fish, although it provided the stable food base that supported the large aboriginal popula-tion, did not figure significantly in the ritual or in the stories. Rather, the pursuit of game animals gave a man distinction, and nothing rivaled the prestige of success in catching the larger food mammals, and most espe-cially among the *Qaluyaarmiut*, the *tungunkut* 'bearded seals.'

Yet seal hunting could be chancy, bound up with variables beyond the control of even the most skillful hunters. The Bering Sea Yupiit and Inuit did not use the breathing hole sealing methods of the Canadian and Polar Inuit. Instead they hunted from kayaks and skin boats, launching harpoons and bladder darts at their prey. The hunter was subject to the elements and an essentially hostile ocean environment; death by exposure or drowning was a very real possibility. Contrary ice conditions, weather, and winds could spell a poor harvest. The sea and broken ice pack is vast and seals by nature are solitary animals. Locating, killing, and retrieving sea mammals required a complex and sophisticated maritime hunting technology as well as extensive training. Seals swim with only the head above water and make small targets; they can easily elude a kayak or boat in a chase. Further-more, they can retreat to the depths of the ocean, with hardly a clue left to indicate their whereabouts. When killed, they often sink if not well se-cured with a harpoon, and even if struck with a harpoon, they can escape to the broken ice pack, where they may break off a harpoon, tear it loose, or hide and die in the lees of the pack ice. And last but not least are the prob-lems associated with butchering large mammals on the ice and transport-ing the meat and hide back to the safety of land.

Thus, the supernatural figured heavily in the success of a hunter. Skill, experience and perseverance alone were insufficient, since the animal, with a mind and inclinations of its own, had some choice in the matter. Consequently, people were careful to placate the animal souls and cultivate a right relation with the game animals. Among the numerous gestures of respect shown to the animal remains were the avoidance of ritual pollution, the careful consumption of the flesh, and burial of the bones in a hallowed place. Besides observance of the animal soul feasts, *Nakaciuryaraq* 'The Bladder Festival' being the most important, there are the various first catch ceremonies, still observed today, which propitiate the animal souls and help to assure future hunting success.

Among the *Qaluyaarmiut* it is customary to have a ceremonial distribution and often a feast at significant first catches, such as a boy's first seal. This is referred to as an *avegturyaraq*. If the boy's first catch is a small seal, for instance, a *nayiq* 'ring seal' or an *issuriyagaq* 'yearling spotted seal,' the mother might prepare a feast, cooking the entire seal, and serve *akutaq* and *assaliaq* 'fried bread,' which are customary at any feast. The boy himself eats nothing of his first catch, but rather it is consumed by the men present. If it is a larger seal — for example, a larger *nayiq* 'ring seal,' an *issuriq* 'spotted seal,' an *amirkaq* 'young bearded seal,' or a *tungunquq* 'bearded seal' — the meat and blubber are distributed among the older men to take to their homes. The family may have a feast of cooked food for the elders as well. Thus, the first catch of any species in a hunter's life span is eaten by and distributed among the old men of the village. It is common to celebrate a boy's first kill or a girl's first gathering of any kind, such as her first time for filling a container with berries or a boy's first edible bird.

Also a young man to become a *nukalpiaq* had to attend carefully to the *alerquutet* 'prescriptions' and *inerquutet* 'proscriptions' of the elders in order to make himself acceptable to the animals so they would approach him and at the critical moment allow themselves to be taken. Young men were to sleep and drink sparingly; they were to work tirelessly assisting older people, emptying chamber pots, clearing away snow from passages, all the while thinking of the seals; they were to avoid substances which could contaminate them (such as the 'bad air' of menstruating women); and they were to persist in good thoughts and avoid certain forms of contact with women.

Finally, hunters had amulets and songs of power that helped them to attract and capture animals. Writing about amulets and sympathetic magic, Margaret Lantis says:

> The concepts of spirit powers and objects containing those powers and of amuletic songs form the core of Nunivak religion.... Nothing that the people considered important could be accomplished

without the help of an inogo.... The shaman possessed stronger powers and a greater variety of powers, yet it is doubtful whether he was as essential to the spiritual contentment of and self-assurance of the people as their own amulets and songs that they had received from their ancestors (Lantis 1946: 205).

According to Lantis, just about any object or material could be used as an amulet: carved images, pebbles, roots, parts of the human body or those of animals. These were worn attached to hunting implements or carried in charm bundles within a kayak (Lantis 1946: 204-205). Undoubtedly, Sir James Frazer's principles of homeopathic magic, the Law of Similarity and the Law of Contagion, were important in determining the virtue of magical procedures and amulets, the supposition being that "like produces like, or that an effect resembles its cause, and, second, that things which have once been in contact with each other continue to act on each other at a distance...." (Frazer 1922: 12). Lantis notes that particularly powerful and intrepid hunters sought human remains, either parts of bodies, or in some cases the body of an infant, which they would secretly steal from gravesites and wrap in charm bundles to store in their kayaks, believing that human remains attracted seals (Lantis 1946: 229). Moreover, each hunter acquired from his father hunting songs and a tutelary spirit, what Lantis calls an 'inogo (perhaps from *iinru* 'amulet, charm'), the image of which was painted on the kayak, *angyaq* 'umiak,' or large harpoon shafts, and these were believed to contribute immeasurably to success in the hunt (Lantis 1946: 239).

In the story that follows, the young protagonist acquires through his father an especially potent and effective amulet, a dried wolverine skin which transforms itself into a real wolverine that stalks, kills and returns with prey. A wolverine skin is an especially apt amulet, since the *qavcik* 'wolverine' is a clever, skillful and relentless hunter. But like all magical and wondrous objects, the wolverine skin comes with a warning and stipulation. The young man is directed to urinate and thoroughly empty his bladder before he sends the skin off to stalk its prey; he must do this before and never afterward. Of course, he eventually forgets the warning and brings about the unwanted consequence.

Many of the figures and images in *Puyangun*'s story point to the existence of a deeper myth. Urine, for instance, is a cleansing agent, but it is also used to ward off and neutralize certain negative spiritual influences. Then there is the wolf who lies for five days curled by her gravesite, a figure of the psychopomp who conducts the shade of the deceased to the land of the dead. The deceased wife and mother, her face concealed, carries on her back a particularly noisy and fretful child who never ceases to cry. In the great winter ceremonies of the Yupiit, noisy and boisterous children, rollicking about naked, faces painted and concealed, signaled the advent of the spirits of the dead. *Puyangun*'s story brings to mind some of the Grimm's fairy tales, for instance, "Brother Lustig," "The Devil and the Three Golden Hairs," or "The White Snake" in which certain elements of the pre-Christian mythology and archaic religion survive as figures and reflexes in the tales, for instance, the hero's descent to the infernal regions, his ability to understand the language of animals, and the disarticulation and rearticulation of skeletons in the healing of the sick, all of which suggest the ancient "techniques of ecstasy" associated with shamanism (Eliade 1964). Is it possible that what we have here is the evidence of a proto-myth, a *qanemciq*, a narrative of religious belief, which has been transformed into a fairy tale, a *quliraq*? Is his journey an allegory of the shamanic descent and ascent from the underworld and the regeneration of his power? What is the totemic significance of the wolf-spirit psychopomp and the wolverine? With the death of many traditional religious practices, we may never know.

Mary Mathias, holding child, and Lucy Sipary, *Umkumiut*, June, 1960. Photo by
Christine Heller, courtesy of the Anchorage Museum of History and Art
B91.11.455.

QAVCIK

Puyangun Tununermiu

***

1
Man'a wangni
quliraunrilngatuq; qanemciuluku wiinga taringumatuaqa,
qanemcikqataqengaqa qulirauvkenani.
2
Nunat ukut uitalriit
nunauluteng,
kuigem taum ceñiini uitallinilriit. Nunat makut kuigem ceñiini
    uitatulriit.
3
Nulirqelriignek ilaluteng.
Tauna tua-i angutii nukalpiaruluni,
piculiuluni,
piculit nukalpianek pitullruamegteki. Piculiuluni taun'
nukalpiaruluni.
Tua-i taũgaam irniangyuunatek tua-i
taukuk nulirqelriik.
4
Tua-i irniangyugyaaqlutek tua-i
kanavirutekliniaqekiik
irniangellerkartek.
5
Pivakarluni atam nulirra qingallinilria.
Tua-i qingaryuklukuarngami paqtaarulluku; tua-i qingauniluku
    makut yurvirtain piaqluku
arnat.
Tua-i ukverciiganatek, ukverciiganatek tamarmek!
Tua-i pilliniuq tua qingallinilria.
Tua-i nunaniryuglutek cakneq.
Tua-i nukalpiaruami-ll' kalukarlutek, nerevkarilutek.
6
Tua-i utaqasciiganatek taumek irniamegnek yuurtellerkaanek.

WOLVERINE

Rose Charlie of Tununak

***

1
To me this one
doesn't seem to be a *quliraq* ; I understand it to be a *qanemciq*,
the one I am going to tell, not a *quliraq*.[1]
2
There was this village,
which being a village,
was situated along the shore of that river. These villages are usually
    situated by the shores of rivers.
3
Living there amongst them was a couple, a man and his wife.
The husband was a *nukalpiaq*,
a good hunter,
since good hunters were called *nukalpiat*. He was a good hunter
    and a good provider.
But they couldn't bear any children,
that man and his wife.
4
They really wanted children
and were despondent
over the fact that they didn't have any.
5
After a while the wife became pregnant.
Because she suspected she was pregnant, she had others check her,
    and those women who checked her confirmed
that she was pregnant.
They were incredulous; neither one of them could believe it!
She was indeed pregnant.
They were overjoyed.
Since he was a good provider they held a feast.
6
They couldn't wait for their child to be born.

33

Tua-i pivakarluni tua-i yuurrnariani yuurtelliniuq tan'gurrauluni.
Tua-i nutaan nunaniryugpallaarlutek tua-i cakneq taukuk angayuqaak
  irniangyugturyaaqngamek.
7
Cunawa-gguq im' tua-i caqackarqan kalukaraqlutek,
  nerevkariaqlutek.
Tua-i cakneq tauna irniartek irniaqsugluku.

***

8
Tua-i-ll' waten
allrakungeqerluku ataucimek—
allrakungaqameng ataucimek
pek'ngalalriit tua-i kangangluteng, aqvaquangluteng tua-i,
allrakuq cip'artaqamegteggu—
tuaten tua-i aqvaquangeqanrakun
aanii tauna erucit iliitni tupalliniuq assirpegnani, tua-i nangteqluni.
Tua-i
angutiin taum tua-i ellmikun piyukluku cangakevkenaku.
Unuaquan tupalliniut arcarikanirluni.

Agayuur, Cecilia Aluska, and *Carriralria,* Peter Aluska, *Tununermiuk,* 1957.
Photo by Christine Heller, courtesy of the Anchorage Museum of History and
Art B 91.11.428.

When it was time for it to be born, a boy was born.
His parents had always wanted a child, but now they were even
    happier.
7
Whenever the boy did any little thing, however insignificant,
    they had a feast and let people eat.
They were really happy to have their child.[2]

***

8
So then
when he was about one year old—
when they're one year old
they start to walk and run around on their own,
a little past the age of one—
just as he was beginning to run around,
his mother woke up one morning not feeling well, being ill.
But
her husband wasn't worried, thinking it would pass.
When they woke up the next morning, she was even worse.

Piunriq, Bertha Hooper, and *Qiuran,* Robert Hooper, *Tununermiuk,* circa 1960.
Photo by Christine Heller, courtesy of the Anchorage Museum of History and
Art B91.11.427.

9
Aren tua-i
arcarikaningarcan
angalkunun, taun' nukalpiaruami nunuliqtuurluki,
tuunritevkaryaaqekii tua-i
tamakut tua angalkut cakaniutekesciiganak', arcariinarlun' taũgaam.
Pivakarluni tua-i tuqulliniluni taun' aaniit.

10
Tua-i taukuk
cakneq aliayuutekluku. (Tauna-gg' irniara aliayugpakanritlilria
    cumikeluaqaumanrilami, angutii taũgaam tua tauna.)

11
Tua-i tuquan piavet kelumeggnun
qungivimeggnun tagulluku
kemga ellilliniluku.
Tamaani tamaa-i kanaranek qantullrulriit, yuk taun' tuquaqan,
    kanarat-gguq naacirturluki erenret talliman[a]
unuut-llu talliman.
Nunat taukut,

Tununermiut burial grounds, 1927. Gravesite is that of *Carriralria* (George
Aluska's younger brother) as identified by *Cuniq*, Jents Flynn. Photo from the
Geist Collection, Anchorage Museum of History and Art B92.33.45.

9

Aren, so
when she got worse,
he had shamans use their power to make her better, rewarding them
since he was a good hunter;
but those shamans couldn't do anything to help; on the contrary, she
    was just getting worse.
In the end their mother died.

10

Those two
were very sad on account of this. (Well, his child was probably not
    so very sad since he was not fully aware [of what had
    happened], but the husband was.)

11

Because she was dead they brought her up to the graveyard,
back there behind the village,
and they placed her corpse there.
They used to say that back then, when a person died, they had a
    mourning period of five days
and five nights.
And the people

The beach at *Tununeq,* circa 1958. *Paningayaq,* Medina Flynn, is bending down;
Ayaginar, Eliza Fairbanks, is sitting on the log in the foreground; *Paniuyaq,* Lucy
Arnakin, is standing in the background; *Nengqerralria,* Katie Walter George, is
standing second from right; and *Ciiskuaryuk,* Martina Walter Wiseman, is at the
far right. Photo by Christine Heller, courtesy of the Anchorage Museum of
History and Art B91.11.786.

nunat yui tamarmeng tua-i yagluteng tua caskulluarqengaunateng,
  caskumek aturngaunateng taukut erenret unuut-llu talliman
  naamavkenaki.
Tua caskumek tegusngaunateng qalqapagngaunateng
  caviggarngaunateng-llu tua-i.
Caskut tua-i aturngaunaki ernerni taukuni tallimani unugni-llu tallimani.
12
Tuaten tua-i kanarat naacirturluki pillratni,
tuani-gguq
maaten pilliniut
qunguan taum, kemgan caniani—
elagucuitellratni tamaani—
kegluneq ungelrumauralria.
13
Cunawa-gguq im' tua-i erenret taukut
unuut-llu talliman naacirtullratni,
kegluneq tauna ayayuunani tuani tua-i ungelrumalliniaqelria.

of this village would fast and they would neither mention nor use
  any tools during the entire five days and nights.
They would touch no tools, using neither axes nor knives,
for five days and five nights.[3]

12
While they were waiting for the mourning period to be over,
there, it was said,
next to the grave where the body was—
this was back when they didn't bury the bodies—
they saw
a wolf lying curled up.
13
And so it was that during the entire mourning period of five days
and five nights
the wolf never left, but stayed there curled up.

Panruk, MaryAnn Hooper, with children *Ak'ak'aq,* Maria Angaiak; *Kaagiugaq,*
David Moses; *Aanall'er,* John Moses; and *Cakayak,* Maggie John, in *Niugtaq,*
1957. Photo by Christine Heller, courtesy of the Anchorage Museum of History
and Art B391.11.560.

14
Tua-i-ll' tallimiitni tua naangata,
unugluni errluni
pian piyaaqelliniut tayim' taun' kegluneq cataunani.
Maaten tua-i
paqluku tauna kemga piyaaqellinia tayim' taum keglunrem
    ayautellinikii.
Tua-i
natmun-llu ayauyuciinaku tua-i.
Taum tua-i angutiin
qivruk'urluryaaqluku-am cali tua tuaken kemga uitavianek
    ayautellranek, tua taũgken tua-i qaill' pisciiganan' tayim'
    ayautelliniluku!
15
Tua-i uitalliniut, tauna tua-i angutii—waten-am tuquaqata-ll' yuut,
tamakut
yut'eng,
allrakuq kassuumavkenaku yuilqumun ayaasqevkenaki
    inerquutaullruan—
tua-i allrakuq tauna aturluku atauciq ayaksaunani yuilqumun.

***

16
Tua-i allrakuq
kassuan, *one year*-aurcan,
ayaganglun' tua-i.
Tua-i ayalliniaqelria.
Waten tua ellakegciaqan tauna-ll' qetunrarrani tua malikluku
    yuilqumun aavurqurluku tua ayangssitaqluku.
Iliini malikaqluku.
17
Tua-i tayim' qakuurrluku ayagpakarluni-am,
ayagluni,
piinanermini pilliniuq
ikamraq un' cam—qemim-gga qaingani uitallermini pillilria.
Ikamraq un'a
kituryartulria;
qamuutarluni-gguq aipaa aipaa-llu kasmurrarluni.
Tua-i
paqnayuami allayugciqaami un'umek nunalgutkenrilngalamiu-llu,
natetmun-llu ayagyaraunrilngurmun ayagngalan,
ciunrakun tua maaggun cukangnaqluni tua atralaalliniluni

14

When the fifth day had come and gone,
night went and morning came,
and when day was done, they checked on the wolf but it was not there.
Then
they went to check on the body, but, behold, the wolf had evidently
    taken it away!
Nor
did they have a clue to where it took the body.
The poor husband of the deceased
was devastated that it had taken the body from its resting place,
    but there was nothing he could do; it had taken the body away.

15

And so they stayed, and that husband of hers—whenever people died,
the members
of their family
were told not to hunt in the wilderness until a year had passed,
    that being their rule—
he didn't hunt in the wilderness for one year.

***

16

When a year
was over, when a year had gone by,
he started hunting.
He would go hunting.
When the weather was nice, he took his son with him, taking the
    boy with him to the wilderness so that he wouldn't be lonesome.
Sometimes he would take the boy with him.
17
So sometime later, since he was still going out,
he went hunting,
and while he was hunting he saw
that there was a sled down there—he was probably on a hill.
The sled down there
was passing;
one person was pulling the sled and the other was pushing.
So
because he was curious and couldn't recognize them,
and since it seemed as though they weren't from his village,
and they seemed to be traveling in an unusual direction,

ciunringnaqlukek.

18
Tua-i-ll' waniw' tekillukek,
ukuk-llu tekillutek.
Tua-i angutii tauna
arulairrluni.
Ingna-gguq-gga arnaq
kasmurrartii, ikamrak taukuk kasmurrartiik, tauna-llu angun
    qamuutarluni.
Tauna-gguq-gga arnaq kasmurrartii
mikelngurmek tunumiayaarluni
atkumi iluakun.
Amna-gguq tua mikelnguq neplirturluni,
tauna tunumiara.
19
Maaten-gguq tang tua-i wavet ingna arnaq piurallinia tuarpiaq-gguq
    imna nuliallra!
Aturainek-llu-gguq aturluni imumi tuqullrani atullrinek.
Tua-i-gguq elitaqluku!
20
Aren tua-i elitaqngamiu
tauna angun pillinia,
"Cunaw' waniw' nuliaqa elpet ayautellruken!"
Tua-i-ll' taum angutem kiullinia nuliaqenritniluku elliin nuliaqniluku.
Tauna tunumiayaara-gguq tua nepaicuunani tua neplirturluni!
Caurluni-gg' tua qiagurluni pillilria wall'u-qa calun' neplirturluni.
    Nepaicuunan' tua neplirturluni kesianek.

21
Taum tua yupiam pillinia,
"Taisgu nulirqenritan! Wiinga nulirqaqa!"
Tua-i taum angutem
qamuutallrem taum tua-i teguvkaryugnaunaku.
Kinguvarluni tua-i imna, taun' arnaq, kegginaa
    uyangtessaagturyaaqellinia pinguarturluni,
    uyangtessaagturyaaqellinia;
uivuciinani-gguq tang
tunutnauraa.
Tua-i tangssaangyaaqellinia.
22
Pivakarlun' tua-i ukatmun piyuguaqerluni ukatmun

he hurriedly went down the hill ahead of them,
trying to head them off.
18
And then he got to where they were heading,
and the two arrived.
Her male companion [who was pulling the sled]
stopped.
Over there was a woman,
who was pushing it, pushing that sled by the handlebars, and that
     man who was pulling it.
And the woman, it was said, who was pushing,
carried a small child on her back,
inside her parka.
That child in there was continuously making noise,
the child on her back.
19
He observed that woman over there, and, lo and behold, it was as
     though she were his dead wife!
The clothes she had on were the clothes she wore when she died.
He recognized her!
20
Aren, so when he recognized her,
he said to the man,
"So it was you who took my wife away!"
And the man retorted that she was no longer his wife, but said she
     now belonged to him instead.
The child on her back was not silent, but kept making noise!
Well, it was doing something, perhaps crying or just making noise.
     Anyway, it was never silent, but kept on making noise.
21
So that real person said to him,
"Give her to me, she's not your wife! She is my wife!"
And that man
who was pulling wasn't going to let him take her.
Going to the rear [of the sled], he tried to peer into her face, tried to
     peer without being noticed;
she would keep her back to him
without seeming to turn.
He tried in vain to see her.

22
After trying for a while, he pretended to go one way,

pileryalliniuq: aren tua-i kegginauvkenani im' kegginaa;
   agluquk-llu igingalutek!
Tua-i tangnirqevkenani alingnaqluni!
Enruluni!
Kemegglirluni ilii enruluni!
Tua-i assirpegnani,
alingnaqluni!
Tuaten-am pingraan tua tangeng'ermiu-ll' taq'ertevkenani
taitesquralliniluku.
Tauna-gguq-gga tunumiara tua-i neplirturalria taqsuunani, taun' mikelnguq.
23
Taitesqurallni cakaniqeryugnaunaku, tua-i-gg' qungvagyugyaaqelria
   cakneq taumek nuliallminek cakneq,
taq'ercugnaunaku-am tungcirturalliniluku.
24
Tuani ima tam tuani angun qanlalria, "Ampi tua-i ayagceskuk,
tumkarpuk amna atuyunairceciiqan!"
Tamaa-i tumkamegnek
qungvagyugluni taun'
qamuutalria
piyaaqluni. Taum tua-i ayagcessngaunakek tauna nuliani
   taiteqarraarumavkenaku.

Agayuur, Cecilia Aluska, with *Tanqiar,* Leo Aluska, on the beach in front of
Tununeq, 1957. Photo by Christine Heller, courtesy of the Anchorage Museum
of History and Art B91.11.417.

then quickly went the other way: *aren*, her face was unrecognizable;
  her jaw was hanging down!
It was not a pretty sight, but was quite frightening!
It was bone!
Some of it had flesh and some of it was bone!
It was not at all nice
but scary!
He kept at it even though he saw how disgusting she was,
and kept insisting that he give her back.
And that child on her back still didn't tire of making noise.
23
He continued to insist on her return even though he was appalled [at
  the sight] of that dead wife of his;
he didn't stop, but kept telling him to give her back.
24
That man would say, "Hurry up so we can go;
you're going to let our trail become unusable!"
The one who was pulling the sled
kept saying
that the thought of losing their trail was giving him the creeps.[4]
But he would not let them leave without first getting his wife back.

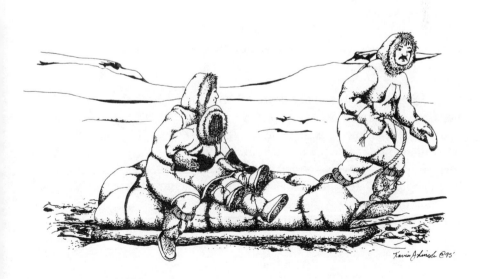

25

Tua-i taum pivakarluni angutem taum qamuutallrem
aqumlelliniuq.[b] "Aa-rra-rra-rraa!" tauna imna
qamuutalleq pilliniuq. "Aa-rra-rra-rraa! Aling, arenqiapaa-ll' elpeni!
Call' pik'ngan taqngaitellinivagciu!
Tua-i taisngaitaqa! Uumek taũgaam tua waniw' cikiqataramken
wiinga-ll' qunukmiyaaqaqa
elpetun una qunukellerpetun pitarrluku.
Tua-i taũgaam taqngaitelliniavet taiteqata'rqa."
Kinguvarluni tua-i ikamramegnun[c] cingyaani ikirrluku,
ancilliniuq
qavciim amianek—
qavciit makut *wolverine*-augut. *Wolverine*-am *skin*-aanek
kinrumalriamek.
"Kitak tua-i waniw' una
tegukuvgu-qa,
tegukuvgu-qa tua-i
uniciiqerpekuk?" taum angutem aptellinia tauna. "Una-q' tua
waniw' qavcik tegukuvgu uniciiqerpekuk?"
Tua-ll' taum angutem pillinia, "Qaillun-gga taũgaam, qaillun pillra
nallunriqumku ayagceciiqekemtek. Nallunriumavkenaku
ayagcessngaitamtek."

26

Tua-i-ll' taum angutem pilliniluku, taum
qavciim pikestiin,
"Pissu'urqavet tua-i pitarkamek tangrraqavet
tungiinun caulluku ellilarniaran; taum tua-i qavciim aqvalarciqaa
taun' pitarkaq.

27

Taũgaam tua-i ayagcetqata'arqavgu
yuqertenqegcaaralaqina tua-i,
yuqertenqegcaarluten cakneq! Cali-ll' agiirrluni maa-i tekitniaraqan
qurrsullange'rpet, agu agu qurqeryaqunak tua-i!
Tua-llu-q' tua-i ayagceciiqerpekuk?"
Tua-i angerluku. Teguluku tauna tua-i pikiitek tayim' ayakpaglutek
taukuk.
Ellii-ll' tua-i uterrluni.

25

After this went on for a while, the man who was pulling the sled
suddenly sat down.[5] "*Aa-rra-rra-rraa!*" the one who was pulling
sighed in frustration, "*Aa-rra-rra-rraa!*" *Aling,* you are so persistent!
You sure don't give up when you want something!
I won't give her back! But I am going to give this to you;
I am reluctant to part with it,
just as you are reluctant to part with this one [your wife].
I am going to give this to you because you will not quit."
He went to the rear of their sled, opened the tarpaulin,
and took out
the hide of a *qavcik*—
qavcik is the *Yup'ik* word for wolverine,
the dried skin of a wolverine.
"*Kitak,*
when you take this,
if you take this,
will you leave us?" that man asked him. "If you take this wolverine,
    will you leave us?"
And the man answered, "Only on the condition that I know the
    purpose of it will I allow you to leave. If I don't find out, I
    will not let you go."

26

And then that man, the owner of the wolverine,
said to him,
"When you go hunting and you want to catch an animal,
point it facing the animal; the wolverine will go get the prey.[6]

27

But before you let it go,
urinate thoroughly,
making sure you empty your bladder completely! Also when it's
    coming back and it's about to reach you,
even if you suddenly have to go, never, never on any account urinate!
So now, will you let us go?"
He agreed. When he took the hide, the other two left quickly.
And he too went home.

***

28

Aren tua-i

taum imum angutem tua-i anglanitekluku taun' pissurrsuutni.

Tuaten tua-i canek pitarkanek tangrraqami,

tungiitnun cautaqatgu, cautaqani tayima

taum pitarkam tungiinun ayagciquq tua-i-ll' keggmiaqluku

agiirulluku taun' pitarkaq.

Ayuqluku imarpigmi nunam-llu qaingani.

Tua-i ayuqluku aturluku. Tua-i taũgaam tuaten alerquuciatun

yuqertenqegcararraarluni ayagcetaqluku. Tua-i-ll' waniw'

tekitniararluni cali, qaill' pitariqertelluku,

qurrsullagglainarluni tua-i agiirtaqan, taũgaam tua-i yuqercuunani.

29

Atu'urqekii tua-i, tauna-ll' qetunraa angturriluni yuilqumun

ayagayaurrluni.

Ayagayaurcan tuaten, ayagciigacimamamarraarluni mikelnguuluni

—mikelnguugaqameng tua yuilqumun ayagciigatetulriit.

Tua-i taũgaam tayima *twenty*-q allrakut ciptaqamegteggu

tua-i ayagyugngariaqluteng pengegnarqessiyaagpegnateng—

taum tua-i qetunraan atungelliniluku.

30

Tua tuaten cali atiin inerqurluku inerquutaminek tua-i.

Tua-i inerquutani taun' nalluvkenaku: tua-i yuqerrngaitellni-llu

agiirrnginanrani ayagcetqataquniu-llu yuqertellerkani.

31

Aren tua-i taum imum tan'gurraam, pissurrsuutekestiin, tua-i

kenekluku tua-i cakneq tauna imna pissurrsuutni! Tua-i

pitarkanek piciatun tua-i

pissurrsuutekluku imarpigmi nunam-llu qaingani,

pissurrsuutekluku.

Tua-i taum caqerviinaku kenekluku cakneq.

***

32

Atam waten pivakarluni uksuarmi qaniqerluni tumliranariqertelluku

kelumeggnun-am pavavet ayangssilliniluni tuntut umyuaqluki.

Tuntut tumaitnek tekicami

tum'arrluki tua-i ayalliniluni. Maaten-gguq tang pilliniuq ava-i

aũgkut tuntut.

Aren tua-i tauna tua-i tan'gurraq pitangyukarluni taukunek tuntunek

48

***

28
Aren
that man was very happy on account of his hunting device.
    Whenever he saw prey,
when he faced it in their direction, it would travel in the direction
of the prey and it would come back with the prey in its mouth.
It was the same on the ocean as it was on land.
It could be used anywhere. Following the instructions exactly,
he would let it go after thoroughly emptying his bladder.
    Then whenever it had almost reached him on its return from
    wherever it had been, he would always have the urge to
    urinate, yet he wouldn't urinate.
29
He kept on using it and then his son grew into a young guy and
    started going out into the wilderness.
When the boy started hunting, after not being able to for a very
    long, long time because he was a child—you know they can't
    go into the wilderness when they are children.
But when they're past the age of twenty,
    they can go hunting without causing too much worry—
that son of his started using the 'wolverine.'
30
Furthermore, his father warned him as he had been warned.
He knew the rules: not to urinate while the 'wolverine' was coming
    back, but to urinate right before letting it go.
31
Aren, how that boy, the owner of the hunting implement, loved his
    hunting tool! He used it to hunt all kinds of game;
it was his hunting tool on the ocean as well as on the land,
his very own hunting tool.
He was deeply attached to it.

***

32
And then one day in the fall it snowed enough so that tracks would
    be visible;
he went out to roam the area behind the village with caribou in mind.
When he came upon tracks of a herd of caribou,
he followed the tracks and then saw that over there was a herd.
Aren, that young guy was really excited about the prospect of

tua-i cakneq!
Tua-i tauna pissurrsuutni anlluku
tungiitnun
caulluku,
aũgna-ll' tua-i tungiitnun caucani[d] ayagluni. Ayakartelluku
    neq'aqalliniluni aling yuqertenritliniluni-ll'. Tua-i-ll' aũgna
    ava-i ayagluni.
Tua-i qessanayullagyaaqelriim tua-i ayaumariluni taũgken.
33
Ayaglun'-am tua-i ava-i, tuntunun tekicami tua-i tuqurqiluni, uterrluni
tua-i—
tuntumek-gga keggmiarluni pillilria.
Tua-i-llu uka-i-am pinariqertelluku
yuqercuum tekitelliniluku, tua-i piqtang'ermi qurrliniluni tua-i
    yuqertellrunrilami ayakatallrani, tua-i caqtang'ermi,
    piqtang'ermi qurrliniluni.
Man'a-ll' agiirtellria
ciuneqluku tailuni,
yaaqsigiinarluni.
Tekitniarallni malikluku caqirrngiinarluni,
tua-i-ll' ava-i yaatiikun ayagluni.

Panruk, MaryAnn Hooper, with *Kaagiugaq,* David Moses, *Tununermiuk. Niugtaq,*
1957. Photo by Christine Heller, courtesy of the Anchorage Museum of History
and Art B91.11.551.

catching a caribou from that herd!
So he took out his hunting implement,
faced it
toward the herd,
and when he pointed the 'wolverine' toward them it took off. Just
  after he let it go he suddenly remembered that he hadn't
  urinated. And there went that wolverine hide!
He regretted his action but it was already on its way.
33
And so it left and when it reached the herd it started to kill,
then came back—
perhaps it now had a caribou in its mouth.
As it was coming
he had the urge to urinate and, although he tried not to, he couldn't
  help but relieve himself because he hadn't urinated before it left.
Here it was approaching,
coming toward him,
and then it began to get farther and farther away.
As it got closer it started to veer,
and then it passed him by.

34
Aren tua-i tauna qessanayullagluni tua-i avavet tangssuaralliniluku,
tua-i tayim' pellaluni.

***

35
Aren tua-i qaillun pingailami tua-i
qivrukngamiu cakneq
tumliranaqngan-llu
tum'arrluku ayalliniluni.
Tua-i-gguq maa-i ayallinilria
qemiq-llu tua-i tekicamiu
qemiq tevvliniluku. Aūgna-gguq-gga cali agaa-i call' qemiq akiani.
    Atrarluni-ll' tua-i.
Atraqataqanermikun
tan'geriani tumet tamakut tangesciigaliamiki
arulairlun' tua-i
unugpak uitalliniluni tuani.
36
Tua-i-ll'
tangerrsugngariuraamiki tanqigiarallranek ayaglun' tuamta-ll' tua
    tumaikun ayalliniluni tum'arrluku.
37
Tua-i-am qemiq tevluku, tua-i tevluku pilliniuq agna cal' agaa-i qemiq,
canimetevkenani-llu.
38
Tua-i tumaikun arvirluni, qemikun tuaggun atrarluni aciakun-llu
    arvirluni qemimun mayurluni.
Tua-i-ll' waniw' qaklitqatarluku
tan'geriluni.
Tua-i ayakarluni, tan'geringraan tuaten
ayakarluni, pilliniuq kenurraq camna,
nem kenurraa.
39
Aren tua-i
tan'geringraan taumek kenurramek,
kenurramek kangpaassiqerluni {qanemcista engelarluni}
atralliniluni.
Tua-i taūgaam tan'gercelan cukasciiganani.
Atrallinilun' tua-i.
40
Tua-i tekitelliniluk' tauna ena.

34

Aren, that young guy watched with regret as it disappeared,
vanishing over the horizon.

***

35

Aren, because there was nothing else he could do,
because he was heartbroken on account of losing it,
and since there were tracks on the ground,
he went after it, following its trail.
So then he left following the tracks,
and when he came upon a hill,
over the hill he went. There on the other side was another hill.
    He went down.
Just when he was about to descend,
it got dark on him and because he couldn't see the tracks anymore,
he stopped
and stayed in that spot the whole night.

36

And then
when there was enough light to see the tracks, he left,
    and again he went following the trail.

37

He went over the hill and saw over across there another hill,
nowhere near.

38

So he went across following the tracks and he went down the hill,
    going across to the other hill, which he ascended.
When he was about to reach the top,
it got dark.
He went on for a little bit, even though it had grown dark,
and after continuing on for a little bit he saw a light down there,
the light of a house.

39

Aren, so
even though it had gotten dark, using that light,
using the light as a compass {narrator laughs}
he went down.
However, since it was dark he couldn't move very fast.
But he went down.

40

He reached that house.

Elatiini-gguq-gga—
cunawa-gguq
pikaggun egalengqerrami taun' ena, taum tua kenurraan,
egalran
kenurraq alaitellran pillinikii—una-gguq elatiini elagyaq,
mayurrvik.
41
Maaten-gguq tua-i amiiga tekicamiu pillinia qamaken tanqik cal'
    man'a piluni!
Amiiga ikingqalliniluni.
Cali tua elaturraa man'a
tanqigceńani
qamaken
kenurram pillranek.
Ayumian tua-i itraaralliniluni.
42
Itrarluni tua-i pilliniuq,
ena alailliniuq,
arnaq un'a
natrani utqetaarturalria, mikelnguyagaq-gguq-gga
tegumiara.
43
Mikelnguyagaq tua neplirturluni, tua-i tayim' ak'anqegcaaq ak'a
    tamaani tayima,
twenty years-am-llu civuani taum tua atiin tangellrulukek cal' tuaten.
44
Maaten-gguq tang imna itraaraqerluni,
nem ilua tangerrsugngariamiu, pilliniuq imna pikna qavcik ak'a tua
    agaurangellrulliniluni, imna tauna yaatairtellra!
Aren tua-i arenqiateqanrakun
waqaalriartanglliniuq. Maaten tua qinqanirlun' pilliniuq angun ikna
acimi—
caa tayima,
uitaurtuq wall'u-qa caliuq—
angun tauna uitaluni.
Ingna-gguq-gga tua arnaq tua taqsuunani utqetaarturalria, mikelnguq
    tua neplirturluni, nepaicuunani.

45
Tua-i-ll'
waqaalliniluku.

Beside the house, it was said—
since apparently
that house had a sky window above, and that light
in the window
made it visible—beside it was this food cache,
an elevated food cache.
41
Lo and behold, when he reached the door [of the house] a light
    shone from within!
The door was evidently open.
And that porch
was bright
from
the light that shone within.
Then he started to go in.
42
He went inside and saw,
when the inside came into view,
a woman down there
who was pacing back and forth on the floor, with a little child
whom she was holding.
43
The little child was continuously making noise, which had been
    going on for a long, long time.
Twenty years earlier his father had seen them in the same state.
44
When he had gone further in,
when he was able to see inside the house, lo and behold, he
    saw the wolverine up there; it was already hanging, the
    one that veered away from him!
Aren, just as he was getting excited about it,
there came a greeting, "*Waqaa!*" When he peeked further in he
    saw a man over there
on a bed—
he was doing something,
working or whatever—
that man was living there.
Over there was the woman who never stopped pacing, with a child
    who was continuously making noise and was never silent.
45
And so
he was asked what he wanted.

Tua-i-ll' pillinia
pissurrsuutni pikna aqvaniluku.
Taum ciunran pillinia, "Aren
pikngamni utertuq!
Alerquutka atunrilavgu
pikngamni pika-i utertuq!
Pikenritan! Wiinga pikngamni taiguq; ataam taiguq!"
46
Aren tauna-am tan'gurraq kasmenga'artelliniuq tua-i!
Taitesqelluku tua-i elliin kenekniluku cakneq.
Taum-am tua ciunran tua taisngaunaku tua-i
taqniluku tua-i pikenrirniluku, atunrirniluku tua-i inerquutni
    atunrilaku.
47
Tauna im' tan'gurraq tua-i,
tua-i kasemlun' tua-i.
Tauna-gguq tua arnaq tua taqsuunani utqetaarturalria mikelngurmek
    taumek tegumiarluni neplirturalriamek—
tua qiagurluni-gg' pillilria.

And the young guy answered
that he had come for his hunting tool up there.
The one who addressed him said, "*Aren,*
it came back because it is mine!
Because you didn't follow my instructions
and since that one up there is mine, it came back!
It is not yours! Since it is mine, it came back; it came back again!"
46
Aren, that young guy became very persistent!
He told him to give it back, saying that he loved it very much.
And that man said that he wouldn't give it back,
that he had forfeited ownership, that it was no longer his and he no
    longer could use it because he hadn't followed his instructions.
47
That young guy,
he didn't give up.
And that woman was continuously pacing back and forth with a
    child on her back who was constantly making noise—
it was probably crying.

Kakgailnguq, Lucy James, with daughters *Pinirraq,* Elsie; *Cuk'ayaq,* Frieda;
and *Makill'aq,* Theresa, *Tununermiut* in 1959. Photo by Christine Heller,
courtesy of the Anchorage Museum of History and Art B91.11.575.

48
Tua-i-ll'
taum angutem pillinia,
"Arenqiapaa elpetegni aatan-llu
pikngatek-lli taqngaitellinivagcetki
unakumavkenaki!
Kasemneruqapiarallinivagcetek!
Taqaitellinivagcetek!"
Tuaten-gguq im' pikiini taun' tan'gurraq ilutequangartelliniuq, tua
    pininriqerrluni,
iluteqngarrluni.
Iluteqngarteqanrakun
arnaq imna, "Enǵ!",
arvirluni tuaten taun' mikelnguq
taumun angutmun tunluku, "Una teguu! Wiinga maliggnauqa!
Qunukvakaucirpetun wiinga maliggnauqa.
Qangvarpak-lli
mikelngiunqegg' cakaniyuilngurmek!"
49
Aren tauna angun kapiallalliniuq nangerrluni tuaten.
"Pivkenak pii tunqatarqa!
Maligcaqunaku! Tunqata'arqa!"
50
Aren tauna nangerrluni itrarluni tauna tua-i
qavcik agalria
atrarrluku tunlliniluku tua-i. Pilliniluku taum angutem, taum
    qavciim pikestiin,
tua nutaan piksagutniluku tua-i.
Umyugaa aturluku pikuraasqelluku tua-i;
cameg' inerquutaunaku tua-i piyugtaciatun tua-i, waniw' tua-i
peggluku nutaan tuneniluku.
Pikuraasqelluku tua nutaan cameg' inerquutaunaku
pissurrsuutekuraasqelluku.
Tua-i nutaan uterrluni
nunaminun tuavet.

51
Tua-i nutaan pissurrsuutekliniluku piyugtacimitun tua-i.
    Agiirrnginanrani-ll' yuqercukuni yuqerrluni tua-i
    cakaniyuunani-ll' taun' pikluku.

48
Then
that man said to him,
"*Arenqiapaa*! You and your father,
when you want something you never quit
until you get it back!
You two are so persistent!
You two will not quit!"
When the man said that to him, the young guy started to sob and
　　broke down.
He was grief-stricken.
Just as he started to grieve,
the woman grunted, "*Enĝ*!"
and went across the floor and
gave the child to the man, saying, "Take this! I shall go with him!
Since you are so reluctant to give up the 'wolverine,' I shall go with him!
I've been caring for this child who never grows
for ever so long!"
49
Aren, that man suddenly panicked and stood up.
"Don't do that; I'm going to give it to him!
Don't go with him; I'm going to give it to him!"
50
He stood up and went over to the
hanging wolverine
and took it down and gave it to him. That man, the owner of the
　　wolverine,
said to him, that now it was really his.
He said that he could do whatever he wanted with it;
there were no rules attached and he could do anything he wanted
　　now that
he was letting it go and giving it to him.
He told him that he now possessed it without any stipulations
and that he could keep using it as his hunting device.
Then the young guy went home
to his own village.
51
Then it was indeed his 'wolverine' and he used it however he
　　wanted to. And he could urinate if he wanted to while it was
　　coming back and nothing would happen since it was now his.

52
Tua-i
tauna cali kingunerluku.[e]
Tua-i-gguq tauna arnaq
irniayaaralria,
cali maa-i ernerpak tauna irniara tuacetun angtangatuq,
cali tua tuaten
akaar tamaani atiin taum
tangellracetun, taum-llu cal' qetunraan tangerrluku cal' tuaten
    angtaluni, nepaicuunan' qiagurluni.
Cali-gguq cali tayima maa-i
ernerpak, cali tauna mikelnguq tuaten ayuquq,
tuaten cali tua-i
neplirturluni cali cakaniyuunani pingatuq.
53
Tua-i iquklituq aūg' qanemcika,
tayim' cameg iqungqerrsaaqellilria.

52
Also
I am going to add something.
As for that woman,
the one with the child,
her child is probably the same size to this day,
just as [it was] in the story,
just as his father saw him
a long time ago and just as that son of his saw it, it was the same
    size, never silent, constantly crying.
Even to this day
that child is just like that,
just like that,
still making noise and probably still the same.
53
Perhaps there is another ending,
but my [version of the] story has come to an end.[7]

Esturngalria, Stephanie Nayagniq, *Tununeq*, circa 1980. Photo by Andrew J. Chikoyak.

YUP'IK WOMANHOOD

"Oh, how they endured back then, those women!"
—Tom Imgalrea, *Cev'armiu* (Woodbury 1984: 27)

Nanugaq, Priscilla Early, *Tununeq*, circa 1980. Photo by Andrew J. Chikoyak.

The Sky Woman

This is the Yup'ik version of the star woman tale, told by Native American peoples in various forms throughout North and South America. In its elemental form, a heavenly being, a woman, descends from the sky country and takes a human husband and then after a time, for one reason or another, ascends again to the sky country. A popular published version of this tale is *The Ring in the Prairie: A Shawnee Legend*, originally collected by Henry Rowe Schoolcraft (Bierhorst 1970). Claude Lévi-Strauss in the *Mythologies, Volume 1*, also gives an entire set of star woman tales gathered from the Amazon region of South America (Lévi-Strauss 1969).

Both Lantis (1946: 265-267) and Curtis (1930: 74-75, 77-78) have recorded versions from *Nunivaar* 'Nunivak' which account for the creation of the island. Two brothers live all alone; while hunting, they are blown out to sea and find shelter on an iceberg. The younger begins to cry and his older brother cannot console him. While he cries, a woman wearing a fishskin parka with a ruff of long caribou hair descends and alights on their kayak. With the soil that is in her lap, she creates land which becomes the island of *Nunivaar*. She becomes the wife of the older brother (in the Lantis version) or the younger brother becomes a woman and marries the older brother (in the Curtis version); the three live together contentedly, hunting, gathering and fishing. One day the younger brother returns from caribou hunting to obtain a replacement for his bowstring, which has snapped. While she is preparing a new bowstring for him from sinew, he attempts to sexually harass her. She pokes him with her sinew separating tool and unintentionally and inexplicably kills him (the wound is only superficial). When the older brother returns and discovers the body of the younger brother buried in soil of the sod house wall, the sky woman returns to her home in the sky despite his wish that she remain. In his loneliness and despair, he covers himself with a wolf skin and becomes a wolf, and this is how wolves came to *Nunivaar*.

Curiously, although the various tales differ considerably in content and emphasis, certain distinguishing features seem to hold over a vast area: the descent and final ascent of the star woman, the theme of food gathering,

65

Cakayak, Maggie Moses John, at left, and *Cuk'ayaq,* Mary Julia Carl. *Tununeq,*
1958. Photo by Christine Heller, courtesy of the Anchorage Museum of History
and Art B91.11.386.

her rejection of her human spouse, the unwanted attentions of an amorous
male which drive her away, and the presence of a furbearing animal.

Arnaucuaq's version which follows does not purport to give an account of the creation of a homeland; a *Qaluyaaq* creation story already
exists (see "*Ciuliaqatuk:* The Ancestor"). Nevertheless, it very closely resembles the *Nunivaar* creation story, although in the end the elder brother
becomes a *qavcik* 'wolverine.' Moreover, when compared to other star
woman versions, it illustrates the way elements of a story set are transformed from one version to another, allowing for considerable local variation while maintaining the constancy of the essential features which distinguish a particular story set.

As we noted above, all the versions of the star woman tale seem to
include the theme of unwelcome sexual advances, harassment, or violation
of the woman, some in graphic and shocking detail. *Arnaucuaq*'s version
only touches upon the subject, saying that the younger brother "bothered"
or "touched her on the body," but the implication is very clear. Lantis's
Nunivaar version is more explicit, dwelling on the harassment by the
younger brother in more detail. Furthermore, the sky woman is specifically directed beforehand by her husband, the older brother, to submit to

the younger brother's advances (a detail missing in *Arnaucuaq*'s account). Polyandry, although very rare, was practiced among the Yupiit in pre-contact and early contact time, and this seems to be what the woman is being asked to do. Yet the woman, and neither of the men, ends up being the one in control. Just as she came, so she returns, leaving the elder brother wifeless and forlorn.

This recording of *"Anngaqelriik:* The Two Brothers" was done December 8, 1993, in the Tununak Catholic Church in front of an audience of high school catechism students and elders. The elders requested that the sessions be conducted in the traditional way, with a partner helper who should sit beside the narrator and assist and correct him in the narration. *Cuniq,* Jents Flynn, was *Arnaucuaq*'s partner.

Yup'ik women making baskets, *Tununeq,* circa 1945. Back row left to right are *Inuguarpak,* Susie Agimuk; *Nalugalria,* Clara Aluska; *Inuk,* Rosalie Pitka; and two unidentified women. In the middle row are *Panigkaq,* Cecilia Flynn; unidentified child; and *Canaar,* Clara Akogtak. In the front row, the only identified person is *Cungauyar,* Winnie Billy, second from left. Photo from the Warren H. Atherton Collection (acc. #90-111-44N) in the Archives, Alaska and Polar Regions Dept., University of Alaska Fairbanks.

ANNGAQELRIIK

Arnaucuaq Tununermiu

***

1
Taukuk tuani
qanemciullermini
anngaqelriik taukuk
tamaani uitallinilriik.
Umyuarteqaqlutek kiimek yuuyuklutek waten
allamek yugtaicukluku.
Tua kiimenatek
tamaani kuigem ceñiini uitallinilriik.
Taũgaam mayurrvigtarluni cali eniignek qainga, mayurrvigmek.
2
Waten-gguq tua malikurlutek
ayagaurarqelriik
yuilqumun.
Waten tua-i
man'a taũgaam ayagayaraq pissuryaraullruami, waten ayagaqameng
    yuilqumun
pitarkaq taũgaam umyuaqluku ayagatullruameng
ca-llu umyuaqevkenaku.
3
Tamana-gguq
kuigak
imarpik un'a yaaqsigpegnaku
piuq.
Tua-i-gguq tamaavet tamaa-i waten maliklutek imarpigmun unavet
ayagaqelriik.
Cali-llu-gguq ayagaqamek
qavartaraqlutek
iliini,
tua utertaqlutek.
4
Tuamte-llu-gguq pavavet kelumegnun

68

THE TWO BROTHERS

Mike Angaiak of Tununak

***

1
There were these two
in this story
who were brothers
living together.
They thought that they were the only people around
and assumed that there wasn't anybody else.
They lived there by a river
all by themselves.
But there was a food cache on top of their house, an elevated food cache.
2
It was said that they would go
together
into the wilderness.
Since such
traveling was the only way to hunt, whenever they journeyed into
    the wilderness,
they were intent only on the wild game while they traveled
and thought of nothing else.
3
It was said
that their river
was
not far from the ocean down there.
They would go there together, down there
to the ocean.
And it was also said that they would
sometimes
sleep overnight when they went,
and then they would go home.
4
Moreover, it was said that they would go up there into the interior,

cali
maliklutek ayaglutek
tamaa-i tuntussurlutek, tuntunek.
Cali tua-i unangaqlutek.
Taũgaam-gguq
tamakut pitatek,
kia aulukngailaki,
tua ellmegnek waten[a]
aulukeqcaararaqluki tamakut pitatek.
5
Waten tamaani
man'a pitarkaq pegcuunaku,
aruvkarluku piyuitellruamegteggu aũgkut
ciuqlimta tayima,
man'a
yuilqumek unangkengaq
tua-i cakneq aulukaqluku
watqapik-llu aruvkarpegnaku
cagmarcetevkenaku-llu piaqluku, tuaten tua ayuqngameng.
Tua-i-gguq
cali
tua amllermek
piyuunatek waten tua ellmegnek taũgaam aulukluki pilaamegenki
taukuk.
6
Tuamte-llu-gguq unavet imarpigmun cali tua waten ayakunek
      taqukanek cali,
cali tua-i
unanglutek,
unangaqlutek.
7
Qavartarlutek piaqlutek unuaquaqan tua-i utertaqlutek.

***

8
Tua-ll'-am caqerlutek tua-i maliklutek ayalliniuk unavet imarpigmun.
Tamana-llu kuigtek
yaaqsiggarluku tua tamaa-i qavartarlutek.
9
Tua-i-ll' tuani arulaingqallragni
ella assiirutliniluni, anuqenglliniluni tua-i,
tua-i ayayunairulluni merkun.

and
going together,
they'd go caribou hunting, hunting for caribou.
And they'd get some.
But
because there was no one to take care of
their catch,
they endeavored to care for what they caught
all by themselves.
5
Since in those days
our ancestors never neglected
the wild game,
never letting it rot,
whatever
was caught in the wilderness
was tended to carefully
and never allowed to spoil
or go to waste, because that was how they were.
It was said,
moreover,
that those two
never got a lot
because they had to take care of their catch themselves.
6
Furthermore, it was said that when they went down to the ocean,
     they would
also catch
seals,
obtaining them as well.
7
They would sleep overnight and then go home the next day.

***

8
So then one day they went down to the ocean together.
They slept over night
a little ways from their river.
9
While they were stopped there,
the weather got bad, becoming windy,
and it was no longer safe to go by water.

Unuaquan tua-i uitalliniuk tamaani
yuilqumi.
10
Tuamte-llu-gguq unuaquan ertuq
cali tua-i anuqlirlun' tua-i.
Tayima ernerni qavcini tuani ayagciiganatek uitalliniuk.
11
Piqerluni-gguq tang una,
uyuraa tauna,
tua cupegtenglliniluni, aliayungluni,
tua utercugyaaqluni
tuavet uitaviggamegnun.
12
Tua-i taum anngaan qanrut'lallinia,
"Tua-i anuqlirturluni pingaituq. Assirikan uterciiqukuk."
Uum-gguq wani cupegtellra arcariinarluni.
Kiituani-gguq tang qiangenglun', qiangenguq; tua-i qarutengraani-ll'
    tua qialuni
pinguq,
tua kayukellikan uterciiqnilutek
qanrutengraani.

***

13
Tua-ll' caqerluni
taum qialuni inerqungraani.
Tauna anngaa piinanrani, tuan' qianginanrani,
cameg' imumek qiallra avungqerrnganani pinglliniuq.
14
Tua-i
qiallra im' avungqerrnganani.
Taringcaungengluku pillinia
tua-i cameg' imumek
qiallra imna
avungqerrngatlinilria tua-i.
Naken-llu piciinani
tua-i.
Tua-i taringamiu tamana avungqellra,
taun' uyurani pillinia,
"Alingnaqvaa, atam qiaviiqnak
niicugniqaa!"

72

The following day they stayed there
in the wilderness.
10
Furthermore, the next day when it dawned,
it was still windy.
There they stayed for the next few days, unable to go.
11
It happened, so it was said, that this
younger brother of his
began to get homesick, began to get lonely,
wanting to go home
to their place there.
12
So his older brother would tell him,
"It's not going to be windy forever. When it gets better we'll go home."
But it is said that his homesickness began to get worse.
Finally, it was said, he began to cry, he began to cry; even though
    [his brother] tried to encourage him, he cried
on and on,
this despite the fact that he tried to convince him that they would go
    home
when it got calm.

***

13
One time he kept on crying
even though he was admonished not to.
While his older brother was there, while he was crying,
it seemed as though his crying was mingled with something else.
14
It
was as though his crying was mingled with something.
He made an effort to understand it and realized
that there was something
which seemed to be blended with
his crying.
And he didn't know where
it was coming from.
When he understood that it was mixed with something,
he said to his younger brother,
"*Alingnaqvaa*! Oh my goodness, stop crying
and listen!"

15
Tua-i
tuaten qanrucani
nepairtelliniuq.
Piqerluni tua-ll' nep'ngelliniluni naken-llu piciinaku tua-i
ca imna neplilria.
Maaten-gguq tang taringnariluni piuq aturturalriarullinilria.
Naken-llu tua piciinaku qasturiinarluni.
16
Maaten-gguq
tamaa-i qasturiluni pilliniuq;
maaken, pagaaken qilagmek
pillinilria!
Nutaan taringluku tamaa-i
kiartengluku man' ella tamaaken tua pian.
17
Tua-i-ll' piqerluni ayumian tua-ll' pagaa-i tangrruulliniuq pagna
atralria pagaaken qilagmek
uivvaarturluni.
18
Canimelliinarluni tua. Tauna tua-i uyuraa qianrirluni tua taumek
    tangssunglutek.
Maaten-gguq canimelliluni piuq
arnaullinilria tauna tua-i
pagaaken qilagmek
atraaralria!
19
Maaten-gguq canimelliluni piuq—
imumek waten atkungqellermeggni—
kenirmiangqerrluni-gguq camek, kenirmiangqellinilria!

20
Uivurluni atraaralliniuq tua-i waniw' caniagnun
tuc'ami, waniw' tua tuc'ami maavet nunamun,
imna taun' kenirmiani
maavet ciqrutliniluku.
Ciqruskii imna nunaurtelliniluni. Tua nunami uitaqalliniuk
tamaa-i!
21
Tua-ll' taum pilliniak, "Tua-i
naklegyagullutek
tua-i waniw' tangercetua; ullagamtek.

74

15
So
as soon as he said that,
he got quiet.
Then it happened that something began to make noise and they
didn't know where it was coming from.
Then it became apparent that it was someone singing.
They didn't know where it was coming from and it was getting louder.
16
Lo and behold,
it was getting louder;
it was coming from there,
from up there in the sky!
They finally understood that and began to search
up in the sky since it was coming from there.
17
And then suddenly it became visible up there,
descending from up there in the sky,
going round and round.[1]
18
It was getting closer. His younger brother stopped crying and they
    began watching that.
It drew near and, lo and behold, they saw that it
was a woman
who was coming down
from the sky!
19
Lo and behold, when she got close, one of them saw—
this was when they used to have parkas like this—
that she was holding something in the fold of her clothing, that she
    was holding something in front of her![2]
20
She descended going round and round [and alighted] next to them,
and when she touched down, when she landed on the ground,
she spilled what she
was holding in her skirt onto the ground.
What she spilled out became land and all of a sudden there they were,
situated on land!
21
And then she said to them, "So,
having compassion for you,
I am allowing you to see me; I have come to you.

22
Kitaki
tua-i nunavtegnek itrarniartutek nutaan
maaggun."
Tua-ll' taum
anngaan
pillinia, arnauluni tua-i, "Alingnaqvaa,
tua-i-qaa
maliksukumegten qessaciquten?"
23
Pillinia, "Tua-i-wa
maliksukuvtegnga maligciiqekemtek."

22
Now,
you may go back to your home at last,
this way."[3]
Then that
older brother
said to her, she being a woman, "*Alingnaqvaa!* Oh heavens,
would you
refuse if we asked you to come with us?"
23
She said to him, "If
you want to take me with you, I will accompany you."

Caqigaq, Christine Post Lincoln, *Qaluyaaq*, 1927. Photo from the Geist Collection, Anchorage Museum of History and Art B92.38.52.

***

24
Tua-i nutaan malikluteng tuavet uitaviggamegnun
utrutliniluku.
25
Tekicameng tua tamaa-i
ilakenga'artelliniak.
26
Nutaan
ayagaqamek,
nutaan tua-i
imkut pissulallmek amllenritnek utrutaqlutek aulukestenga'arcata.
Taum-am cal' arnam tua-i elluarrluki
aulukluki tamakut unangkengakek,
unkut taqukat cali-ll' pavaken
tuntut
cali
pitalkek waten uksuarmi.
Nutaan tua-i ilaganga'arrlukek.

***

27
Tua-i-ll' caqerluku
uum
anngaan tauna
arnaq pillinia, "Alingnaqvaa,
tua-i tang aipaqsaguskumegnuk wangkuk taugaam atawauyalria!"
28
Tua-llu
pillinia, "Kitak-wa tua tuaten
aipaqsukuvnga."
Nutaan tua-i aipaqsagutelliniluk' tua-i.
Ayagaaqlutek tua-i
maaken
cailkamek
tuntunek tuaten
ayagaqamek pitaqlutek.[b]

***

24
So bringing her along, they went back to their home,
the three of them together.
25
When they arrived back there,
they began to live with her.
26
Then at last,
when they went out traveling to hunt,
they started
to return home with more than what they used to catch, since they
    now had someone to take care of the catch.
Indeed, that woman carefully
tended to what they caught,
those seals from down on the coast and caribou
from up inland,
as well as
to what they caught throughout the fall.
She finally became part of the family.

***

27
Then one day
that
older brother of his,
said to that woman, "*Alingnaqvaa!* Oh dear,
it would be a good thing if we became husband and wife!"
28
So then
she said to him, "All right then, if you want it that way,
if you want me for a wife."[4]
So finally they became husband and wife.
They [the two brothers] began to travel around
and from the land,
deep in the wilderness,
they would get caribou.
Whenever they went out they would catch some.

***

29
Tua-ll'-am[c]
caqerlutek tayim' ayalliniuk.
Tayima tua-i.
Ak'anun tua pivkenani tauna
uyuraa
tekitelliniluni.
30
Tekicara'arluni tua-i
itliniluni.
Iterngan pillinia, "Waqaa,
qaill' pilriaten
tekicara'arcit?"
Tua-ll' pillinia urluvra-gguq qelutairtuq,
qelutii kevkartuq.
31
Aren tua-i kevkartellinian,
pikaitenrilami yualunek
qelutekiulliniluk' tamaa-i,
imkurluki
qunavutmek,
qupurrluki.
(Tuatnatullruameng yualunek, tuatnatullruut tangvatullrulua-llu wii
    tuatnalrianek.)
Piirriluni
qelutekiulliniluk', qelutekiurturalliniluk'.
32
Qelutekiurinanrani taum
tan'gurraam
tauna tua-i ullagluku
cangllinikii tua-i, maaggun tuaten qaingakun
piaqluku, tua-i
piaqluku.
33
Tua-i qelutekiurluk' imumek tua piirriluni takturringluni
tuatnallrani-am
tamatumek qelutekiuraminek
kegginaakun waten
tua-gg' uluryaciqallinia. "Tua-i
qaripiiqnii
pii!"

***

29
Then
one day they [the brothers] left.
So they were gone;
it wasn't long before that
younger brother of his
came back home.
30
He arrived early
and entered.
When he came in she said to him, " *Waqaa!* Hello,
why are you
back early?"
So then he said to her that his bow string broke,
that his bow string had snapped.
31
Aren, so because it was broken
and since she didn't lack sinew,
she began to make a string for his bow,
doing this
with a sinew separator,
separating them.
(Because that was the customary way to work sinew, that's what
    they used to do and I used to see them doing it.)
Braiding some,
she made a bow string; she began to make a bow string.
32
While she was making a bow string, that
young man
came to her
and began to bother her; he would touch her here
on her body,
bothering her.
33
She was busy making a string for him, braiding it, and it was
    getting long,
and when he annoyed her,
she did this [lashing him] on his face
with that bowstring she was making,
causing him to wince. "Stop
slowing me
down!"

34
Imna-gguq tuaten pikiini
pus'a'rtelliniuq wavet natermun.
Tua pus'a'rcan,
qaillun-llu pivkenaku, qaill' pinrilamiu tamatumek taugaam
qelutekiuraminek uluryacirluku pillruamiu.
35
Tua-i-llu-gguq
tamana tamaa-i qelutekiurani
taqngamiu pillinia, "Kitak, tua-i maa-i
urluverpet qelutekaa taq'uq.
Elliluku cali ayagyukuvet ayii!"
Una-gguq qanrucaaqekiini uitaluni tua waniwa.
36
Tuamte-ll' tua pillinia, "Alingnaqvaa,
maa-i qeluten
taq'aqa.
Elliluku
ayagyukuvet cali ayii." Qanrucaaqengraani-gguq
uitalliniluni.
Maaten-gguq kiuyunrilani
ullagluku
pillinia
ak'a-gguq tuqullrulliniluni!
37
Kegginaa tua man'a
imutun tamatum qelutem tuarpiaq-gguq
piqerrluku pilleq.
38
Aren qessanayullalliniuq taun' arnaq.
Tauna tua angutni
umyuamikun tua pillinia tua-i alingluni cakneq,
qaillun pillerkaunani!
39
Tua-i-ll' qaill' pillerkailami,
imumek waten enet
kangcirangqetullruameng
tupiganek,
mat'um maani acim kelua pakigluku
elalliniluku man'a enem,
kangcirat amatiit,
ellinguaqaqluku tua-i.

34
It was said that when she did that to him,
he quickly bent down to the floor here.
Then after he bent down,
that's all she did to him, because, except for having made him wince
with that bowstring, she didn't do anything more to him.
35
Then, it was said,
when she was done making
that bow string, she said to him, "Now then, this
string for your bow is done.
Put it on and if you want to go, then go!"
When she tried to tell him, he just stayed there.
36
Again she said to him, "*Alingnaqvaa!* Oh dear,
I'm done now
with your bow string!
Put it on and
again, if you want to, go!" Although she tried to tell him,
he just stayed there.
When he wouldn't answer her,
she went over to him
and saw, lo and behold,
that he was already dead!
37
His face
appeared as though it had been whipped
by the bow string!
38
Aren, that woman really regretted it!
She thought of her husband
and was very frightened,
not knowing what she ought to do!
39
So then, because she didn't know what she ought to do,
since these sod houses
used to have grass mats
for paneling,
she drew it back here behind the bed
and began to dig a grave in the house,
behind the grass matting,[5]
measuring him occasionally.

Engelqayagucan-llu tua-i,
imkut tamakut kangcirat ayuquciicetun
ellilliniluki.
40
Arnaq tua tauna arenqianani umyuarrluuqerrluni cakneq
taumek anngaanek.

***

41
Tua-i-ll' piqerluni
anngaa tua tekitelliniluni tauna.
42
Tua-i kenillruami
tekipailgan tua-i neqkiurluku
tekiutarkiurluku.
43
Ner'lliniluni,
waniwa tua tua imumek tua neru'urluni.
44
Tua-ll' imumek taqluni
aqsiqerrluni.

Panruk, MaryAnn Hooper, *Niugtaq,* 1958. Photo by Christine Heller, courtesy
of the Anchorage Museum of History and Art B91.11.548.

When he was able to fit,
she put the grass mat curtains back
the way they were.
40
That woman was very worried and anxious
about his older brother.

***

41
So then in a short while
his older brother arrived.
42
Since she had already cooked
before he came home, she got his food ready
to give him his welcoming meal when he arrived.
43
He ate,
you know, he continued to eat.
44
Then, getting full,
he stopped.

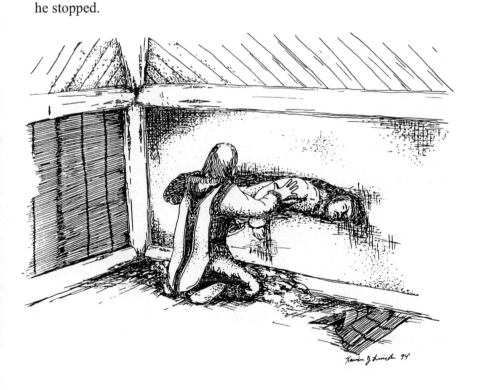

45
Tuavet tua-i tamaavet taklara'artelliniuq waten tamaavet kangciranun.
Taklara'arteqerluni,
qaillun una
pilliniuq
qanerluni, "Aling, ca, ca tanem pamna
pamani aviranaqvakarta?"
46
Tua-i tauna-ll' qaneqsaunani tua
tauna
aipaa arnaq.
47
Tua-i pamavet pirraarluni, "Aling, ca pamna?"
Tua pivakarluni
tauna tua pakilliniluku,
tamakut kangcirat.
Tua pakigluku tua tanglliniluku tauna tua-i.
Tua-i-ll' qanlliniuq, "Waqaa!
Qaillun una pia?"
48
Tua-i-ll' taum
arnam pillinia, "Tua-i-w' arenqialnguq!
Qelutaircilliniluni
urluvminek unuaq,
qelutekiullemni tua-i
pivakaanga
mat'umek maa-i urluvrem qelutekaanek uluryaciqerluku pilqa
pitekluku tua-i tuaten,
tuaten tua pillinilria.
49
"Tua-i arenqiatuq!
Tua-i-w' waniw' maannģaitua!"
50
Tua-i-ll' taum
angutiin
pillinia, "Arenqiapaa,
qaillun pivkenak!
Canrituq!
Tua-i piami waniw' waten piuq. Canrituq!
Ayagpegnak!"
51
Tua-i pillinia, "Arenqialnguq-wa

45

He lay down on those grass mats, on those woven grass curtains.
Laying down,
he felt around
and said,
"*Aling*, what, what in the world is behind me
that's so uncomfortable?"
46
That woman,
his wife,
didn't say a word.
47
Then after looking behind he said, "*Aling*, what is back here?"
Feeling around
he peeled back
that grass matting.
Peeling it back he saw him.
And he said, "*Waqaa!* What!
What's wrong with him?"
48
So then that
woman said to him, "It is unfortunate!
He had broken his bow string
this morning,
and while I made him a bow string,
he kept on bothering me
and on account of the fact that I made him wince with the bow string
    I was making,
he ended up like that.
49
It is unfortunate!
So I won't stay here!"
50
And so that
husband of hers
said to her, "*Arenqiapaa!* Oh heavens,
don't worry!
It's okay!
This happened to him because of what he did. It's okay!
Don't go!"
51
Then she said to him, "Unfortunately,

umyuan assirrlainarngaituq cam iliini.
Umyuan assiilkan
qaillukuarlua piciqngatarpenga."
Aren tua-i pingaitniluku tua!

***

52
Tua-i-ll'
piqerlun' anllinilun' tayima
tauna arnaq.
53
Anellran kinguani,
tua-ll' qakemna
niitnariqertelliniuq imutun
agiirtellmitun.
Qakma niitnariqertelliniuq qakma.
54
Anqerrluni
pillinia ak'a-gguq tua-i maa-i
qerratartelliniluni.
Aren talliminek-llu piyaaqekii tua-i enurluk' tua-i!
Imutun-am tua-i atullminek tamatumek yuarutmek aturluni.
Pillinia, "Arenqiapaa,
ciin waniw' ayagcit?"
Tua-ll' taum arnam pillinia, "Arenqialnguq-wa tua-i
umyuan eq'engkan
taumek uyu'urpenek,
uitasngailavnga!
Tua maancuumiilama kingunemnun tua waniw' ayakatalrianga!"
55
Aren tua-i enurluku!
Ayagturalliniur-am tua pagaa-i uivurluni quletmun tua tayima
tangssugluk' kiituan' tayim' tangrruunrirtuq pagaavet qilagmun.

***

56
Aren tua-i cacirkairteũrlulliniuq kinguani!

57
Tua-i
uitaqerluni, uitaqeryaaqerraarluni...
Tauna-gguq

you won't always be well-disposed.
If your thoughts turn bad,
you may do something to me."
Aren, he said he wouldn't do anything!

***

52
Then
that woman
right then and there went outside.
53
After she left,
there was something that could now be heard outside,
like the first time
she had come.
Outside something could be heard.
54
He quickly went out
and saw that she was already
ascending.
Aren, he tried to reach her with his arms, but in vain!
Again she was singing the same song she sang before.
He said to her, "*Arenqiapaa*! Oh my goodness,
why are you departing?"
So then that woman said to him, "It is unfortunate, because
if you become enraged
about your younger brother,
you will not leave me alone!
So since I don't want to be here, I'm going back to where I came from!"
55
Alas, he couldn't reach her!
She began to go up there, rising upwards, going around and around
while he watched her and at last she could no longer be seen in the sky.

***

56
Aren, with her gone the poor thing was beside himself, with nothing
     to do!
57
So
he remained for a minute, and having waited there a while to no avail...
That

mayurrvik
qavciim amianek
pitangqelartuq.
58
Tua-i-llu
qanlliniuq, "Aling, arenqialngua-gg' tua-i waniwa
waten kiimenii tua-i piyuumiitua."
Tauna tua qavcik
aqvaluku
kenitelliniluku mermek,
amiq,
amiq tua-i amiungan.
Kenilluku tua-i nengugtaarluku.
Nengugtaarngamiu
pilliniuq, "Ataki tua wii
makuurrlii taũgaam."
59
Aiparmi-llu-gguq kegginalga
man' navgurluku[d]
cetukluku, cetui tamakut
piluki.

Uliggaq, Susie Angaiak, *Tununeq*, circa 1980. Photo by Andrew J. Chikoyak.

elevated food cache, it was said,
had a wolverine
skin.
58
So then
he said, "*Aling*, I find it depressing
and I don't want to live alone like this."
He went and got
that wolverine
and soaked it in water,
that is, the pelt,
because it was a pelt.
He soaked it and stretched it.
As he was stretching it,
he said, "If only I could
become one of these!"
59
And, it was said, [taking] his wife's *uluaq*,[6]
he cut the *uluaq*
and used it for claws, using those [shards]
for claws.

Apalciq from *Niugtaq*, 1958. Photo by Christine Heller, courtesy of the Anchorage Museum of History and Art B91.11.442.

60
At'elliniluku tauna tua-i qavciim imna amia.
Tua-i qavciurrluni tuani.

61
Tuamte-ll' tua-i pilliniuq, "Tua-i-w'
wani uitangailngua
ingrinun taũgaam ayaglua tamaani
pikuma nutaan
uitaciqelrianga."

62
Tua-i-gguq
tamaa-i tauna qavcik
tamaa-i tuaten qavciurtellruuq tauna tua kiimellirngami.

***

63
Aũgna ava-i qanemciq tua waten waniw' taktaluni
ayuquq.
Tayima uum wani iluracungama elitaqlikii
niitetullikii-ll' tayim' iliini.

64
Tua waten waniw' pitaluku;
iquklituq tua-i.

65
Tua-i-gguq qavciurrluni tuani[e]
pillruuq
tauna tua-i,
angun tauna.
Tua-i iquklituq; waten waniw' taktauq
una waniw' qanemcika.

66
Tua-i aũgna ava-i qanemcika iquklituq.

60
He put that on, that wolverine skin.
So he became a wolverine right then and there.
61
Furthermore, he said, "I won't
remain here;
rather I shall go into
the mountains
and there I shall stay."
62
So, it was said,
back then
he thus became a wolverine when he found himself all alone.[7]

***

63
That's how long that story
is.
I suppose my cousin here recognizes it
and perhaps has heard it at some time.[8]
64
This is how long it is;
it is over.
65
So it was said he became a wolverine that day,
that one,
that man
did.
Well, it is the end; this is how long
my story is.
66
The story I just told is over.

Children listen as a girl tells a story knife story in Hooper Bay in the 1950s.
Photo from the Alfred Milotte Collection (acc. #90-045) in the Archives, Alaska
and Polar Regions Dept., University of Alaska Fairbanks.

Domesticity And Violence

Yup'ik children used to tell stories together, using story knives to draw figures in the sand, soft clay, soil or snow. The story knives can be elaborately carved ivory knives or something as simple as a metal butter knife. *Cingarkaq,* Eliza Orr, said that when she was young, children liked to use strips of metal banding for story knives. Generally the stories were told by girls who drew stylized stick figures in the ground to accompany their narrations. *Aparpak,* Victor Kanrilak Jr., remembers as a small boy having to spit on the dry ground to dampen it so the girls could make their story knife figures. Children in *Tununeq* told story knife stories until fairly recently, but nowadays, with television in the village, children are rarely seen using story knives.

When the older generation of people living today told story knife stories as children, they would tell *qulirat* and *qanemcit,* that is, traditional stories. In *Cingarkaq's* time (she was born in 1958) the girls made up *Anuurluqelriik* 'Grandmother and Orphan' stories, improvising on traditional stories. They also told "playhouse" stories; that is, they made up fantasy stories about families, homes and children, just as other American children do.

We decided to reintroduce the tradition of story knives to the primary and middle-grade students in Tununak. Using clay soil which we had gathered before freeze-up, we invited groups of older women to the school. Each elder had a group of several students, some plastic butter knives from the cafeteria, and a shallow box of soil. The students seemed to enjoy the activity very much; the small groups were conducive to the kind of intimacy that is ideal for storytelling exchanges, and they got to use their hands and move about. This story, recorded on October 17, 1994, is the result of one session.

Although the story may at first appear as innocuous, in fact the story as *Kakgailnguq* tells it deals with content which is deeply disturbing, especially to a child. Like the popular fairy tales of *Bluebeard* or *Hansel and Gretel,* the story of "*Negairpak* 'Big Spider'" is hardly light entertainment, with its evocations of domestic violence, abuse and dismemberment. It brings to mind that fairy tales, albeit ingenuous, often deal with the inner conflicts and the dark underside of the personality, posing issues and dilemmas that children encounter and must of necessity work through in order to achieve integration, a point well made by the psychoanalyst Bruno Bettelheim in *The Uses of Enchantment* (1975). Further on we encounter the figure of the intrepid and resourceful heroine in "*Uqurilria Neviarcaq: The Obese Girl*," the female who is always equal to her predicament. Here we meet her counterpart, the woman who is completely at the mercy of a domineering and violent male. In such situations a woman's position could be difficult, with little or no remedy. As Lantis writes, "Although there were customs of kindness and tolerance toward children, the society centered in the adult males. The good hunter or shaman could take or discard women and children as he wished, short of physically mistreating them" (Lantis 1960: 167).

As always, there is very little in the way of commentary to help us know the narrator's attitude toward the material. The narrator sticks pretty much to recounting the events and leaves the evaluation to the audience. Yet there is something very pathetic, for instance, in *Kakgailnguq*'s portrayal of the flounder-woman's resignation to her fate, and the daughter's terror when her mother is led away is deeply affecting and all too familiar. *Kakgailnguq* tells this story in a very soft and quiet voice, with little modulation and barely detectable emotion; yet, paradoxically, this only adds to our sense of revulsion.

Nep'ik 'sod house' in *Umkumiut*, 1950s or 1960s. Photo by Christine Heller, courtesy of the Anchorage Museum of History and Art B91.11.457.

NEGAIRPAK

Kakgailnguq Tununermiu

***

1
Tua-lli-gga-gguq una
negairpak atralria ellami pagaani, *spider*-aq angelria!
Atrarluni.
Anuqengaqan-gguq
tengtaqluku.
North-amek anuqengaqan tengtaqluku.
Anuqet-gguq tamalkuita atrainanrani
tengtaqluku.
Anuqet tamalkuita tenglluk' tua-i-llu quunengluni.

2
Quunengan-llu-gguq
atrainanermini qavaqalliniluni.
Qavarlun' tua-i
anglaniluni quunermek puqlerpagmek.
3
Tua-i-ll' tupagyungami tupalliniluni.
Tekiteqatalliniluni nunamun.
Maaten-gguq kiarrluni piuq, acini un'a tangrraa,
aciani
kuik ameltuluni!
Ellriini kuigpall'er ameltuluni.
Tua-i kiarrluni nall'arteqatalliniamiu,
un'gani uakaramini pilliniuq muragpall'er un'a
kuigmi caningqaluni.
4
Tua-i-ll' ullangnaqluku
negairpiim piqtaarluni—tangrruallemni—
piqtaarluni
murak tamana tekitelliniluku, nallairluku *spider*-am.

BIG SPIDER

Lucy James of Tununak

***

1
Once upon a time there was this
big spider coming down from the sky up there, a big spider!
He was coming down.
It is said that when it got windy
the wind would blow him away.
When it blew from the north, he got blown away.
The winds from all directions blew him away
while he was descending.
He was blown away by the wind from every direction and then it
    became calm.
2
When it got calm,
he fell asleep as he was going down.
So he was sleeping,
enjoying the calm weather and the warm air.
3
And then, when it was time to wake up, he woke up.
He was about to get to the earth.
Lo and behold, he glanced around and looked below
and there beneath him
was a wide river!
At least to him it was a big, wide river.
So he looked all around because he was going to land on it
and when he looked downriver he saw a big piece of driftwood
lying across the river.
4
And then the big spider tried to go to it,
swinging back and forth—the way I imagine it—
swinging back and forth,
the spider reached the mark right above the wood.

5
Tua-i-llu nall'arcamiu tua uitaluni atrarluni
tull'uni-llu-gguq tamaavet muragmun, muragpall'ermun.
Tagluni tua-i
kiartelliniluni: imarpiim ceñii un'a
qaũgyarluni.
Tua-i-llu-gguq atrarluni, atraqcaarluni,
qaũgyami yaaruilliniluni muragaarmek yaaruicirluni
caarkaicuami.
6
Nel'inguarluni yaaruiluni
acililuku-llu
cat-llu ellinguarturluki
umyuartequ'urluni,
"Ukut wani piugut, ukut piugut..."
Kiirrarmi-gguq tua-i *spider*-auluni.
7
Tuamte-ll'-am yaani yaatiini
neqivilinguarluni, neqivigmek, elagyamek.
Qaingani-llu-gguq
yul'inguarluni—
icigg' pilinguarluni yuguamek, arnaruamek.

100

5

Then when he was above it he stopped and went down,
landing on that piece of wood, on that huge log.
So he went up to the shore
and looked around: the shore of the ocean down there
was covered with sand.
And then, it is said, he went down, slowly working his way down,
and told a story knife tale on the sand, using a piece of wood,
because he had nothing else to do.
6

He made an imaginary house with the story knife,
drawing in a bed
and putting in other things as well,
thinking all the time,
"These represent these, these represent these..."
He was the only spider there.
7

Furthermore, over there, in the area beyond it,
he drew an imaginary food storage place, a *elagyaq*.
On top of it
he made an imaginary person—
you know, he drew a make-believe person, an imaginary woman.

Fishing for *iqalluarpiit* 'herring' between *Uyalget Igvaat* and *Uyaqurruaq* near *Tununeq*, circa 1980. Photo by Andrew J. Chikoyak.

8
Pirraarluni amiigakun tuaggun amiinguarakun itliniluni.
Iterngami-llu-gguq acilinguallminun
inartellriim tayima qavaqalliniluni.
Tua qavarluni.

***

9
Tupagyungami tupalliniuq:
nerpall'er man'a!
Cat-gguq tua ellillri makut piunguarluki
piurtelliniluteng.
Cat tua-i ellinguallri piurrluteng.
Tua-i uitaluni quyaluni
pilinguallni neng'urtellinian—quliraungami.
10
Tauna yul'inguallni ellami
paqtellinia,
arnaq pikna
akluunani matarmi qerruyuaralria uqutmun caugarrluni, anuqii
    tunulluku,
qerrulluni qungingaluni.
11
Tua-i-llu
quyaqerluni
teguluku itrulluku
aturalivkarluku
spider-am
arnaq tauna.
Wife-aqsagutelliniluku.
12
Tua-i
uitalutek tua-i irnianglutek-llu-gguq *boy*-amek,
irniayagarluni *boy*-amek. Unuaquan-gguq tupagtuk:
irniacuariik takuskegcirluni quuyurniaqluni-llu.
13
Tuamte-ll'-am-gguq
aipirilutek tupagtuk:
uyaqurri tegg'illinilriit, ak'a tua-i tegg'iluteng.
14
Tuamte-ll'-am-gguq tua-i tupanqiggluteng,
three-aani ernerni:

8
Having done this he went in the door, the imaginary door.
Upon entering he went to the imaginary bed he had drawn,
and laying down he fell asleep.
So he slept.

***

9
When it was time to get up, he awakened:
here was this big house!
The things he had drawn in as imaginary things
had become real.
Everything he had drawn had become real.
So he was happy and he stayed there
because the house he had drawn had become real—since this is a *quliraq*.
10
He went to check
that imaginary person he had drawn outside,
that woman up there,
who was without clothes, shivering with her back to the wind,
curled and cold.

11
And then
he was delighted
and he took her and brought her inside,
and that spider
had that woman
make clothes.
She became his wife.
12
So
they stayed there and they had a child, a boy,
a little boy child. It is said that they woke up the next day:
their little child was easily able to turn his head sideways and smile.
13
Furthermore, it is said,
they woke up on the second day:
his neck was already strong enough to hold his head up.
14
And again they woke up
on the third day:

aqumgayangiirluni ak'a, aqumgayaurrluni.
15
Tuamte-ll' tua-i
qavarluteng.
Tupagtut-gguq-am:
aurrsaurtellinilria natermi—
icigg' waten piqcaarluni pekcaurtelliniluni.[a]
Tua-i-gguq cukak'ayagluni tauna qetunraak.
Tupanqigtut-ggur-am: kiimiirluni, *all alone*-arluni.
16
Tua-i-ll'
tupanqigtut: ak'a pekluni,
aqvaquanguq; uqilariuq cukanrarluni.
17
Tua-i-llu-gguq atiin, *spider*-am,
pinarian
qayaliluku, tangerrluku-gg' tua-i qayaliluku,
muragnek
imarpiim ceñiinek.
18
Qikertartangqertuq-gguq imarpiim kanani iluani,
nuna, qikertaq.
19
Ayagaqluni-gguq[b]
pissurluni qayani aturluku.
Taqukaculuni, piciatun, tengmianek
reindeer-anek-llu pitaqluni.
20
Atiin pilalliniluku
qikertamun kanavet piqaasqevkenaku camek taqukamek
    malirqangraan.

***

21
Niiculuni tauna
irniara.
Aatami inerqurqani niitaqluni.
Tua-ll' caqerluni
pivakarluni taqukamek malirqalliniluni.
Tauna-llu-gguq nunapik, qikertaq,
tekiarrluku,
tekiartelliniluku. Maaten-gguq piqertuq qayam ugircaraa una,

he was already able to sit on his own.
15
And then again
they went to sleep.
It is said they all woke up:
the boy was able to crawl on the floor—
you know, he was able to move about doing this.[1]
It is said that son of theirs grew quickly.
They woke up again: he could be by himself without toppling over.
16
Then
they woke up again; already he was walking
and beginning to run; he had quickly become fleet-footed.
17
And then it was said that his father, the spider,
because it was time,
seeing [how fast] he was growing, made a kayak for him
out of wood
from the ocean shore.
18
There was an island, it is said, down in the ocean,
a piece of land, an island.
19
He would go out
hunting, using his kayak.
He was good at catching seals, all kinds of different game, geese,
and even reindeer.[2]
20
His father would tell him
never to go to that island down there even though he might be
    chasing something, like a seal.

***

21
That child of his
was obedient.
When his father warned him not to do something, he listened.
Then one time
he was pursuing a seal.
It was said
that he happened upon a tundra island,
having gotten there accidentally. Lo and behold, he saw this place

tangvak'arraarluku
umyuarteqliniluni,
"Una-gga
aatama inerquutaq'lallikii
pisqevkenaku!"
Tangssuararraarluku-gguq tuavet ugircaramun tagluni ugirtelliniluni.

22
Maaten-gguq piqertuq tumyarat makut!
Yuuluni. "Aatama waniw' inerquutaqlikii."
Tuani niicuiteqerluni.
Yuuluni tumyarakun ayagluni.
Ayainanermini-am piqertuq akret makut,
nevuq akruluni, *stairs*-arluni.
Mayurluni,
qavcinek piqerluni piqalliniuq: pelatekaq ingna, *tent*-aq.
Tua-i-llu-gguq
nangerngaluni umyuarteqluni, "Una-gga waniwa aatama
    inerquutaqtullikii
ullaasqevkenaku."

23
Niicuiteqaami taum nalliini ullalliniluku.
Amiigakun qinquussaakalliniuq:
arnaq kiugna
acimini
mingqelria, iqrelria
imarnitegnek,
raincoat-aliluni taqukam qiluanek.
24
Tua-i-llu iterluni.
Iterngan taum arnam pillinia,
"Waqaa! Aatavet inerqularaaten taiqaasqevkenak."
Nalluvkenaku-gguq tauna inerquutaqtukni.
25
Tua-i-ll' yaatiinun, akitiin yaatiinun, aqumqalliniluni tangssuarluku
    mingqellria.
Pilnguami-gguq
caarrlugmek tegulluni yualua amugaqaku
caranglluk, *grass*-aq,
yualuanun

where kayaks were beached
and after looking at it briefly,
he thought to himself,
"Perhaps this is the place
my father has warned me
about!"
It is said that having looked at it for a while, he went up there and
    beached his kayak.
22
When he got there, lo and behold, he saw this path!
He got out of his kayak. "Perhaps this is the place my father warned
    me about."
This time he was being disobedient.
He got out and followed the path.
While he was going he came to these stairs,
stairs dug into the soil.
He went up
and after a few steps he saw a tent over there.[3]
And then, it is said,
while standing there he thought to himself, "Perhaps this is the place
    my father has warned me about,
saying not to go there."
23
Because this time he was being disobedient, he went to it.
He peeked in through the door:
there was a woman inside,
on her bed,
sewing, sewing a waterproof seam
on a raincoat,
making a raincoat out of seal gut.
24
And then he went in.
Upon his entrance the woman said to him,
" *Waqaa*! Your father warned you not to come here."
She knew of his father's repeated warnings to him.
25
Then he sat down next to her pillow and watched her sew.
When he tired of watching,
he took a piece of discarded grass and as she pulled her thread in,
he would put a piece of grass
[through the loop] of her thread
and she would pull it in with her thread.

piqaqan tapqarulluku mingqutaqluku.
Kiituan-gguq tauna arnaq qennguq.
Utercesqevvakaani tua utertelliniluni.
26
Tua-i tekilluni tua-i
camek pivkenan', pitevkenan', taqukatevkenan' taqukacuyaaqelria.

27
Tuamte-ll'-am-gguq unuaquan atrarluni
qamigaruarluni tuavet cal' arnamun pilliniluni.
Tuaten-am tua-i.
28
Tua-ll'
mingeqnginanrani-am tua-i
caarrlugmek piqa'aqluku.
"Arca-gguq! Aatavet tuquciiqaanga!"
"Tuqusngaitaaten;
nalluuq."
29
Pivakaani-am tua-i qenrutengengani anlliniluni uterrluni.
Tauna-gguq
angun
picuirulluni.
Ayaktang'ermi-llu-gguq picuirulluni
tuavet piqtaarngami arnamun
aatami inerquutaanun.

30
Tua-i-llu
tuaten-am ayallrani
aipani,
wife-ani, [Negairpiim] pillinia,
"Qetunrarpuk tekiskan
ellimeqaqiu
pavaken tuntumek nutaramek aqvacesqelluku!"
Tuntuyungniluni.
Tua-i tekitellrani aaniin pilliniluku,
"Kaaka-gguq aatan
tuntumek nutaramek neryulria. Aqvaskiu-gguq unuaqu."

Finally, it is said, that woman began to get angry.
Since she kept telling him to go home, he went home.

26
So he got back
with nothing, having caught nothing, not even a seal, although
    he was one who usually caught seals.
27
And then again, it is said, he went down the next day
and pretending to go out seal hunting, he went to that woman again.
The same thing happened.
28
And again
while she was sewing,
he took some grass and did what he did [the other time].
"I said stop it! Your father will kill me!"
"He won't kill you;
he doesn't know."
29
Because she kept telling him to go and was angry with him, he
    went out and returned home.
That
man, it is said,
never caught anything anymore.
Although he went out, he never caught anything,
because he kept going to that woman,
the one his father warned him about.[4]
30
And then
when [the son] went out as he was accustomed to do,
[Spider] said
to his wife,
"When our son arrives,
direct him
to get a fresh caribou from up there!"
He said that he was craving for caribou.
So when [the boy] arrived, his mother said to him,
"Listen, your father said
that he wants to eat fresh caribou. He said to get him some tomorrow."

***

31
Tua-i-llu
tuaten piani tupagngameng
upluni urluvni teguluku ayalliniluni pekluni
pavavet kelumeggnun.
Tua-i-llu-gguq ipluni tayima. Atii-gguq *house*-ameng tunuani
nacarrlugteqluni ellami
inanglilria,
ellami tua-i inangqaurluni nem mengliini.
32
Tua-i-ll' qetunrani aŭgna tamarngan
maktelliniluni,
alirluni,
qayamun aglaalliniluni.
Tekicamiu makluku atrarrluku
ayalaalliniluni tuavet arnamun, qikertamun.
(Qenercami pillilria.)

33
Tua-i-llu-gguq
arnaq tekicamiu callulliniluku *spider*-am
aunrarqelluku, talliik qecugluk', iruk qecugluk' qamiqurra-ll'.
Unguvaarkaunrian unilluku. Tuamte-ll' taglaalliniluni

***

31

And then

since [the son] was asked to, when they woke up,

he got ready, took his bow and departed, walking

up toward the area inland.

Then he disappeared out of sight. His father was behind their house,

afflicted with gloomy thoughts,[5]

lounging around,

lying down outside next to the house.

32

And then when his son was well out of view,

he got up,

slipped his arms into his sleeves,

and he quickly went to the kayak.

When he got to it he set it upright and dragged it down [to the
    water's edge]

and he quickly went to that woman on the island.

(Perhaps he did that because he was angry.)

33

And then, it is said,

when Spider got to the woman he fought her,

making her bloody, tearing off her arms, legs, and also her head.

He left her for dead. Then he quickly went up

Mellgar (Apac'iq), Jimmy Short, *Tununermiu*, 1957. Photo by Christine Heller,
courtesy of the Anchorage Museum of History and Art B91.11.430.

111

nem'eggnun,
qetunrani tekipailgan.
Tagqerrulluku qayaq ayuqucillratun
akiviggluku,
palurrluku.
Taqngamiu nem'eng-am tunuanun uitavillminun
aqumluni nacarluni iggangliuralliniluni.

34
Tua-i-llu-gguq qetunraa tekilluni maa-i, agiirrluni maa-i.
Tekican tua-i iterluni.
Pitliniluni tuntumek.
35
Tua-i-llu
inarrluteng-am tua-i.
Tupagngameng-am tauna angun,
qetunraa,
qayani makluku atralliniluni.
36
Atrarluni tuavet arnamun
imarnicilriamun.
Maaten-gguq qinqeryaaquq
auggluut-gguq taũgaam unkut!
Itqerrluni
kiartelliniuq:
cai makut cagtellriit,
qamiqurri makut kepumaluteng!
Tua-ll' tauna angun qanlliniluni,
"Kia-gga pinrilkii aatama pikii!" Taggliniluni
tua-i umyugaa assiinani.

***

37
Iterngami
aatani, *spider*-aq,
tulukaruum *skin*-aanun—
icigg'
kinrumallikii tauna tulukaruum *skin*-aa—
ekliniluku *spider*-aungan
mik'lan *spider*-aq ek'arcuumaan. Ek'arcuumiin

to their house
before his son arrived.
He quickly brought the kayak up and put it back the way it was,
propping it on its side
with the bottom side up.
When he was finished with it he went behind their house, back to
    where he was before,
sat down, put on his hood and lay there on his side, resting on his side.
34
And then his son was arriving, there he was, coming.
When he got there, the father went in.
His son had caught a caribou.
35
Then
they went to bed.
When they woke up, that man,
his son,
set his kayak upright and went down [to the island].
36
He went down to that woman,
the one who was making a raincoat.
Lo and behold, when he peeked inside, it is said
that all he saw were some traces of blood down there!
Rushing in,
he looked around
and saw her body parts scattered about
and her head cut up into bits and pieces!
Then that man said,
"No one else but my father did this to her!" He went back up [to the
    mainland],
feeling very angry.

***

37
When he entered,
he placed his father, the spider,
into the skin of a raven—
you know,
maybe that raven skin
was dry—putting him in because he was a spider,
because a spider is small and can easily be put in. Since he could easily
    fit,

qillerrluku, atraulluku imarpigmun
eggluku
aataūrluni!
38
Aling tua-i-gguq nanikualuni taun' atii.
Ayalliniluni tua aterrluni
qairetgun naluurturluku.
Ceñakunᶜ ayaulluku imarpiim.
39
Tua-i-ll' tuaten-am qailiurturallermini
qavarningami qavaqalliniluni.
40
Tua-i-ll' tupagyaqliami tupagtuq ayuqucia quunirluni.
Pektevkenani-gguq tua uitaluni.
Tua-i-llu
allganermek kiartelliniluni. "Qaill' pisia; kitua-qa?"
umyuarteqliniuq.

41
Allganruarmek kiarcaaqvigminek
cetugmiaqcaarturalliniluku *skin*-aq tamana
cayaqlirluni alcuayagarluni.
Pissaagluku qinertelliniuq tepumaluku ceñami.
Kelutmun-gguq kiartuq muragugaat paūgkut amllerrluteng.
Tua-i anengnaqluni tuaggun allganerkun anluni.
42
Tagluni nel'iluni, *house*-alilun', muragnek
qayaliluni-ll' muragpallraat angenqurriitnek.
43
Taqucami
ayalliniluni ceñarrarkun, imarpiim ceñiikun.
Tua-i ellmikun ayangssiinanermini
ingna neqa tagqertelliniuq, naternaq,
cauga-ll' tayim' kass'atun, naternayagaat.
Tauna ugirtelliniluni ceñamun waten-llu-gguq piurluni.ᵈ
(Icigg' *fish*-at aūgkut piuratulriit.)
44
Tua-i-llu-gguq ullagluk' anguarturluni,
narulkani teguluku
tuqucaaqevkenaku, maaggun mengliikun
pitaqluku.
Teguluku-llu-gguq qayaminun,

he tied it up and brought it down to the ocean
and threw
his poor old father away!
38
Aling, it is said his father was desperate.
He drifted away,
going up and down with the waves.
The ocean [current] was carrying him along the coast.
39
And then while he was going up and down with the motion of the waves,
he got drowsy and fell asleep.
40
When he finally woke up, he realized it was calm all around him.
He wasn't moving anymore.
And then
he searched for a tear [in the raven skin]. "What happened to me;
    did I sink?"
he thought to himself.
41
Having searched for a little tear to no avail,
he strove to scratch that skin with his nails
and finally made a little tear.
He tried to peek out and saw that he had washed ashore along the coast.
Looking towards the mainland, he saw a lot of driftwood.
So after struggling to get out, he emerged from out of that tear.
42
He went up and built a house out of the wood
and made a kayak out of the biggest log.
43
When he finished,
he traveled right along the shore, along the shore of the ocean.
So while he was going along to no particular purpose,
a fish flopped up on the beach, a flounder,
whatever they call it in English, little flounders.
That one beached on the shore and they say it went like this.[6]
(You know how those fish move.)
44
And then, it is said, he paddled toward it,
and taking his spear,
being careful not to kill it, he caught it
here on its side.
He took it into his kayak,

qayami kinguanun,
nep'artelluku, alrapaqluku,
utrulluku.
45
Tua-i-am *spider*-aungami taun' *wife*-aqsagulluku
fish-aungraan.

***

46
Tua-i-llu-gguq tayim' piinanermegni
irnianglutek arnamek.
Tua-i angturriqcaaralliniluni.
Uksurluni tua-i.
Angturriqerrluni atiita-gguq,
taum *spider*-am,
aanateng qenrutaqluku
assiilkengluku.
Kiituan-gguq kiliq'eryaurtaa aunrartelluku puvturluraqluku-llu-gguq.

47
Tua-i-ll' caqerluni
panini pillinia, *daughter*-aani,
"Waniwa aatavet tekiskuni
nutaan tuquciiqaanga! Akwaugaq tuqutenritqalqaanga!"
48
Tua-i-llu piinanrani qakemna yuk yulkialuni.
Tua-lli tua akngirtelliniluni ircaqũrra!
"Nutaan qakma tuqutarkaugaanga!"
49
Itertuq-gguq maaten
nukalpiaq ugna picarnaunani!
Tua-i-ll' arnam taum pillinia, naternam,
"Waqaa?"
Tua-ll' taum nukalpiam pilliniluku, angutem, "Aqvaamken!"
Tua-ll' arna[m pia], "Aqvanritarpenga;
imum tekiskuni piciqaanga!"
"Tua-i-gg' aqvakemken!"
50
Qessaurlungraan—pania-gguq-gga aqumgauralria—
qessaurlungraan tayarnerikun
teguqerluk' anqerrutelliniluku.

into the stern of his kayak,
and stuck it there. Sitting back to back,[7]
he took it home.
45
So because he was a spider he took that one for his wife,
even though she was a fish.

***

46
And then, it is said, sometime later
they had a baby girl.
So the poor thing was growing up.
Then winter came.
As she got bigger, it is said their father,
that spider,
would get angry at their mother
and started to dislike her.
As time went by, he began wounding her, [physically abusing her]
 by giving her cuts which made her bleed, leaving the poor
 thing swollen and puffy.
47
Then one time
she said to her daughter,
"When your father arrives
he will surely kill me! He nearly killed me yesterday!"
48
And then a little later a person made sounds out there.
Her heart skipped a beat!
"This time the one out there will kill me for sure!"
49
When he entered,
lo and behold, it was a worthless looking hunter![8]
Then the flounder woman said to him,
" *Waqaa* ?"
Then that man, the hunter, said to her, "I'm here to get you!"
Then the woman replied, "You're not going to take me;
my husband will do something to me when he arrives!"
"Well, I'm here to get you!"
50
Although she didn't want to—her daughter was sitting there—
although she didn't want to, poor thing, he took her
by her wrist and quickly dragged her out.

Panian-llu-gguq maligarrluku qalrillagluni.
51
Atraulluku imarpiim tungiinun.
Tua-i-llu-gguq kana-i meq tekicamegnegu
mer'em mengliinun nangerrlutek.
Angulvallraam-gguq taum nukalpiam
iqelquni alqimaqeraa, iqmiglukek.
Waten-llu-gguq piluni[e]
iqmiggaarlukek.
52
Tua-i-llu-gguq
imarpik mengelmikun ikirrluni, meq ikirrluni.
Tayima-llu-gguq ayaglutek. Panian-gguq tangssugluku.
Ayiignek-llu-gguq imarpik tamana ayuqucillmitun utqerrluni.

Qirvan, Willie Angaiak, fishing for *cagiq* 'halibut' near *Tununeq,* circa 1980.
Photo by Andrew J. Chikoyak.

Her daughter, it is said, burst out crying and ran after her.
51
He took her down towards the ocean.
Then when they reached the water down there,
they stood by the edge of the water.
It is said the great big man, that hunter,
put his little fingers in his mouth.
After he put his little fingers in his mouth,
he went like this.[9]
52
And then, it is said,
the ocean borders [rose up and] opened; the water opened [and
    exposed the bottom of the ocean].
Then they departed while her daughter was watching.
As soon as they left, the ocean immediately went back to the way it
    was originally.

***

53
Tua-i tayima. Tagluni qiaqcaaralliniluni
aanami putuskaa teguluku.
Pull'uni qianginanrani
aatii qakma tekilluni.

54
Tua-ll' pilliniluni qakma,
"Qailluqtar-kiq qama-i piagu? Unguvaciquten? Tuani pii!"

55
Tua-i-llu-gguq iterlun' qanerturluni; nutaan waniw' callukatarluku!
Iteryaaquq-gguq
pania kiirrarmi qiaqcaaralria.
Tua-i-ll' ullagluku pillinia, "Naugg' aanan?"
Kiuvkenani-llu-gguq.
"Naugga-gguq aanan?"
Kiuyuunani
apqaungraani.
Tua-i-llu-gguq tauna arnaq nangerrluni
anqatangartelliniluni.
Atiin-llu-gguq maliggluku.
Maligcani tua imarpiim tungiinun atrallinilutek.

56
Panicuariin-gguq
tuaten tangvallmitun waten piqerluni.
Pillrani imarpik ikirtuq:
aaniin makut tumai
kina-llu maliklutek.

57
Tua-i-llu panini pillinia, "Utaqanga!
Aanan aqvanauqa."
Tumaikun ayagluni. Ayainanermini
avani
teggarvall'er
mer'em
aciani, imarpiim aciani, terr'ani camani
teggarvall'er ing'. Tekicartullinia tumaikun tua maliggluku.

58
Amiiga ikircesciiganani.
Egalerluni pikaggun.

***

53

And so it was. The poor thing went up to their house and cried and cried,
taking her mother's pillow.
While she was bent over and crying,
her father arrived out there.

54

Then he said from out there,
"Darn her, what did she do to her in there? You live? Hah, stay
    right there!"

55

Then he went in talking the whole time; now he was really going to beat
    her up!
He entered;
however, his poor daughter was crying and crying all by herself.
Then he went up to her and asked, "Where is your mother?"
She didn't answer.
"I said, 'where is your mother'?"
She never answered,
even though he kept asking her.
And then, it is said, that girl stood up
and got ready to go out.
Her father followed her.
Because he followed her, she took him down toward the ocean.

56

His little daughter, it is said,
did what she had previously observed.
When she did that the ocean opened up:
there were her mother's tracks
accompanied by someone else's.

57

Then he said to his daughter, "Wait for me!
I shall go get your mother."
He followed her tracks. As he was going,
[he saw that] over there
was a big rock
under
the water, at the very bottom of the ocean down there,
a great big rock. He approached it following her tracks.

58

Its door couldn't be opened.
It had a window on the top.

Uyangtelliniuq-gguq maaten egalerkun:
aanii kana-i aqumgalria
cissirpallraam-gguq, ciissim,
tauna nemrumaluku
pekcesciiganani.
Kanani-gguq-gga natermi
teggalqurraq;
mel'irluni man'a.

It is said that he peered down through the window:
there, lo and behold, was her mother down there, sitting;
a big serpent, a serpent,
was wrapped around her
and she couldn't move.
Down there on the floor
was a little rock;
there was water around there.

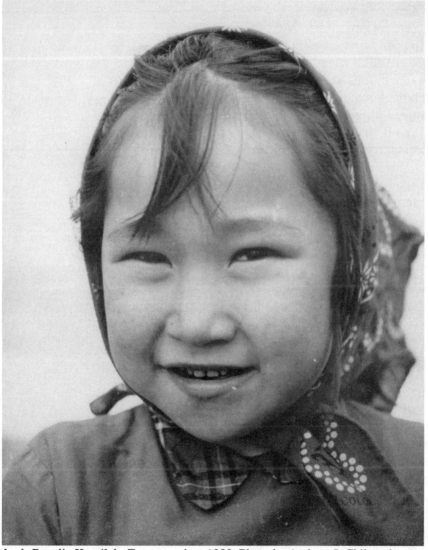

Inuk, Rosalie Kanrilak, *Tununeq*, circa 1980. Photo by Andrew J. Chikoyak.

59
Naruyaq-gguq misngauralria,
nayurtiik taukuk.[f]
60
Tua-i-llu
kanavet pillinia,
"Nulirqa taisgu!"
Tua-ll' pillinia taum cissirpallraam,
"Nulirqekuvgu elpenek aqvau!"
"Kiiki nulirqa taisgu!"
"Elpenek aqvau; nulirqan!"
Tua-i-ll' umyuani assiircan
teggarvall'er tauna
waten pilliniluku.[g]
Pikiini-gguq qup'artuq
amiiga-llu-gguq mermek imangarrluni.
Tua-i-ll' *wife*-ani
teguqataryaaqekii naruyalkuum ullagarrluku neqnguan
        kegqalliniluku. {qanemcista engelartuq}
Yagtellrani-llu-gguq
naruyam igluku
naternaungan, neqnguan, igluku.
Aũgna-llu-gguq tengluni.

***

61
Tua-i-ll' uterteũrlulliniluni unakevkenaku naruyam anrutaani
        uitanga'arcan.
Panini tua-i qanrulluku
aanii naruyamun nerniluku.
Taglutek-gguq nem'eggni uitauqcaaraũrlullinilutek.
62
Pania-gguq iqangtangluni;
manullerii iqangluni.
63
Ayumian-gguq naangualiaqekii-gguq muraggarnek tua-i piciatun.
Iqangengan manua
caviggani, aũgna akaartaq mellga'rmek atlek,
manullerii teguluku kelikcaaralliniluku iqairluku, iqaq aũg'arluku.
Akagartaqluteng-gguq iqat,
iqauluteng tua akagartaqluteng.
Tuaten piluku.

59
It is said that a sea gull was perched there,
the one who was guarding those two.
60
And then,
he said to him down there,
"Give me my wife!"
Then that big serpent replied,
"If she's your wife, get her yourself!"
"*Kiik*! Hurry up and give me my wife!"
"Get her yourself; she's your wife!"
Then, because he got mad,
he went like this
to the big rock.[10]
When he did that, it cracked
and the entrance suddenly filled with water.
And then, when he was about to take his wife,
that darn sea gull quickly went to her and snapped her up because
    she was actually a fish. {narrator laughs}
When she reached out,
the sea gull swallowed her
because she was a flounder, a fish.
And that one, it is said, flew off.

                            ***

61
And then, the poor man went home without his wife because she
    was now in the stomach of the sea gull.
He told his daughter
that the sea gull had eaten her mother.
The poor things went up to their house and there they stayed.
62
His daughter, it is said, was getting dirty;
the front [of her parka] got filthy.
63
Meanwhile, it is said, he made various toys for her out of wood.
Because the front [of her parka] was soiled,
taking his knife, that old-time curved knife which they called *mellgar*,
he took the front [of her parka] and scraped it, cleaning the dirt off.
The dirt rolled down
as little balls of dirt.
He did that.

Wavet-llu elliluki,[h]
waten piluni, iqat akagenqeggluteng,
cupqaqiiteng
egturyauluteng teng'aqluteng.
64
Tua-i-llu wanigga iquklilluni.
Iqat tua makut,
egturyat icigg' iqarraulriit,
iqarrauniluki
pilaqait.
Pinguallrullilriit-gga
akaar-gguq quliram iqaqai. {qanemcista engelartuq}

65
Iquklituq.

He put them here,[11]
placing his hand close to his mouth and blew
the little balls of dirt,
which would fly off as mosquitoes.[12]
64
This is the end of the story.
As for the dirt there,
you know, these mosquitoes are like dust;
they say
they are dust.
Perhaps they pretended
that they were the dirt from the *quliraq* from times past. {narrator
    laughs}
65
This is the end.

The two girls on the far left are unidentified. Next to them from left to right are
Nengqerralria, Katie "Walter" George; *Ciiskuaryuk*, Martina "Walter" Wiseman;
Nuyalran, Bessie Arnakin; and *Paniuyaq*, Lucy Arnakin. *Tununeq*, 1957. Photo
by Christine Heller, courtesy of the Anchorage Museum of History and Art
B91.11.410.

Nayagaq, Caroline Post, left, and *Ellaar,* Anastasia Albert, blowing up a seal poke, 1930s. Photo from the Jesuit Oregon Province Archives, Gonzaga University, negative number 504.21.

Yup'ik Womanhood And The Figure Of The Heroine

Of all the traditional virtues, perhaps none rated higher than the reputation of being a good worker, one who was always busy and occupied with one task or another. As Lantis writes of the *Nunivaarmiut*, "No adult could be lazy. Regardless of status, lineage, age, or physical condition, one had to work to the limit of one's capacity" (Lantis 1946: 245). The woman's sphere of responsibility, according to Lantis, was the conversion of raw materials into consumer goods. She butchered, cut and stored most of the meat and all of the fish, rendered the blubber and stored it in pokes, converted the raw hides into tanned skins, which in turn she made into clothing. Then she cooked and served the food, usually serving it to her husband, fathers, brothers and sons over the age of five in the *qasgiq*. She gathered, dried and stored the grass, weaving it into mats, tote bags and baskets. In addition to her ordinary household and child-care tasks, she gathered a significant portion of the family's food, including greens, roots, berries, mussels, clams, eggs, and more. All ethnographers seem to agree that Yupiit and Inuit women were remarkably industrious and productive.

Yupiit elder informants told Ann Fienup-Riordan that parents of a prospective bridegroom carefully examined a girl before accepting her as a mate for their son. She must be respectful and attentive to her parents, and, most importantly, she must display the right attitude toward food; she must be someone who meticulously cares for food and who is assiduous in avoiding waste (Fienup-Riordan 1994: 172-173). In other words, she would be a hard-working and productive member of an economic partnership.

Traditionally, girls married soon after puberty and even before, sometimes as young as eleven or twelve. Lantis, however, in a revealing collection of personal reminiscences of *Nunivaarmiut*, noted evidence of resistance on the part of girls to early arranged marriages:

Girls lived apart from adult men even more. Hence there was a sense of strangeness that amounted even to fear. Moreover, it seems that in many cases the men were not tender or considerate and the girls had reason to be afraid. Most of the girls were childlike, dependent, unwilling to leave the relation of dependency on parents. They were given little chance to go through a normal adolescence, and rebelled against being forced into adulthood. Finally, there are indications that there was, anciently, greater hostility between males and females than there is now. (Lantis 1960: 41).

In the last three decades, marriages have been occurring at a later age, more in conformity with general American customs, so that nowadays it is highly unusual for a girl to be married before graduation from high school and quite often women may wait until their mid-twenties or even early thirties before contracting a marriage. Moreover, a woman is free to choose her husband, and marriages no longer are arranged by parents. Yet some things in regard to the above still hold true. Yup'ik women are generally still quite hard-working and they are expected to assume household and child-caring chores at an early age. Furthermore, the stereotyped image of Eskimo women as passive and compliant, virtual chattels of a husband, as portrayed by popularizers like Peter Freuchen in *The Book of the Eskimos* (1961), has never been quite accurate. Yup'ik women were always vital in the economy of subsistence, having gender-proscribed but essential roles

Asvaicuk, Bessie Menegak Jackson, left, and *Angalgaq,* Margie Tom Kassaiuli, *Tununeq,* circa 1980. Photo by Andrew J. Chikoyak.

in the economic partnership, and they had considerable autonomy and control in many of their affairs.

The protagonist in the story which follows fulfills some of the ideals of Yup'ik womanhood, being energetic, strong and resourceful. She is a type of Gretel or Cinderella figure, since fate deals her a bad hand. Yet she is equal to her situation; with intrepid courage, the power of her spirit songs, and not a little guile she overcomes all odds. Interestingly, *Puyangun*, the narrator, also is such a person. Although a tradition-bearer and elder of the community, she fulfills in an exemplary way all the traditional roles of a woman. Along with her husband, she owns and operates a successful small business and, in addition to her excellent narrative skills in Yup'ik, she is fully literate in English and is known as a capable and assured person. For many the challenges posed by rapid change and acculturation have proved profoundly disturbing and disruptive; in her case, these have served as a stimulus to greater strength and resourcefulness.

UQURILRIA NEVIARCAQ

Puyangun Tununermiu

***

1
Qanemcikaqa maa-i man'a
mat'um tua-i yuucimta,
tua-i-gg' qanemciungermeng yuuciput aturluki
qanemciutulriit.
2
Tua-i qanemcimek niitaqamta
piciqukut yuucirput,
yuucirput ayuqluku.
Wangkucicetun yuut tamakut pitullrulliniluteng.
3
Man'a maa-i qanemcikaqa
tua-i-gga
ciuliqagcilriit,
ciulirnerulriit,
yut'eng
elluarrluki yuullerkaatnek alerquamaarkauluki.
Makut-llu pisteteng
alartaqata
kitugcilluki,
nunat taũgaam
nepaitlerkaatgun
calivkarluki.
Ilait
aassaqutevkenaki,
kinkuunivkenaki alerqualaasqelluki
callermeggnek-llu, callritnek-llu qanrutesqaqluk', camek-llu
     taqutellratnek qanrutesqaqluku
yuut tamalkuita quyurrluki.
Nalluinanermeggni ca,
ca puglanritnaurtuq nuniitni tuani,
yuut-ll' ilait qiperrlugyaaqluteng tuaten pisqevkenaki.

THE OBESE GIRL

Rose Charlie of Tununak

***

1
This story I'm going to tell
relates to our life;
so even though these are stories, they do illustrate
our way of life.
2
So when we hear a story,
we will be hearing about our way of life,
illustrations of our way of life.
Those people [in the stories] evidently did what we did.
3
This story I'm going to tell
concerns
those who are leaders,
the ones who are foremost;
they are supposed to
show their people the right way to live.
And when their leaders
make mistakes,
the people would correct them,
making them work exclusively
for the peace
of the village.
They weren't secretive
with any people,
but would inform them [without partiality], whoever they were,
and they would tell them about what they worked on and what they
    did. And they would discuss whatever they came up with,
gathering all the people together.
If they had just come up with something
without the knowledge of the village,
some people would fuss and complain about it, telling them not to

4
Taukut-am tua-i nunat
waten
pinariaqateng
yugmek kipussaalriartangqetullinilria.
Taukuk tua nulirqelriik kipussaaglutek ikamratek ucilirluki
    aklurugarnek,
yugmek tua-i aqvailutek,
tamakunek kipulluku piarkauluku.
5
Tua-i-am taukut tua nunat
tuatnalliniut
tua kipussaagvikluki tekitarkaulutek maa-i.
Taukut tua-i nalluvkenakek tekitarkauciak.
6
Tua-am tamakut ciulirnerit
quyurqelluteng
arenqiirturluteng nallunairiluteng tauna tua-i akikarkauluku.
Angayuqaak-llu qanrullukek
tauna tua-i akikeciqniluku, akiliutekciqniluku.
Nalluyugnaunateng nunat imkut tauna tua-i nasaurluq
akiliutnguarkaullinillra.
Taukuk-llu angayuqaak cangalliurpegnatek tua nallunrilamek
    qiperrlugpegnatek-llu
nallunrilamek tua piarkaungan.
7
Tua-i taukuk
nulirqelriik tekitelliniuk piinanermegni uksuumainanrani
ikamrakek tua-i uciakacagarluteng
aklurugarnek.
Tauna tua-i nasaurluq
kipucarturluku
tamakunek akilirlutek.
8
Tua-i tauna nasaurluq
kiputelliniluku.
Tauna-ll' tua nasaurluq
nalluvkenani,
ellii tua piarkaullni tuaten
nalluvkenaku.
Tua qiperrlugpegnani tua-i maligtaquuraulluni

    do it that way.
4
In this particular village,
when
the time had come for them,
there would be someone who came there to buy a person.
That couple, a man and his wife, came with their sled filled with
       goods to buy [someone];
they came to get a person
and they used those goods to trade with.
5
So this village
was evidently doing that sort of thing,
and they were supposed to arrive to buy from them.
So the villagers knew they would be arriving.
6
So their leaders
met together
to confer and decide who it was that must be given in exchange.
Her [a certain girl's] parents were informed
that she was to be given away, that they intended to use her in trade.
That village knew exactly that she was the girl who was to be traded
       in exchange.
And her parents were not perturbed or bothered since they were
       informed about it, and they didn't fuss or complain
since they knew that that's how it must be.
7
So the other
couple, the man and his wife, arrived one day during the winter
with their sleds full
of goods,
having come to buy
that girl
and use those goods in exchange.
8
So they
bought that girl.
That girl
knew
what was to become of her,
knowing all about it.
She didn't fuss or complain but did what she was told

taukuk angayuqaagmi tayima alerquaguralaagni
   maligtaquurautesqelluku.
Pilalliagni tayim' qiperrlugpegnani-llu
maligtaquuraullun' tua maligglukek,
maligtarkaurtellinilukek.
9
Taukut tua-i
aklurugaat
taukut tua-i nunat pikluki.
Tua-i cakneq, cat piciatun,
tamaani cat nurnarqetullratni!

***

10
Tua-i unuaquan
ayalliniluteng.
Ayiignek tua taukuk
taum nasaurluum
maligglukek ayalliniluni.
11
Ayalliniaqelriit tua-i
qavartaraqluteng.
Cali-ll' ellaseng assiitaqan tua capurciurluteng uitaaqluteng.

12
Tua-i imna tauna nasaurluq qessailami
tua-i cayugpagluni, tua-i caliyugpagluni, ikayualukek taukuk
ayaucestegni,
caliaqelria.
13
Tua-i pivakarluteng ayalngungameng
nem'un uumun tekitelliniut.
Elatiini-gguq-gga elagyaak.
Tua-i taukuk nek'elliniluku tauna.
14
Maaten-gguq tang im' itertut,
ena man'a tua-i
akiqliqelriignek aciluni—
akiqliqelrianek nepiat acingqetullruata!
Tuavet tua-i
acikniluku tauna ikna pilliniluku
elkek-llu cal' tua-i

because her parents were instructing her to do as she was told.
Since they instructed her she didn't fuss or complain,
but followed along and did as they told her,
since accompany them she must.

9
So that village acquired
those
numerous goods.
There were so many, all kinds of things,
back in those days when things were scarce!

***

10
So the next day
they left.
When those two left,
that girl
went with them.
11
They traveled on
and slept overnight.
And whenever their weather was bad and they were weather-bound,
    they remained [where they were].
12
Since that girl wasn't lazy,
she couldn't stay put, but worked and helped those two
who had taken her away;
she was always working away.
13
One day, having traveled on and on,
they came upon this house.
Their food cache, it was said, was right by it.
It was evidently their house.
14
Lo and behold, when she went in,
the house here
had two beds across from each other,
since sod houses used to have beds across from each other!
There
they told her was her bed on the other side
and they too,

taukuk
akiani ikani cali
acimi,
acingqerrlutek.
15
Arenqiapaa-ll' tua-i tauna imna
nasaurluq
taukuk
nerevkalliniaqekiik
neqkegtaarrlainarnek taũgaam!
16
Cayungraan-llu caliyungraan canek uqamailngurnek,
calivkayuunaku.
Tuarpiaq-gguq imna
uquringyartullra cukanrartacia,
neruraami.

17
Tua-i imkuk taukuk,
taukuk ayaucestellregken,
camek tua neqmek
nerevkaraqamegnegu
uqungellra
cukairartaqan
tua-i tauna neqa nerevkanqigcuunaku.
Tua-i uqungellran cukairarutekestiinek nerevkaryuumiinaku.

18
Cali tua-i caaksuartura'arqami waten,
caksuarturallran iliini
kemga
uquringyartullra cukairarutekekaku,
tua-i cal' tauna
calillra,
caliaqellra caliaqevkanqigcuunaku.
19
Tua-i taũgaam
canek mingqeksuarturluni,
allganernek-llu mingqeksuarturluni.
Taluluni tuaten imkunek
yualunek,
makut

the couple,
had a bed
across
from hers.
15
Arenqiapaa! Oh my goodness, that
girl
was fed,
by those two,
but only with the very best food!
16
And even though she wanted to do something, even though she
    wanted to work on heavy things,
they didn't allow her to work.
It was as though that [girl]
was gaining weight rapidly
since she was eating a lot.
17
So those two,
the couple who had taken her away,
whenever they had her eat
a certain kind of food,
they would never give her that food again
if that food slowed down
her weight gain.
They didn't want her eating anything that would slow down her
    weight gain.
18
Again when she kept herself busy,
sometimes occupying herself with small tasks
and her body
slowed down in gaining weight on account of that,
then whatever
she was working on
would be stopped and she would not be allowed to work on it again.
19
But she only
sewed a few things
and patched a few tears.
She also split
sinew,
splitting the sinew

ungungssit cat, tuntut taqukat-llu yualuitnek
waten qupurrluki,
qupurrerraarluki qip'iluki,
qip'urluki yualuktullruit tamaani.
(Wiinga-ll' tamakut tangtullruluki tuaten yualilriit.
Makunek
yualukapianek aturpegnateng—
atulangermeng-gga tua-i
pitangenrakun ellangellruama.
Taũgaam tamakut
ukvekenruluki yualut yualuktuluki.)

20
Tamakunek tua caliangqelliniaqelria
allganernek-llu tua-i
mingqaqluni.
21
Taum-llu imum
aqvastellran, aqvastellran angutiin taum,
kegginalelilliniluku
taluciluku-ll' cali,
tamakunek yualunek talukan, qupurrikan, atuusqelluki.
    (Talutet imkuulartut cingickeggluteng tua ellegluteng taũgaam.
Ayuqevkenateng-am tua tugkararrarnek ilait kangingqerraqluteng.
Tua waten ipegluteng mingqucetun
taũgaam ellegluteng. Taũgaam kankut iquit cakneq ipeckeggluteng
    tamakut tamaa-i
talussuutekluki, qupurrissuutekluki.)

22
Taum-llu tua-i arnam,
ayaucestellran nulirran,
kakivililuku cali.
Tua mingquterluni tuani kegginalni-ll' tauna
tauna-ll' talutni tuani
uitavkaraqluki. Canek cal' tua-i ilaluki yualukanek, canek, pinek,
    tua-i. Mingqaqami-ll'
ilakuarrani tuavet tua-i
kakiviminun ek'urluki.
23
Aren tua-i imna tauna tua-i uquringlun' tua-i. Kiituani-gguq
maani-ll' avat'mini

of these
animals, of caribou and seals,
twisting them after having split them,[1]
and using them for thread after twisting them.
(I myself, used to see them make thread.
They didn't use
this modern thread—
well, some of them used it,
since I first became aware of my surroundings just when they were
    acquiring it.
But they
had more confidence in that sinew and used that.)
20
She evidently worked on that [sinew]
and also would sew up
tears.
21
And that one
who took her away, the husband,
made her a woman's knife
and a sinew-splitter
so that she could use them when she split sinew and when she
    separated the strands. (Sinew-splitters are very sharp and
    pointed, but also thick.
They were all different and some had pieces of ivory for handles.
They were sharp like needles,
only thick. But their points were very sharp and those were used as
    devices for splitting,
for separating the strands.)
22
That woman,
the wife of the one who took her away,
also made her a needlecase.
She had a needle, a woman's knife
and also a sinew-splitter,
all of which she kept there. There were also other things, thread and
    other stuff. And when she sewed
she would put all her scraps
into that needlecase.
23
Aren, that one began to get fat! Pretty soon,
whenever she sewed, her things

cani imkut mingquqcaarqami-ll'
kegginalni-llu
tauna-ll' talutni
tamariyaurtak mat'um tua-i uqum
tamarivkaryaurrlukek, man'a tua-i uqurissiyaangami.
Pekcuirulluni-ll' tua-i uqurissiyaangengami.

***

24
Taukuk-gguq tua-i imkuk,
taukuk uitaviik,
ertaqan tua-i ayagaqelriik tayima.
Ernerpak tayim' mulumalutek atakuaqan
tekitaqlutek.
Taugaam tua-i
ellalliutaqatek, ella assiitaqan,
ayagpegnatek erniuratulutek.
25
Tua-i-gguq taukuk imkuk,
taukuk aqvastellrek,
ayakataqunek,
kiani
nem kiatiini—egkuitnek pitukaitnek—kiatiini kiani
tupigat ikirrluki,
ikireskanki nem man' ilua
tua-i neqniriqerciiquq cakneq, neqniqlun' tua-i.. ˪
Tua-i-gguq taugken,
tamaa-i pekcugngallermini
ellminek arturyagutsiyaagpailegmi,
tua-i-gguq taugken
meq'erlutek.
(Angassacuaraat ellaita tamaani luuskaacuarqellrukiit.)
Angassacuaraq imiqetaaqerluku tamarmek meq'etaaqerlutek, tua
    meq'erraarlutek tayim' ayagaqlutek.
Tua-i cakneq neqniqluni tepii!

26
Tua-i inerqurturalliniaqekiik
agu tauna, agu tuaken,
tauna paqnakqaasqevkenaku
tauna tua-i
neqnirqelria cakneq!

here around her,
her woman's knife
and her sinew-splitter,
would get lost on account
of her fat, because her midsection was getting too fat.
She couldn't walk anymore because she was getting much too fat.

***

24
It is said that those two,
those two with whom she was staying,
would go away whenever daylight came.
They would be gone all day and when evening came
they would return.
But when
they were weathered in, when the weather was bad,
instead of going out they would stay all day.
25
It is said those two,
those two who had fetched her,
whenever they were about to go out,
in there,
from inside the house—from what they call *egkuq*, the back wall—
    from in there,
upon opening the hanging braided mats,
when she opened them, the interior of the house
would suddenly be filled with a delicious and appetizing aroma.
Then it is said,
back when she was able to walk,
before she had become unable to move about,
then it is said
the couple would sip a little.
(In those days they used small wooden ladles for spoons.)
They both filled the small ladle and took sips from it, and having
    drunk they left.
The aroma was extraordinarily delicious!
26
They continually warned her
never, never
to be curious about
that one
with the delicious aroma!

***

27
Tua-i-am caqerluni tayim' ayiignek,
niiculnguami,
ayumian itrarluni
tua-i pilallragcetun
tupigat ikireskai anllullalliniuq tua-i neqniqluni cakneq man'a tua-i.
Maaten-gguq tang im' ikirrluku pia
uqumek imarluni!
Tua-i tauna angassacuar elkegtun qaluarrluku
meq'alliniuq. Tua-i neqniqluni imna cakneq tua-i,
tauna imna
muriim qantam imaa!
Tua-i cakneq neqniqluni!
Tua-i pirraarluku
pinqigtevkenani-ll' tua-i neqnilinge'rmi. Piyaraagtun tua tuaten
    ataucirrarmek piluni.
Patuluku tuamte-ll' tua-i
uterrluni, arvirluni tua-i,
tua-i caliqcaaralliniluni.
[Uquq tailallinilria tamaaken yugnek uqungcaarallragnek.]
28
Atam-gguq tuaten tua pirraarluni
uqungellra man' cukairtellria.
Imumek tua-i
uquringiinarluni cukanrarluni
pirraarluni,
tuaken tua-i ayagnirluni
uqungellra man' cukairtellria.
Tua-i cukaircan qaillukuaqeryaaqerraarlutek
taum arniin aptellinia,
"Kiaken-qa pillruuten?"
Tua-llu-gguq pillinia,
paqnayulnguami elkek piuralaagnek
ellii-ll'
pillruniluni ataucirqumek.
Tua-i arenqianaku uum kinguakun,
uum kinguakun waniw' nallunrirniluku
pinqigcesqevkenaku!
29
Tua-i pinqigtevkenani tua-i. Tua-i taugaam uquringluni cakneq taum
    kinguani cali.

144

***

27

And so one day after they left,
since she was tired of being obedient,
she went in,
just as they had done,
and upon opening the braided mats a very delicious aroma rushed out.
Lo and behold, when she opened it she saw
it was filled with oil!
Then just as they had done, she dipped in that small ladle
and drank some. It was very delicious,
that stuff
in the wooden bowl!
It was scrumptious!
After sampling it,
she didn't do it again although it was very delicious. Following
    their example, she just tried it once.
After covering it,
she went back across [the room]
and continued with her work.
[Evidently, the oil came from the people they fattened up [and rendered.]²

28

Atam! It is said that after having done that,
the rate at which she had been gaining weight began to slow down!
Initially
she had gained weight very fast,
but after she did that,
from there on out
the rate at which she had been gaining weight began to slow down.
When it slowed down, after having tried to do something about it,
that woman asked her,
"Did you take some of that in there?"
And then she told her
that since she was tired of being curious and since they had done it,
she too
tried it once.
They became very agitated about that and told her never to do that again,
never to do that again after this
now that she knew about it!

29

So she didn't do it again. But after that she again became very obese.

Kiituani-gguq tang caliaqami-llu uurpallraam, aqeckutagpallrami
  uqum qaingani
caliyaurtuq tua estuuluqluku,
inguqaqluku.

***

30
Tua-i-gguq taukuk
uitaviigken
waten mingqutmek ugg'un kap'aqkiik.
Tua-i-gguq taugken akngireskan
qanerlutek
pinariksaitniluku.

Arnaqulluk, Martha Flynn, performing a dance, *Tununeq,* circa 1980. In the
background are *Caqigaq,* Christina Patrick; and *Pinirraq,* Elsie Hooper, holding
Ussugan, Joseph Hooper. Photo by Andrew J. Chikoyak.

Finally, she would work using the top of her big, fat, huge stomach
as a table top whenever she worked,
using it as a work surface.

***

30
It is said that those two
with whom she lived
would poke her here [on the nose] with a needle.
If she felt the pain,
they said
that it was not time yet.

31
Kiagluni-ll' tua-i, kiagluni qakem' elliit.
Kiagulnguami tuamte-ll' uksurluni.
Uksuqanrakun tua-i
kapvakartelluni elpeknanrilliniluk' tua-i; kaputengraaku-ll'
camek akngircuirulluni.

32
Tua-i qanlliniuk ukuk tua nutaan pinariniluku;
ellakegciqallerkaa atanqessugluku,
pinariniluku tua.

***

33
Tua-i tayima tua-i.
Pivakarluni atam
unuakut iliitni
arnii tauna,
taum aqvastellran arnii, nulirra
unuakumi
anrraarluni
iterngami qanlliniuq,
"Nutaan atam keggna ella!" angutni piluku.
"Egavayunarquq nutaan ellakegciami cakneq;
egavayunarquq!"
Tua-i angutii
ilumunqaarluni, "Ilumun tua-i
egavagnaurpuk ernerpak!"
34
Tua-i
nulirra tauna, arnii,
anrraarluni
camek tua-i qemaggviucillugmek—cauga-ll' tayima—
imumek tua-i *sack*-arpall'ermek, qemaggviucillugpall'ermek
itrulluni!
Tuavet tua-i ekengnaqluku, ekluku.
Ekraarluku-ll' tua-i
anutengnaqluku tuamte-ll' tua-i.
35
Anuqurainaamegen'gu tua qakma,
ikamragnun tuamte-ll' qakma, ikamraullinilriignun
    ekengnaqenglliniluku qakma tua-i.

31
And then summer came, the season of summer arrived.
And again when summer ended, winter came.
Just as winter arrived,
after having poked her several different times, she no longer felt it;
    although the woman would stick it in
she no longer felt any pain.
32
So they said that the time had finally come;
they should wait for a nice day,
since she was ready.

***

33
And so the days went by.
And then it happened
that one morning
that woman of his,
the woman of the one who had come to get her, his wife,
in the morning,
after having gone out,
upon reentering, she said,
"Now what a nice day it is!" speaking to her husband.
"It is a good time to have a big cookout since the weather is very good;
it is a good time for a big cookout!
Her husband
agreed saying, "Indeed,
let's cook her today!"
34
So
his wife there, his woman,
having gone out,
brought in
a big old bag—I don't know what—
a big sack, a big old bag!
And with difficulty they put her in it.
After stuffing her in,
once more they managed to take her outside.
35
When they finally had her outside,
she felt them straining to get her into a sled, into what was apparently a
    sled.

Tua pivakarluku
ekliniluku qakma tua-i.
Ayangartelliniut qakma. Ikamraulutek tua makuk uitaviik qakma.
36
Atam-gguq tauna,
tauna nasaurluq,
yuarullugmek
nallunrilkengangqelria!
Tamana tua-i yuarulluk ellalluggsuutnguluni.
Ellalliisqumakuniu tua tamana yuarulluk, yuarun-gga tua tamana,
atulriaruarkauluni.
37
Tua-i tuani ayallermeggni
yuarulluk tua tamana tua-i
ircaquminek qamaken atuumalliniaqekii.
38
Atam-gguq qakemkuk pivakarlutek arulairlutek,
ikamrak makuk arulairlutek,
qakemkuk qanngartelliniuk,
"Alingnaqvaa,
aũgna avani asguani
cauga?
Tuar ava-i ellalluk!"
39
Tua-i-llu
pirraarlutek, tuamte-ll' qakma,
tuamte-ll' tua qakma ayaglutek.
40
Tuamte-ll' tua-i arulairlutek pilliniuk,
pilliniuk qakma,
"Arenqiatuq aũgna!
Tua-i ella qakemna assirngailngatuq;
assiqatanricugnarquq!"
Tua-i naspaayuglutek
tuamte-ll'-am tua qakma ayaglutek.
Ak'anivkenatek arulairlutek piuk,
arenqiapaa-ll' qanuksuarangluni-llu-gguq tua-i,
tua-i
utercuglutek.
Tua-i assirngaicukluku ella piluku
utercuglutek.

After working at it for a while,
they got her in.
She could sense them begin to move. She was on a sled.
36
Atam, it is said that that one,
that girl,
knew
an old song!
That old song was for conjuring bad weather.
If one wanted bad weather that old song
was supposed to be sung.
37
And there as they were going along,
from inside she sang that old song
with all her heart for the whole time.
38
Atam, after a while those two out there stopped,
that sled stopped,
and those two began to say,
"*Alingnaqvaa*, my goodness,
what is that
over there on that side?
It looks like bad weather over there!"
39
And so
after they said that, [she sensed] that out there,
out there they had again begun to move on.
40
Again they stopped and said,
[she heard them] say,
"That is very unfortunate!
It seems as though the weather won't be good;
it is probably going to get bad!"
They wanted to keep trying
and again they continued on.
It wasn't long before they stopped and exclaimed
how unfortunate it was that it was beginning to snow lightly and
that
they would have to go back.
Thinking the weather wasn't going to hold,
they wanted to go back.

41
Tua-i qakma qaillukuangartelliniuk,
"Aling,
qaillun atak piqerluk,
utrulluku
wall'u-qa unilluku?"
Qakma aipaak pilliniuq,
"Utrucaaqekumegnegu-gga
ellalluum anguvallaarciqlikiikuk.
Cukaipallaarciqelriakut
waten utrucaaqekumegen'gu
taũgaam unilluku pikumegen'gu
cukanruciqukuk. Ellalluum anguvakarngaitaakuk.
Cukanrarlunuk uterciiqukuk unilluku pikumegen'gu."
42
Tua-i qakma unicunga'artelliniak.
(Petugluku-ll'-am unitellrunritaa!) {qanemcista engelartuq}
Unicungarrluk' tua qakma tayim' nepairullutek.
43
Nepairucagnek tua-i akassaangelliniuq
yuugarcessaagluni. Ellminek-llu tua artuami
qaill' tua-i
uqurissiyaagngami qaillun pisciiganani.
44
Tua-i akassaagpakarluni,
qaillukuarpakarluni,
qakma tua akagartelliniluni.
45
Aren akagngami tua akangelliniuq tua-i ellani ellakenrirluku tua-i,
akak'acagarlun' cukanrarluni.

***

46
Tua-i piinanermini
arulairlun' tua qakma.
47
Arulairngami tua-i uitaurallinilun' tua-i pekcesciigalami.
Tua-i qakma tua-i!
Tua-i tayim' unuut-llu erenret-llu nalluluki
tan'germi tua uitiimi taum iluani.
48
Pivakarluteg' atam, tayima tua-i erenret tayim' qavciurtellruat—

41
She could hear them deliberating about what to do,
"*Aling*,
what shall we do,
bring her home
or leave her?"
[She heard] one of them say,
"If we attempt to bring her home with us,
the bad weather might catch up with us even faster.
We'll go even slower
should we attempt to bring her home with us;
however, if we leave her behind,
we'll go faster. The bad weather won't overtake us so quickly.
We'll get home faster if we leave her behind."[3]
42
So evidently they had abruptly decided to abandon her.
(They should have tied her up!) {narrator laughs}
After having decided to leave her, there was silence out there.
43
When they became silent, she started to try to roll,
trying to get out. And because she couldn't help herself,
being
much too fat, she was unable to do anything.
44
Because she kept on trying to roll,
trying in numerous ways,
she started to roll.
45
Aren, when she started to roll, she really started to roll and became
disoriented, rolling really fast.

***

46
After a while
she stopped.
47
When she stopped she just stayed there since she couldn't move.
And there she was inside!
She couldn't distinguish nights from days
because she was there inside in darkness.
48
Atam, after they were gone for some time, after so many days—

qanikcam qaingani uksumi pektaqamta neplitulria
qerqiugtemek wangkuta,
qerqiuggniluki aptuaput—
ayumian qakma qerqiugtellriartanglliniuq.
Qakma tua-i qanelkek alaunatek.
Arenqianatek tua-i
qivruyaaqlutek, qunuyaaqlutek aũg'umek
ciin-llu unitellmegnek qanaagaqlutek.
Qakma tua-i
muragmek
qanikcam qainga kapurluku
piyaaqluku taũgaam nall'arteksaunaku yaatiini pilutek.
49
Tua-i tayima
pilnguamek
tayim' tua nepairutlinilutek.
50
Tuamte-ll' tua unuaquan tuaten cali,
yaaqvaqanirlutek taũgaam.
Tua-am cal' tua-i nalkevkenaku tayima
nepairullutek.
51
Tuamte-ll' unuaquan
picuaqerlutek,
tua-i qama-i qanelkek alailamek tua-i nalkumangairutniluku,
nallekngairutniluk' tua-i taqsugluku.

52
Tua-i tayim'
nepairullutek.
Tua-i-ll' pinqigtevkenatek tayima.
53
Aren im' tuantelliniaquq.
Uquriami-ll' paluyugnaunan' tua-i
qaini tamana uqurugaq amllessiyaagan.

***

54
Pivakarluni atam
man'a maani ayuqucia
tuarpiaq-gguq
pagna qulii

(in the winter when we walk on the snow it makes noise
and we call it *qerqiugtellria,*
crunching sounds on the snow[4])—
there was finally this crunching noise out there.
Their conversation above was audible.
They were very sad
on account of their loss, having been reluctant to lose her
and were talking about why they had left her behind.
She heard them out there
using a piece of wood
to probe the snow,
but they were unable to hit upon the right spot, being far from her.
49
When they were finally
weary of doing that,
there was silence out there.
50
Again they did the same thing the next day,
but in an area which was further away.
Again they didn't find her and there was once again
silence out there.
51
Again the next day
they searched briefly,
and since their conversation above was audible, she heard them say that
    she would never be found,
that they would not find her and that they should quit.
52
There
was silence again.
And then they didn't come back again.
53
Aren, she evidently stayed there.
And because she was fat, she wasn't about to starve
since there was so much fat on her body.

***

54
Atam, time passed
and she became aware
that above her
it appeared that

tanqigmek-wa tua-i,
tan'gercetkacagarpegnan', tanqigmek
caksuaralria-gga tua tanqivyugteksuaralria.
55
Teguqallrukai ima tam[a] tuani ayauteqatallratni,
kakivini,
mingqucivik. (Kakiviit nallunritaci?)
Kakivini teguqallrukai
ekqatallragni tuani.
56
Kakivini taukut teguluki
ikirrluki
kegginalni teguluku
man'a tua-i caqutni
ullirtelliniluku,
kegginalegmek caviggirluni.
Aren tua tanqig' imna
ikireskii, tanqig' imna tua pillrani,
tua-i uisngasciigalami tua-i uitauralliniluni!
Tanqiqitsiyaagluni.
57
Tua-i tangellni man'a
assiriuraan
nangerrlun' tua-i imucetun-gguq
ellminek arturyugnairutliniluni.
Nangercami pilliniuq
qanikcaq tua urullinikii.
Ellii tua-i urugyaaqekni una,
una tua-i
caqutiin nallii engelkurluku qanikcaulun' tua-i,
uruucaaqellinikiini.
58
Tua-i nangercami
mayussaangelliniuq tua tuaggun,
uitaviminek.
59
Aren mayurturainaami imna,
tuaken nugcami, up'nerkauluni!
Nangercaaqelliniuq
aren man'a tua-i
irugken amia kanavet
cingillrinun imgumaluni,

some light was showing through,
that is was not totally dark,
that a little bit of light was showing through.
55
Oh yes! When they were going to take her away, she had grabbed
her needlecase
where she kept her needles. (Do you know what a needlecase is?)
She had grabbed her needlecase
just as they were going to stuff her in.
56
She took that needlecase of hers
and opened it
and took out her woman's knife
and cut open
the sack she was in,
using a woman's knife to cut.
Aren, after opening it,
the light, the light was so bright
that as she was unable to keep her eyes open, she just sat there!
The bright light was too much for her.
57
After her vision
began to adjust,
she stood up; but unlike before,
she was able to manage herself.
She noticed when she stood up
that the snow had melted.
All about her it had almost melted,
but the area
bordering her sack still had snow,
although it had almost melted around her.
58
When she stood up,
she tried to climb up
from where she was.
59
Aren, when she finally climbed out,
when she got out of there, it was spring!
Aren, when at last she managed to stand up,
the skin
of her legs was all rolled up in folds
down there around her ankles,

uqum tamaa-i, uqurrlugugaam pillra.
60
Ayumian tua-i
ukatmun kangivarrluku,
natmun maavet qillerrlukek. Tamarkeggenka pikek asqigiqerrlutek.
Ukuk-llu cal' talligni
cali cal' tua-i qillerrlukek natmun tayim' piakek.
Man'a cal' aqeckutagpallrallni cali mayurrluku maavet cali qillrulluku.
61
Tua-i amia imna
arenqianani
qacuk'acagarluni uqurissiyaallruami.

from that fat, all that fat!
60
So then
she pulled [the loose skin] up this way,
and tied it here. Having done that to both sides it felt better.
And her arms as well,
again she tied [the loose skin] up, I don't know where.
And this here, [the skin of] her once huge stomach, she also tied it up here.
61
Her skin was
incredibly
loose because she had been so very obese.

Cungauyar, Winnie Billy, distributes the meat and blubber of a *tungunquq* 'bearded seal' at an *uqiquq* 'seal party' in *Tununeq*, circa 1980. Photo by Andrew J. Chikoyak.

Qamiquni-ll' tua tamana aqevliin cal' tua, qamiquni, pakmavet
   qillerrluku
piluku.
62
Tua-i umyuarteqliniuq taq'ercami,
"Waniwa-kiq
natmun ayakuma
yugnun
tekitniarcia?"
63
Tua-i uitaqeryaaqerraarluni
elliin tua-i piyukurallminun
ayalliniluni.
64
Tua-i tamaa-i
ima tanem
urunqinek tua canek
tan'gerpagnek-llu nerqaqluni tamaa-i tumemini
pingluni tamaa-i.
Kaingurainalliami tayim'
how many months. {qanemcista engelarluni}

                        ***

65
Tua-i-ll' im' ayagpakarluni
nunanek ingkunek tekicartulliniluni.
Tua-i tekicamiki
nem'un uumun
ciuqlirmun tekitellminun
itliniluni.
66
Itliniuq-gguq maaten
nulirqelriignek yungqellinilria.
67
Aren tua-i taukuk
quyaqautekluk' ciunregken. Allanrukluku tua-i
quyakluku.

68
Aren qaneryaaqelriim-gguq
taringnaitkacagarluni. Tua-i qamna cali uqurillruami, qamna cali
   qaneryaraan kangia

And because the skin of her head was also sagging, she tied it up
as well.

62
When she was done, she thought to herself,
"Now I wonder
in which direction I should go
in order
to encounter people?"
63
After remaining there for a moment,
she left in the direction where she thought
there might be people.
64
Oh yes,
it was then
that she started
eating crowberries and other kinds of berries along her way
from patches where the snow had melted.[5]
Perhaps she had finally become hungry
after 'how many months.' {Narrator laughs}

***

65
Having traveled a long time,
she was about to reach a village over there.
When she reached the village,
she entered
this house,
the first one she got to.
66
She entered and, lo and behold,
it was occupied by a man and his wife!
67
Aren, those two
whom she encountered were very glad to have her. She was a
     stranger to them
and they were happy to have her.
68
Aren, it is said that when she tried to speak
she couldn't be understood. Since there was fat inside there as well,
     inside at the source of her voice,

uqurillruami wall'u-q' ulua uqurillruami,
qaneryaaqelriim-gguq tua-i qaill'
ikiukacagarluni qanellra.
Kavcagglun' tua kavtalleggluni,
caluni-gg' tua-i assirpegnani.
Qamna qaman' agtuqtaarusnganani natii, uqurissiyaalleq taman' pillilria.

***

69
Aren tua tuanteqalliniuq.
Taukuk tua-i,
tekisviigni taukuk nulirqelriik,
nulirra tua tauna tua-i
kevgiurluku tua-i aqumlluku
qessaitkacagaami-ll' tua-i.
70
Tua-i
taukuk imkuk nulirqelriik tauna
assikluku cakneq tua-i qessailan kevgaqngamegnegu.

***

71
Tua-i-am pivakarluteng
taukuk imkuk uitaviik,
nulirqelriik taukuk,
angutii pillikiit wall'u-qa tamarkeggenka piagket,
qasgisqelliniagket.
72
Tua-i qasgisqenġacetek
tayim' anlutek.
Tauna-ll' tua-i,
tauna nasaurluq tua-i,
tuani uitaluni eniigni.
73
Tua-i-ll'
qasgirraarlutek
aanii imna itliniuq
tua-i man'a pillra... nunaniryugpegnatek-wa tamarmek.
74
Pilliniak

or on account of her tongue being fat,
upon attempting to speak
her speech sounded terrible.
It made a rattling sound
and didn't sound right.
It seemed like it was vibrating inside where there perhaps had been
    so much fat.

***

69
Aren, so she ended up there.
[As for] those two,
the married couple whom she had come upon,
she served and waited upon his wife,
letting her take it easy around [the house],
since she herself felt very much like working.
70
And
those two, the man and his wife,
liked her very much because she wasn't lazy and because she served
    and waited upon them.

***

71
After some time passed
the people sent for her husband or perhaps for the two of them,
those two with whom she was staying,
that husband and wife,
and evidently told them to go to the *qasgiq.*
72
And since they were told to go to the *qasgiq,*
they went out.
And that one,
that girl there,
stayed behind at their house.
73
Then
after having gone to the *qasgiq,*
her "mother" came in
and she wasn't...well, they were both rather unhappy.
74
The couple told her

ingkunun yaani,
arenqiirtulriani-gga tua-i, arenqiirturluteng pillilriit,
neqcaqsugniluku, ellii tauna,
tauna nasaurluq!
Yaa-i tua-i
neqcaqerkaurrluku taqniluku tua-i!
Elkenka tua-i
cakneq qunuksaaqniluku kevgaqngamegnegu tua-i,
cakneq qunuksaaqniluku.
Taũgaam
ingkunun yaa-i
neqcaqsugluku
quyurrluki qanaaniluki.
75
Tamakut-am tamaa-i,
unaken-gguq imarpigmek qakvalriit,
ellaita-llu-gguq tangyuilkait qaillun
ayuquciit nallukait
unaken imarpigmek tagelriit;
tua-i-gguq-am
nasaurlurmek
wall'u tan'gurrarmek
tamakut tamaa-i akilituit
tagelriit tamakut.
Ellaita-llu-gguq nallukait qaillun-ll' ayuquciit, nalluluki.

76
Tua-i taun' ellii
akikeqatarniluku.
77
Tamaa-i cal' tua-i
qanellra cali
assiriksaunani.
Qamna tua-i
ayuqucimitun
ayuqliriksaunani.
Qanraqan cal' tua-i
qaillun neplituluni.
78
Taukut tua-i
nunat
Qaũrrngimek acirluku. Qaũrrngiulun' tua tauna

that they,
the ones who were conferring [in the *qasgiq*],
wanted to use her as bait, her,
that girl [they wanted to use her as bait]!
Over there they
had decided to use her as bait!
The couple themselves
said they really didn't want to part with her because she was their helper,
saying that they were extremely loathe to lose her.
But
those over there, they said,
had conferred together
and wanted to use her as bait.
75
[They spoke of] those there,
who emerged from the depths of the ocean;
they themselves had never seen them
nor did they know what they looked like,
those that emerged from out of the ocean;
it is said
that they placated them
with a girl
or a boy,
[presenting them to] those there who were coming up.
And they themselves, it is said, didn't know what they looked like,
    not knowing anything about them.
76
That said that they were going to use her
in sacrifice.[6]
77
At that time
her speech, moreover,
still hadn't improved.
Her throat
hadn't gone back
to its original state.
Whenever she spoke it still
made a strange noise.
78
The
people of that village
named her *Qaūrrngiq*. They called her *Qaūrrngiq*

nasaurluq tuaten tua qantullra pitekluku.
Qaillun tua-i allakarrarcetun,
qamna uqurissiyaallruami, qantuan
Qaũrrngimek acirluku.

***

79
Tua-i tayima pivakarluteng
taukuk uitaviigken pilliniak
tua-i pinariniluku.
Qanerniluki cama-i
ciuqliq
alairniluku, taukut nugelriit.
80
Maaten-gguq tang imna
qasgim elaturraanun
aguteqataagni
un'a imarpik
takuyarluk' pillinia
ellriini un'a yuk ataucirraq
tagelria.
Ataucirrauluni-gguq tua-i.
81
Tua-i agulluku
itrulluku
pilliniak
tuani tua-i
utaqauraasqelluku.
82
Tua-i qasgimiut
qanerluteng, iliit anluku,
yuut qakemkut qanrutesqelluki
tua-i anqetaanermek taqesqelluki.
Anenqigtesqevkenaki
unuaqu taũgaam anesqelluki ereskan.
83
Tua-i aqumluni utaqaluki taukut tua pistekani.
Piinanermini piqalliniuq
qasgim elaturraani
qimugtet tua-i makut anait amllerrluteng,
imkut tua-i anat teggelriit,
cetengqilluki

because of the way she spoke.
As she spoke differently,
since her throat had been so fat,
they named her *Qaûrrngiq*.[7]

***

79
After a while
those two who she was staying with told her
that the time had come.
They said
that the first one
of those who were coming up out of the water had appeared down there.
80
Lo and behold, it is said
that when they were about to take her
to the outer room of the *qasgiq*,
she craned her neck and looked at
the ocean down there;
it seemed to her that there was just one person
who was coming up.
She saw, it is said, just one person.
81
So they took her,
brought her in
and told her
to wait
there.
82
The people in the *qasgiq*
sent someone out to tell
the people out there
to stop going outside.
They told them not to go out again
until the next day, when daylight had come.[8]
83
She sat there and waited for the ones who were going to get her.
While she was there she noticed
in the outer room of the *qasgiq*
that there were a lot of dog feces,
the kind that had frozen
and gotten hard

uksumi.
84
Umyuangarucami tua tamakut—
qillrutarkarrsurraarluni-gg' pillrullilria—
anat imkut tamakut qillerqurluki
qaiminun maavet
agarquralliniluki tua-i, amlleriluteng.
85
Camna imna yuk at_aucirraq taggleq umyuaqengengamiu
qinerrluku pillinia
maa-i canimellillinilria.
Aren yuut-gguq imkut yugugglugglugugaat amllerrsaaqellinilriit
	ataucirraam taūgaam tua tumiikun
atauciunganateng taguralliut. Waten tua caqircarpiarqata
ik'ikik tua-i cama-i, iquit-llu-gguq cal' cama-i
iik engeliignun, mer'em engeliinun,
ilai cal' cama-i mer'em mengliini uitaluteng!
Amelkacagaryaaqelliniluteng-gguq tua-i!

86
Tua-i cama-i uyangartaqluk' piuraamiki
tua-i kana-i
ceńamun tekilluteng.
Maavet tua mayuata tua qaillukualaagluni piqainanrani piqalliniuq
qaltallrunrilkuni qurrutngungatuq...
(Muragnek tamaani qaltangqetullratni,
qurrutekluki tuaten.
Muriit imkut
qantaliluki
mertarrsuuteliluki-ll' piaqluki qurruteliaqluki ilulirluk—tamakuciq.)
....aren tua-i aqvaluku
all'uku qamiquminun
uitauralliniluni.

87
Tua-i-ll' cakma! (Naūgg'un-gga tangerrsuutengqellilria.)
Tua-i-ll' cakma,
man'a maa-i atakuqercelluku,
cakma tua yill'uku!

in the winter.
84
Since she had an idea, she took those
feces and tied them—
she probably got something to tie them with—
here on her body,
and she kept on hanging them until there were a lot.
85
Since she was wondering about that one person who was coming up,
she peered out and saw
that he was getting closer.
Aren, there were apparently, it is said, many, many people, but
they were following one person's tracks,
making it seem as though there was only one person who
was coming up. Thus, when they turned slightly,
ik'ikik, oh my, [she noticed that there were] so many down there;
the end, it is said, reached all the way
as far as her eyes could see, right to the edge of the water,
and some were still at the water's edge!
There were so, so many of them!
86
Since every once in a while she would look out to check up on them,
she saw that they
had gotten to the shoreline.
When they were coming up onto the land she quickly looked
around and saw
what may have been a water bucket or a urine bucket...
(At the time when they used to have buckets made out of wood;
they used them for urine buckets as well.
They made wooden
bowls,
making water buckets and urine buckets by carving them—[it was]
that kind.)
....and, *aren*, she went and got it
and put it on her head
and waited.
87
And there they were out there! (Maybe she had some way to see.)
There they were out there!
Just as it was getting dark,
he was there, right outside!

88
Aren maaten-gguq tang imna igvaartut, aren quy'uqerrluteng tua
    ilaseng igvaqaan igvaartut,
yuuyaaqelriameng
qengait taũgaam cillarrluteng, qaill' maatekiirluki
    nuyangqerrninganaki[b]
ciutait-llu waten ayuqluteng.[c]
Naryaniurluteng-gguq qengait cuq'iqtaarluteng, naryaniurluteng,
igvaartellriit.
Igvaarcata imna
anelraqataaralliniluni
tamakut tuaten anat,
alngani tamakut anat, arulalluki. Taum tuaten
iluani uitaluni. Qanellra-ll' cal' tua-i ikiuluni cal' tua-i.
"Aa-rrii-i,
yuut-ggem tamakut neqniqniaqa-a-it!" Arulalluki cukariinarluni,
    "Aa-rrii-i, yuut-ggem tamakut neqniqniaqait!" Ugkut-llu-
    gguq tayim' aũg'arluteng!
89
Tua-i itrarluni
aqumluni uitaqanrakun
ak'anivkenateng-am tuaten igvaartelliniut.

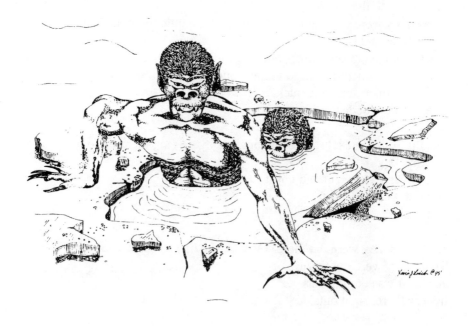

88

Aren, lo and behold, as soon as one of them appeared, *aren,* they
   started to come in all together, one after the other,
and although they appeared to be human,
their nostrils were flared and it seemed that their hairline went down
   to here, [to their eyebrows],
and their ears were like this, [pointed].
It is said that they were sniffing, their noses twitching about, sniffing
when they appeared one after the other.
When they appeared she
slowly advanced toward the exit while she shook those feces,
her dangling feces,
shaking them while she was
inside that thing. Her speech was still harsh and ugly.
"*Aa-rrii-i,*
I heard that these people are delii-cious!" Shaking them, going
   faster: "*Aa-rrii-i,* I heard that these people are delicious!"
   And those who were by the exit took off!

89

Then she went in,
and just as she sat down,
they appeared again shortly afterwards.

Qukailnguq, Maria Fairbanks; *Nanurniralria,* Mary George; and *Cakataar,* Julia
Charles, in *Niugtaq,* 1957. Photo by Christine Heller, courtesy of the Anchorage
Museum of History and Art B91.11.776.

Igvaarcata imum cukanranek nangerrlun' tua-i arulaluni anelrartuq,
    "Aa-rrii-i!" {engelarluteng}
Ilalqerluku-ll' taum qanellra
qurrutem iluani ekumiimi
qaltaryagtellria ilalqerluk', qanellran cali ilalqerluku. Tuaten tua-i
    anelraqertellinilun' imum cukanranek.
Imkut tayim' taukut
egmian tayima
catairtelliniluteng.
90
Itrarluni tua aqumluni atanqingyaaqelliniuq
imkut tua igvaryugpegnateng. {qanemcista engelartuq}
Igvaryunrilata-gguq maaten imna
anelrarluni qinertelliniuq:
ak'a tua-i cali tuaten tagellmegcetun
ak'a tua kinguqliqu'urluteng ava-i kingutmun peksagcugnaunateng-llu
kingutmun cal' ava-i ketmurtellriit.
91
Tua-am taukut qanrutekluki:
alingeqtararamitullinilriit-gguq-am taukut; alingetungermeng tuaten
    pitullinilriit, alingyugngang'ermeng.

Dried herring racks in *Tununeq*, 1957. Photo by Christine Heller, courtesy of the Anchorage Museum of History and Art B91.11.381.

When they appeared, she stood up and advanced toward them,
    shaking and thrashing around, "*Aarii-i*!" {laugher}
It made matters worse when she spoke,
being inside a urine bucket;
the echoing sound and her [coarse, ugly] speech made it worse.
    She rushed toward the exit even faster.
They
disappeared
instantly.
90
Then she went back in and waited,
but they didn't come back. {narrator laughs}
Lo and behold, it is said that when they didn't appear she
went to the exit and peered out:
already they were going back
just as they had come up, in a single file, not scattered all over the place
as they went back down to the ocean.
91
So this is what they would say about them:
that they too could be frightened, that although they got scared,
    although they could be frightened, they would do that,
    [that is, come out of the ocean to get a human being].

92
Waten kingunengqertuq.
Qaillun-gguq tayim' piat.
Pinqigtellrullilriit-gguq-gga wall'u-gguq-qa alingellruameng cakneq
pinqigtellrunritut.
Tuaten tua tauna kingunengqertuq.
Cali aũgna imna
qantarpallraam iluani
neqnirqelria cakneq
tua-i tamakuciuluni,
yuk,
uquringcarraarluku cakneq uquringengan-llu
kenirluku.
Uqua tua tuavet ekluku meq'etaarturatulliniluk' taukuk nulirqelriik.
Cali-ll' tua-i ellii tuani
keniryarturyaaqeksek
pinariaku tua-i,
keniryarturyaaqeksek
ellallungullukek, tua kenirpegnaku anagiluku, keninritngurrluku.

***

93
Tua-i
tamaa-i tamana,
taukut-am nunat maligtaquurautelliniameng
kenkutellrianek tayim' aprumallilriit.
94
Tuaten ilateng nalluitni
camek piyugnaunateng,
nalluvkarpegnaki.
Tamakut-llu akiliutekateng yuut
angayuqritnun
tungelqurritnun-llu nalluvkarpegnaki piaqluki.
Kapiayugnaunateng tamakut;
nepliryugnaunateng
nallunrilamegteki
atanqaqluki tua-i.
95
Wiinga-kiq tayima,

92
This is how it concludes.
No one knows what they did after that.
Perhaps they did it again, or maybe since they were so scared,
they never did it again.
But this is how it ended.
Furthermore, that [oil]
inside that huge bowl,
which was so delicious,
was of that kind,
a human being,
whom they fattened up
and made obese, and when fat enough,
cooked.
Evidently that couple, that man and his wife, put it in there and took
        sips from it.
Furthermore, they were on their way
to cook her,
since the time had come and she was ready,
and they were on their way to cook her
when the weather got bad; thus, they didn't cook her but lost her,
        and in the end she didn't get cooked.

***

93
So
back then,
because the people of that village did as they were told and got along,
perhaps they were referred to as a loving and peaceful community.
94
They wouldn't come up
with anything
without the knowledge of others.
And as for those people whom they were going to use as a sacrifice,
they informed their parents
and their relatives.
They didn't become desperate;
they didn't raise a fuss;
they waited patiently
because they were informed.
95
If they did this

tayima irniaqa nallumni
tuaten pikatgu
qaillun nepaunii uitaniarcia?
Neplirciqua cakneq
tuaten piyaaqekatgu nallumni!
96
Tamaa-i tamana,
maa-i elpeci
ciuliqagtengurciiqelriaci tayima.
Wangkuta—
niitetukci una—wangkuta-gguq piugurngaitukut.
Elpeci tayim' cam iliini
makunek ciuqlirrarpeceńek
ak'allaureskata
calistengurciiquci!
97
Tuamte-llu cal' tua-i calistengurraarluci tamakut nangkata
elpeci tuamte-ll' tua-i ciulirnerurrluci,
cali kinguqlirpeceńek calistengluci.
Tuaten yuk
maa-i ak'arpak man'a tuaten ayalriaruluni, *cycle*-amek aptukiitnek,
    cycle-auluni tua taqngaunani.

98
Kitaki tua-i
elpeci tamana *school*-auceci-ll' murilkelluku cakneq, *school*-arci.
School-autevci mat'um
maryarcillerkarpeceńek ilavceńek;
alerquagillerkarpeceńek ikayuumaaci.
99
Qinuitnaq taŭgaam kiingan, qinuinaki yuc'i
yuullerkait umyuaqluki pilarniartuci,
nepaunaci yuuniartuci,
nepaunaci nunauniartuci,
nepaunaci Tununermiunguniartuci.

to my child without my knowledge,
how could I,
I wonder, remain silent?
I would rant and rave
if they were to do that without my knowledge!
96
As they were,
so you
will become leaders some day.
We—
you have heard this before—we will not go on living forever.
Some day,
when the present generation of leaders
become old,
you will take up their work!
97
Moreover, after you take up the work [of being leaders] and the
    [elders] are gone,
then you will become elders yourselves,
and the ones who are younger than you will work for you.
That is how people
have been since time immemorial; it is called a cycle,
    It is a cycle and will never end.
98
Now then
attend carefully to your schooling while you are a student.
Your schooling here
will help you when you lead the others;
it will help you when you teach others.
99
Live tranquilly, with only harmony
in mind for your people,
so that you may live without strife,
so that you may have a village without strife,
so that the people of *Tununeq* may be without strife.

Qaluyaarmiut in front of St. Joseph's Catholic Church in *Tununeq*, circa 1934. Photo from Jesuit Oregon Province Archives, Gonzaga University, negative number 504.10.

1. *Iraluq*, George Hooper
2. *Qirvan*
3. *Maklak*, Edward Hooper
4. *Qengaralria*, Dora Fairbanks
5. David Sipary
6. *Ermianguaq*, Henry Albert
7. *Tumailnguq*, Michael Albert
8. *Kakgar*, Alice Post
9. *Naulalria*, Ruth Chakuchin
10. *Arnaqulluk*, Stella Jimmie
11. *Atsaq*
12. *Apurin*, Leon Flynn
13. *Kumangulria*, Louise Kanrilak
14. *Qang'allugaq*
15. *Tumailnguq*, Gabriel Kylook
16. *Taulan*, Paul Agimuk
17. *Piiyuuq*, Francis Usugan
18. *Ayukun*, Nona Albert
19. *Tumaralria*, Priscilla Fairbanks
20. *Inuk*
21. *Tanqiar*
22. *Uassuuk*, Agatha Nevak
23. *Kaagyugaq*, Adeline Panruk
24. *Kilirrnguq*
25. *Cingyukan*, Albertina Dull
26. George Sipary
27. *Carriralria*, Charlie Post
28. *Ingamuralria*, Anna Kailukiak
29. *Allirkar*, Nancy Usugan
30. *Anguyacungaq*
31. *Nuuniq*
32. *Paniyagaq*
33. *Qilangaq*, Jojean Charlie
34. *Unangik*, Jane Ocsar
35. *Qailiuq*
36. *Kangrilnguq*
37. *Napaqtaq*
38. *Panayuq*
39. *Ceturngalria*, Stephanie Nayagniq
40. *Maniggaq*
41. *Panikpiaq*
42. *Nusailaq*, John Fairbanks
43. *Ac'urun*, Urban Albert
44. *Nalugalria*, Clara Aluska
45. *Inuguarpak*, Susie Agimuk
46. *Naniruar*, Magdaline Jimmie
47. *Qulvarkaq*, Bob Hooper
48. *Qiuran*
49. *Tulukaq*
50. Maggie Sipary
51. *Qanrilaq*, George Kanrilak

Memory, The Oral Tradition, And The Written Word

Arnaucuaq's account of the revenge of the jealous wife (see "*Piciuvkenani Uingulleq.* The Unfaithful Husband" [Tennant and Bitar 1981: 221-233]) combines scripts and motifs from several stories we have already encountered. The entry of the heroine follows the familiar scenarios of the Star Woman motif. In "*Anngaqelriik:* The Two Brothers" the sound of singing in the wilderness announces the appearance of a woman from the sky, who subsequently marries one of the brothers. In the following story, however, the woman does not actually descend from the sky; she appears at the entrance to an elevated den. In either case, she comes from a high place and attracts his attention through singing. The practice of making an *aviukaq* 'food offering' at the den of an animal is also a familiar motif in Yup'ik stories; such attentions are always recompensed (see "*Nuliaq Teglegcilleq.* The Stolen Wife" [Orr and Orr 1995: 100-125]). The fact that he leaves food offerings suggests that she might be a *tuunraq,* an animal or helping spirit who can appear in human form.

The jealous woman's revenge is also familiar. In "*Tutgara 'urluunkuk Nukalpiartayagaq-llu:* The Granddaughter and the Young Hunter," a young man breaks his promise to marry a girl when he returns from the wilderness. She appears at the *qasgiq* to dance before the men and, just as in the story above, she refuses their musical accompaniment. In the end, she shames the young man, who then proposes to her.

Edward W. Nelson's story "The Red Bear," recorded a century ago, bears a close resemblance to *Arnaucuaq*'s account of the jealous wife's revenge (Nelson 1899: 467-470). A woman is jilted by her husband, who takes up residence in a distant village with two new wives. His first wife finds them, destroys them, and then turns into a bear. In either case, "The Red Bear" or "*Ciknalleq Nuliaq.* The Jealous Wife," the jilted woman wreaks destruction on those who abandon her.

The similarities among the various existing accounts would seem to underscore the accuracy and fidelity of the oral tradition. We have examined Yup'ik texts of traditional stories collected by Francis Barnum, S.J. a century ago and we are struck by their similarity in style and content to our

Tununermiut texts. Although every oral performance of a given story differs somewhat from all others, many constants remain over long periods of time. Elders stress the importance of faithfully rendering the traditional stories: if one cannot accurately recall a particular story, they say, then one must not attempt to tell it.

An oral tradition that does not rely on written records or documents, but instead depends on the fidelity of active memory, must devise various mnemonic aids. Conventionalized scripts are one means. Stories are com-

Arnaucuaq, Mike Angaiak, circa 1980. Photo by Andrew J. Chikoyak.

posed of episodes, many of which are highly stylized and invariant. Examples of these found in the stories are the formulaic beginnings, the standard marriage proposal script, the adoption script, the youthful apprentice's sea mammal and land mammal hunting script, and the wronged fiancee's requital.

Another tactic employed in assisting memory and recall is the custom of reciting stories in the presence of knowledgeable elders. When the principal narrator has concluded his narration, the audience is given an opportunity to bring to mind those parts that have been left out. "*Nakaciuryaraq.* The Bladder Festival" in this volume is an example of this collaborative narration. Finally, it should be noted that the participants of an oral tradition have developed unusual powers of memory. Again and again, in working with the *Tununermiut* elders, we are impressed with the depth and breadth of their knowledge and their ability to recall information, much of which they have gleaned from the oral tradition and retain without the assistance of written records.

One should be cautioned, however, that the literate and oral traditions are not always distinct and separate. We were struck by the great similarity between a narration of *Arnaucuaq*'s and a story told by Michael John of *Niugtaq* (Tennant and Bitar 1981). *Arnaucuaq*, being originally from *Kayalivik*, grew up in the same area as Michael John; they presumably shared the same oral sources. The two accounts agreed not only in the general plot and characterization, but in detail as well. When we brought this to *Arnaucuaq*'s attention, he told us that this was so because he had gotten his account from reading Michael John's story! Indeed, many of the stories *Arnaucuaq* tells in our corpus of *Tununermiut* stories can be found in written Yup'ik sources elsewhere. He said he had heard the story as a youth in the *qasgiq*, but had forgotten many of the details; reading Michael John's published version had refreshed his memory. *Arnaucuaq*, although a monolingual speaker of Yup'ik, is a Catholic deacon who often reads the New Testament selections in the service from the Yup'ik translation of the Bible. He is indeed literate, not in one but in two systems of orthography! We had attributed the remarkable similarities in the existing texts to the fidelity of the oral tradition. We had not taken into account the possibility that his sources were not only oral, but written as well. In our way of thinking the oral and literate traditions were distinct and separate. Not so with *Arnaucuaq*. He moved freely between the two, using one to supplement and enrich the other.

CIKNALLEQ NULIAQ

Arnaucuaq Tununermiu

***

1

Tauna-gguq angun
tamaantelliniuq
kuigem ceńiini.
Tamana-gguq kuik
imarpigmun anumauq yaaqsigpegnani.
Ugna-gguq kuigem painga, anqatallra,
camek qertulriamek pitangqertuq
imumek tua ingricuartun ayuqluni, anqataqallra una kuigmun.

2

Tamaa-i kiimenani tua-i taũgaam ayagaaqluni taun' angun.
Ayagaqami-gguq tamaavet imarpigmun
imna tauna qertulria tekitaqamiu
qantaminek, qantami imaa,
aviukarqetulria. Aviukarqaqameng tua-i teguqaulluteng maavet
pitunillrularait waten.[a]
Aviukarqerraarluku tua-i
ayaglun' kiturluku.

3

Tua-i taũgken unani imarpigmi pirraarluni uterrluni waten kiagmi
nem'inun tua-i uitaluni.
Tuamte-ll' tuntussuraqluni tua-i
piyugteqaqami;
taũgaam-gguq
tuaten ping'ermi
kia aulukngaitelaaki tua-i
amllerivkenaki tua pituuq
elliin taũgaam taum
angutem auluktuamiki.
Tuaten tua piciryaraqluku.

182

THE JEALOUS WIFE

Mike Angaiak of Tununak

***

1
There was a man, it is said,
who lived
by the banks of a river.
That river
flowed out into the ocean, which wasn't far away.
Downriver, by the mouth of the river, where it was about to empty
    into the sea,
there was a rise in the land,
like a little hill, right where the river was about to empty into the sea.
2
There this man lived all by himself, although he would go out hunting.
It is said that whenever he went out to hunt on the ocean,
as he came upon that high ground,
he made food offerings
from the contents of his bowl. When they make ritual food
    offerings, they take a little bit
and place it here; they say they did that.[1]
So, having made offerings,
he would proceed along his way .
3
During the summer, after he ventured out to the ocean, he would
return home and remain in his house.
Furthermore, he would hunt for caribou
whenever he wanted to;
however, it is said
that even when he did that,
since there was nobody to take care of his catch,
he didn't get too many,
because he was the only one
that took care of them.
That was the way he lived.

4

Kuik taman' cetuluku tauna tua tekiteqatarqamiu
qantaminek tua-i,
qantami imaanek wall' akutaminek
wall' canek allanek neqnek,
aviukarqeqarraarluku tua kituraqki. Waten-gguq tua kuigem taun'
    ceńaqaa
qertuluni waten
tua tangvallrani-ll' cataitaqluni tua.

***

5

Atam tua pivakarluni
unuakumi anlliniuq;
an'uq-gguq tua-i quunirluni tua-i qakemna, ellakegciluni.

6

Tua-i-ll' qurrliniluni nakaciami.
Qurrnginanermini camek imumek niitelliniluni
unegken kuigem tamatum paingan tungiinek.
Tuarpiaq-gguq tang aturturalria.
Taringcaurluku pilliniuq
tua-i atulriarullinilria.
Umyuarteqliniuq, "Alingnaqvaa!
Cunaw' tang ella allamek cal' yugtangqelalria!"
Umyuarteqaqluni kiimi tua yuuyukluni.

7

Aren qayani tua upluku
ayumian uatmun
ayalliniluni.
Qasturiinarluni.

8

Wani-gguq tua yuarun iquklitqataqerluni
imumek tua-i cuy'aqerrlun', cegqerrluni tua-i,
nangyartuqernaurtuq. Tua-i-gguq tua nangyartuqallra tua-i cakneq
    qastunaurtuq.
Qasturiinarlun' tauna
paillitqatallni malikluku.

9

Tua-i-ll' tuavet igvalliniluku tauna tua-i.
Maaten-gguq tang
igvarluk', tekiteqatarluk' piuq,
qacarnerani

184

4

When he traveled downriver and reached that high ground,
from the contents
of his bowl or his *akutaq*
or any other food,
he would make food offerings and then pass on by. It is said that
    place was on the shore of the river,
along a rise,
and when he observed it there was nothing on it.

***

5

Time passed and then one day
he went out in the morning;
upon going out he saw that it was calm and the weather was nice.

6

So he urinated because his bladder was full.
While he was urinating he heard something
downriver, down toward the mouth of the river.
It sounded as though someone were singing.
Listening carefully he realized
that it was indeed someone singing.
Then he thought, "*Alingnaqvaa!*
So there are other people in this world!"
He thought that he was the only person.

7

Aren, so he got his kayak ready
and then proceeded
downriver.
It was getting louder.

8

It is said that when the song come to an end,
it terminated
with a very high-pitched sound. The conclusion of the song was very
    loud.
As he neared the mouth of the river,
it was getting louder and louder.

9

So that high ground came into view.
Lo and behold, when it
appeared to him and he was about to reach it, he saw,
along the side,

185

amik pikna,
makut-gguq-gga tupigat
kanavet tua kuigem ceñiinun.
Maaten-gguq
pikavet tangrraa
arnaq una
waniwa!
10
Aturai-gguq tua makut
assirluteng. Tua-i aturai makut imumek-gguq tuarpiaq
tangellrat imumek,
blue -arrluaraulun', qiugara'arturlun' pilria tamakut
aturai.
11
Tua-i ketiinun arulailliniuq,
tua-ll' qanlliniuq tauna, "Alingnaqvaa! Cunaw' tang yugtangqertuq!"
Tua-ll' taum arnam pillinia, "Alingnaqvaa!
Kitu'urtaartura'arqekevnga unavet ayagaqavet.
Nerevkarturalararpenga
neqevnek
waten arulaiqerviklua
unisvikerrlainalararpenga neqkamnek.
12
Tua-i tang
naklegyagulluten wanigg, tua-i tangercequrainalrianga.
Waniwa
waten elpenek-wa tua-i aulukurallerpenek
naklegyunglua tangerceskemken."
13
Tua-i-ll' ullalliniluku
arnaq una tua-i.
Umyugaan tua qam'um
pilliniluku
tua-i-gg'
qamavet nem'inun itrautnaluku umyuartequtelliniluku.
14
Tua-i-ll' umyuartequcamiu
aptellinia, "Waniwa-qa
maliklua
kiavet nemnun itraryuumiituten?"
Tua-ll' tua pillinia, "Tua-i-gg' pisqumakuvnga maligciiqekemken.
Kitak ayagpailemegnuk qamavet

a door up there,
and there were these braided grass mats, it is said,
rolled down to the bank of the river!
Behold,
he looked up
and saw
this woman!
10
She was wearing beautiful
clothing. Her apparel, it was said,
seemed to be somewhat
of a bluish color; her clothes
were bluish.
11
So he came to a stop in a spot down below from the woman
and said, "*Alingnaqvaa!* So there are indeed people here!"
And then that woman said to him, "*Alingnaqvaa!*
You are always passing by me whenever you go down there to the ocean.
You always give me something to eat
from your food,
stopping where I am
and always leaving something for me to eat.
12
So look,
I've finally made myself visible because I feel compassion for you.
Here now,
I'm revealing myself to you because I am feeling compassion for you
because you have been taking care of things all by yourself."
13
So he approached
the woman.
Upon reflection,
it occurred to him
that he might
bring her back with him to his own house.
14
And then, when he considered the matter,
he asked her, "If I ask you
to accompany me
upriver to my house, would you want to come?"
She said to him, "Well, if you want me to, I'll come along.
Now then, before we go let's go into

nemnun itqernaurtukuk."
Tua-i itrutliniluku: ena man'a tua maa-i.
15
Tua-i taum qanenqegcilluku, "Tua-i tangerciigat'laqevnga tua-i."
Tua-ll' pillinia, "Akutamnek nerqerraarluten ayagniartukuk."
Tua-i-ll' kiaken
qulqika'arnek waten
qantaq una taitellinia akutamek imarluni.
Ner'lliniluku nangevkenaku-ll' tua elliqerluku tua-i taqluni.
Taum arnam
ayakataami aũg'umek
ekviucillugmek, imkut cat qemaggviit,
neqet qeltait—
tamaa-i ekviucillugnek pitullrulliniit;
imkuuluteng tua missuukluk' ellaita—
tauna tua-i teguluku, ang'aqluku.
Aturani taukut yuulliniluki,
yuungamiki taumun tua caquluki
allanek-ll' all'uni
pilliniluni.

16
Tua-i
maliklutek itrallinilutek.

***

17
Nutaan tua tauna angun
nutaan tua pissulanga'artelliniuq,
tua-i amlleriluki taum-ll' tua aulukluki tua-i.
Pavaken-llu tuntunek cal' tua aqvataqluni tua-i.
18
Tua-i atam pivakarlutek
aipaqsagutellinilutek nutaan,
aipaqsagullutek tua-i.
Piinanermini taun' aipaa qingalliniluni.
Maaten-gguq tang tua-i
pinariani an'uq tan'gurraraullinilria tauna
irniara.
19
Ayagaqelria-gguq tua taun' angutii
tekitaqluni.

my house."
So she brought him in and, behold, here was this house!
15
So the woman talked to him nicely saying, "Until now you have
    been unable to see me."
Then she said, "We will go after you eat some of my *akutaq*."
She brought a bowl
from inside the shelf
filled with *akutaq*.
He ate without finishing it and when he was done he put it down.
That woman,
since she was about to leave,
took an *ekviucilluk*, a container for things,
made of fish skin—
they called that an *ekviucilluk* in those days;
it was like a burlap sack to them—
and she took it to bring stuff along with her.
Taking off her clothes,
she put them in that container
and she put on some other
clothing.
16
So
together the two of them went upriver [to his house].

***

17
Thereupon that man
finally started to hunt in all earnest,
increasing his catch, and that woman took care of them.
He also went inland to catch caribou.
18
So from that time on
they became partners in marriage,
becoming a married couple.
Thereafter his partner became pregnant.
Lo and behold,
when the time came, her child, a little boy,
was born!
19
Her husband, it is said, would go out hunting
and then would return.

Tua-i-ll' un' irniarak-gguq imumek
angturriqerluni,
taũgaam-gguq
ayagatnaqluni imumek teguluku,
tamaani
irniateng
tunumikluki piuratullrata nalliini,
tuaten tua elliqerluku
waten kiagmi
ayalriim imna tayim' tekitenritliniluni
qavartarluni nani tayima.
20
Nutaan unuaquan tekilluni.
Cangalliurpegnani-ll' ellii tauna nulirra.
Cunawa-gguq im' icivarpak
ayaucimi iliini tayim' tekitenritnaurtuq.
Unuaquan-llu tekitevkenani, qavartallri-gguq
amlleriinarluteng taũgaam.
21
Tua-i-llu-gguq waten caqerluni
makunek aturainek
wall' kelugartellrianek tauna arnaq
mingqaqamiki
kelukenrilkeminek makunek
tanglanglliniluni
qaillun-ll'-am tua piksaunaki elliin tua-i makut kelukevkenaki allam
    kelukluki.

***

22
Tua-i-ll' caqerluni,
waten tua uksuaryartungenrakun-gga tua-i,
tua-i tayim' ayalriim tua tekitenritliniluni tua tayima.
Tua-i kiimellirlutek tua-i
tauna-llu irniarrani-llu.
23
Tua-i uksurluni-llu
tua-i taũgaam neqkaitenrilamek
kaigyugnaunatek.
Tauna tua-i arnaq
umyugaa qamna
nekayuum tekitellinia taumek angutmek.

And then, when their child
got bigger,
but still
had to be held to get about,
back
when they packed
their children on their backs,
when he had reached that stage,
during the summer,
the husband left and didn't return,
but slept somewhere overnight.
20
Finally he came home the next day.
And his wife didn't seem too concerned about it.
So that's how it was for the next few days:
sometimes he left and wouldn't return for some time.
Then once he failed to return on the following day; in fact
his overnights were becoming more frequent.
21
And then it is said that one time,
when the woman
was sewing torn stitches on the
man's clothes,
she saw these stitches
that weren't hers;
she wasn't the one that made those stitches, but they were someone
    else's stitches.

***

22
Then one time,
just as it was getting on towards early fall,
the man left and didn't return at all.
The woman and her child
were now all alone.
23
Then winter came,
but because they had a supply of food,
they didn't starve.
That woman
began
to harbor angry, resentful thoughts towards that man:

Yugmek kepqerraarluni waten tayim' natmun ayagluku
　　tekitenritellranek.
24
Tua-i-ll' imumek kiagyungluni kiagluni
qanikcairulluni-llu
arnaq tauna
waten ivrucililliniluni (qavcinek tayim' pia, atauciungunrilnguugnek).

25
Tua-i upluni
taqngami,
tua-i tauna irniacuarani pillinia,
"Tua-i
aatan im' natmun ayagluni tayim' tekitenrita?"
Tua-i tangerqeryugyaaqniluku waniwa.
Upcamek engelqiluni tua-i taquamegnek tamakut-llu ivrucit ayaulluki
imkut cal' taukut aturani
qemaggviucilluum iluanelnguut cali malikluki.
Anngami,[b] waten kiagmi,
anngami keggavet
uivvaalliniuq
makut anuqet
cauqetaarluki waten
qanerluni,
"Natmun-kiq wanigg' ayakuma,
ayakumegnuk,
tangerrsarceńuk?"

26
Tua-i-ll' uivluni
unavet kan'a tua kana-i icigg' keggakneq,
keggaknermek piaqekiit kan'a,
caungamiu arulairluni pilliniuq,
"Tua-i
kat'um tungiinun ayaguaqerluk."
Ayalliniuk imarpiim ceńiikun,
kanarngamiu imarpik.
27
Cunawa-gguq im' kiagpak
tua-i pektaqelria! Taukuk ivrucini-gguq
nat'rairutaqata tua-i allagnek all'uni
ayagaqluni. Tua-i tua taquarratek taukut aninqurluki.

having had a need for someone else, he went somewhere and
    didn't return.
24
And then it got warm and it was tending towards summer and the
snow began to melt and finally the snow was gone;[2]
that woman
made waterproof skin boots (I don't know how many she made, but
    more than one pair).
25
When she was finished
with her preparations,
she said to her little child,
"Well,
I wonder where your father went to stay?"
She said she yearned to see him.
When they got ready, they took the right amount of provisions and
    they also brought those waterproof boots,
as well as those clothes
that were in the *ekviucilluk*, taking those along.
When she left, and this was in the summer time,
she went outside
and turned a full circle,
facing each
wind direction
as she said,
"Which direction, I wonder,
should we go
if we are to see him?"
26
Then she turned a full circle
and when she faced the northwest coast down there,
the one they call northwest,
she stopped and said,
"So
let's try that direction."
When they came down upon the ocean,
they traveled along its shore.
27
So she walked
for the entire summer! It is said that when the soles of those
waterproof boots of hers were worn out, she would don another pair
and travel on. They conserved their provisions.

Kuigmek-llu capenricuunatek
camek-llu yuc'illruarmek tangyuunatek
kiagpak.
Atam tua kiagumainanrani kuigem uumek painganek tekitellinilriik.
Nutaan tekicamek
muragnek ukunek,
muriullernek,
tangerpaalullinilriik.
Qanlliniuq, "Aling tua-i yugtangqelliniuq ca imna tayima!"
Man'a-llu-gguq atakurluni.
Camek-gguq ayaruarangqelartuq tua-i.
Tua-i mernurluni
imumek tua qayugga tua pektelnguluni
ciungani-llu-gguq tuaten piksaicaaqluni.
Ayagturaqerlutek
ukunek mimerniullernek
tekitelliniuk.
Tuavet tua-i arulailliniuk tua-i taukut uqrutaqeqerluki.
Qanlliniuq, "Tua-i wavet arulairluk!
Cali unuaqu
ayagniartukuk; tua-i
yugtangqelliniuq ca imna."
Imumek tua mernurluni,
nerqerraarluni
imumek taun' irniani
aamarrluku wavet ciuqerminun, aqumluni.
Aamarrluku waten pimaurallermini,
aren, tua qavarniami, mernuami,
tua-i tayim' qavalliniluni.

***

28
Tua-i-ll' tupagyartuqalliniuq imumek waten tua-i maavet
put'ellrullinilria,
tauna tua irniani
piluku wani,
ellminek tua patulluku!
Qessanayullagluni
taun' irniani
pillinia eptellinikii. Tua-i tuqullinilria taun' irniara.
Arenqianani tua-i nutaan tua-i umyugaa qamna
taumek angutmek,

Moreover, they were never obstructed by any river
and they never saw any other people
all summer.
Sometime during the summer they arrived at the mouth of a river.
Luckily, when they finally got there,
they saw
driftwood
that had been piled up by someone.
Then she said, "*Aling,* so there is at least someone here!"
Then evening came.
It is said she had some kind of a cane.
Surprisingly, she was tired,
tired of walking
although she had never been before.
After traveling a bit further,
they came upon some old tree stumps
that someone had worked on.
So they stopped there and used those as a shelter from the wind.
Then she said, "Well, let's stop here!
We can continue on
tomorrow; there
are people somewhere."
Being exhausted,
she ate first
and placing her child
in front of her, she nursed him as she sat there.
While she nursed him in that position,
aren, being sleepy and tired,
she fell fast asleep.

***

28
Then it was time for her to wake up and she discovered that
she was bent forward
and she had done something
to her child,
covering him up!
She was overcome with remorse
when she realized that
she had smothered her child. Her child was indeed dead.
Now she was really feeling distraught about
that man,

umyugaa tua nutaan qamna imkurluni tua-i
tangerqeryugyaaqluku.
Qaillun tua pingailami
mikelnguq tauna taukut muragat keluatnun piavet
nuna man'a elakarluku tuavet tua elliluku, ellingamiu-llu
tamatumek ayarurrarminek canianun kapuarrvikluku.
Qiaqcaaraūrlurrarluni tua-i
nutaan ayalliniluni
kuik tua taman' asgurluku.
29
Kiani-llu-gguq tua-i ukatmun qipluni,
qipteqerluki,
tua-i-ll' kiugkut nunat.
Tua-i nuuqerluki arulaillrullinilria.
Itraaralliniluni tua-i
maaten-gguq itraarainanermini taukut nunat,
tekiteqarraallruluni tua waniwa
ena una,
aūgkut akuliitni uitavkenani, uatiitni ena una waniwa.

Left to right are *Angayiq*, Bob Flynn; *Ciquyaq*, Bob Charlie; and *Ciquyaq*, Paul
Flynn, *Tununeq* in the early 1940s. Photo courtesy of the Anchorage Museum of
History and Art B91.11.415.

feeling distressed and
wishing she could see him right then and there.
Since there was nothing she could do,
she dug a shallow grave behind those stumps of wood
and placed that child in and after placing him there,
she stuck that little cane of hers into the ground next to him.
After the poor woman cried for a while,
she finally left,
heading upriver.
29
Further upriver, they say, the river bent to this side,
and having got past the bend,
she saw that there was a village upriver.
She stopped short of the village.
Then she went further upriver
and having gone further inland,
she arrived first
at this certain house,
which wasn't in the midst of the village, but was downriver from
     the village.

Teddy Tom (deceased); *Pamsuq,* Tommy Angaiak; and *Nuriulria,* Billy Flynn, in
Tununeq, 1957. Photo by Christine Heller, courtesy of the Anchorage Museum
of History and Art B91.11.413.

30
Ikna-gguq-wa tua nallunaunani qasgiat tua-i
nunat taukut qukaatni.

***

31
Tua-i tekiteqarraallruan tauna
arulairluni qinerrluni pilliniuq
qimugkauyartangqellinilria
kiugna.
Piqerluni qimugkauyaraam taum tangerqaamiu
qiluksuggluku pilliniluku.
Tua-ll' piqerluni qamna qanlliniuq,
arnauluni,
"Cakemna qimugten
cam piagu?
Piciqaat-ll'-am paqesgu."
32
Tua-i-ll' tuaten qanqerraartelluku
amik ikirrluku, ikirtuqat
pakigluki,
anlliniuq
tan'gurrar' una,
yun'erraq tua waten
waniwa.
Tangvakarluku uavet
allayukngamiu qanerpegnani
tayim' itliniuq.
33
Tua-ll' iterngami qama-i qanrutlinia,
"Ugna-gg' ua-i arnaq, maani tang nutaan tangerqeka;
ua-i uani amiigmi uitalria."
Tuamte-ll' tua taum kiullinia,
"Arenqiapaa! Naken tekitellriarulliuq;
itresqiu;
iterli-gguq!"
Tuamte-ll' tua-i itresqelliniani tua-i itliniluni,
qimugkauyaraam-llu taum qiluggaarluku qaill' pivkenani tua kiturluku.

34
Maaten-gguq itertuq
tauna tua yun'erraq, una-gguq-gga arnassagaq aipaa!

30

It was said the *qasgiq* was visible across the river,
in the middle of that village.

***

31

Since she came to that house first,
she stopped and when she peered in she saw
that there was a puppy
inside.
Right away when the puppy saw her,
it started barking at her.
At that, someone inside, a woman,
said,
"What's bothering
your dog out there?
They might do something to it; go check it!"

32

And then, after that person said that,
the door opened and someone pulled back
the braided grass curtain that hung over the door
and out came
this boy,
a teenage
boy.
After he took one look at her,
he went in without saying anything,
since she was a stranger.

33

Having gone back inside, he said,
"There's a woman out there, whom I'm seeing for the first time,
and she's by the door out there."
Then the woman replied,
"*Aren!* She must have arrived from somewhere;
tell her to come in;
tell her I said to come in!"
Therefore, because she was told to enter, she went inside;
the puppy, which had barked at her before, didn't bark this time
    when she passed by.

34

Lo and behold, she went in
and there was that male teenager along with this old woman!

Cunawa-gguq taum tua maurluqlinikii tauna.
Tua-i iterluni.
Tuani tua neraqcaaraqarraarluni_itrallruami,
arulairluni
tuavet, pillinia, "Kitaki neryugciquq;
neqkainek piu!"
Tua-i-ll' taum arnam pillinia, "Tua-i tang neryuumiilngua
uani nerqerraarlua ayiima.
Tua-i tekiteqatarluci waniw' tua-i arulaillrulliniunga mernuama."
Tua-i waniw' kiagpak pekcimaniluni.
Nutaan qanemcilliniluni tauna,
taumek tua mikelnguq tekiuteqatarluku tua-i elliin tua-i
mernuami eptelliniluku tuaten aamartellerminiu.
Aipangqellruyaaqniluni,
waniwa taũgaam
tekitnanrirluni,
tua-i-gga ayallermini ataucirqumek qavartarraarluni
   amlleriinarluteng qavartallri,
tayima natmun pillra.
Taumek tua-i aipangqellruyaaqniluni.
35
Tua-i-ll' tauna
arnaq, maurlua, pilliniuq,
"Kia-i-ngullilria ima-qa.
Angun kiugna
tua-i uksurpak tekitaallruuq.
Tua-i pivakarluni tekiteqerluni tua-i
kia-i maantuq.
Kiugkut alqaqelriit
uyuraatnek kia-i
pingqertuq.
Tua-i taungungatuq tua-i."
Tua-ll'
taum aptelliniak,
"Qaillun
ukut nunat
atakumi-qa qaillun tayim' piyuitut?"
Tua-ll' pillinia, "Qama-i-ggur' atam
yurarceciniartuq tauna
wanikuarqu; qama-i-llu-gguq pingllilriit.
Atam-gguq yurarceciniartuq."
Tua-ll' pilliniuq,

It turned out the old woman was the grandmother of that boy.
So in she went.
Before having come up the river, she had first stopped
to eat,
so when the old woman said, " *Kitaki*, she'll want to eat;
get her something to eat!"
The woman said to her, "Look, I have no desire to eat
as I ate downriver before having come.
I had stopped right before I got to you because I was tired."
She told them that she had walked all summer.
She eventually told them what had happened,
about how she was about to arrive with the child and she had stopped
because she was tired and had smothered the child when she nursed him.
She said she had had a husband,
but he hadn't returned
after going out,
that once when he left he had stayed overnight and having once slept
    overnight, his overnights had then become more frequent,
wherever it was that he went.
She said that such a one had been her husband.
35
And then that
woman, his grandmother, said
"That must be him up there.
That man upriver
has been coming and going all winter.
One time he came
and he's been there ever since.
He's with the youngest
of those sisters
upriver.
He might very well be the one."
Then
the woman asked them,
"Is there something
going on
in this village tonight?"
Then the grandmother said, "That one upriver
will arrange for them to have a dance
in a little while, if they have not already begun.
Atam, that one will make them have a dance."
And then she said,

"Tua-i
wiinga itrarciqua
tuatnatukata."
Tuatnaqataami imkut taukut
aturani
anlluki
at'elliniluki qulilluni-llu.
Tua-i atkuut ukut assirluteng tua-i cakneq.
Aqaarluki nutaan
qasgimun taumun tua-i ayalliniluni.

***

36
Maaten-gguq itertuq
elaturrami ukut arnat qavciuluteng waniwa,
qamna-gguq-gga qama-i atulria.
Tua-i-llu-gguq piuraqerluni
yuarun tamana iquklican
iliit tayim' itliniluni.
Qama-i tuamte-ll' tua-i aturluteng, tuatnauralliniut imkut.
37
Tua-i ellii kiimi ellirluni aipaa-llu augna tua-i iterluni.
Qama-i tua-i aturluni.
38
Tua-i-ll' yuarun man'a iquklican qanlliniuq qamna angun,
"Waqaa, tua-i-wa nangllilriit yurararkat?"
Tua-i-ll' qamna qanlliniuq,
"Ugna-gg' ua-i
yurararkaulliami itellria ugna arnaq;
maani-ll' tangrruuyuunani
ua-i.
Tua-i tayima
piyukuni iterciquq."
Tua-i qanrraartelluki itrarluni amigkun
puggliniluni.
Pugngami tamana qasgiq kiarrluku pilliniuq egkumi
kia-i kiugna imna angutii
arnaq-gga kiug' caniqlia.
39
Tua-i-ll' tua qanlliniuq tauna, "Tua-i-gg' yuraqatallilriaten?"
Tua-ll' pilliniuq, "Tua-i-gg' piyarturlua wanigg' itellrianga."
Yuarutmek aturyaaqelria

"Then
I will go up there
if they are doing that."
Since she was going to do that
she took out
those clothes of hers
and put them on and she washed her hair.
Her parka was very beautiful.
Having put it on,
she went to the *qasgiq*.

***

36
When she went in,
lo, there were a few women in the porch
and there was someone singing inside!
After a while,
when that song was concluded,
one of the women went in.
Thereafter they would sing in there, and that's how it went.
37
She was alone at last, when the last of the other women went in.
There was singing in there.
38
And then, when the song ended, the man in there said,
"*Waqaa,* is that the last of the dancers?"
Then someone in there said,
"There is a woman by the door
who probably came to dance;
I have never seen her
here before.
Well,
she'll come in if she wants to."
Then after that was said, she came through the entrance
and appeared.
When she appeared she glanced around the *qasgiq* and in the back
against the wall there was her husband
and next to him was a woman.
39
And then the man [in charge] said, "So, you're probably going to dance?
She replied, "Well, I came in order to dance."
When the man started to sing,

inerqullinia
atuusqevkenaku
ellminek atuulluni
piciqniluni.
Atungartelliniuq
taum-llu tua-i angutem elitaqluki imna tua yuarun tamana aturluku.
Iquklitqatallrani tua yaan' quyigiqerluni
pillrani tua-i niitellngunaqluni iqukliartelliniluni.
40
Qavcirqunek-gguq tua tuatnauq.
Arcariinarluni taun' iqua qukilngunarqellra.
Tua-i-ll' wanigg' nangenruqatalliniluku-gguq cunawa aturluni
imumek-llu tua-i
quyigiqerlun' cegerrluni pillrani
qasgiq man'a arulallagangartelliniluni kaimallagaluni tuaten
    nevurrlugmek.
Tuamte-ll' tua-i atunqiggluni
tua-i-ll' tuatnaluni
qasgiq man'a arulallagluni, iqukliaruciatun
ellii taun' yural' nacaqerluni amigmun uavet
anqertelliniluni.
Aqvaqurluni tua taukugnun
tukugminun pilliniluni.
Itqertelliniluni-ll' tua-i.
41
Tua-i anerteksuarluni
qanertuq, qanlliniuq,
"Quyanaqvaa-ll' tua-i aũgna umyuama eqruutekvakaqii
tua-i ava-i piaqa!
Kitaki atakurpak
agu anyaqunatek!"
Ilagni pilliniak
unuaqu taũgaam anesqellukek.
Tua-i inerquatek taukuk atakurpak tua-i anyuunatek nem'etlinilutek.
42
Tua-i-ll' tupagngameng
pilliniak, "Kitak nutaan ankitek." Imna tua tauna tan'gurraq anlliniluni
    tayima.
Ak'anun pivkenani itliniuq,
iterngami qanlliniuq,
"Aling arenqiapaa!
Imkut tang nunat tayim' nunaunrillinilriit;

she told him
not to sing,
saying
she was going to sing herself.
Then she started to sing
and that man recognized the song she was singing.
As the song came to an end, the pitch of her voice
got so high that it was painful to hear.
40
She did that several times.
The high-pitched ending was getting worse and worse.
Then, it is said, she was going to sing for the last time,
and as before,
when she concluded in a high-pitched shrieking voice,
the *qasgiq* started shaking suddenly and bits of soil dropped down.
Then once more she started to sing again
and when she concluded the song as she did before,
the *qasgiq* shook as soon as she ended the song.
She put on her hood and went to the door
and dashed out.
She ran to those two,
to her hosts.
She quickly went in.

41
Panting and out of breath,
and she spoke,
"*Quyanaqvaa-ll'*, thank goodness, I just fixed that one over there,
the one that so infuriated me!
Kitaki, neither one of you go outside
all through the night!"
But she told them
they could go out the next day.
So, as she bade them to do, they stayed in the house all night.
42
Then when they woke up,
she said to them, "*Kitak*, both of you may go out now." So the
    young man went out.
Shortly thereafter he came back in,
and upon reentering said,
"*Aling arenqiapaa!* Oh my goodness!
The village is no longer a village;

cataituq; nunataituq!"
Maaten-gguq tua taun' maurlullrii-ll' anlun' piuq imkut tua-i nunat
    cataunateng tua-i.
Naparyallret-gguq taũgaam maani
uitaluteng.
Taukut tua nunaunrillinikai tuani tua-i.
Quyaluni taun' arnaq tua-i taumek eqruutekvakaqminek piniluku.

43
Kiimelliirtelliniut tua taukut.
Tauna tua ayagaluni
tutgara'urlua tauna.
Tua-i-am tamaantelliniaqut.

***

44
Atam tua pivakarluni taum maurluagnek pillinia, "Alingnaqvaa,
tua-i aipaqsagutek tua-i! Arenqiatutek allamek ilaitutek, ilaitukut!"
Nutaan-am tuaten tua piagni,
nutaan aipaqsagutellinilutek.
Pivakarluni tua qingalliniluni-am tua taun' arnaq.
Maaten-gguq-am tua-i
yuurtuq tan'gurrauluni.
Tua-i tamaanlluteng. Tua-i-ll' pivakarluni
maurlua tauna
yuugurngailami tua-i yuunrilliniluni.
Elkek tua kiimelli'irtellinilutek tua tuani.

45
Tua-i-ll' caqerlun' uksuarluni waten imumek tua cikuqerluni
aarnairulluni
pillrani taum arnam pillinia, "Alingnaqvaa!
Waniwa-qaa kingunemnun
ayakumegnuk cangata? Ayagyuumiituten-qa?
Wiinga-ll' tua kingunengqertua waniwa."
Tua-i-ll' pillinia
taum angutem, "Tua-i-gg' piyukuvet."
Tua-i ikamrivkalliniluku
waten uksuarmi.
Tua-i
erucit iliitni
upluteng

there's nothing; there's no village!"
When his grandmother went out, lo and behold, she saw that the
    village was gone!
Only the foundation posts of the houses
remained.
She had evidently made the village disappear.
That woman was glad that she had gotten even with the man who
    had so infuriated her.
43
They were now the only ones there.
That boy, her grandson,
would go out hunting.
So there they remained.

***

44
Soon afterwards their grandmother said, "*Alingnaqvaa!*
You two can be husband and wife! How unfortunate that there isn't
    anyone else here with us!"
When she told them that,
they became man and wife.
Soon afterwards the woman became pregnant.
When it was born, lo and behold,
it was a boy!
So they remained there. Then sometime later
their grandmother,
because she wasn't going to live forever, died.
They were now alone in that place.
45
And then once when fall came and it froze up
and it was safe
to be on the ice, the woman said to the man, "*Alingnaqvaa!*
How would it be if we went back
to my home? Do you not yearn to go?
I too have a home."
Then the man
said to her, "Well, if you want to."
Then she had him build a sled
during the fall.
Then
one day
they got ready

ayangartelliniut tamakuk qamuutarlukek.
Aling aren unugpailgan-gguq tang
tuavet tua tekiskilit kiagpak imna pekcimallra imna.
Tuavet tua-i ciunilliniuk nem'inun taum arnam.

46
Tua-i
arnam pillinia, "Tua-i tang waniw' wii nunaka una!
Augna tua-ll' ava-i
piunrilleq
qamaggun kiatemkun cali nunangqertuq."
Tuaten tua ikirtuqaq [pakigluku] iterlutek pilliniuk
imna-gguq cal' taun' akutaq
cali tua nem'ini, ilakuallra taum, uitaurallinilria cali
ayuqucirmitun tua-i.
Nutaan tuaken-am neresqengani nerrliniluni.

47
Nutaan tua tuantenga'artelliniuk.
Tuamte-ll' irniangluni
arnamek.
Aren taukut tua-i imkut nunaurtelliniut.
Nutaan taukuk tua-i irniakek tamakut, irniakegnek ayagluteng,
nunarrluurrluteng tua-i.
Tua-i
tuatun tua-i
nunaurcameng,
aipangaqluteng maaken ilameggnek.
48
Tuaten tua-i
man'a maa-i taktaluku
maa-i qanemcikaqa. Tua-i iquklituq.

and started heading out pulling a sled behind them.
Aling aren, it is said that they arrived at their destination
before night descended, whereas she, on the other hand, had walked
    all summer on the same trail!
They arrived and went into that woman's house.
46
Then
the woman said to the man, "So you see, this is my village here!
The one back there,
who died,
had a village too, which was further upriver from here."
She drew aside the braided grass mat that covered the entrance and
    when they went in they saw,
it is said, that the *akutaq*,
that was left over [by the man who had died], was still there,
just as he had left it.
So when she told him to eat, he ate from that.
47
They finally settled and remained there.
Then she bore another child,
a girl.
Aren, from that family a village was made.
From their children's children,
a contented community began.
Thus it was,
because they
became a village,
they acquired spouses from amongst their relatives.[3]
48
That is how
long it is,
the story which I am telling. It is ended.

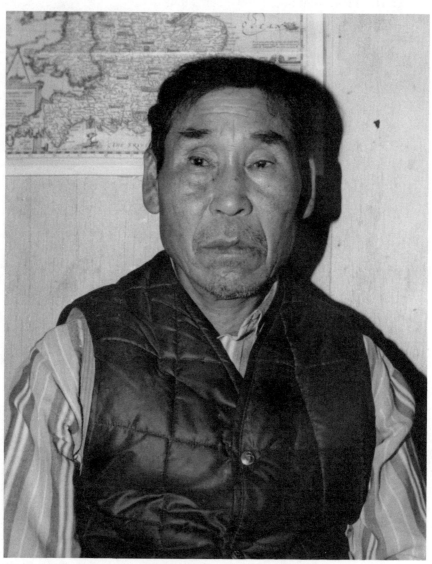

Cuniq, Jents Flynn, circa 1980. Photo by Andrew J. Chikoyak.

TULUKARUK
'RAVEN'

"Well, this Raven character, I always say this, he just doesn't rate high in my estimation; but then nowadays there are quite a few who want to hear about him, quite a few of them; especially Kass'aqs, *white men, are eager to hear about the one named* Ciuliaqatuk."
— *Cuniq*, "The Ancestor"

"Oh no! It looks like the guy with scaly legs from down that way who always tricks people."
— from "The One Who Took Back the Sun":
traditional Koyukon tale (Attla 1983: 93)

Arnaqulluk, Martha Flynn, circa 1980. Photo by Andrew J. Chikoyak.

The Two Faces Of Raven

The two stories in this section are about the same character, *Tulukaruk* 'Raven,' the trickster of Alaska and the Northwest Coast. Raven is an important figure in the folklore of all Native Alaskan peoples, as well as in that of the Chukchi, Koryak, Itelmens, and Siberian Yupik across the Bering Strait. Yet as the following two stories reveal, *Tulukaruk* has two quite different personas. In our first story, told by *Cuniq,* Jents Flynn, he appears as *Culiaqatuk* 'the Ancestor,' the culture hero who created *Qaluyaaq,* Nelson Island. In numerous other like tales, Raven the creator gave people the light of the sun and the moon, game animals, and the Milky Way. He instructed them in the rudiments of their culture. In our second tale, told by *Uyuraurluq,* Andy Charlie, we encounter Raven under a different aspect. Here he is the comical, gluttonous, ever-hungry trickster who usually ends up as the butt of humor because he tries to pull one trick too many.

For a long time we had, with little success, been urging the elders to tell some Raven stories. Many elders, such as *Cuniq,* expressed a reluctance, saying that they could not remember the Raven stories well enough to tell them, which was certainly the case with some. Another reason given for the reluctance was that such stories were not particularly important to remember, which *Cuniq* seems to suggest in his introduction to the *Qaluyaarmiut* creation story. We suspected that the implicit religious content of the Raven stories — Raven is after all the Yup'ik creator — presented a problem. Initially, *Cuniq* said he didn't hold much stock in "this Raven character," but the reader will note that as the story progresses the narrator's implicit attitude toward the subject matter changes. Both he and *Cakataar,* Jack Angaiak, continually cite examples of the existence of one thing or another as evidence that *Ciuliaqatuk* was more than just a fanciful character in a story. The translators are of the opinion that many elders continue to believe to some extent in the veracity of the Raven creation accounts, and this presented a problem for some, since they are all devout Catholics. There is little humor in *Cuniq*'s creation account. The focus is on place names, facts and evidence, and Raven does not come across as the hilarious trickster always tripping over his own cupidity, but as a powerful creator.

Uyuraûrluq, on the other hand, is not interested in true explanations, as his aside comments indicate; rather he is primarily interested in entertaining his audience. His narration is funny and full of laughter. Indeed, he refers to his story as a fairy tale, where the impossible happens and logical explanations don't apply. Nelson records a version of the same story (Nelson 1899: 464-467), and although many incidents and characters in it are the same, the hilarity that we encounter in *Uyuraûrluq's* version is largely absent. Both accounts emphasize Raven's cupidity, but it is clear that Nelson's version — perhaps as a consequence of the compiler's interest, editing, or perception of the function of myth — has the intent of explaining the nature of things in the world. For example, Nelson's account tells why ravens today never eat minks.

Yup'ik traditional narratives are often divided into two categories, *qulirat* and *qanemcit.* Explanations of the difference between the two vary considerably. According to some, a *quliraq* is a story that originates in the distant past, is passed down from generation to generation and has the stamp and authority of collective tradition and authorship. A *qanemciq,* on the other hand, can be attributed to an individual author, although he or she may have been forgotten (Woodbury 1984:13). Thus, what we call myth and fairy tale in the Indo-European tradition is included in the category of *qulirat.* Personal and historical narratives are *qanemcit.*

According to an alternative classification (which we subscribe to), a *quliraq* is a traditional narrative that has a framed and formulaic introduction ("A long time ago there was a village which was situated on the banks of a river, which flowed out into the ocean. On the far extremity of the village there was a grandmother and grandchild..."). A *quliraq* is perceived as being fictional, and therefore the actuality of events and characters is not predicated. On the contrary, a *qanemciq* tells of events that are perceived as actually having occurred, that were "believed *sometime,* by *someone, somewhere"*(Degh 1976: 119). Thus, myths and legends are *qanemcit,* since they were at one time viewed as narrations of events that actually took place. Framed stories, however, are *qulirat,* since everybody understands them as narrations of essentially fictional events.

Basically, the boundaries that separate *qulirat* from *qanemcit* are hazy and the explanations vary. For instance, elders have variously referred to the Raven creation story as a *quliraq* or a *qanemciq,* perhaps depending on how they view it, as a fictional account from the remote past, or as a story about actual events and happenings that are no longer accepted as true. Serov (in Fitzhugh and Crowell 1988: 242-243) writes that among the Chukchi, with whom the Siberian Yupik share a common folkloristic tradition (although they are linguistically distinct), Raven the creator, who appears in the myths, is distinguished from Raven the trickster, who appears in the tales. It is possible that the same distinction holds in the Central Alaskan Yup'ik tales. The tales of Raven the creator are narratives of religious belief, or *qanemcit*, and the trickster tales are *qulirat*. Certainly the levity and tone of the latter would indicate that they are told primarily to amuse (see *Ackiar*'s "*Tulukaruk Iqlunqarli*: The Lying Raven" [Orr and Orr 1995: 78-97]). Moreover, they have a type of formulaic beginning, such as Raven walking along the beach in one of his perpetual quests for food. Here is how *Uyuraũrluq* begins his narrative:

And now to begin it as a *quliraq*. This darn raven here
was strolling along the shore of the ocean.
He was strolling along the shore, and since he really loved to eat, he was
    strolling along the shore of the ocean.

Cuniq's creation account, on the other hand, begins like any other personal or historical narrative.

One more point of difference between the two types of Raven stories should be noted. In *Uyuraũrluq*'s trickster tale, Raven clearly appears under the form of a bird, a true raven; he *q'ruq*s 'croaks' like a raven and flies about. However, in *Cuniq*'s creation account, we cannot be sure because — except for his name, *Tulukaruk* 'Raven' — nothing would indicate that he is a bird. Serov (in Fitzhugh and Crowell 1988: 243) notes that in some of the Siberian creation texts Raven's anthropomorphism is strongly marked and his identity as a bird is less noticeable. The anthropomorphism of Raven is also accentuated in Nelson's creation account, and there is a notable lack of humor or levity.

Cuniq's account of *Ciuliaqatuk*, Raven the creator, was told in the Tununak Catholic Church on February 28, 1994, before an audience of high school catechism students, elders and a few *Tununermiut* adults. *Uyuraũrluq*'s story of Raven the trickster was recorded in the Paul T. Albert Memorial School in Tununak on November 11, 1994, before an audience consisting of Chris Meyer's fifth and sixth grade class, one Yup'ik speaking associate teacher, and the translators.

CIULIAQATUK

Cuniq Cakataar-llu Tununermiuk

***

Cuniq:
1
Tua-i-gga
tamana pisqumakengaat
una Tulukaruk
wanigga wiinga [qanrutkeqata'rqa], una wani Tulukaruk.
Ciuliaqatugmek avani
qanrutketullrukiit,
tau͡gaam
pirrlainarpegnaku akultuluku una tua-i
qanqerqelriit
Ciuliaqatugmek.
2
Una wani Ciuliaqatuucia
wii pirpakenritaqa,
tua-i-gga
imumek
tua-i-gg' pirpakenritniluku wanigg' qanlartua una wani Tulukaruk;
amta-llu maa-i mat'um nalliini
amlleriluni niicugtai,
amlleriluteng.
Kass'arpalluut tau͡gaam waten
niicuumirluku una pilaraat
Ciuliaqatugmek
at'lek.
3
Qagkut tau͡gaam Kuigpagmiut
niicaurteqerraallemni, Kuigpagmiut qagkut,
una pirpakellruat
cali paqnakenriyuunaku
una Ciuliaqatuk.

216

THE ANCESTOR

Jents Flynn and Jack Angaiak of Tununak

***

Jents Flynn:
1
Because
they want me to tell about
this Raven,
I am going to talk about this Raven here.
They used to talk about *Ciuliaqatuk*, the Ancestor
back then;
however,
they spoke of him infrequently,
speaking now and then
of *Ciuliaqatuk*.
2
As for his being the Ancestor,
he doesn't rate very high in my estimation.
Well,
this Raven character,
I always say this, he just doesn't rate high in my estimation;
but then nowadays
there are quite a few who want to hear about him,
quite a few of them;
especially *Kass'aqs*, white men,[1]
are eager to hear
about the one named
Ciuliaqatuk.
3
But the people over there on the Yukon,
when I first heard of this, those people over there on the Yukon
revered
and never stopped speculating about
Ciuliaqatuk.

4
Waken wanigga,
una nallunritlemnek waken,
qakmaken Iqugmek—
natiini tayima Kuigpiim paingan natiini
Iqug' una uitalarta Iqugmiut—
tua tuaken ayagnirnaluku umyuartequa
wavet
Qaluyaanun.
Tuaken tua-i
taq'erkaulua Qaluyaanek,
waken wanigga.
5
Tua-llu tua wanigga ayagnirlua
qanqatartua tuaken Iqugmek.
Tua nallunritetacirramtun wanigga

4

According to the way I know [the Raven story],
I shall begin from over there,
from *Iquk*, Russian Mission over there—
I'm not exactly sure where Russian Mission is situated, perhaps
someplace around the mouth of the Yukon—
and so I shall begin the story from there,
progressing from there
to *Qaluyaaq*, Nelson Island.
So I shall proceed
from here
and conclude with *Qaluyaaq*.
5
So then starting at this point,
I shall narrate from Russian Mission onwards,
to the extent I know about

Standing is *Qukailnguq*, Maria Fairbanks. Seated left to right are *Nanugaq*, Elsie
Tommy; baby *Laakautarkaq*, Lucy; *Naunraq*, Andrew Tommy; and *Tutgaraurluq*,
Pete Tommy, in *Niugtaq*, 1957. Photo by Christine Heller, courtesy of the
Anchorage Museum of History and Art B91.11.564.

piaqa;
amller' nalluyaaqaqa;
taũgaam tak'uq.
Una wani qanelqa iquklitevsiaqata'arqa watua qanrutlemni.
6
Tuani
qasgimi qavaryaurrlua,
tua-llu tua-i unisturluma
qanemcikekii quliraqluku
qasgimiut-llu niicugniluku tua-i elgarcameng.
7
Tua-i niicuarluku tua-i.
Tua-i-llu tayima
piinanemni qavallinilua.
Tua-i tayim'; maaten tupagtua
cali qanenermek taqeksaitellinilria
qanerturaumaluni cali tua-i.
8
Tuamte-ll' qavallinilua.
Maaten cali tupagtua cali tua taqeksaunani wanigg' maktaurluni
    qanerturalliniaqelria.
9
Tua-i-ll' tayima qavaama
tupagqenǵatnga taũgaam tupaglua, tupagqenǵanga unisturluma
tupalliniameng.
Tuaten tua-i
wanigg' ayuqellemnek
qanertua.

***

10
Tua-llu tauna tua-i Tulukaruk
Ciuliaqatugmek pitukiit,
kegga-i qakma
Iqugmi
tua-i uitallrulliniuq tuani.
11
Tua tamaa-i
aipangqellruyaaqluni
tauna Tulukaruk.
Irniarluni-llu panigluni, arnauluni tauna irniara.

it,
and I don't know a lot;
however, it's still lengthy.
I shall complete what I was speaking of just a while ago.
6
I had reached that age
when I had begun to sleep in the *qasgiq*
and my dear late father[2]
told the story
as the people in the *qasgiq*, having settled down, listened to him.
7
So I listened to him very carefully.
Then after
a while I fell asleep.
He continued, and lo and behold, when I woke up afterwards,
he still wasn't done
but continued to talk even longer!
8
And once more I fell asleep.
When I woke up again he still hadn't stopped, but was sitting up
    talking on and on.
9
Since I had fallen asleep,
I awakened up only when they woke me, when my dear late
father woke me, since they were all awake.
I'm telling you
how it was
with me.

***

10
And so Raven
whom they call *Ciuliaqatuk*, the Ancestor,
was staying over there
at *Iquk*,
at Russian Mission.
11
At that time
Raven
apparently had a wife.
And she had a child, a daughter, a girl.

221

12
Tua tuani nunamegni uitallermegni,
waten up'nerkarqan,
tua tauna Ciuliaqatuk
tua qamigarluni tua pissuraqluni
unani imarpigmi.
13
Tuarpagaqluni.
Tua-i
aqvalgitullratni
makunek
imarpillarnek,
tungunqunek,
tamaa-i
aqvalgiraqluteg' maliklutek
tamaavet
pitaa aqvaluku.
14
Ukut-ggur' wani wanigga,
tua-i-gg' nallunritlemkun,
ukut Qaluyaat
wanigga tamarmeng
evunrullruut-gguq,
evunruluteng tua-i
avatii taũgaam nacarrangqerraqluni
tuamek.
15
Tua tamaavet ukut mallegluki aqvalgiraqlutek tamaa-i
unangkengaminek taumek tauna-llu panini maliklutek
    ikayuqluku.
16
Tua-ll' tayima qaill' pitariluku tua-i tamaa-i
caqerluni waten atakumi
atiin
ellimelliniluku,
qavaken
nem'eg' egkuanek nevumek
urravnermek
pisqelluku tua-i,
naklegyagutniluku
waten aqvalgiqtaarturallra.

222

12
As they were living there in their village,
when spring came,
Culiaqatuk
would go seal hunting
down there on the ocean.
13
The sea ice would extend far out.
Back then
when a hunter used to get someone from the village to help him retrieve
his catch
of sea mammals,
tungunqut, bearded seals,
they
would go there together
to get his
catch.
14
Now the way
I understand it,
it was said that *Qaluyaaq*, present-day Nelson Island,
was all
piled-up ice;
the hills were piled-up ice,
only these had ice extending
all around the base.
15
They would go close to these ice pileups when they went to retrieve
the game that he had caught, that daughter of his having gone along
    to assist him.
16
So then on a certain day
in the evening
her father
asked her to do something for him,
requesting her to take
some soil
from the back wall of their house,
some very fine soil;
he said he pitied her
for having to help him retrieve his catch.

17
Tua-i-ll' pisquciatun tua urravnermek nevumek, nevuq'apiarmek
    urravnermek
kenini imirluku, kenia imirtelluku.
Tua qanrulluku
anesqelluku kenirmiaqluku tua-llu tua-i
keggaken
ukatmun,
tua-i-gg' mat'um tungiinun,
kenia tauna kenirmiara
ciqrutesqelluku, tua-i ciqrulluku.
Taugaam tangvagpegnaku ulurluku egmian itresqelluku.

18
Tua-i tuatnaluni tua-i.
Kenirmiani tauna anngami
tua pinertutacirramitun ciqrutliniluku ukatmun tua tangvagpegnaku-
    ll' tua ulurluku
egmian iterluni nem'un.

17
Then, as directed, she took some very fine soil, that is, fine,
    crumbly top soil,
and holding up the hem she filled up her skirt.
He told her
to go out carrying what was in the fold of her skirt,
and from out there
to throw
what she was holding in the fold of her skirt
in this direction,
towards us [here on Nelson Island], flinging it out.
But he told her to avert her eyes and to reenter promptly without
    looking at the dirt.
18
That's what she did.
Taking what was in the fold of her skirt she went outside
and with all her might she flung it toward this area, not
    watching but averting her gaze.
Then immediately she reentered the house.

Nep'ik 'sod house' in *Niugtaq*, 1959. Photo by E. Clements, courtesy of the
Anchorage Museum of History and Art B91.11.549.

19
Nutaan tua piamiu,
nutaan atiin piluku
elgarquraasqelluku
pivkenaku.

***

20
Tua-i tayima qavarluni.
21
Tupiimek
paqnakesqelluku,
anluku kiarcartuusqelluku.
22
Tua-i-ll' tauna imna pania
anlliniluni.
Anngami tua-i ciqrutellmi tungii
pillinia
tua-i camek cikumek tangerrnarqevkenani,
nevuuluni taugaam man'a tua-i
avavet tayima.
23
Tua-i
iterngami qanrulluku
tuaten ayuqniluku tamana tamaa-i ciqrutellra.
24
Tamaa-i
imuuluni maaten pillinia,
imuuluni naugga maani nunam qaingani
ilii nunam aayaarrluugaqelria waten, aayaarrluuluni;
tamaa-i tuaten ayuqluni
mamturivailegmi tamaa-i
nuna tamana.
25
Qaillun tua pitarian
tayima
wavet wanigga
ingriurrluteng,
evunrunrirluteng.
Tuaten ellillratni
wavet
ingrinun nugtarrlutek,

19
Then at last, after she had done that,
her father told her
to settle down
and to forget about it.

***

20
So she slept.
21
When they woke up,
he told her to check on it,
telling her to go out and look around.
22
And then that daughter of his
went out.
After she had gone out she saw over there in the direction where
she had flung [that fine soil]
that there was no ice to be seen,
but rather land here
and beyond.
23
So
when she entered she told him
what she had thrown out had turned into land.
24
She noted
that it was
similar to what in some places
is known as *aayaarrluk;*[3]
that is, that land
was like *aayaarrluk*
before it thickened and solidified.
25
With the passage of time
they
became
mountains,
ceasing to be piled-up ice.
When they became thus,
those two
moved here to the mountains,

nugtarrlutek.
26
Tua wanigga
una wani ateq,
atrat ukut
uitavimta,
Qaluyaaneg' avaqlimta
aterpagtetuit,
Qaluyaaruniluki, Qaluyaarnek.
27
Tua tamaa-i evunrullruyaaqluteng.
28
Tua-llu tua-i wavet elkarcamek,
kia-i kiugna
Engelullugarmiunek pitukvut,
tua tuani tua tuanllutek.
29
Tua-i wanigg' niiyutacirramtun,
nallunritnertutacirramtun-llu una qanrutkaqa maa-i.
30
Tua-i tuani tua-i, kiani kia-i, Engelullugarmiunek arivatukemteńi
    nunangqerrlutek.

***

31
Aa-a, katagilliniunga tamaani tamaa-i aqvalgiraqamek,
caqerlutek aqvalgillermegni
una wani pania
meqsunglliniluni, meqsunga'artelliniluni, meqsungluni mermek.

32
Tua-i-ll' im' atiin
una wani
miineq, maani qacarnermi,
miineq
tugerluku tua-i
ukiuvailegmi-llu
cikuliurutii ayimlluni.
33
Tamaa-i tugglerminiu tua
anqulleq tua [amlleriluni].

228

changing their place of residence.
26
Thus
the name
of this place here
where we live
is *Qaluyaaq*, Nelson Island, as the people around us
are wont to refer to it,
saying it is *Qaluyaaq.*
27
So back then [the mountains] had once been piled up ice.
28
And so when they settled here—
up there
is what we call *Engelullugaq*[4]—
that's where they settled.
29
I am telling this just exactly the way I heard it,
as much as I know about it.
30
So there they lived, back there in what we call *Engelullugaq.*

***

31
Oh, I omitted the part when they, Raven and his daughter, used to
    retrieve his catch together
and one day when they went to do that,
his daughter
got thirsty and having suddenly become thirsty,
    she wanted to drink water.
32
And so her father,
using an ice pick,
was chipping away
at a spring
of water on the side of the hill,
and before he made it through,
his ice pick broke.[5]
33
When he was chipping away at it,
the chips [piled-up].

Tuaten tua-i
cikuliurutni tauna ayimcan
cingilga
anqullmi qaingatnun
tua elliqalliniluku, tua elliqerluku.
34
Una wanigga
tauna cikuliurutiin ayimnera arcaqerluku
qagkut paqnakumallruat.

35
Tua qanerluni ellilliniluku pikavet
anqullmi qaingatnun
qanerluni,
"Tua-i wantaurli una.
Akwaku
kinguliat
tukuurutekniaraat."
Wanigg' una qanellra.
Una wani
arcaqerluku
maa-i umyuama
qanruteksuumiitelaryaaqaa.
36
Tuavet tua-i katagilliniunga
uumek wanigga.
Kia-i kiugkut,
Nulirqelriik kiugkuk ingrik akuliik cegnayuuluni, una-gg' uaqlia
ua-i tanglararci
yaatiinek,
tua-i taukut,
Ciuliaqatuum tugellra.

37
Tua ukiingnaqluni ukiivailegmi-ll' ayimlluni
panini taun' meqsullrani.
Kia-i Cikuliullernek atengqerrutekaa kiugum kia-i
Nulirqelriik,
cegnayuum uaqlia,
Carliaqutat quliit pikna.
38
Maa-i aterpagtelararput Cikuliullernek kiugkut. Makut ingrit

When he
broke off his ice pick,
he put its point
on top of
his pile of chips, placing it there.
34
It is this one here,
especially that broken part of his ice pick,
that those ones out there, [the people from the Yukon] especially
    wanted to know about for some time.
35
He put it up there
on top of his chippings
saying,
"Let it stay here
so that
generations to come
can become rich from it."
This is what he said.
On account
of this
I was especially reluctant
to speak on this matter.
36
That
is what I omitted.
In those hills up there
is a valley between *Nulirqelriik*[6] and [another mountain] which is
    closer [to *Tununeq*],
they can be viewed
from a distance;
that is where
Ciuliaqatuk, the Raven, dug with his pick.
37
When his daughter got thirsty,
he tried making a hole but before he could make it his pick broke.
That is the reason why it is called *Cikuliullret*,[7]
the hill which is
one valley over on this side from *Nulirqelriik*,
just above *Carliaqutat*.
38
We now call those mountains up there by the name of *Cikuliullret*.

caqallret tamarmeng atengqertut wani Qaluyaanek pitukaitni. Cingiit-
llu tamarmeng aterluteng agkut-llu agaavet.

***

39
Tua-i-llu tamaani tamaa-i wani wanigg' uitainanermegni kiani,
pania [agleqerraarluni].
Naugga maa-i
nasaurluut makut, arnat,
pinariaqateng tayim' cuqseng tekitaqan
tua-i augmek qaneryarangqerraqelriit,
tamaa-i
makut nasaurluut arnaurteqata'aralriit,
tua-i tauna arnaurtellrata
engelii.
40
Tua-i-am
atiin taum
maani nem'ini uitavkaryunrilamiu,
uitavkarngailamiu—ciuqlit, tamakut tamaa-i ciuqliput augkut tamana
    tamaa-i atutullruat,
alerquutet aturturatullermeggni mat'um Yupiim—
tua-i
nel'illinia kia-i,
nel'iyarturluku
qulmegnun pikavet;
kia-i kiugna
Engelullugarmiut quliitni,
kiugna cuginqurraq waten
yaatminek alaitaqelria.
41
Tua-i tauna
wangkuta aterpagtelararput maa-i
Qilengpagmek.
Kia-i Qilengpauguq kiugna
Engelullugarmiut quliitni.
42
Tua-llu tua-i tamaa-i
tuani tua-i
aqumgaluni,

These mountains
where things happened all have names here in what they call *Qaluyaaq*.
    All the points of land have names, as well as those points across
    there.

***

39
And so while they were staying up there,
his daughter [had her first period].
For instance,
these young girls, females,
when their time comes,
they would speak about an issue of blood,
at the time
when these young girls were just about to become women,
having reached the point
when they were able to bear children.
40
So then
her father,
because he didn't want her to be in the house,
because he wouldn't let her stay—our ancestors back in those days
    used to follow all those rules,
when they used to follow all of the Yup'ik rules[8]—
he
evidently made a house back there for her,
going up there above from where they were
to make a house for her;
it's that one up there
above *Engelullugarmiut*,
the tallest one,
which is visible from a distance.
41
We now
call it by the name of
Qilengpak.
That's *Qilengpak* over there,
above *Engelullugaq*.
42
And so back then
there [at *Qilengpak*]
she "sat";

apqiitnek "aqumgaluni"
tamaa-i.
Yup'ik avani
kencigtaqapiarallran
nalliini, alerquutet aturluki tamalkuita pitullermini.
43
Tua-i tayima
cuqengqerrluni
tuaten arnam aqumgallra
tuani
uitavimini,
cuqengqerrluni ernernek tallimanek.
Tallimiitni-llu tua nutaan
nem'un iluvarluni
tamaa-i.

***

44
Kiugna kia-i
Qilengpak,
avatii,
ukut Qaluyaarmiut
uitercaraqellruat.
Waten tua-i
elagluku, waten
muragamek taũgaam kapurrsuucirluteng
uitertaqameng,
tua-i
camavet itqan
tauna nallii elagluku.
Tua-i-ll' imna kavirpak tua-i,
marayaq kavirpak,
nutaan
waten qet'aliluki akaguiluki
cumertaqaqluki.
Tamaa-i uiteq
taum tua-i
nasaurluum
yuqerqaq'lallra.
45
Maani-llu kialirnerani avani imna tangtuksi cali peñaruarraq Iqallugtulim
quliini,

that is what they referred to
as "sitting down" in those days.[9]
Back in those days
when the Yupiit were very careful and observant,
they scrupulously followed all the rules.
43
There
was a fixed period of time
during which a woman had to sit
when
she remained in seclusion,
the number of days being five.
On the fifth day
she could reenter her home,
back in those days.

***

44
Further up the coast,
the area around
Qilengpak
is where the *Qaluyaarmiut*, the people of Nelson Island,
used to gather red ochre.
They
dug for it,
but they used a piece of wood to pierce the ground
when they searched for red ochre,
driving it
into the ground,
then digging around the place where they drew the stick out.[10]
So the highly regarded red ochre,
the bright red mud,
would then.
be squeezed into balls
as they respectfully gathered them.
That red ochre there
results
from that young girl
relieving herself.
45
Moreover, further upriver is a little cliff which you see
above *Iqallugtuli*,

peñaruarraq qaũgna.
Tamaa-i
tamakut kaimneret
tanglallruanka-llu wiinga. Tua tamaaken-llu tua-i cumertaqlua,
tegkacagalriit uiterret.
46
Tuaten tua-i ayuqellruluni
tamana. Maa-i cali pitangqertuq qava-i tamana.
Uiteq-llu cali ama-i uitauq maa-i
mat'um nalliini.

***

47
Tua-i ukuk
tuanllutek tua-i.
48
Taũgaam
wanigga
nallunritarallemkun qanrutekngamku
camek ilasciigataqa,
wavet tua umyuarteqlemni Qaluyaanun tekiskuma taq'erkauluku
    qanruteknermek.
49
Tua-llu tua-i una wani aipangqellra,
tua wanigga yaaken teguqerluku
pilriatun wanigg' qanrutkeqata'rqa.
50
Aipangqellruyaaqluni, nuliangqerrluni.
Tua-i tayima tamaani kingunrani nalluani
tegulliniluku
tua pistiin.
51
Tua camun piciinaku tua-i.
Tua-i yuaraluku ayagaluni, yuarayaaqluku.
Tua-llu tua caqerluni—nateqvani-llu tayima pillrua—
uumek teggalqumek tekitelliniluni tua net'un tua angtaluni.
Tua-i teggalqurruluni. Pikna-llu kangra pika-i
paqnakluku pillinia
egalrullinilria,
egalruluni.
52
Tua-i-llu

236

a little cliff upriver.
There
are fragments of red ochre that have broken off,
which I have seen. From there I would respectfully gather
that very hard red ochre.
46
That is how it was
back then. There is still some back there.
And the red ochre to this day
is still there.

***

47
So those two
lived there.
48
Now
however,
because I'm relating as much as I know,
I can't add anything more to the narration,
since I thought I should stop when I got as far as telling about *Qaluyaaq*.

49
And as to the matter of his having a wife,
I am going to tell that
by excerpting a piece from another story over there.[11]
50
He once had a partner, a wife.
Without his knowledge, in his absence,
someone came
and abducted her.
51
He didn't know what happened to her
and looked all over, searching everywhere, but to no avail.
Then one day—I don't know where exactly—
he came across this rock which was the size of a house.
It was rock. He checked the top
and saw
what apparently was a window;
it was a window.
52
And then

uyanglluku pillinia:
nulirra kan'a.
Aipani tauna tangerrluku kana-i.
Nukalpiaq-gga un'a tua-i nukalpiarpall'er caniani
taklaluni.
Tauna-gga imna
aipaa, nulirra,
imkunek qunavciuralria yualunek,
caliurluni.
53
Tua-llu tua-i
piuraqerluni tua-i piinanermini, qaillukuarluni piinanermini,
tua ciugtelliniluni
pilliniuq
tungulria pagna atralria
uskurarluni, uskuraa-gga qevlerpak tua quletmun tayima.
54
Tua-llu
tangerrnarilliniuq, elitaqnarilliniuq, tekicartulliniuq,
negairpak!
Naugga negairnek maa-i tanglartuci uskurarluteng pilrianek
caqam iliini.
Tamakucirpak, negairpak!

55
Tua-llu wanigg' tut'eqatartelluku
imum taum angutem elpeka'artelliniluku.
Kan'a-llu
nem kalvagyaraa
tua mermek imarluni tua muiqaaraumaluni.
56
Elpeka'arcamiu mak'arrluni tua ciukirmi tuavet tua-i kanaqalliniluni;
nat'rak qercurpak.

57
Tayima tua cer'elluni kanavet.
Ak'anun-llu pivkenani man'a tut'eqatarluni.
Yura'artelliniuq, puggliniuq,
uyalegpak,
uyalegpauluni!
Tua-i nengqerluni kiavet kegqerluku
anglluulluku. Tauna-ll' tull'uni

he peered down:
there was his wife down there.
He saw his spouse down there.
This *nukalpiaq*, a great hunter, this great big *nukalpiaq* was lying
next to her.
That mate
of his, his wife,
was working on some sinew,
splitting the strands.
53
Then
after this went on for a while, as he was trying to think of what to do,
Raven looked up
and saw
a black thing up there descending
attached to a thread, which was glittering all the way up.
54
So when
it became visible, when it was finally recognizable, as it was about
    to touch down,
it was a huge spider!
You know, you have seen spiders with their thread
now and then.
It was that kind, a great big spider!
55
So then just when it was about to alight,
that man inside became aware of it.
And the underground entrance
down there
was filled all the way up with water.[12]
56
Suddenly becoming aware of it, the man jumped up and dove
    head first into the water;
the soles of his boots were very white.[13]
57
That man splashed right down into the water and was gone.
In a moment the spider was about to land.
When the man reappeared, when he emerged,
he was a double-crested cormorant,
a big double-crested cormorant!
And the cormorant stretched its neck out and took the woman with
    its beak,

teggalquq-llu tauna
qupluni.

58
Tua-i
tauna ngellekluku wanigga
qanrutkaqa.
Wanigg' tua-i
ilavkenaku wanigga taq'aqa.
59
Cali tua-i ilavci tayima nallunrilkuniu
nallunrilkengani ilaqautekluku pikuniu atawauyartuq.

***

Arnaucuaq:
60
Kiani-llu-ggem
Yaaruillernek qantullruut.

Cuniq:
61
Tauna-gg' tua avauqeka.

Camp at *Engelullugaq*, five miles northwest of *Tununeq*, 1958. The camp was
used by *Niugtarmiut* for herring fishing in the late spring. Photo by Christine
Heller, courtesy of the Anchorage Museum of History and Art B91.11.600.

plunging back into the water with her. And then that spider landed
on the rock,
splitting it in two.
58
So now
I have reached the point
in my narration
where I finish up
without adding any more.
59
It would be a good idea if one of you who knows [the story]
would supplement it with what he knows.

***

Mike Angaiak:
60
They used to talk as well
about *Yaaruillret* up there.[14]

Jents Flynn:
61
I have forgotten about including that part.

Cakataar, Jack Angaiak; and *Cuniq,* Jents Flynn, at the Toksook Bay Mask
Festival, January, 1996. Photo by Andrew J. Chikoyak.

Arnaucuaq:
62
Ii-i!

Cuniq:
63
Kiani kia-i
Engelullugarmiut wani
kiugum Ceturcullrem
ukatmun uatmun qiptellrani teggarvallraak malruuguk.
Taukut tua tanglallruanka
qainganun mayurlua;
imna tua teggalquq, teggarvak,
allirenqeggluni manigceńani.
64
Makut-gga tevagneret
waten tua-i
ayuqnganateng;
tanglallrullikci.
65
Tua-i-gguq
tamakut
taum Tulukaruum panian yaaruillri.
Tua-i arivalarait Yaaruillernek taukunek.
66
Tauna tua-i avauqerluku wanigga, quyana,
avauqalqa.
67
Tua-i
taukut wanigga mat'um qanemcima
ilakai Yaaruillret
kiugkut-gga Cikuliullret
kia-i.
68
Una-gga Angyaruaq
ilaksukluku pilaraqa cali,
Angyaruamek pitukiit.
Ingna,
ikanelnguq-gga,
taukut Cikuliullret keluatni
yaatiini uitalria, Al'aqucim
ciunrani pagaani.

Mike Angaiak:
62
Yes indeed!

Jents Flynn:
63
Up there
by *Engelullugaq*,
below *Ceturculleq*
on this side of the point are two big rocks.
I used to see those
and climb up on top;
that big rock
had a flat and smooth surface on the top.
64
Also there were ditches
looking something
like this;
you must have seen them.
65
Those, it is said,
were
where Raven's daughter told her story-knife stories.
They call that place *Yaaruillret*, 'the one with former story knife pictures.'
66
Thank you,
that's what I forgot to mention.
67
So
that place *Yaaruillret*, 'the one with former story-knife pictures,' is
included in my story here,
as well as *Cikuliullret*[15]
back up there.
68
This *Angyaruaq*[16]
I think is a part of it too,
the one they call *Angyaruaq*.
That one,
the one that is over there,
the one which is beyond *Cikuliullret*,
that is the one which is above and beyond
Al'aquciq .

69
Tuaten tua-i pitaaqa
picimtun qanruteknayukluku
piama.
70
Cali
allamek avauriyaaqelliunga?

***

Cakataar:
71
Cali-llu
wii cali tua niitellemnek usguqaqata'arqa.
72
Wii cali niitellemni aũg'um qanemcikuraqertellran cali
tauna
Tulukaruum pania,
kiaken-gguq kia-i
uitavillerminek
Qilengpagmek
ayallruuq.
Ayagluni, kiugna kia-i Angyaruamek pilaqengaat Ciisqurrnam
    kiatiini imna kiugna Angyaruamek pilaqiit,
natiini-llu tua tayima
ayallermini tuani pania
tua-i mernuinercirluni aqumqallruuq;
aqumqerluni tua-i natiini-llu tayim' pia.
73
Tua-i-llu nangercami cali ayagngami
tua-i tauna aqumqallra uitengqerrluni;
cali tua-i aunrarluni tamaa-i-gguq uniciqerluni.
74
Cali-ll' ayagluni.
Yaavet-llu cali Cakcaarmiut
quliitni Ingrirpagmek kiugna pitukengaat,
tuani-gguq cali aqumqerluni
mernuinercirluni.
75
Tua-i-llu cali tua-i
ayagluni.
Tuaken tang tua natetmun taum qanemcikestiin ayallra
qanrutkenrilkii.

244

69
That is how long I'm making it
because if I tell anymore I might not be
right.
70
Maybe
I've forgotten something else?

***

Jack Angaiak:
71
What's more,
I'm going to supplement with more of what I heard.
72
When I heard this story from the one who was telling
about
that Raven's daughter,
this occurred when she
was staying up there,
having left from
Qilengpak.
As she was going, at that place up there that they call *Angyaruaq,*
     beyond *Ciisqurrnaq,* at what they call *Angyaruaq,*
somewhere around there,
his daughter
sat down to rest;
she sat down somewhere around there.
73
And then when she stood up again she went away,
and there where she sat down was some red ochre;
she was still bleeding and it is said that she left a little bit there.
74
And again she went,
going back there above *Cakcaaq*
to what they call *Ingrirpak,*
and there again, it is said, she sat down
to rest.
75
And once again
she left.
After she departed—the person who told the story didn't tell
where she went.

Cali-gguq tauna
uiterrartangqertuq
taũgaam-gguq amllerpegnateng; taukuk-gguq tuan' aqumqallrek tamarmek
uiterrartangqertuk,
taum tua panian ayallra kiaken
Qilengpagmek.
76
Wii tua nalluagka taukuk uitengqellrak. Taũgaam taum
qanemcikestellran
tuaten qanemcikellrua.
77
Cali-llu taum qanemcikestellran pillermini
neq'lillruniluku
iqalluarpagnek,
iqalluarpillruniluku.
78
(Imkunek egcetaarqelriit avani tangtullrulrianga-llu;
uqur' imna ceteqtayagartuqarraarluku
tua-i-llu waten ekelriani tua egluni.)
79
Tauna-gguq tua-i iqalluarpaliani
pillrua,
melulillrua taukugnek
panimi egcetaallregkenek.
80
Tua-i-llu-gguq
neq'liluni tua-i iqalluarpaurrluni.
Tuaten-am cali taum
niicugniurallma
pillrua.
Taukugnek tua wanigg' ilaqerqa-am
tayima. Cali tayima
avaurillemnek cali
elpeci ilavci ilaqerniaraa.
81
Tuaten-am tua-i wanigg' pitaluku piaqa.

***

Cuniq:
82
Ii-i!
83
Qanellruutek

That place also is said
to have a little red ochre,
but not a lot; both of those places where she sat down
have a little red ochre,
those places where his daughter went to
from *Qilengpak.*
76
I myself don't know whether or not they have red ochre. But the
    one who told the story
told it like that.
77
Furthermore, the one who told the story also said
that Raven made fish,
herring fish,
that he created herring fish.[17]
78
(They rendered oil and I used to observe them doing it back then;[18]
they would first slash the blubber
and then render it by frying it in a pan.)
79
As for that herring he made,
he
made roe for it
from the leftover rinds of fat that his daughter had rendered.
80
So then, it was said,
he made a fish which became a herring.
That is what the one
whom I was listening to
said.
So I have augmented [the story]
with those two [additions]. Again
one of you can add
what I have forgotten.
81
So that's all I have to say about it.

***

Jents Flynn:
82
Yes!
83
You two told us

waten tua-i
kepuqaciurangraan
nallunritlemteggun qanrutkesqelluku, qanellruutek,
waten kepuqaciurangraan.
84
Tua-i-llu
tuaten ayuqerkaungan una umyuaqekngaqa
qanrutkeqatarqa
mat'um ilii
qanemcim.
85
Ayalliniluni
ceńirrluni.
Naugga
ilaci qanemcillruuq; kalikani uitauq
qanemcia tangla'rqa, tangssugluku
qanemcia
camani nemteńi tangla'rqa
terr'et kitengkaqluki ayagniluku.

86
Tua-i tamaa-i mat'um ilakaa.

Cakataar:
87
Aa-a!
Quliraulliuq tauna. Quliraulalria tang tua tauna,
wii qulirauluku, quliraqevkarluku teq tauna pilaqeka.

Cuniq:
88
Ilakaa tamatum!
89
Quliraulria-gg' tua man'a, qulirauguq.
90
Tua-llu tua-i tauna
katagaqa wanigga:
tamaani ceńirtellermini
enetnercilliniluni capenricami,
enetnercirluni.
91
Tua-i uitaluni

to tell what we knew
even though it is fragmentary like this; you said
to do so even though it is in bits and pieces like this.[19]

84
And so
because it must be like that, I will narrate
the one I'm thinking of,
which is an episode
in this story.
85
He [Raven] was walking
along the beach.
You know,
one of you told a story, which is in a book
and I've seen his story, having seen
his story,
which is down there at our house,
the one that says that he was walking along
kicking sea anemones.[20]
86
It is an episode of this [narrative].

Jack Angaiak:
87
Oh yes!
That might be a *quliraq*. That is told as a *quliraq*,
I let them tell that sea anemone story as a *quliraq*.[21]

Jents Flynn:
88
It is part of that!
89
Well, this one is a *quliraq*, it's a *quliraq*.
90
And so then
I omitted that episode:
when he was walking along the beach,
waiting for low tide being obstructed from crossing,
he waited for the tide to recede.
91
So he stayed there

enetnercirluni
tuani.
Canaurluni, canallri makut
waten
egtaqateng
cikaaruluteng ayagartaqluteng tua, cikaaruluteng. Makut maa-i cikaaret.
92
Tua-i piinanermini tuamta-llu tua-i qavarnim tekitengani qavarangluni.

93
Tua-i-ll'-am ceggaumangnaqngami,
egturyalilliniluni.
Tua-i nutaan pinga'arcami, makut egturyat keggsungartaqatni,
qavarniyugnairulluni. {engelarluteng}
94
Tua-i tamaa-i
kinguakun taum
ayagngatuq
terr'et kitengkaqluki.
95
Tua-i-llu pivakarluni
iliita
keggluku, {qanemcista engelartuq}
quumkaulluku.
Aũg'arciiganani.
96
Tua-i
yuarutnguluni taũgaam tauna
pillra
waten aturluni, yuarutnguluni:

Tii'iq, tii'iq, pegesnga, pegesnga! {qanemcista engelartuq}
Angama,
angama,
imarnitegken aipaigketnek nunulirciqamken!
97
Tua maa-i mat'um ilakaa.
98
Taum ciunran pegcugpegnaku.
Tua nunulirturyaaqluku;
waken wanigga
uunguciirtaqa.

and
waited for the ebb tide.
He was whittling
and when
his shavings fell,
they became capelin and swam away. These are the present-day capelin.
92
And then after a while when a feeling of drowsiness came over him,
    he started to get very sleepy.
93
And because he was struggling to stay awake,
he made mosquitoes.
When the mosquitoes began to bother him, when they started to bite him,
he was no longer drowsy. {laughter}
94
He apparently
left
after that,
kicking the sea anemones.
95
After a while
one of them
bit him, {narrator laughs}
closing around his foot.
He couldn't get it off.
96
But
when they talked to each other,
it was
by singing, through a song:

Sea anemone, sea anemone, release me, release me! {narrator laughs}
My maternal uncle
my maternal uncle,
I will reward you with one of his gut raincoats!
97
That's part of this [narrative].
98
The one he was pleading with wouldn't release him.
He tried to give him different rewards;
yet from this point onwards I am not sure
about the rest.

99
Qulirauguq tua-i, qulirauluni.
Tauğaam tak'uq; tua takliniuq.
100
Tuaten pitaluku [piaqa].

***

Cakataar:
101
Iillayukallemnek piunga qanrutkeqernaluku.
102
Atam cali kiugna tua qanemcikqaqerlaku ilakenrilengraaku,
    yurvillruamku
Qilengpak kiugna
kiantellemni.
Waten
nekniluku-am niitelalqa umyuaqluku mayullemni mayullruunga.
103
Tua-ll' kiugna Qilengpak, man'a tauğaam neglirnera alaituq, teggalqut.
Teggalqunek iillayungellruunga; iillayugturallruunga;
man'a neglirnera maaggun uivurallruaqa!
Aling, aren teggalqunek iillayullruunga:
atam imkut teggalqut
waten tua mamtutangatellruut,
waten, qaillun-llu waten angtaluteng,
waten tua kangirairumaluteng.
Qulliqurluteng ukut tua pitatekluteng mayurnaurtut pikavet
yaaqliqu'urluteng.
Imkunun tua-i ayuqeltassiigutellruanka
icigg' makut maa-i,
ingna school-arvilleq,
puyirvii tangrraqamki neq'aqatuanka.
Tamakucirtun tua ayuqut.
Cali-ll' qaterrlugluteng
tamakucicetun.

104
Makut-llu akulait piqalriit qava-i
tamakucit tamaa-i pinaurtut.
Yaaken tua alaitlermeggnek tua yaaqliqu'urluteng tua-i.
Tamakunek iillayungellruunga.

99
It is a *quliraq*, a traditional story.
However, it is long; it is apparently quite lengthy.
100
That's how long [I'm making it].

***

Jack Angaiak:
101
I would like to tell about what really amazed me.
102
Allow me to tell about that one back up there, even though it isn't
    properly a part of the story, since I was up there examining
Qilengpak
once when I was back there in that area.
I
climbed up there remembering that they say it was her house.
103
Only the rocks on the north side of *Qilengpak* are visible.
I was awestruck by the rocks; I was continually amazed;
I went around to its north side!
Aling, I marveled at those rocks:
those rocks
seemed to be about yea thick,
like this, and about so big,
with the corners rounded off like this.
They were the same size and stacked one on top of the other and so
    on as they went up,
all in rows.
I compared them with those [bricks],
you know, with that
school over there,
with the old school's chimney and whenever I see its chimneys I
    remember them.
They were like that kind [of brick].
Moreover, they were also whitish
like that kind [of brick].
104
And between them [the rocks] in there
there would be that kind there.
From where they were visible they were in rows.
I was utterly astounded by those.

Cuniq:
105
Nateqvani?

Cakataar:
106
Qilengpagmi kiani yurvillruaqa.
107
Nani-ll' maani ayuqaitnek tangeqsaitua waniwa,
tamakut.
Tua-ll'-am cali tua-i
egalengqerrnilaatgu
cetamanek,
avaggun qerkitarallrakun uivlua
uqvigarmek tegumiangqerrama
kangranun mayurlua piunga tua kangra una tua-i
manigcecaaqelriami allirenqeggluni, manigcecaaqelriim taũgaam
    maniaterrluarluni.
Apertullruitki tua tuani waten kangiraitni, waten
    kangirenqenricaaquq waten taũgaam ayuquq,
piaqa una
ukiner' una ukatmun taũgaam cauluni.
Qinercaaqekeka kiavet qamna tua tunguluni.

108
Tua-ll' uqvigarmek
kauluku
piaqa tua qamna tua qama-i,
tarviaskilaku. Ikavet cali arvirlua piunga tuaterrarpiar-am cali.

109
Tua-'m piaqa tuaten tua-i cali tua-i
qamna nequtunruluni.
Piuraranka taukut cetaman tua ilumuullinilriit:
tua-i-gguq
egalri
cetaman.
Tuaten tua qamkut
nequtunaurtut
taũgaam tua-i waten man'a
pivkenateng qamna taũgaam nequtuluteng.
Wa-gguq egalri

Jents Flynn:
105
Where precisely is it?

Jack Angaiak:
106
Up there at *Qilengpak*, I examined it.
107
I haven't seen anything like those anywhere
around here.
Furthermore,
because it was said that it had
four windows,
I went around where it was lower
and since I was holding a piece of willow,
I went up to the top and saw that the top
was somewhat flat and leveled; it was somewhat flat although a bit
    uneven.
Since they mentioned that they [the windows] were in the corners, [I
    investigated them]; it [the structure] was not exactly square
    but somewhat squarish,
and there
I saw a hole, but it was facing this way.
When I attempted to look in, it was dark inside.
108
So I stuck
the willow stick in
and I could feel [that it was hollow] inside
as I moved it side to side. I went across to the other side [to check
    the other window] and it was just the same.
109
When I checked it again it was the same inside,
only wider.
As I continued to examine those four I could tell that it was indeed true:
those, it was said,
were its four
windows.
The hollow areas inside
would be wide,
but not the openings;
only the inside parts were wide.
Behold, these were

taum tua-i panian!
110
Taukunek tua teggalqunek iillayullruunga.
111
Tua-i tuaten ata pitaqerluku wanigg' taq'aqa tua taumek
yurviarallemnek kiugna.
Tua-i tauna Tulukaruum pania umyuaqurallruaqa. Tulukaruk taun'
    nel'illruami,
nel'illra
panini.
112
Nel'illrullinikii pengegnailngurnek kiugkunek. {qanemcista engelartuq}
113
Ii-i, tuaten atak tua pitaqerlii kina cali tayima nallunrilkengavci
ilavci
tayim' qanrutekniaraa.

***

Cuniq:
114
Uitertenraralriit-llu tamaa-i
tamatum nalliini kegginateng mingugaqluki.

Cakataar:
115
Ii-i, aa-a, tua cali tamakut pillrulua cali.
Waten-gguq yuk-gguq uitermek tua pissuqerraalria
ayagyuaq
kegginani-gguq uiterciiqaa,
uiterrluku tua-gg' nutaan pitellria.
Tua wii tua takumni tuatnalriamek tangerqallrunritua taũgaam
    qanrutellruanga uum
yuut iliita tayim' tuqullrem.
Uitertenrrayagalria nutaan tan'gurraq
kegginani-gguq, kegginaa-gguq mingugciquq uitermek.
Qaillun-llu kangianek qanrutevkenii.
116
Calria-kir' tuaten tua minguusqelliniagu
uitermek kegginaa?
Cali-am tuaten alerquutengqerrsaaqluni tamana.

his daughter's windows!
110
I was astounded by those rocks.
111
So this is where I stop, at that point
when I investigated it up there.
I had been thinking about Raven's daughter, that Raven had made
 a house,
had constructed a house
for his daughter.
112
He apparently made her a very sturdy house back there. {narrator laughs}
113
Yes, that is how much I shall say and someone else, one of you
who is knowledgeable on the matter
may narrate it.

***

Jents Flynn:
114
In those days those who picked red ochre for the first time
would smear some on their faces.

Jack Angaiak:
115
Oh yes, they also told me that.
Indeed it was said that if a person, a young person, were to gather
red ochre for the first time,
he must smear his face with red ochre,
smearing his face with red ochre upon gathering it for the first time.
I myself haven't seen anyone do that, but one of the people
who has since died, told me about it.
When a young man picks red ochre for the first time,
he would smear his face with red ochre.
Nevertheless, I was not told the meaning of it.

116
I wonder why they wanted them to
smear their faces with red ochre?
They obviously had a rule for that.

TULUKARULLER

Uyuraŭrluq Tununermiu

***

1
Wiinga qulirapiggarmek nanitkacagalriamek, *fifteen minutes*-aq-ll'
    una takciqliuq. {qanemcista engelartuq}
2
Qulirat makut ilait tua pinguarutuut, icigg' imkuni cani...
Canek ima tanem imkut qanemcingssaarallraat pitukait,
imkut igararraat
nanitkacagarluteng?
3
Cingarkaq: *Fairy tale*-at.
4
Uyuraŭrluq: Ii, tamatumek. Tamatuuluku qulirapiggaq
    tua-i camek-llu pivkenani. {qanemcista engelartuq}
Qulirapiggauluku, *fifteen minutes*-aq una malkassaagarluku piqatartuq.

5
Imkut ima tanem tulukarulleraat canek [pilaqait kass'atun]?
6
Cingarkaq: *Raven.*
7
Uyuraŭrluq: *Raven,*
raven-at, tulukaruut.
Tulukarulleraat makut ikiukacagalriit tengmiat! {qanemcista engelartuq}
8
Waniwa-llu kia nerkiinek niiteksaitua,
tulukaruut tamakut.
Cali-llu
qanrutkumatuluteng
akusrarutekesqevkenaki makut
tulukaruut,
nangcikesqevkenaki.

THE MISCHIEVOUS RAVEN

Andy Charlie, Sr. of Tununak

***

1

I'm going to tell a real *quliraq*, a very short one, and this fifteen
    minutes might be too long. {narrator laughs}

2

Some of these *qulirat* are fiction, you know, those...
What do they call those short tales,
those books
that are very short?

3

Eliza Orr: Fairy tales.

4

Andy: Yes, that kind. This story is a real *quliraq* and there's no
    moral to it. {narrator laughs}
It's going to be a real *quliraq* [and we're going] to try to use up
    fifteen minutes.

5

What do they call those *tulukaruut* [in English]?

6

Eliza: Raven.

7

Andy: Raven,
ravens, *tulukaruut.*
These darn ravens are very ugly birds! {narrator laughs}

8

To this day, I haven't heard of anybody eating
any ravens.
Also,
they told [us]
not to tease these
ravens
or abuse them.

9
Tamakut-gguq
tulukarulleraat nangcikesciuraqameng,
cami
akinaurutii tukniuq;
cauluni, picurlaullugpauluni tuc'ugngaluni,
tamakullraat tamaa-i
tulukaruut.

***

10
Tua-i-ll' qulirarrauluku ayagnirluku. Tulukaruller una
imarpiim ceñiikun cen!iquuyaaralliniuq.
Ceñiquuyaarluni neryunqeggurluami-ll' tua-i ceñiquuyaarallralliniuq
tua-i.
Pivakarluni atam
imkunek
belukha-nek, cetuanek,
qaktaalrianek tangllinilria. {qanemcista engelartuq}
Tangerrngami tua ayariyaaqellinii, cucuyaaqellinii,
neryunqeggurluami. "Qaillun-kin una-i pitaqluki nerqerlii
unaken?" {qanemcista engelartuq}
11
(Tua-i-gg' qulirat makut
pituameng.) Tua-i-am taukut cetuarugaat murilkengllinii, taum
tulukaruum tua-i murilkelluki. Ilait tua-i qanerciruarluki, "Aling
qaktaqavci-llu tang aitarteqvaarluci-ll' pilarci!" {qanemcista
engelartuq}
Tua-i-am nall'arulluteng ilait aitangayaggluteng qaktellininaurtut.
"Aling qaktaqavci-llu taktuamek ayakarluci aitarteqvaarluci
piaqluci!"
12
Tua-i atam pivakarluteng tuaten-am aitarteqvaarluteng
qakcimalallin[inaurtut].
Tuatnaata tua-i
murilkenglliniluki.
13
Tua-i...
(Aling epenrilnguq-ll'-am anrutam iluani!) {qanemcista engelartuq}
Pivakarluni tulukaruk tamakucilriamun qanranun tua-i ellminek
cuukcautelliniluni aitangqallrani.
Aling quliraungami-am tua-i anrutaani uitaqalliniluni! {qanemcista

9
It is said that when
ravens are mistreated,
their retaliation is greater
than the deed done to them;
it is as though a great misfortune may come as a consequence,
[from] those
ravens.

***

10
And now to begin it as a *quliraq*. This darn raven here
was strolling along the shore of the ocean.
He was strolling along the shore, and since he really loved to eat,
    he was strolling along the shore of the ocean.[1]
As he was walking along,
he saw those
belukhas, *cetuat*,
surfacing and submerging. {narrator laughs}
He desired them when he saw them, wanting them because he loved
    to eat. "I wonder how I can catch those down there and eat
    them?" {narrator laughs}
11
(This is because anything is possible
in *qulirat*.) That raven started to observe all those belukhas,
studying them carefully. He pretended to talk to some of them,
    "*Aling*, behold, when you surface open your mouths wide!"
    {narrator laughs}
Some of them did open their mouths wide when they surfaced.
    "*Aling*, when you come to the surface, stay up longer with
    your mouths wide open!"
12
After they had submerged they started to surface longer with their
    mouths wide open.
When they started to do that,
he began to watch them very carefully.
13
So...
(*Aling*, he wasn't suffocating inside the stomach!) {narrator laughs}
As he was watching, the raven popped himself into the mouth of a
    whale that was surfacing with its mouth open.
Aling, because it's a *quliraq*, the raven was all of a sudden in the

engelartuq}
Aling epenrilnguq! {qanemcista engelartuq}

***

14
Tua-i piinanrani tuani (anrutani-gg' tua-i pillilria iluani),
ayumian tua-i ayuqucia man' qinuirulluni,
man'a maani uitavia. Piuraqerluni qakemna qanelria,

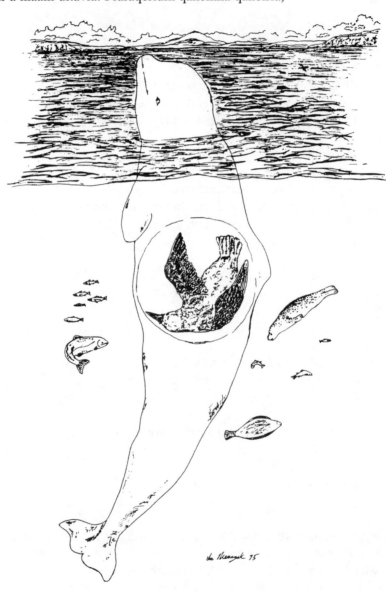

whale's stomach! {narrator laughs}
Aling, he wasn't suffocating! {narrator laughs}

***

14
While he was staying there (apparently in its stomach),
suddenly he felt it was calm
[in] this place where he was staying. While staying there,

Qang'allugaq, Hazel Lincoln; and *Aassanaaq,* Massa Paul, *Tununeq,* circa 1978. Photo by Andrew J. Chikoyak.

"Alingnaqvaa-ll' mat'umi, caluni man' tuqullrullinia?" Yuut
iliita ceńirtellriim mallukluku.
Tauna tua-i cetuaq tauna itqerrvillra tuquluni tua-i. (Aling
epsuipagta tauna {qanemcista engelartuq}
tulukaruller!)

15
Qakma tua-i pilangelliniluk' tua-i.
Tang-llu ayuqucia tanqigmi utertenglliniluni tua qakma tua-i,
ullirrluku tua pillrani.
(Aling tengyugngallinilria-am anrutaani uitang'ermi!)
Piyugngariuraami tua-i ullircan tua-i,
pirraminek tua qulmun tua ellminek tua anpecilliniluni qulmun.
    {engelarluteng}
16
Tua-i
piyugngaami, yaatiinun mic'ami,
qaini tua essuqcaararlulliniluku.
Tua essuqcaararraarluku elluariurangami ayumian tua tungiinun
    ayalliniluni
taum tua-i.

somebody out there said, "*Alingnaqvaa,* how did this thing
ever happen to die?" Somebody walking along the shore
had found the carcass.
The belukha he entered had died. (*Aling,* how was it that he didn't
    suffocate, that {narrator laughs}
 raven!)
15
The person out there started to butcher the belukha.
And behold, [the raven] was aware of the return of daylight when
    the person out there
disemboweled the whale!
(*Aling,* he could fly even though he had been in the stomach!)
When he was able to [fly], when it had been cut open,
he shot upwards with all his might. {laughter}
16
Then,
since he was able to, when he landed behind [the man],
the poor thing managed to scrub himself off.
Having scrubbed himself off, after he came back to his senses, he
    went towards
that man.

Ayaginar, Maggie Short, braiding and hanging *iqalluarpiit* 'herring' to dry in
Tununeq, circa 1958. Photo by Christine Heller, courtesy of the Anchorage
Museum of History and Art B91.11.403.

17
Tekicartullinia angutem uum tauna tua-i
cetuaq, *belukha*-q, pilallinikii tua.
Tua-i tekicamiu tua, "Aling arenqiapaa-ll' piluaqalliniuten-am
　　mat'umek cetuamek!"
Aren tua-i-gguq man'a ceturpakayall'er tua-i tuqullrullinilria-gguq tua-i,
ekiinani-llu-gguq tua-i. {qanemcista engelartuq}
18
Uqurikayagluni-gguq tua-i tamana cetuaq tua-i.
Kemga-ll' tua amllerluni angengami.
Qanrucaqturcani
pillinia,
"Aling tua-i-qa pilainanerpeni tayim' camek-llu tangerqanrituten?"
　　{qanemcista engelartuq}
"Arenqia,
aqsiik ima tam ullirrlukek piinanemni ca tuar tang maaken
　　anqertellrulria melmun tua-i tayim' pinganani." {qanemcista
　　engelartuq}
19
"Aling tuatnallrukuni-ll' tua-i neryunaiciiqellinilria tua-i!
Caciinani-ll' tuqullrukuni cali neryunaiciiqelria."
"Aling ilumun tua-i tuatnallrukuni neryunaiciiquq; kemga man'a
　　piyunaiciiqngatuq.
Tua-i uitalli, tang tua man'a qaillun pivakartuq." {engelarluteng}
20
Taum tua-i imum,
mallukestellran,
tua-i cakaarluku nat'ariinek-llu tegutevkenani
unitelliniluku tauna
belukha-rpall'er.
21
Ayaguallliniluni-'m tua. Elliin-llu ayiin unisnguarluku.

***

22
Arenqiapaa-ll' tua-i amlleran tua-i kiimecuumiilami—naugga-mi ilai
　　tulukaruut ilakai?—
ilakarrsuavakarluni
imarmiutayagarmek arnacaluarmek aiparkanglliniluni, unayaqluku.
23
Aren taumek tua-i cetuam kemgugiinek uqurugarmek-llu tua-i

17
As he got close, this man
was butchering the belukha.
When he reached him, [he said], "*Aling aren*, oh my gosh, you are
     very fortunate to have found this belukha!"
Aren, this great big belukha, he said, evidently died of something;
it had, he said, no entry wounds. {narrator laughs}
18
That belukha, it is said, was very fat.
And it had a lot of meat because it was big.
When he didn't say anything,
[the raven] asked him,
"*Aling*, did you see anything odd since you started to butcher that
     belukha?" {narrator laughs}
"*Arenqia*, as a matter of fact,
while I was opening the stomach, something suddenly shot out and
     it seemed as though it flew upward." {narrator laughs}

19
"*Aling*, if that's the case, then it is not suitable to eat!
And if the cause of death is unknown that too makes it inedible."
"*Aling*, you are right! If that is the case then it is not good to eat;
     this meat is evidently inedible.
Let's leave it; there are too many things wrong with it!" {laughter}
20
This person
who had found the carcass
let it be and without taking any part of it,
he left
that great big belukha behind.
21
The raven pretended to leave. As the man left, he also
     pretended to leave it behind.

***

22
Arenqiapaa, since there was a lot and he didn't want to be alone—
     where were the other ravens that he could share with?—
and searching around for somebody to share with,
he found a small female mink as a companion, inviting her [to join him].
23
Aren, with that belukha's flesh and fat they had a lot of food. They

neqaucirlutek. Avegluku tua-i tauna tua-i imarmiutayagaq-llu.
Avgullutek tua-i
neqautekliniluku.
24
Aren-gguq tua-i im' tulukaruller tua-i umyugiukacagarluni;
ukatmun takuyaqa'arqami waken kegqaulluni tamuqsuararaqluni.
{qanemcista engelartuq}

25
Tua-i cakneq anglaniluni tua-i
taumek neqminek.
26
Tua-i atam pivakarluni ak'a un' neqii nangyukalria cetuarugar' im' avga,
taumun imarmiutayagarmun tunellran avga.
27
Tua-i
nangulluni civuani,
tua-i cakairulluni.
28
Tua-i arenqialami, cakailami, imarmiutayagaq tauna neqaucian,
uitayaaqerraarluni akutelguan-llu-gguq taun' imarmiutayagaq
    arnacaluar, {qanemcista engelartuq}
tua-i atakumi-am tua caqerluni ullagluku tua,
alangruunguarluni tua-i pilliniluk' tua qaillukuarlun' tua-i.
Alingcetaarluku tua (qaillun tayim' erinarluni pillrua).
Tua-i atakumi tan'gerian, qaill' pitarian, agluni tua-i
pilliniluni,
"Aaaa!"
Elatiinun pirraarluni:
"Aaaa!
Aaaa! Akutaarpenek-gguq atam cikinrilkuvnga[a]
    nervagniaramka-a-a-n!" {engelarluteng}
29
Imarmiutayagaam alingqallermini akutaaraūrluni eggluku elatmun,
    {engelarluteng}
elatrutaa neqni.
Tua-i
tanqigian caarkaunrilan pillinia imna tua-i qantallra tua
    painqegcaaraumaluni.
30
Tua-i neqii cukariqerrlun' tua-i.
Atakut anagivakayuunak' alangrunglun' tua-i. {engelarluteng}

split it in half, he and that little mink.
They split it in half
and kept it for their food supply.
24
Aren, that raven was really indulging himself, eating whenever he
    felt like it;
he faced this way [and that], taking a bite out of this and leisurely
    chewing [on that] for a while. {narrator laughs}
25
He was enjoying his food
immensely.
26
Since he was eating a lot, his half was almost gone,
his half of what he had shared with the little mink.
27
Then
his half was gone first,
and he had nothing left.
28
Since he had nothing left and the mink had a lot of food,
having waited in vain, and since it was said that small female mink
    always made *akutaq,*[2] {narrator laughs}
once during the night he went to her,
pretending to be a ghost somehow.
He tried to scare the mink (by altering his voice in some way).
At night, sometime after dark he went over and
said,
"Aaaa!"
Having situated himself outside her house:
"Aaaa!
Aaaa! If you do not give me your *akutaq,* I will eat you u-u-p!"
    {laughter}
29
When the poor little mink got scared, she threw the *akutaq* outside;
    {laughter}
she threw her food outside.
Then
when it was daylight and there was nothing to fear, she went out
    and saw her bowl was licked completely clean.
30
Her food was rapidly being depleted.
Practically every evening she was visited by a ghost. {laughter}

31
Akutaaraûrluni tua-i ciqrutaqellinikai tua-i cakmavet!

***

32
Umyuangengluni taringerrlugluni.
Tauna tua-i qantaq,
kangiplugnek,
arallermek,
kangiplugnek avukluki,
utaqanerrlugtelliniluku tua-i caqerluni atakumi.
33
Tua-i-am pinarinariqerluku-am tua-i cakma nepengssak cakemna
    tua-i arenqiatelliniluni, "Akutaarpenek atam tua-i
    cikinrilkuvnga nervagniaramken!"
34
Tauna tua-i aralleq kangiplugnek ilalek ciqruskii, cakemna
    nep'nguq, "*Q'ruq!*
Q'ruq!" {engelarluteng}
35
Tua-i tayim' tuaten q'ruqaaraluni tua-i catairutliniluni.
36
Unuaquan emutelliniak iigni.
(Iiliurtemun piyugnaunani!) {qanemcista engelartuq}
Taumun tua imarmiutayagarmun emutelliniak iigni.
Maaten tua-i imna
iik {qanemcista engelartuq}
yurvilliniak, arallermek kangiplugnek-llu
evrut'rugai amllerrluteng!
Elleqtiin pilallinikii! Katengvalliniluku wavet,
"Ik'atak tulukarucilleqtaq neqkaarapuk cukateqtarluki!"[b]
    {engelarluteng}
37
Aûgna tua-i waten pitaluku nallunritlemkun qanemcikqerqa.
    Qulirauguq.
Yaa, tua-i-gga.

31
Poor thing, she kept on throwing her *akutaq* outside!

***

32
She more or less figured out what was going on.
So she mixed charcoal and ashes,
[mixing it in] that bowl,
charcoal
and ashes [to make it seem like *akutaq*],
and waited anxiously for him one night.
33
So then at about the time he was supposed to be there, something
    out there was making noise, wailing, "If you don't give me
    your *akutaq*, I will eat you up!"
34
Then after she threw out the mixture of ashes and charcoal, the thing
    outside started croaking, *"Q'ruq!*
Q'ruq!"[3] {laughter}
35
He was still making that croaking sound as he went away.
36
The next morning he took his eyes to be fixed.
(Without even going to an eye doctor!) {narrator laughs}
He took his eyes to be doctored by that mink.
When she checked
his eyes, {narrator laughs}
lo and behold, she saw that they were full of ashes and charcoal
and there were a lot of foreign objects in his eyes!
So it was he who was doing it, darn him! She
    flipped him the big bird right here [on the nose],[4]
"You lousy raven, you made our food supply go faster!"[5] {laughter}
37
So that is the extent of that story; I told it according to the way I
    remembered it. It is a *quliraq*.
Yes, it is over.

Caingilnguq Allen Chikoyak with *tungunquq* 'bearded seal,' *Tununeq*, circa 1980. Photo by Andrew J. Chikoyak.

ANIMAL SOULS

"The greatest peril of life lies in the fact that human food consists entirely of souls."
—*Ivaluardjuk* to Knud Rasmussen (Rasmussen 1929: 56)

Tununermiuk with two seals and a *tungunquq* 'bearded seal' hide with blubber, circa 1980. The man on the left is *Nanugaq,* Simon Billy; the man on the right is unidentified. Photo by Andrew J. Chikoyak.

Nakaciuryaraq 'The Bladder Festival' And The Story Of The Boy Who Went To Live With The Seals

The following narrative was recorded in *Negeqliq*, St. Marys, in March 1995 during a bilingual conference of the Lower Kuskokwim School District. Several elders from the LKSD villages were invited. It had been arranged beforehand that *Nuqarrluk*, David Lewis, of *Cevv'arneq* would begin with a story that would be particularly illustrative of Yup'ik traditions and values. *Cingliaq*, Paul Gregory, of *Mamterilleq*, Bethel, *Arnaucuaq*, Mike Angaiak, of *Tununeq*, *Uyuraũrluq*, Andy Charlie, and *Puyangun*, Rose Charlie, of *Tununeq* joined in, elaborating David's reminiscence on *Nakaciuryaraq* 'The Bladder Festival' by adding the well-known Yup'ik story of the boy who lived with the seals for a year. As is the case with folklore from many hunting and gathering societies, this story concerns a culture hero or mythic figure who leaves the society of men to live among the principal game animals of the people. He returns later to establish rites and ceremonies connecting predators and prey in a perpetual relationship of exchange and respect. Often the protagonist marries an animal-woman and goes to live among his in-laws, thus viewing everything from the perspective of the hunted, as is the case with Paul Goble's magnificently illustrated *Buffalo Woman* (Goble 1984). In *Nuqarrluk*'s story, the Yup'ik protagonist's journey beyond the limits of ordinary experience is accomplished through participation in ritual. This is a time when the boundaries separating everyday reality from the mythic world of animals and spirits are most easily crossed.

Nakaciuryaraq was the most important and elaborate of the great midwinter festivals. There are fairly detailed accounts and reconstructions of the ceremony from several sources. The principal ones are, Nelson (1899:379-393) among the *Tacirmiut* 'St. Michael dwellers,' the *Kuigpagmiut* 'Yukon dwellers,' and the *Qissunarmiut*, who lived near the present day village of Chevak; Curtis (1930: 58-66) on *Nunivaaq*; Lantis (1946: 182-187; 1947: 153-158) on *Nunivaaq*; and Fienup-Riordan (1994: 266-298) on *Qaluyaaq*. Although there was much regional and local variation, some essential features held throughout the Central Yup'ik area. *Nakaciuryaraq* was a ceremony during which the souls of animals, principally seals, were invited into the community of the Yupiit. There they were hosted and treated as honored guests and afterward returned to the ocean, thus recycling the souls of the animals killed during the preceding year and assuring their return in the coming year as *pitarkat* 'future game or quarry.' It took place during the winter solstice, when the days were shortest and hunting was most restricted, in either December or January. The Yupiit believed that seals lived beneath the ocean in communities that paralleled the structure of Yupiit communities. The various species of seals were ranked according to whether they were *teggenret* 'elders,' *nukalpiat* 'great hunters,' *nukasegaucit* 'hunters of lesser skill,' or just young men of no particular importance. Young seals were admonished by their elders, the *tungunqut* 'bearded seals,' who instructed them in the *qasgiq,* to keep awake and at the moment of death to focus their *ella* 'consciousness' in their bladders. This would assure the possibility of reincarnation, since the Yupiit believed that the locus of the soul in animals was the *nakacuk* 'bladder.'

Slain seals were ceremoniously treated upon their arrival in the village. They were given a ritual drink of fresh water and there were various and strict rules governing their treatment. They were not to come in contact with dogs, menstruating women or other unclean things. Their flesh was to be consumed entirely and with due respect (with silence and concentration during meals), and their bones were to be buried in a special place, not simply cast out. Most importantly, there were the rules for ritual distribution, the various first catch rites, and the taboos regulating human conduct toward game animals, assuring a right relationship with the most important (at least ceremonially) food animals.

The bladders of all sea mammals (and some land mammals) were inflated and dried, then deflated and stored. When the approximate time of the solstice had arrived or, as *Nuqarrluk* notes, when the ice on the lakes was thick enough to walk on, the people would begin the preparations for *Nakaciuryaraq.* The inflated bladders were hung from the ceiling of the *qasgiq,* then later attached in bundles to *nanerpiit* 'seal spears' which were hung on the back wall. During their sojourn in the *qasgiq,* the seal spirits, as represented by the bladders, were treated with the greatest respect and circumspection. Songs were composed and sung to them, special dances were performed in their honor, they were smoked with *ikiituut* 'wild celery' (*Angelica ludica*), edible plants that the men gathered on the tundra and used for ritual fumigation in ceremonies. Throughout the time they were in the *qasgiq* , they were never left unattended, great care being exercised to avoid loud noises or activities that were offensive to the animal souls residing in the bladders. On the final day of the festival, the bladders were removed through the sky window at the top of the *qasgiq,* along with a ceremonial staff on the end of which was bound a sheath of *ikiituut* 'wild celery,' called a *kangaciqaq*. The latter was set ablaze and borne by a specially designated bearer, usually a young man dressed in fancy ceremonial clothing (a woman's squirrel parka in *Tununeq*). He ran ahead, pursued by a crowd of men who thrust their animal bladders into the flaming mass of the *kangaciqaq*, causing great clouds of sparks to fly aloft, and since it was dark when all this occurred, it was by all accounts a truly spectacular sight. Earlier a hole had been cut in the ice, and when the celebrants reached the spot, they punctured their animal bladders and thrust them underneath the ice, returning the animal souls once again to the sea and reincarnation. Quite often the *Nakaciuryaraq* festival ended with the *angalkuq* 'shaman' being bound with thongs in a fetal position and placed in the firepit in the center of the *qasgiq*, where he was covered with a woven grass mat. The oil lamps were then extinguished. From there he journeyed beneath the sea to visit the seal people. If all went well, he would return to report that the seals were well pleased with the treatment they had received and would return again to the hunters in the coming year.

There are other stories associated with *Nakaciuryaraq*. Both Lantis (1946: 182-187) and Curtis (1930: 56-58) include stories that explain the supernatural origin of *Nakaciuryaraq*. But the story of the boy who went to live with the seals is certainly the best known and the most entertaining. It is a kind of manual for hunters, explaining the type of person and the behaviors that the seals look for in their human predators. The Yupiit believe that animals have some choice in the matter of their death and that animals give themselves only to those hunters who they believe will treat them with respect and consideration.

NAKACIURYARAQ
CALI-LLU
TAN'GURRAQ UITALLEQ TAQUKANI

**Nuqarrluk Cevv'arnermiu, Arnaucuaq Tununermiu
Puyangun Tununermiu, Uyuraũrluq Tununermiu
Cingliaq Mamterillermiu**

***

Nuqarrluk:
1
Tua-ll'
waniwa tua wii
aũgna nakaciutullrat
amllerqunek atullrunritaqa
malrurquuyugnarquq tangvalqa taũgaam
tamakunek nakacugnek makut wani
taqukat nakacuitnek pilallrit.
Waten aũgkut murilkengqerraallemni
upakutullruut unegkut Caninermiut,
up'nerkiyaraluteng-gguq
unavet imarpiim ceñiinun.
2
Tua-i-llu tamaani upiimeng makut pissuryugngalriit-wa tua-i ilait-llu
    tayim' nutaan qayangluteng,
pissuryugngalriit pissuata,
waten taqukamek tagutaqata,
ayuqenrilngurnek tua taqukanek tagutaqata,
egmian tamakut
nulirrita wall'u paniita
egmian tamakut tua caliaqevkarluki tanglallruanka.
Waten uitangiinarcetevkenaki nem iluani.
Tekicata cali, aũg'um ava-i watua imum unuaq qanqallermini,
mermek piuratullruit.
Taqukaq imna natermun
qavavet egkumun elliluku.
(Nepianek nengqertelluki cal' angullruanka
aũgkut aulukestellrenka.)

3
Nepiaq imna maaggun waten akiterluni

THE BLADDER FESTIVAL
AND
THE BOY WHO LIVED WITH THE SEALS

David Lewis of Chefornak, Mike Angaiak of Tununak
Rose Charlie of Tununak, Andy Charlie of Tununak
Paul Gregory of Bethel

***

David:

1

Well,
I myself here
didn't experience very often
the way they celebrated the Bladder Festival,
but I probably observed it a couple of times
when they used those bladders
of the seals for the ceremony.
When I first started to observe those people from *Canineq*
they used to move from one place to another,
moving down to the coast,
to their spring camps.

2

Then, after they moved there, the ones that were able to hunt and
　　some of those who had just acquired their first kayaks,
when they hunted, those who knew how to hunt,
when they brought up a seal,
when they brought up different kinds of seals,
I used to see their wives or daughters
immediately
set to work on them.
They never let them remain in the house unattended for long.
Furthermore, when the seals arrived, as someone said previously
　　this morning,
they always used to give them water.
They put the seal on the floor
near the back wall.
(I, too, happened to live in those sod houses,
amongst people who took care of me then.)

3

The sod house had low wooden benches here,

un'a taũgaam amiigem nunii muragtaunani.
Man'a taũgken tua-i aci,
aci man'a, acim ketii man'a ngelii muraganek waten
aqumyararluni.
4
Itrutaqamegteki tua-i tamakut taqukat ayuqenrilnguut,
    pirrlainanrilngermeng piqa'arqata,
tua-i tamakut taqukat elluarrluki ciuniulallruit arnaita.
Egmian-llu tuavet qavavet muriim qainganun
tulurcamegteki
imna aũgna angassaq, murak piliaq,
mermek imiqerluku
ugg'un
ungalruggen'gun mermek kuvqerluku
tallian-ll' ingluakun.
Tua-i-gguq merrilluki.
5
Tua-i-llu caliaqngatki
nakacuit imkut wangkuta tan'gaurlurni
tamakut-llu aulukestellemta arnat,

The *qasgiq* at *Tununeq*, drawn from a photograph by Xavier Lincoln.

except that the area of the entrance had no wooden benches.
Here there was a sleeping platform,
along the edge of which were low wooden benches
for sitting.
4
Occasionally, when they brought in those different kinds of seals
their women received them and took care of them properly.
And as soon as they placed them there on the wood planking,
leaning them against the back,
they filled that ladle made of wood
with water
and here
on the nose they spilled a little bit
as well as on the front flipper.
It is said that they were providing them with water to drink.[1]

5
Then when they worked on
the bladders, we young boys
along with those women who took care of us,

Man with bladder harpoon and *maklak* or *tungunquq* 'bearded seal.' Photo from
Jesuit Oregon Province Archives, Gonzaga University, negative number 504.14.

angayuqallemta aūgkut...(wiinga-ll' aanaka una elluarrłuku
   tangellrunrilkeka
taūgaam tuquqatallrani ika-i tangvakallruaqa tamatum
akitem waten keluani.
Qaūgkut-wa taqukat qavani egkumi tamatum akitem keluani,
arnaq ikna
caumakiit,
cunaw' ika-i tuquqatalria. Wiinga-wa tua wani
tamatum egkum iquani, naparyarluni aūgna uitalria,
waten nangerrlua tulungqalua ikavet tangvaurkeka.
6
Cunaw' tua taun' aanaka. Aanaka tuani tuquqatallinilria.
7
Tua-i-ll' tayim' kinguani taum
tangvalqa uunguciirulluni.)
...tamakut tamaa-i nakacuut
aūg'arqatki imkut arnat
egmian qerruqalallruaput.
Tamakut taūgken makut angtuat makliit wall' tungunqut,
ukug-am makliinkuk tungunquq-llu—
atauciuyaaqelriik taūgaam
allakarmek atengqertuk, ilait makut aperyarat
aptuamteki allauqaqluki wani nunani—
tamakut angtuat
tamakut pitaqestaita caliaqetuluki. Makut taūgken nayiit, issurit,
piyagaat, imkut anqiiyagaat,
piyagait nakacuit egmian qerrurturluki wangkuta,
pegcuunaki cailkamun,
qavavet egkum pianun agarqurluki. Tua-i ilait piliqelriit tamakut
   nakacuit amlleriaqluteng qerruumalriit.

8
Tua-i-llu pissunermek taqngameng
waten aipangeksailngurnun makunun tan'gurrarnun
ataita tunluki
tamakut qillrutait
keniqurluki angiquraasqelluki
imairturluki.
9
Tua-i-llu tuaten qaqicata
qemaggluki.
Qemaggluki tua-i kiagpak qemangqaluki.

our deceased parents...(I myself wasn't fortunate enough to have
    known my mother,
although I saw her when she was dying above that
low wooden bench.
There were those seals inside near the back wall and behind them
was that woman
being taken care of;
actually, she was about to die. I was here,
at the end of the back wall which had a post,
standing and leaning against it as I watched her.
6
As it turned out, that was my mother. My mother was about to die.
7
And then after witnessing that
I'm not sure what happened.)
...when those bladders
were taken out by the women,
we immediately inflated them.
However, the bladders of the big ones, the *makliit* or *tungunqut*,[2]
two different names for the bearded seal—
they are actually the same mammal,
but with different names because some of the names
are said differently in some places—
those big ones
are taken care of by the ones that caught them. But as for these hair-
    seals, spotted seals
and newborn seals,
we immediately inflated the bladders,
not just leaving them anywhere,
but hanging them on the ridgepole of the back wall. Some of those
    who caught a lot of seals accumulated numerous inflated bladders.
8
Then when they stopped hunting,
the fathers of the young men, the ones who hadn't yet acquired spouses,
gave them the bladders
to soften and loosen the
sinew strings
and empty the contents.
9
And then when they had finished,
they put them away.
They stored them for the summer.

***

10
Tua-i-llu
uksuaran cikuqami, waten cikuqaan, imumek nanvat makut
    piyuayunariqercata,
ukut wani
qanqaqungluteng nakaciurnariyaaqniluku amci
mamturivailgan nanvaq.
Nanvamek,
tauna tua mamturillerkaanek qungvagyugluteng.
11
Tua-i-llu tuaten qanaaguraqerluteng
tamakut imkut nakacuut paivvluki nutaan.
Paivcamegteki,
teq'unun...
(Teq'ut tamaani wiinga-ll' cumacikellrunritanka qasgimi, piciatun
una wani
teq'uq imangqengraan yuut ayuqenrilnguut teq'urritnek.
Imallrit-llu tamakut, imallritnek,
qecit, qeciitnek tamakunek
qayiqungaqata waten
imkunek aũg'aqallritnek eliqnerrarnek
teguluki tamakut wangkuta tan'gaurluni
tamuagaqluki. Ilaitni-ll' neqnirqelar! {engelarluteng}
12
Tua-i camek qanyuunateng ciissimek-llu qanyuunateng.
Imkut tua-i tamakut-llu waten
ataurtellriit, temirtenǵurtellriit tuaten, qayiuraqata,
nerluki tuaten aũg'alteng makut piaqluki.)
13
Tua-i-llu taukut imkut nakacuit keniqaarluki—wall' mermun
    pilaryaaqellikait tayima,
akurrviit taukut cauciitelaranka tua wall' teq'urruut
wall' meruut—
keniata
ataam qerrurluki.
14
Qerruamegteki
qasgilluki qasgimun.
Tua-i
ilai tayim',
pilriit,

***

10
Then,
when autumn came and the lakes were frozen and were safe to walk on,
the elders
began saying that it was about time for the Bladder Festival,
that is, soon before the ice thickened on the lake,
since they were concerned
that the ice in the lake might get too thick.

11
And then, having discussed the matter,
they then brought out those bladders.
When they brought them out,
they put them in urine.
(Back then I didn't find the urine in the *qasgi* repulsive,
though
the containers were filled with different people's urine.
And as for what they were filled with,
that is, the skins to be used for
making kayaks,
we would take
bits of the scrapes that were cut off
and chew them. My, some of them were really tasty! {laughter}
12
They never said anything bad about it or mentioned germs.
And even those
who had become fathers or adults, when they made kayaks,
would chew on the scrapes which they cut off from the hides.)
13
After that the bladders were soaked—perhaps they were soaked in water;
I'm not sure what they put them in, either urine
or water—
and once they were softened,
they again inflated them.

14
After they inflated them,
they took them into the *qasgiq*.
There
were some people
that

285

tua-i-gg' nuqlitellriit, ayuqsuilameng pissulriit tuaterrlainaq piyuilamta
maa-i-llu cali tamana aturluku ayuqerrlainarluta cali
maa-i pissuraqamta unangyuunata, ilait unangnerkitaqluteng, ilait
   taugken unangnertuluteng.
15
Tua-i-llu
qerruamegteki qasgimun,
tua-i murilkelluki ukut wani.
Maqiqata'arqameng-llu tamaaggun
qasgitgun,
yugyagluteng maqitullruameng,
teggalqutgun maqiqungvailgata,
elaturramun anucamegteki nayuusqelluki tamakut nakacuut.

16
Qerruumaluteng tua-i.
Taqngata-ll' tua-i ataam qasgimun itrulluki.
Tamaa-i nakacugtangqerraqan
yuitevkanritengnaqluku tamana qasgi pituluteng, pitulliniluteng.
17
Tua-i-llu piqerluteng erenret qavciatni, amlleret erenret
   tegularpeknaki,
qavciatni tayima...
(Kankut kana-i nunallrenka ellangvillrenka wii tuatnalallruut
Calitmiullret-ggur' ukut.
Ukut Qipnermiut kellirraqait kana-i
alaunateng,
taukut tua-i wii ellangvillrenka, Calitmiunek piaqluki.
Kuigem tamatum ceniini ikegkut
nunalleruaraat taukut
yungqerrnanrinratgun wii
murilkengluki.)
Keluatni im' nanevpaar augna angluni, angssauluni,
waten anluamek callarciluteng imkut
augkut tan'gurraat
ilait aipangumariluteng ilait-llu tua aipangqatarluteng.
Tamakut tamaa-i nakacuut aulukluki tamakut ayagyuarita.

***

18
Tua-i-llu
cali

286

weren't able to keep up [with an equal number of bladders], because
    hunters are all different and they don't all catch the same amount,
and even today they are like that; some hunt and don't catch
    anything; some catch a few, and then there are those who catch a lot.
15
Then
when the bladders were inflated in the *qasgiq,*
the people would watch over them.
And when they were going to take a firebath in that
qasgiq,
because many of them took firebaths together
before they started using stoves with rocks on them,[3]
they took the bladders out to the enclosed entryway and asked
    someone to watch over them.
16
They were still inflated.
When they were finished bathing, they brought the bladders in again.
Back then, when there were bladders in the *qasgiq,*
they made sure that there were people in there all the time.
17
And then, on a certain day, not too long after the bladders had
    been taken into the *qasgi,*
on a certain day...
(Those people down there[4] in my old village where I first became
    aware did that
at the place they called *Calitmiut.*
It is right below *Qipneq*
and it is visible from there;
that is where I first became aware, at *Calitmiut.*
It is by the shore of the river
and I started to observe
that little old village
at the time it was being abandoned.)
There was this big lake up away from the river, quite a big one,
and those young men
that were married and the ones that were about to get married
would open a hole in it.
Those young people were the ones that took care of the bladders.

***

18
And
furthermore,

287

atakumi waten upluteng ikiitugteqatarluteng-gguq
imkunek makunek naumalrianek nunami.
Ikiituut nallunritaci-qa tua-i?
Tamakutqatarluteng
upluteng cali.
19
Tua-i-llu
waten tanqigpallra cali nall'arrluku tuatnatuut,
tamakut tua tan'gurraat—qavciuluteng tayim' naaqeksailamki
nallukenka,
taũgaam talliman ukut cipingangatelarait nangerngalriit
tan'gurraat tamakut waten egkumi—
ukut tua-i cauyateng makut waten piluki upluki.
Upluki tua-i yuarutmek aturluteng; elitellrunrilkeka tamana
elicaaqengramku-gg' tua-i taũgaam uunguciirutaqa.

20
Tuaten pirraarluki
tus'aksuaraqarraarluteng, maani nacitet iquatni tus'aksuarluteng
ukut kaugtuaksuarallratni.
Tus'aksuarraarluteng tayim' anluteng
tamakussurluteng tayim' maavet
nanvat ceñaitnun piciatun makut naumatuata.
Wangkuta-ll' tua tan'gaurlurni kinguatni yuarutmek atungarrluta
elliurturluta ukatmun caugaqluta. {engelartut}

21
Tua-i-ll'
mulussiiyaagpeknateng cali ataam itrata
taqluta tua wangkuta, taq'errluta.
Nutaan tua tuaten piqataameng,
tauna imna aũgna qanrutkelqa nutaan anluaq
nanvami tuani,
anliiyartuusqelluki ukut qasgimiut qanerluteng.
Tua-i-ll' anliingameng,
meq tauna
nanvaq ukicamegteggu
tupiganek patuluku.
(Tupigat ilaita makut nalluyugnarqait.
Tupiumalriit aũgkut,
qayat makut—ikaraliitaitnek pilaryugnarqait tamakut—

in the evening they would prepare to pick wild celery,
those plants that grow on the land.
Do you all know about wild celery?[5]
They were preparing to pick that kind,
getting ready for that too.

19

And
they would do that while it was still bright outside,
those young men would—I don't know how many there were
    because I didn't count them,
but there seemed to be over five who were standing
by the back wall—
and other men would get their drums ready.
They would prepare the ones who were going picking by singing.
    I didn't learn that song;
actually I did learn it, but I have forgotten it.

20

After they did that,
the young men who were going to go picking would stand at the end
    of the floor planks, bending and rocking their knees rhythmically[6]
while the drummers were softly beating the drums.
Having done that, they would leave
to gather the wild celery
by the lakes, since it grew all along the lakeshores.
We young boys, who were left behind, would begin to sing a song,
and while we were doing this, we would face this way and that.
    {laughter}

21

Then
not too long after that when they entered again,
we would suddenly stop singing.
Now when they were going to do
what I mentioned before, about the hole in the ice
on the lake,
those *qasgimiut* would tell [the young men] to go make the hole.
Then they worked on it
and when they
cut through the ice on the lake
they would cover the opening with a braided grass mat.
(Some of these people probably don't know what *tupigat* are.
That grass that is braided,
the kind they used in kayaks—I think it's called *ikaraliin*—

289

mer' imna tauna patuluku.)
22
Tua-i-llu atakuan, tan'gerian,
nalukatangarcameng imkut tamakut nakacuut
quyurrluki muragamek waten epulirluki,
iquatgun wavet qillerrluki. Atauciuvkenateng cali unani
nangerngalriit nacitet qaingatni,

Ngel'uralria, Sam Tangkak, *Tununeq,* circa 1980. Photo by Andrew J. Chikoyak.

they covered the ice hole with that.)
22
Then in the evening when it got dark,
when they were going to push those bladders under the ice,
they all gathered them, and using wooden poles for handles attached
the bladders, tying them to the pole ends. There was more than one
person standing on the floor planks;

An unidentified woman from Hooper Bay, 1950s. Photo from the Alfred Millote
Collection (acc. #90-045) in the Archives, Alaska and Polar Regions Dept.,
University of Alaska Fairbanks.

qavciuluteng tua-i,
talliman cali cipinganganateng.
Tua-i-gguq nalukatarluki.

23
Tua-i upcameng waten
imkut tamakut piqatalriit tamakut imkut nakacuit waten quukarluki,
qerruumaluteng tua-i.
Aũgna-llu ciuqlirkaat, aũgkut ayut ikiitugnek avuluteng
    qillengqalriit cali muragamek epuluteng,
wavet kenurramun uumun—waten kenurraitellratni uqurrarnek
taũgaam kenurrangqelallratni—
kuma'arrluki, kuma'arqaarluki tus'aksuarluteng
ukut-am tua-i cauyat makut piluki kaugtuarluki tua-i qaillun.
Kuma'arqaarluki taum ay'uqercata amigmun uavet anelraqerrluni
    elliurluki taukut,
elliurraarluki tayim' anluni.
Anqercan-ll' imkut tamakut nangerngalriit tayim' anluteng tamarmeng.

24
Tayima tua-i muluuraqerluteng
iterluteng tua camek tegumiarunateng.
Cunawa tuani anluaq tauna ullagluku nutaan tamakut
nakaciit qagerqetullinikait
qagerqerraarluki-llu cikum acianun qerrluki.
Tua-i-gguq nalugluki.

***

Puyangun:
25
Atam aũgna avani,
imarnitnek-ggem all'uteng piningat'lallruit.
Nuqarrluk:
26
Tua-i, ii-i!
Yaa, tua-i-gg' tamakut murilkeluaqallrunrilkenka.
Tamakut
kituggluki
piaqluki unitellrenka!
Puyangun:
27
Qasgimek anuteqatarqamegteki imarnitnek all'uteng

in fact there were several,
seemingly more than five.
That was when they were about to go and push the bladders under
    the ice.
23
Then when they were ready,
the participants took their poles with the bladders, which were inflated,
and placed them on their shoulders.
And their leader, holding the staff that had *ayuq* 'Labrador tea'
    combined with *ikiituk* 'wild celery' tied onto it,[7]
went to a seal-oil lamp—this was when they didn't have electricity
    but only seal-oil lamps—
and ignited it as they bent and rocked their knees rhythmically
while the drummers beat the drums.
After igniting it and letting the fire grow, while moving the staff
    from side to side he rushed toward the entrance,
and having done that, made his exit.
When the leader went out, all the other ones who were standing
    around went out too.
24
Having been gone for awhile
they would re-enter empty-handed.
So then, apparently they went to the hole in the ice
and punctured all the bladders,
and having punctured them, they stuffed them down under the ice.
This was *nalugluki*, pushing the bladders under the ice.[8]

***

Rose:
25
Atam, in regard to what you said earlier,
I thought they put on a gut raincoats when they did that.
David:
26
Yes indeed!
Yes, I really didn't observe those too well.
Why don't you
set those things right
that I left out!
Rose:
27
I think they put on those gut raincoats

[pingatelallruut].

Nuqarrluk:

28

II-i, taqukat qiluitnek imarnitnek.

Mecungyuitqapiarnek nutaan ellalliurcuutnek.

Tamakut tamaa-i ava-i aũg'um qanrutkellri,

imarnitet

ellalluum qaillun metuluni-ll' pingaunaki maaggun-llu

pengegnairluku pikani

mer' iterngaunani cang'ermi ellarvang'ermi.

Tamakut tamaa-i

aũgkut apertullma makliit, tungunqut

qiluit.

29

Waten carrirluki cali

tamakukiutuit tamakut makliit qiluit.

Wa-gguq imarniciluki, ellalliurcuuciluki.

Unani-llu qayarluteng pitullratni

aturarkaurtelluki qayaitnun cali wavet eksaraatnun

man'a neqututaciat

Qayaq frame on *tatkik* 'rack,' *Tununeq*, circa 1980. Photo by Andrew J. Chikoyak.

before they went out of the *qasgi*.
David:
28
Yes, seal-gut raincoats.
The finest waterproof raingear.
Those things that she just referred to,
the raincoats,
the rain will not soak through and
when they are fastened here,
the water will not go in even if it rains hard.
Those are the ones
that I mentioned, the bearded seal's
intestines.
29
They cleaned those and
prepared them
to make the raincoats.
And when they used kayaks,
they made the raincoat so that it was ready for use and
the width [of the raincoat]
was the same as the width of the cockpit of the kayak, and it was

Maggie, David, George, and Evan Sipary in *Tununeq*, 1927. Photo from the Geist
Collection, courtesy of the Anchorage Museum of History and Art B92.3357.

neqututateksagulluki calturngairulluku painganun.
Tua-i-gguq anuqliuqata
tamatum qayami una painga
ket'garluku
mermun itercessngaunaku tua-i.
Tamakut
anuqengutaqateng
nunam tungiinun tua ayagturatuut
meq tua-i qailingraan, anuqlirlun' tuaten.
Tamakunek tamaa-i pikiutuit.

***

30
Tua-i-llu tuaten pirraarluteng
wa-gguq
makut arnat
elaturrami camek cakma nepengluteng!
(Aũgkut amiingqetullratni
waten ikiqetaanrilngurnek ilait kalvagyarauluteng aciqvaarkun
    ayatuluteng
cakmani-ll' elaturrami
cali aũgna elaumaluni tuaggun pugluteng antullratni.)
Angukar tuavet amiigem
canianun aqumluni,
cakemkut elaturrami qaalruangluteng
arnanek tuaten avuluteng, arnarpalluut.
31
Tua-i-ll' piqerluteng ugna pusngauraqerluni
qantamek ug'umek naluulluni,
akutaq-wa imaa.
Tua-i-ll' wavet
tuc'aramun elliqaami
kayimqerluku qanercarluku,
aterpaggluku tauna,
una-gguq
kia taum naluutekaa.
32
Tua-i
tuaten im' taun' piurluku. Ilait ang'aqluteng qantav'allraat,
makut imkut
tutgarameng-wa tua pillilriit
wall'u makut yung'eqarraarutmeng

made to fit.
So whenever they encountered windy weather,
the raincoat was put on and tied around the
coaming of the kayak,
which prevented the water from going into the kayak.
Whenever
the wind picked up,
the [men] could gradually go towards the land
even though the ocean was choppy and windy.
The raingear was made that way for that very purpose.

***

30
Then after they pushed the bladders under the ice,
behold,
the women
started making some sort of noise out there in the enclosed entryway!
(This was when they had entrances,
not like doors of today, but some were deep tunnels
with closable entryways
through which they entered and exited the tunnel.)
An old man sat there
near the floor opening, inside,
and the ones in the enclosed entryway started making different
    murmuring sounds,
these being mostly women.
31
Thereafter the man bent down for a moment,
then lifted up the offering of a bowl
filled with *akutaq*.
Then when
he stepped up,
he pushed it in,
naming the one who presented it
and saying this offering was
from so and so.
32
So
he kept on doing that. Some of the bowls were large,
perhaps those
which [were offered on behalf] of their grandchildren
or the firstborn of a couple,

piyaurpailgata,
tamakut naluutait
anglallruut tua-i akutamek pakmaararaqluteng
muriit qantat.
33
Maa-i tang makut
wangkuta elissautekaqsugngayaaqekngaput cali!
Aũgkut qantat cali tamakut assigtallrit aũgkut ciuliamta
canun piciatun tamakunek-llu
qilunek
imirluki waten up'nerkami assigtaqluki
tamakut taqukat qiluitnun,
kenugteqatarqamegteki
tamakunek assigcirluteng muragnek. Ilait anglallruut,
qaill' tua waten angtaluteng,
qantat aũgkut muriit
angutaita caliarit. Wangkuta cali tua-i tamakut
nallunritarkaqsaaqekngaput tamaa-i wangkuta
waten ellilriani,
tanglartellritni.

Kumangulria, Louise Kanrilak, *Tununeq*, circa 1980. Photo by Andrew J. Chikoyak.

before these children were able to do things on their own,
and those offerings made on their behalf
were large wooden bowls heaped up high
with *akutaq.*
33
Look, these are some ideas
that we can also use as tools for teaching!
Those bowls that were used by our ancestors
for different things were also used as containers for
intestines
in the spring time;
when they prepared
those seal intestines
they used those wooden bowls. Some were big,
about this big,
those wooden bowls
which were made by the men. Those are also some of the things
that we ought to know about,
those of us who have reached this age,
having seen them.

Left to right are *Nayagaq,* Caroline Post; *Tulukaq (Iraluq),* Joe Post; *Canirraq,*
Charlotte Post; and *Caqigaq,* Christine Post Lincoln. The child in front is
Carriralria, Charlie Post. *Tununeq,* 1927. Photo from the Geist Collection,
courtesy of the Anchorage Museum of History and Art B92.33.51.

34
Taũgaam tua-i arenqiatukut wangkuta.
Tua-i-gg' nen'i piqalaryaaqengramteki taũgaam
makut maa-i qanruteknanriraput wangkuungramta
nallunrilengramteki tua-i ukut-llu waniwa
tanglarait. Ava-i-ll' aũg'um, ing'um arnam [Puyangutem], ava-i
    tanglallminek cali
tamakunek
qanqertuq.
35
Nutaan aũgna qaill'
amllerrsaaqeng'ermi-wa tua-i
taum tungiinun
qaneryararpakairutua aũg'umek.

***

36
Iliit yuut aptuq:
Iluq, apcugyaaqua ataucimek.
37
Nuqarrluk:
Ii-i.
38
Aptenqigtuq:
Aũg'umek wani
nakacuut ayagcet'lalliniatki atakumi
erenrani pivkenateng, tamatum kangianek nallunricugyaaqua
    atakumi ayagcet'lallratnek.
39
Nuqarrluk:
Tua-i-wa tamana kangia nallunrit'luaqanritaqa
taũgaam tua-i tuaten
atakumi pituut
erenrani piyuunateng,
atakumi taũgaam, atakurrlainarmi.
40
Cali aũgkut,
wa-gguq nakaciruarluteng cali piaqameng, tuaten cali pituut. Makut
nunamiutaat, makut
imarmiutaat
cat piciatun
nakacuit cali tuatnatuit kinguatgun taukut.

34
However we are in a difficult and awkward situation.[9]
We may teach a little in some of the homes, yet even we,
the elders, nowadays no longer talk about these things here,
despite the fact we have the knowledge about them, and these people here
see that.   And that one there, that woman [*Puyangun*], just
    mentioned the things
which she used
to see.
35
Now then, although what I talked about
has a lot more to it,
I don't have much more to say
about the Bladder Festival.

***

36
A member of the audience:
Iluq,[10] I'd like to ask one question.
37
David:
Yes.
38
A member of the audience:
Concerning those
bladders being sent away in the evening
instead of during the day, I'd like to know the reason why they sent
    them away in the evening.
39
David:
I really don't know the exact reason why,
but they did it
in the evening,
never during the day,
only in the evening, always in the evening.[11]
40
Furthermore, those people in the past,
whenever they celebrated what they called *Nakaciruaq,* the Lesser
    Bladder Festival, they also did it like that. These
land animals, these
minks,
or whatever species of land animals,

Kinguatgun pingatelallruit.
Tuaten tua-i cali naluucirturluki
akutanek.
Aren, caqtaallrit augkut
ciuliamta amllerrsaaqut.
Aanirluteng tuaten
tamaa-i.
Akutaryungaqameng-wa pilaryugnarqelriit. {engelarluteng}

41
Arnaucuaq:
Iluq, qanrutkenritelten augkut qanqautekqerlaki?
42
Nuqarrluk:
Yaa, assirciquq! Makut niicugait.

***

43
Arnaucuaq:
Ii-i, man'a maani Nakaciuryaraq
tak'uq.
Elluarrluku waten elisngastiin
qanrumaqerciqsugnarquq.
Tamaani nakaciutullermeggni
uksuarmi tamaa ayagnitullruut.
Wiinga malrurqugnek tangvallruunga.
Una ciuqlia tangvagyaaqekeka imutun tuarpiaq qavanguqsukluku
      pillruaqa.
Una tua-ll' kinguqlia nutaan murilkenruluku
pillruaqa, tayim' niitelarngatuci Kayalivigmiunek, tuani
      Kayalivigmiuni ak'a tan'gurracualleraullemni tayima
nakaciulriit.
44
Atam cayarait amllertut,
caqtaarturallrit
makutgun-llu kalukarluteng.
Ava-i cal' qanrutekluki, waten
ikiitugtaqluteng tua-i
kinercirluki qasgi.
Murak-llu caliluku
tamaa-i tamakut ikiituut
uitavigkaat

their bladders were also treated ceremonially after the Bladder Festival.
It seemed that they did it [*nakaciruaq*] after the Bladder Festival.
They also presented offerings of
akutaq.
Aren, there were a lot more activities
that our ancestors did.
They also celebrated what they called *Aaniq*[12]
in those days.
I guess they did that when they yearned for *akutaq.* {laughter}
41
Mike:
Iluq, may I say a little about those things you didn't talk about?
42
David:
Yes, it will be good! These people here want to hear it.

***

43
Mike:
Yes, the way of celebrating the Bladder Festival
is not brief.
I think a person who really has the knowledge about it
may talk about it for a lengthy time.
Back then, when they used to celebrate the Bladder Festival,
they began soon after freeze-up.
I watched a couple of them.
The first one that I watched seemed as if I dreamt about it.
The second time I was more observant.
You probably have heard of *Kayalivik*; there at *Kayalivik* when I
    was a little boy
they had a Bladder Festival.

44
You see, their customs were numerous;
they did different activities,
and they also had feasts.
And he was just talking about how
they used to gather wild celery
and dry them in the *qasgiq.*
And they worked on a piece of wood
where the wild celery
would be placed,

wa-gguq kangaciqaq, kangaciqamek taun' acirluku.
Takarnaqluni tamana qasgimi.
Tamatum-gguq nakaciullrata nalliini
waten nacartuumaluteng ityuunateng yuut, angutet.
Picsaqa'artevkenani
nacartuumaluni
itquni,
itqan maaken qanerciquq,
"Nacaqegcilliami!"
Tua-i taun' neq'aqaami nacani yuugarrluku.
Cali-ll' qasgiq yungqetullruluni
tua yum'inek.
Agkut qasgim inglua
angutnek yugluni qaũgna-ll' cal tua qava-i inglua-llu cali man'a.
Waten-llu tamaavet
uitavikenrilkemeggnun piyuunateng.
45
Tua-i-ll' pitsaqa'artevkenani tayim' iliit itquni
alarrluni agaavet
aqumluni,
aqumyaaqekan-am
ellangarteng'ermi tauna uitaluni,
agkut-am akiqliit,
akiqliita wa-gguq aqvaluku,
cauyanek tegulluteng,
ingulautmek aturturluteng.
Tamaa-i nakacuum nalliini cali ingulatullruut makut arnat.
Cukariyuunateng, cukaunan' kaugtuarturluni.
Unaggun qasgim natrakun tauna aqvastii,
tamaa-i ingulautmek atuqata,
anguaruarturluni uyungkassiarturluni arvirturciquq.
Tua-i-ll' tull'uni, nacitet tull'uki.
Tuskaki-llu
imna tauna nutaan alartellrem taum maliggluku
agaavet
qasgim ingluanun tamaa-i nunaminun tua-i nutaan uterrluni. Tuaten
    tua ayuqluteng cal' pillruut wii tangvallemni.
Cat caciqtaaryarait amllertut
mat'um nakaciullratni.

a staff, which they called a *kangaciqaq*.
One had to show respect in the *qasgiq*.
At the time of the Bladder Festival,
the people, the men, never entered with a hood on.
If someone entered
wearing a hood
accidently,
someone else would say,
"As if he has a nice hat!"
So, when he suddenly remembered, he would quickly remove his hat.
Also, the *qasgiq* used to be occupied
by its own people.
One side of the *qasgiq*
had men in it and so did the other side.
And they didn't
sit where they didn't belong.
45
If one of them came in and accidently,
by mistake,
sat across there,
and, although he might have become aware
that he was sitting in the wrong place, he remained there,
then the ones over there across from him,
the ones on the other side, would do what they referred to as
    'fetching him,'
by taking drums
and singing old time slow songs.
At that time, during the Bladder Festival, the women used to dance
    to them.
They never quickened their pace, and the drums were beaten slowly.
When the one 'fetching' him came on the *qasgiq*'s floor,
as they were singing a slow song,
he would slowly go across, bending his knees rhythmically to the
    beat, pretending to row.
Then he got there, got to the floor planks.
And when he got to them,
the one who had made the mistake would follow him
to the other side
of the *qasgiq*, finally getting back to his rightful place. That was
    how they were when I observed them.
There were many activities
which they performed during the Bladder Festival.

46
Nakacuut cali
qasgimun piaqamegteki imkunek
nanerpagnek,
imkunek malirqessuutnek,
tamakunun petugturluki
pitulqait nakacuut
qasgim iluani. Cali qasgim ilua,
itrumariaqata,
yuicesqumavkenaku
cali inerquutnguluni.
Qasgi yuicesqevkenaku tamaa-i
tuaten ayuqellruuq,
man'a nakaciuryaraq.
47
Nakaciuryaram mat'um qanerkai amllertut
caqtaarturallri.
48
Tuamte-llu-gguq cali piqerluteng qecegluteng
tan'gurraat.
Tua-i-am
tamaa-i tamakut qetgutet
waten picimegtun ayuqevkenateng.
Avaken tayim' ciuliameggnek ayagluteng tamana tamaa-i yuarun,
    qetgun,
kinguvarturallinilria,
tua-i tamaa-i
elissautekaqluku-llu.
Tuaten tua-i ayuqelliniluni, wa-gguq qecegluteng.
Qecgaqameng man' tua yuarutait tangssunaqluteng taringumalriani,
canguarluteng tua, calluguarluteng wall'u-qa tuntussunguarluteng.
Tamaa-i muraggarnek waten
ayarirluteng
qecetullruut.
Waten elliurturluteng
piaqameng tayima qaillukuangaqluteng. Tamaa-i tua-i
tuaten pitullruut.

49
Tuamte-ll' kinguakun
wa-gguq cali iinrilluteng.
Cali qecegluteng cal' qecegyaaqelriameng

46

Also, when they took the bladders
into the *qasgiq*,
those spears,
the ones they used for pursuing game,
they would tie
the bladders to them
inside the *qasgiq*. Furthermore, they didn't want the *qasgiq*,
once the bladders had been taken in,
to be without people,
which was a proscription.
They didn't want
the *qasgiq* to be without people at any time
during the Bladder Festival.

47

There is much to say about the Bladder Festival
and the activities associated with it.

48

Moreover, the boys
would perform what they called '*Qecek.*'
And those
activities they did in '*Qecek*'
weren't done in any old way.
The songs used for '*Qecek*' were passed down from their ancestors
to their descendants,
and were used at that time
for teaching.
That is how it was with this activity that they referred to as '*Qecek.*'
When they performed '*Qecek*,' their songs were interesting if one
could comprehend
what they were pretending to do, for instance, pretending to fight or
pretending to hunt caribou.
At that time they used a piece of wood
as a cane
when they performed '*Qecek.*'
They motioned like this
when they did that, and they would start to do different things. That is
what they used to do.[13]

49

And then after that
they performed what they referred to as '*Iinriq.*'
And although it was like '*Qecek*'

tamakut cali ayaniillritnek qecegluteng cal'
tuaten tua iinrilluteng.
50
Tuamte-ll' tua piqerluteng wa-gguq ingularluteng arnat.
Imumek tua-i ingularqameng
cukaunateng imumek tua qaspertulaameng
imumek waten qaspeteng teguqerluki maaggun
tua-i waten piurluteng
pinaurtut, cukaunateng. Wa-gguq ingularluteng,
tamaa-i arnat pitullruluteng
tamaani.

51
Mat'um cali
nakaciuryaram, mat'um,
caqtaarturallri amllerrluteng.
52
Tuamte-ll' aaniquneng cali
aanirciqut.
Ukuk-gguq-gga aanak
imarniterlutek pakmani-llu
egalermi piaqlutek.
Wangkuta-am tan'gurrarni
pinauraitkut
wa-gguq qimugtenǵusqelluta.
Elaturrami tamaani uitaluta
makut-gga qantat ayuqenrilnguut akutat
tamaa-i tamakut aaniutekait.
Pinauraitkut,
"Piyullerpeceńek unaken nerluci qantanek!" {engelarluteng}
Tua-i
tamatum-llu nalliini anuraqu'urluta yuullruamta
pisqaqaitkut tauǵaam neqkegtaarnek tua neraqcaarnaurtukut.
    {engelarluteng}
Wa-gguq tua qimugtenǵuluta. Ilii tua-i
qantam angenrilnguum
amllermek imangqeksaituq. {engelarluteng}
Kia-ll' inerqurngailakut tua-i umyugiuqapiarluta. {engelarluteng}

53
Tua-i tauǵken
taukuk aanak nutaan

it was a simpler form of it, not so elaborate;
 that was the '*Iinriq.*'
50
Again, after a while the women did what they called '*ingulaq,*' a
    slow dance.
When they did the '*ingulaq,*'
they moved slowly and since they used *qaspeqs* 'parka covers,'
they would take hold of their *qaspeq* skirt hems,
and would do thus,
slowly.[14] They called
what the women did
at that time '*ingulaq.*'
51
There are many activities
associated with
the Bladder Festival.
52
Again, when they did '*Aaniq,*'
they would make provisions for the ceremony.
There were two "mothers," it is said,
dressed from head to toe in waterproof garments,
and they would be there at the sky window.
They would
tell us boys
to be "dogs."
We would be in the *elaturraq* 'enclosed entryway'
and there were bowls of different kinds of *akutaq,*
which were symbolic of their [the "dogs"] being provided with mothers.
They would tell us,
"Eat whatever you want from those bowls!" {laughter}
And
since we were living under such restrictions in those days,
it was only when they told us to that we would we eat from those
    delicious foods. {laughter}
We were what they called "dogs."[15] Some
bowls, the ones which were small,
didn't contain a lot of food. {laughter}
And since nobody was going to scold us, we ate as much as we
    wanted. {laughter}
53
Then finally
those two "mothers"

qantaq teguluku, kayimluku
qama-i qanerciquq, "Kia taum aaniutii
qimugtet nanglliniat!" {engelarluteng}
54
Taugken tua-i ilii
itruciiqaa qantaq ilangarcimavkenani, "Kia una aaniutii qimugtet
nerenritliniat. Neqniatellian-gga nerenrilkiit!" {engelarluteng}

55
Tuaten tua neqnek cikirnauraitkut
pinariaqan tua-i,
tamaa-i wa-gguq aanirluteng.
56
Augna ava-i ilii cali qaqitenricaaqaqa
aug'um ilu'urma qanrutkenritellran ilii,
niicugniurallemni.
Ava-i qanrutkeqa'arqa.
Tua-lli?

***

57
Uyuraurluq:
Tua-llu-qa cali
ilaqeryugngauq?
58
Cingliaq:
Iqungqertuq cali.
59
Uyuraurluq:
Ilayugngauq?
60
Cingliaq:
Ayautellrat imna
nakacugnun?
61
Uyuraurluq:
Ii-i.
Augna
iquknguaqaaku
tayima elluarrluku qanrutkenrilkumku ukut iliita
pinritellrenka
arulairrlua qanrutekniaraa.

would take a bowl, push it in
and say, "Whoever brought this in,
the dogs have eaten it all!" {laughter}
54
However some of
bowls brought in were untouched. "Whoever brought this "mother"
    in, the dogs
apparently didn't eat it. They didn't eat it since perhaps it is
    unpalatable!" {laughter}
55
That is how they gave us food
when the time came,
in what they referred to as '*Aaniq.*'
56
I realize I didn't complete everything I intended to,
having heard what my *iluq*
just talked about.
I just said a little bit about it.
Well?

***

57
Andy:
Well then,
can more be added to it?
58
Paul:
There is more to it.
59
Andy:
More can be added?
60
Paul:
[How about] the one they brought
to the bladders?
61
Andy:
Yes.
This is related
to the ending there
and if I don't tell about it correctly one of these people here
can stop me and talk about
what I left out.

***

62
Tua-i-'m waten
nakacuum nalliini
taukuk nulirqelriik
qetunrangqelliniuk tan'gurrarmek
qaillun-llu tayima angtaluni-ll' tauna tan'gurrauga.
Waten tamaani ak'a
makut wani
yut'eng,
qetunrateng,
paniteng
tua-i
tua-i-gga mat'umek pingnaqurallratnek amllermun
nuqlicesqumavkenaki ilaita cingumatullrulliniamegteki.
Kiingan man' pissuryaraq, neqsuryaraq, pissuryaraq
    yuuciqellruamegteggu-gguq tamaani.
63
Taukuk-am nulirqelriik tauna qetunrartek
tua-i qaillukuarluku.
Tua-i-gga pingnatugyaureskan nuqlilluku pisqumanricaaqluku
    pitacirmegni,
kiingan yuk'engermegen'gu
angalkut iliitnun....
Kitek ayagniqaqerru!
64
Puyangun:
Tauna tua-i,
qetunrartek tauna,
qaillun-gga tua-i
nuqlitevkenaku ilainun
yuusqumayaaqluku.
Miknani taũgaam tauna qetunraak
taukuk.
Tua-i qaillun nuqlitevkenaku taukuk angayuqaagken
    pisqumayaaqetacirmegni,
tuaten tua-i umyuartequlluku angalkumun taũgaam piluku
qaillun tayim' angalkum piyunarqellrakun
apertuutarkaulukek qaillun pillerkaagnek.
Taum tua-i atiin
qaillun umyuarteqluni tayima angalkuluaqamun taũgaam piyugyaaqluku
cakneq angalkuulriamun.

***

62
Well then,
[this happened] at the time of the Bladder Festival;
there was this couple
and they had a son, a boy,
and how big that boy was, I don't know.
A long time ago,
these
children of theirs,
their sons,
and their daughters,
well,
their relatives really encouraged all of them
to be able to keep up with whatever they tried to do.
At that time hunting and fishing was their only livelihood.

63
This couple was deliberating
over a matter concerning their son.
When he reached the point of being able to do things on his own,
    they really wanted him to be able to keep up with others,
and although he was their only child,
[they went] to one of the shamans....
Please, would you continue.
64
Rose:
Well that one,
their son,
they wanted him to live his life
in such a way
as to be able to keep up with others.
However, he was small,
that couple's son.
His parents really wanted him to live without having to be in need of
    anything,
and since they thought like that, the only thing for them to do was to
    take him to a shaman
who would look into possibilities about what could be done,
and point out to them what they ought to do.
That father of his
thought about it and wanted the task entrusted only to a real shaman,

Taũgaam tua-i elliin nalluluki makut angalkut
qaillun tuknitatekenritellrit, cat tuknillrit cat-llu tukniatellrit.

65
Tua-i qaillukualnguami taum atiin
caviggani
qasgim tunuanun
elagulluku ellilliniluku tua-i nalluatni yuut elliin taũgaam kiimi
    nalluvkenaku.
Ellirraarluku tua-i
nutaan tua-i angalkut *check*-aqatalliniluki.
66
Cingliaq:
Tauna,
aũgna,
maani
kiaqvani niitelallerput,
taum wani aaniin,
aaniinun tauna pinilaraat.
Uluani,
uluani pikavet
egalrem
mengliinun iirluku.
Nutaan-gguq tuani
yuaqatarluni angalkupiamek.
67
Puyangun:
Ii-i, wangkuta caviggauluku
pimaarput.
Tauna caviggaa
tuavet tua patu[lluku] atiin.
68
Cingliaq:
Aaniita-qa?
69
Puyangun:
Aatiin.
Ii-i, tua aaniin piklinia. Quyana.
70
Wangkuta taũgaam niitlemteggun pirraarluku elpet cal'
niitlerpeggun pikuvgu assiryartuq.

a truly powerful shaman.
However, he didn't know
how much power each one had, which were strong one and which
    were weak.
65
So, because the father got tired of deliberating over the matter
he took his cutting knife
and buried it
behind the *qasgiq* without people knowing; only he knew.
So, after placing it there
he was ready to check out the shamans.

66
Paul:
That one,
the one you talked about,
here
in the upper areas the way we heard it is
that the mother of that boy,
they say his mother did that.
She hid her *uluaq*,
her semilunar knife,
on the edge of
the sky window.
Now, they say, was her time to go in
search of a true shaman.
67
Rose:
Yes, but the way we say it is
it was a cutting knife.
His father
covered the cutting knife there.
68
Paul:
Was it their mother?
69
Rose:
His father.
Yes, so it was their mother. Thank you.
70
It would be good, however, if we tell it the way we heard it and you
can tell it the way you heard it.

71
Cingliaq:
Ii-i.
72
Puyangun:
Wangkuta ciumek niitlemteggun piluku
ava-i aũgna iquklitevsiarluku
tua-i-ll' elpet cali
niitlerpeggun cali
pivsiarluku
taqkumta.
Ataucikun pivkenaku.
73
Cingliaq:
Ii-i, *okay.*
74
Uyuraũrluq:
Ava-i aũgna
uum wani,
caviggaq tauna tua-i yuarulluku
pillra.
Tua-i canun angalkunun tukniuralrianun piyaaqengermiu
nataqesciiganaku.
Nutaan aũg'um angalkukeggnerunrilngalnguum nutaan tua-i
aperturluku nataqluku.
Tua-i tauna nutaan tua-i taukuk nutaan
ukveqluku taumun qetunrarmegnek
pilliniluku.
75
Tua-i waten
uksuarmi nakaciullrata nalliini,
nalullrata nalliini,
tauna tua qetunrartek taukunun
nakacugnun nalullratni malikluku tua-i taum
angalkum ayagcetellrullinia taun' tan'gurra'ar.
Taũgaam ayagcecamiu
taukuk angayuqaak qanrutellrulliniak
pisqumaciagtun
aliayuutekeksaunaku kinguani paiguraasqellukek.

76
Tua-i-'m uksurpak

316

71
Paul:
Yes.
72
Rose:
First, we tell it the way we heard it,
finishing the rest of the story,
and then you can also
tell it the way
you heard it
when we're done,
not doing it all at once.
73
Paul:
Yes, okay.
74
Andy:
Now back to the story
we started
and the [hidden] cutting knife he was using to seek
[shamans] with.
Well, although he had different shamans with more power look for
    it, they couldn't find it.
Finally, a seemingly worthless looking shaman
        pointed it out and found it.
And so, that couple now
believed in him and they entrusted their son
to him.
75
And so,
at the time of the Bladder Festival in the fall time
when they were going to push the bladders under the ice,
that shaman had them take their son along with those bladders
and the boy went along with the bladders
when they were pushed under the ice.
Once he had sent the boy away,
he told the parents that
since they wanted so much for their son,
they should just remain behind without being sad on account of
    missing him.
76
So, for the whole winter

taukuk tua qetunrarmek kinguani pailliniuk.
Waten erucim iliini tangrruarlutek taumek qetunrarmegnek
aliayugnalutek piyaaqaqagnek ak'a iterluni tauna, taum angalkuum,
    inerqualliniaqekek, "Inerqullruamtek-ggem
aliayuutekesqevkenaku pisqelluku."
Tua-i piaqatek
utermun
tua-i tuaten piyugnairtaqlutek.
77
Arnaucuaq:
Aũgna qanrutkenritellren qanqautekqerlaku?
78
Uyuraũrluq:
Ii-i.

                     ***

79
Arnaucuaq:
Tamaani-gguq
tamaa-i nakacuut pillratni

Qaguak, Paul Carl, left; and *Agiyangaq,* Mark George, with *pitaq* 'catch' at the
edge of the ice, circa 1980. Photo by Andrew J. Chikoyak.

they remained behind after their son was sent away.
On some days when they visualized their son
and started to miss him, the shaman would enter their home and
    warn them saying, "I thought I told you
not to miss him."
When he told them that
they would return to their original state
and not miss him.
77
Mike:
Can I say something about what you missed?
78
Andy:
Yes.

***

79
Mike:
At that time, it is said,
during the Bladder Festival

Qaluyaarmiut 'Nelson Islanders,' 1927. Photo courtesy of the Anchorage
Museum of History and Art B92.33.53.

tamaani waten
nalugniarallratni,
waten-gguq cal tan'gurraq iliini—
qaillun tayim' angtallia—
tamaa-i nalugniarallratni qavani egkumi nakacuut uitalriit
ullagluki-gguq
ullagnaurai
matangqaluni.
Tua-i-gguq tau͡gken nakacugnun tuavet mayu'urqami tayima
akuliitgun piluni iquakun kiaggun ig'arrluni,
tamaa-i nalugniarallratni, tauna tan'gaurluq.
Tamaa-i tamakut nakacuut ak'a nallunrirluki maliggluki tua-i
ayagarkaulliniami. Au͡gna ava-i qanrutkenritellren qanqautekaqa.

80
Uyurau͡rluq:
Yaa, quyana. Tua-i
unimtauyuama ilaitnek waten wanigg' katagiaqama pilarciqaat.

***

81
Tua-i im' taun' tan'gurraq
taukut ayautelliniat nakacuut.
82
Maa-i-llu
tamaani tamatum nalliini
qaneryarangqetullruut
waten arnaq
tan'gurrarmun nuyurriltaarutekluku pisqevkenaku
uqriraluku-llu pisqevkenaku
mallguuraluku-llu pisqevkenaku
tepii-llu narumayugngaluku kangaasqevkenaku.
Tamaa-i kencikluki picirmeggni
tamakut pissurteteng.
83
Tauna im' tan'gurra'ar
tamaani ellangqellermeggni
taum tua-i tukuan,
auluku'urtiin,
taukuni tua-i cani nunani, qasgimi uksurpak uitatlinikii, tauna

at the time
before they pushed the bladders under the ice,
it is said that sometimes the boy would—
he must have been this big—
before the time they pushed the bladders under the ice, he would go
    to the bladders
situated near the *qasgiq*'s back wall,
going to them
naked.
So, when he climbed up to those bladders, he would go
in amongst them and fall out through the other end,
doing this before the time they actually pushed that boy under the ice.
You see, the boy already knew he was to
go with the bladders. That is the part you missed that I wanted to
    include.
80
Andy:
Yes, thank you,
I tend to forget some parts and if I miss anything the others will do
    right by me.

***

81
So, the bladders took
the boy along with them when they left.
82
And now
at that time
there used to be a saying
that young men should be cautious
about approaching any fertile females.
And they should not be around the down wind side of women
or walk too close to them
in order to avoid smelling their scent.
At that time they showed great respect
for their hunters.
83
While they were in their "other" world,
that little boy
was watched over
by his host,
who kept him in that [undersea] village, in a *qasgiq*, all winter long.

tan'gurra'ar.
Tua-i imna yugyagglainarluni qasgi tamana pilallinilria.
Taqukanek-gga tua-i yugyagluni. {qanemcista engelartuq}
Tua-i-gguq uksurpak uitallratni imkut makut wani ilait
kumeksuaralguluteng, ilait. Cunawa-gguq useqniit imkutuseqnagaat
issuriurteksailnguut.
Asriuluteng-llu.
Tua-i nakuksugluku-llu ilaita.
Tamaa-i tua uksurpak uksilliniaqelriit tamaani
taukuni nunani.

***

84
Tua-i atam pivakarluteng makut wani angullualleraat ilait, uksurpak
    pivakarluteng,
qaillun tayima ella pitarian
qanqaqungellinilriit,
ella-am keggna uitaurayunairucaaqniluku piarkaulriani.
85
Tua-i pinarian imkut tamakut
angutet ayakaquuranglliniut cukatatkevkenateng.

That *qasgiq* was always crowded.
It was crowded with seals [although perceived by the boy as
    people]. {narrator laughs}
They say that all through the winter some of them there
were always scratching themselves. It turned out that they were
    two-year-old spotted seals, those young spotted seals
which have not reached adulthood.
They were also naughty.
And that boy would get picked on by some of them.
They apparently spent all winter there at
that village.

***

84
Time passed and towards winter's end,
at that certain time of the season, some of the old men[16]
began to talk occasionally, saying that
the weather outside was right and they should do what they were
    intending to do and not wait around.
85
When it was time,
those "men" began to go out in intervals at various speeds.

Young dancers at the Toksook Bay Mask Festival, January, 1996. *Cingarkaq,*
Eliza Orr, is in the left rear. Photo by Andrew J. Chikoyak.

Kiituani man' qasgim ilua yugyanringuq.
86
Tua-llu tua pivakarluni taum auluku'urtiin pillinia, "Amci tua wangkuk
eglengnariyaaqaakuk!"
87
Aren tamaani, ima-tanem,
tamakut angullualleraat qanlallinilriit,
"Kitaki ata
egilraukuvci
qavaryugpiiqnaci pilaqici!
Qavarci man'a atussiyaagpiiqnaciu
pilaqici!"
Ilaita-gguq kiugartelliniaqut,
"Qairek-qaa nepliagurallrak
ceggamanarqelartuq, niiskengaqurallrak?"
Tuaten tua kiulalliniluteng.
88
Tua-i imna
ayaucamiu taum
tukuqestiin ayautellinikii
tua-i unaggun tua-i imarpigkun, ayautellinikii.
Iliini-gguq nunat ketiitnun tua-i tekillutek,
mayurlutek cikum qainganun, qavarlutek. Mayurlutek-gga tua
    piaqameng,
qayat-gguq uperquralliniaqameng pamani tua ilait atrarciqliniut,
kanaryarturciquq-gguq tua-i neplik'acagarluni imna qamigaq canek
    qamurluni piciatun inianek-llu uyampagluni
tua-i camek tangerciiganani, avirlurrluni cakneq.

89
Tuamte-llu-gguq tua-i mermun kanaami
ayakuni
anguarutni mermun agtuuteksailngalengraan ayaagarnaurtuq ilii-
    gguq carraquinermek mulga akurcecuayaaqernaurtuq.
Aren tangerrnaqngalengraagnek-gguq
menglaraagnegun-llu kituraqluni pagg'un-gguq taũgaam quliikun
    kiarrluni.

90
Naugg' imumi
qanrutellrulaqaitkut-llu iniat aciiranrilkurrluki pilaasqelluki,

Eventually the inside of the *qasgiq* was no longer crowded.
86
After a time his host said to him, "We should hurry up and
get going!"
87
Aren, oh yes, at that time
those old men would say,
"As you
travel,
please try not to sleep too much!
Try not to succumb
to sleep!"
Some of them would retort,
"Is it hard to stay awake
listening to the sound of waves?"
That was how they responded.
88
So when
the host took the boy
with him, they traveled
in the ocean down there.
Sometimes when they arrived below a village,
they climbed on to an ice floe and slept. When they climbed up and
     were on the ice,
they say that some of the village men would get their kayaks ready,
some of them coming down making so much noise, dragging
     different things, and having things including clotheslines
     wrapped around their necks and hanging so that they were
unable to see anything, and making tremendous noise.
89
And when he [a villager] came down to the ocean
to go out hunting,
though he would row on water as usual, it appeared [to those
     below] that just the very tip of his oar would slightly
     penetrate the ocean surface.
Aren, they say that although it seemed [to the host seal and boy] that
     they should be seen,
with the two being so near the hunter, he would pass them by
     looking only above them.
90
You know, back then
they used to tell us to try not to walk under hanging things,

cat-gga tua-i iniat.
Tamaa-i-gguq
iniat aciiravakarluki pistait tangvallratni ellangqellermeggni caneg'
    inianek uyampagluteng {qanemcista engelartuq}
tava-llu pitarkaq cali taun' tangerciiganaku.
Ellakun-ll' anguarluteng qulruarqaqluku pitaqsugnaitem ugaani
    kituraqluku pilallinilriit.
Tuaten tua ayuqevkenateng. Ilaita-gguq taugken tua anguaryaaqaqluteng
ping'ermeng
tua-i tangerpegnakek ayagaqluteng.

***

91
Tua-ll' tua-i pivakarlutek,
nunat
up'nerkillret ketiitnun pivakarlutek tekicamek, taukunun nunat ketiitnun,
taum tua-i pillinikii nutaan pistekamegnun
wanigg' tekitnilutek.
92
Tua-i im' tuaten tua-i qayat uperqaqelriit ayagayaaqelriameng
yaatairlukek, qulruarqaqlukek tangerrngalngermegtekek
ayalallinilriit tamakut qayat.

93
Atam tua pivakarluni uptellriartangllinilria.
Nunani caurallra tua-i, caurallra, qayarpallaraurallra, caurallra
    qaskepiarluni niilluku anglanaqluni.
Pinariani man'a tua-i angun qamigarluni atraralliniluni. Tua-i-ll'
    ceñamun atraami
qayani atrarrluku. Menuunani tua-i tauna angun tua-i cataunani
    man'a ayuqucia.
Ayumian man'a anguarluni
mer'agen'gun anguarluni ayaagangaartelliniuq.
Ayumian-llu ukaqsigiyartuan ayumian qavarningyarturluni.
94
Tua-i-ll' tua-i
maa-i canimelliqertelluku
tua-i tayim' ceggaumauviirucamek tua-i tayim' qavallinilutek.
Tua-i taukuk taum tua-i nukalpiam
pitaqlukek. (Waten unani imarpigmi amirkat pingaqata
niitelartukut una-gguq aanalegtuq.

different things that are hanging on lines.
It is said that a person who
keeps walking under such hanging things would be seen, from the
     seal's perspective, as if he had things wrapped around and
     hanging from his neck, {narrator laughs}
and he wouldn't be able to see any game.
And he would row through the air, passing above them, giving him
     no chance of catching them.
There were various things like that. And though a hunter
would row intent on hunting,
he would pass without seeing the two of them.

***

91
And so after a time,
when
the two arrived below a spring camp, a village,
the one who cared for him said that they had finally arrived at the
village of the one who was destined to catch them.
92
And so, as happened before, after these [hunters] got their kayaks
     ready, they too would go beyond the two of them,
passing above them, although it seemed [to the two below] that
those kayakers traveling should be able to see them.
93
Then later they noticed a person getting ready to go out hunting.
The things he did in the village, the sounds of preparing his kayak,
     whatever he did had a clear sound and was fun to listen to.
Then it was time, and here was a man coming down to hunt seal.
     When he came to the edge of the shore,
he launched his kayak. He was spotless and there was nothing
     wrong with the way he was.
Here he came rowing,
traveling on their water surface.
And then as he got closer, he [the seal boy] started to feel drowsy.
94
And so
as he got closer,
because they just couldn't stay awake, both of them fell asleep.
So that *nukalpiaq*, a good hunter, caught
those two. (When they start seeing young bearded seals in the ocean,
we hear that so and so caught "one with a mother."

327

Tua-i irniartuumaan maklak, amirkaq, tapeqlukek pitaqlukek.
Tua-i aanaleggniluku
una qanrutektuat, tua-i-gguq aanaleggluni.)
Tua-i elkek tua-i taungulutek,
amirkauluni ellii tauna-ll' tua aipaa tua-i tungunquuluni.
Tua-i taum
qamigam taum nukalpiam pitaqlukek.
95
Ilavci tang usguliqerliu.
96
Cingliaq:
Aũgna nutaan
naspaaqerlaku?
97
Uyuraũrluq:
Aũgna wani,
waken wani usguliqerraartelluku.
Ava-i
pitaqngakek taq'aqa,
pitaqngakek, aũg'um
nukalpiam taukuk tua-i pitaqngakek.
Icigg'
itqertellrulria
tauna angalkuq
qetunraak tekiteqatarniluku.
98
Arnaucuaq:
Ii-i.

***

99
Taum-gguq tua-i
angalkum taukuk tua-i murilkaaqellruak cakneq.
Waten-gguq
tauna tua qetunrartek
angniinatek piyaaqngagnek ugna-ll' ak'a iterluni
qanrut'lalliniak,
"Kitaki icigg'
piqatallemni qanrutellrukemtek
aliayugarkaunrilkuvtek taũgaam piciqniluku."
Tua-i-ll'
tauna nukalpiaq

So, they catch a bearded seal along with its baby,
and they say that
a person caught "one with a mother.")
And so, those two were that kind,
the boy was the young bearded seal and the host was the adult.
So that
nukalpiaq, a good hunter, caught those two.
95
One of you can add further comments to it.
96
Paul:
May I now
try what I was going to say?
97
Andy:
You may after they continue
from where I left off.
I stopped at the part
when they were caught,
when that *nukalpiaq*
had caught those two.
You know
that shaman
rushed in
to tell them [the couple] that their son was about to arrive.
98
Mike:
Yes.

***

99
It is said that
the shaman watched that couple very closely.
When they
thought about their son
and started to miss him, that shaman would come in
and say to them,
"Well, you know
I told you when I was going to send him off
that I was going to do it only if the two of you wouldn't miss him."
So now
that *nukalpiaq*, the good hunter,

tekiutelliniluni tua-i
tamaa-i.
100
Tua-ll'-am taulleraam itqerrluni
qanrutliak,
"Kitaki qetunrartek tekituq!"
Nang'errlutek tua-i
anlutek
piyaaqelliniuk
amirkaq taũgaam man'a tua maa-i.
101
Tua-i-am arenqiacaaqlutek.
Tua-ll' taum pilliniak,
"Tua-i tayima tekituq.
Nakaciurciqut cal' tayima.
Nakacium taũgaam nalliini nutaan
tangerciqertek cal' tamalkuan." Tuaten-am tua qanrutliniak taukuk.
102
Tua-i umyuamegnek nangteqeũrlurlutek kiingan-ll' irniaqngamegnegu;
amta-llu-gguq tua taum angalkum tua-i murilkellukek cakneq.
Umyuaqluku waten angniicaaqaqagnek ullaglukek
qanrutaqatek tua-i
pinriqertaqlutek.
(Tauna tua-i tuaten, tua-i wii tuaten,
niitellrua-qa aũgna.
Nakacuum-gguq taũgaam nalliini tua-i
nutaan tua-i tangellruak taukuk angayuqaagken nakaciullratni.
Aũgna ava-i
tua-i tuaten pitaluku qanrutkaqa.)

***

103
Puyangun:
Cali-ll' aũgna
taum tua-i angalkum
tuani tua ayagcecamiu
aanii pillinikii
qilurraq mermek imirluku
piavet
acian keluanun

had apparently arrived with
what he caught.
100
So that shaman came in
and told them,
"Well, your son has arrived!"
They quickly stood up,
went out
and saw
that it was only a young bearded seal.
101
They both felt anguished.
Then that shaman said to them,
"Well, he did arrive.
They will have a Bladder Festival soon.
Only at the time of that Bladder Festival will you finally
see him whole again." That is what he told the couple.
102
The poor couple were sick at heart, suffering because he was their
    only child;
however, the shaman was watching them very closely.
Whenever they felt unhappy thinking about their son, the shaman
    would go to them
and when he talked with them,
they would stop feeling unhappy.
(That is how
I heard that part.
It is said that only at the time of the Bladder Festival
would they see their son.
That is all
I have to say about that part.)

***

103
Rose:
Also the part
when that shaman
sent the boy off,
he instructed his mother
to fill a section of dried seal gut with water
and place it
up behind

elliqalaasqelluku. Murilkelaasqelluku taũgaam imairutlerkaa.
Mermek imiqerluku
tauna pillra murilkelaasqelluku imairutaqan imiraqluku pisqelluku.
Tauna-am cal' tua yaatiikun,
tauna mikelnguq,
waten meqsugluni pillrani
taum cal' tua pistiin
keluliuqerluni keluanek piaken
aũg'umek ukinermek mer'esqellinia
tallimarqunek qanra imirluku.
104
Tua-i meqsuami tallimarqunek imirluku qaneni mell'iniluni.
Camirtenrilami-llu
arvinliryaaqekai taryuuluni.
105
Tuaten-gguq cunaw' im' uksurpak:
aaniin tua-i taum
tauna qilurraq imairutlerkaa
murilkaaqaqkii.
Tauna-ll' cal' tua-i tan'gurraq
elicami,
mer'aqami tua-i
qaneni tallimarququtagpall'ernek imirluku meryaurrluni camirrluni.
Tuaken tua mengqerrluni.
Talliman taũgaam cipcaaqaqamiki taryuugaqluni qaillun
    meyunaunani. Tuaten cal' tua-i
taum aaniin merquratullrulliniluki taum angalkum
alerqullracicetun. (Pingatqapiggluni-am tua-i
piluni cal' tauna meq
imairutaqluni ak'anivkenani
tuani mer'aqani.)

***

106
Cingliaq:
Good morning.
Good morning-aarurrluni. Quuyuarluci cali.
Quuyuarrsuutekaci amlleret uka-i agiirtut.
Quliranek niicugniyukuvci,
eliterrlainarngaicaaqaci taũgaam ukut,
waniw' ciulirneret,
kelgiluci,

her bed. However, she was to make sure that it didn't get empty.
She filled that thing with [fresh] water,
and was told to tend to it, filling it whenever it got empty.
Besides that,
when the boy
got thirsty
his caretaker
reached up behind him
and told him to drink from a hole there,
filling his mouth five times.
104
So because he was thirsty he filled his mouth five times and drank.
Since that didn't satisfy him,
he drank a sixth time but it tasted salty.
105
So that's how it was for the whole winter:
his mother
watched that section of seal gut
very carefully.
And also,
since he learned his lesson,
whenever the boy drank,
he would drink contentedly by filling his mouth with five big gulps.
That was his source of fresh water.
But whenever he exceeded the limit of five, it tasted salty and was
     not drinkable. That is how
his mother provided him fresh water as the shaman
had instructed. (And it seems it really happened
that way, that the water
was emptied quickly
each time he drank it.)

***

106
Paul:
Good morning.
It is a good morning. Keep smiling.
There is more coming to smile about.
If you want to listen to stories,
although you may not learn them all,
invite
these elders here,

neqkegcarluki,
akutarturtelluki
saayumek-llu nutaan assilriamek culriamek saayirilluki
atlilirluki yuurqertelluki nurusngairulluki saayumek.
Yuurqainanermeggni nutaan meng'arkaugut.
Quliranek maq'erkaugut.
Tauna cali iquliqerluku.
107
Tua-i-ll' una cal' ava-i,
imuken pikaken,
"Qaill' atak una
qetunrarpuk,
makunun
yuullgutminun,
maligtaqulluni yuuqerli."
108
(Nutaan tua tuani waten aparpiinkut aũgkut,
yuurqerraaluteng aqsiqertaqameng,
qanngartaqameng tuaten pitullruut
ukucetun, waten wangkucicetun, kitugtauguqu'urluteng.)
109
Aũgna ava-i cal' niitelqa waten,
taum-gguq tua-i aaniin
uluani pikavet
qasgim egalran mengliinun elliluku, elaulluku.
Tua-lli-wa-gguq tua yuaraqellria.
"Canek tua-i atak piqerlii maklagnek, amirkanek?"

110
Atam tua pivakaqerluni
(aũg'um ava-i qanrutellruciacetun)
angulluacualler-gguq un' igvaqili,
kemyunaunan' (wangtun).
Tua-i-gguq una angulluaq,
angulluacualleraqtaq.
Taum-gguq pia,
"Pikna uluan
cairutvakaqen
am atraresgu
wayarivakalria!" (Tuaten wangkuta pilaraput.)
Nutaan cal' tauna
tan'gaurlu[q]

prepare good food for them,
let them have *akutaq*,
and finally make plenty of good strong tea and
let them drink from a saucer.
While they drink their tea they will begin to talk.
They will start telling stories.
That is my comment [before I start].
107
Well then, back to
that part [where the parents were deliberating over their son]:
"I wonder how this
son of ours
can live
a life equal
to his peers."
108
(Now those grandfathers,
having drunk their tea and feeling full,
would start talking and used to do it like
these guys, like us, correcting each other.)
109
Also, this is the way I heard that part [about the knife].
The mother of the boy, it is said,
put her *uluaq* knife up
near the edge of the *qasgiq* window, burying it.
And so they say she kept searching [for the right shaman].
"I wonder what I'll have him become, a full grown or a young
     bearded seal?"
110
So one day
(like that elder said)
this worthless looking old man appeared.
He looked incompetent (like me).
And so, it was an old man,
a shabby old man.
He said to her,
"Your *uluaq* up there
has brought you nowhere,
hurry up and take it down!
It has done enough damage [exposed enough shamans]!" (That's
     how we tell the story.)
Then finally that

nutaan tua tunllinia.
Nutaan tua tunngani
tuaten tua taum angulluacualleraam,
(wangcetun ayuqellriim),
pillinia,
"Qaillun ayuqengraan agurrluk"
(aũg'utun qanrutkellruciatun)
"umyuartek uqamaiteqercecaaqunategu.
Nakacugnun ayaucetqata'arqa."
Nutaan tua tuani
nakaciurraartelluki paqrilluni tayima.

111
Tua-lli-wa-gguq tua tayima
cataunani ngelaunani.
Angniiteqeryaaqaqata angulluacualler ugna itqerrnaurtuq,
"Angniicesqumallrunritamtek!
Inerqullruamtek!" (Tang tua makut qanruyutet, inerquuteput wangkuta
aturarkaput.)
Taukuk ukveqngamegnegu tuaten pirraarluku ataam tua
    pingnatuktarlutek piaqlutek.

***

112
Tua tamaani
uksurpak. (Ava-i aũgkut tekilluki
aũgkut-llu cali
pilugull'ernek
uyamigluteng ayatulit
tekilluki.)
Aũgna-ll' tua-i
ayagpakarlutek nunat ketiitnun tekituk,
"Nutaan waniwa
pistekamegnun tekitukuk."
Tua-i uitalutek. Pia-gguq,
"Atam pingna nukalpiaq
tangerqerru!"
Maaten-gguq piavet tangrraa
pilugumikun,
asguruamikun, alimikun
tanqigmek anllugquralria.

boy
was given to him.
When they gave the boy to him,
the shabby old man
(the one like me),
said to her,
"No matter what it's like don't ever"
(as they narrated before)
"burden your minds worrying about him.
I'm going to let the bladders take him away."
Then at the time
after they had that Bladder Festival, they found him missing.
111
And so, it is said, he
was gone with no trace.
Whenever they started to feel sad, that shabby old man would come in,
"I told both of you not to be unhappy.
That was my admonition!" (See, these are admonitions that were
    told to us
that we should follow.)
Since that couple believed in him, after he told them that, they again
    tried to remain happy.

***

112
So, they were there
for the whole winter. (I have reached the point
about those
that hunted
with shabby old skin boots wrapped around and hanging from their
necks.)
And now that part [which begins]
after they traveled for some time and arrived below a village,
"Here we finally
reached the one destined to catch us."
So they stayed. The host said,
"Notice that *nukalpiaq*, a good hunter,
take a look at him!"
Lo and behold, when he looked up at him
he saw light gleaming
from his skin boots,
his parka ruff, and his sleeves.

"Ping'um uitasngaitaakuk!"
113
Tuamte-llu-gguq tangrresqaa,
"Atam qayaa tangerqerru!"
Tuaten-gguq tua ayuqluni, tengrunaqpiaq cakneq!
Menuunani meniutem-llu ugaan'
tanqigmek anllugqurluni.
114
Tua-ll' pillinia taum tukuan,
"Pingna
nukalpiaq mulngakellriaruuq.
Menuurutevkenani makunun maa-i nunamiutarnun yuuguq.
Nulirran-llu elluarrluku
auluktuluku.
Unatminek-llu
akutaq una akucuunaku."
(Naugg', ava-i inerquumalallruukut
arnaq una agiireskan
uqlirnerakun kituusqevkenaku.
Nallumni
kituraqata *perfume*-arnimek narlartua. {ngel'arluteng}
Ilaitni tua narniqnaurtuq
taũgaam aqespagalartua ilait piaqata. {ngel'arluteng}
Tamakunun ellangellrunrilamta.
Tamana tamaa-i
una wani
tan'gaurluq
mulngakluku aulukarkaulliniarput
pissuqataaralria.)
115
Tua-i tuaten tangvaurarraarluku pia-i,
tua-i-gguq tuaten ayuquq
taun' nulirra.
Una-llu-gguq cali
tauna uinga tuaten ayuquq.
Tuaten tua tamakut-llu
alerquutni aturluki, inerquutet.
Tamatum-gguq tamaa-i tanqigcetaa, tamatum-gguq tamaa-i
tuaten ayuqevkaraa.
"Murilkekina
usuuq, uitasngaitaakuk!"

"That one up there won't leave us alone!"
113
Then he told him to look again,
"Look at his kayak!"
It was like that too, very exciting!
It was very clean, and being very clean
light was gleaming from it.
114
Then the host said to him,
"That
nukalpiaq up there is a very careful one.
He lives by not tainting himself with these land animals.
And his wife always
takes proper care of him.
Also she doesn't use her hands
when she makes *akutaq*."
(As an example, we used to be admonished
when a woman comes our way
not to pass her on the lee side of the wind.
Sometimes when I don't realize it
they pass by me and I smell perfume. {laughter}
Some of them smell good,
but I sneeze when others pass by. {laughter}
As we were growing up, those things weren't around.
So that is why
this
young boy
is supposed to be watched over carefully,
the one that is just starting to hunt.)
115
So, after observing the husband he told the boy that
that's how she is,
that wife of his.
And this one too,
her husband is like that.
He heeds those
instructions and admonitions.
That is why he emanates brightness, that is why
he is like that.
"You!
Be alert for he won't leave us alone!"

Tua-ll' pillinia,
"Cam tus'uciacetun
wavet tunumnun cukatacirpetun itqerreskina!
Uitasngaitaakuk
nallunaituq tua-i."
1
Pia-i upluni qayaminun
ekluni anguangarteqerluku,
canimelliluku
qavarninglutek.
Atam ilait qavatuut
ullalriani,
qavaryupiarluteng.
116
"Tuaten
cam imum tuskaten qamanqumnun cukatacirpetun pikina!"
Tuaten tua-i
qanruciacetun canimelliinauciacetun ak'a tua qavaryupiarlun'
    kiituan' qavaqalliniuq. Tuaten tua piciacetun
qamanqurranun itqerrluni tua-i-ll' tayima.
117
Nutaan tuani
angulluacualler taun' up'nerkanrakun
itqertuq,
"Qetunrartek tekituq! Cangairutuq!
Cangaituq, qaill' pingairutuq!"
118
Tua-i-am
quyaurlurlutek agqertuk.
Maaten pilliniuk
maklak una
irniaminek caniqlirluni.
Tua-i-am tuaten ping'ermek pingnatuktarlutek.
119
Tua-llu,
tua-i-llu
nakaciunqigtut-am.
Tuani tua nakaciurraartelluki aanii-am tuaken mertarluni
nakacuut
anluaratnek.
120
Tuani tua

He then said,
"As soon as something hits you
I want you to enter my back as quickly as you can!
He isn't going to leave us alone,
it's obvious."
1
The man up there got ready and got into his kayak
and as he started to row
and got close,
they both got drowsy.
See, some seals sleep
when they are approached,
sleeping very soundly.
116
"As I told you,
when something hits you, enter my back as quickly as you can."
As soon as
he said that, as the hunter got closer, they both got drowsy and fell
    asleep. As he had been instructed,
he [the boy] quickly entered his host's back, and so it was.
117
And now was the time
during that spring for that shabby old man to
enter quickly,
"Your son has arrived! Nothing is going to happen to him anymore!
Nothing will happen to him, nothing is going to be wrong!"
118
So,
they quickly went over, filled with joy,
and when they got there,
they saw only this bearded seal
with its baby next to it.
So, although they were saddened they tried to stay happy.
119
Then
they had
a Bladder Festival again.
After the Bladder Festival the mother of the boy packed water
from the hole
where they had pushed the bladders through.
120
At the time

mertallermini tan'gurraqegtaarmek uumek tekituq mangllegturluni.
Pia, "Ciin qiasit?"
"Tua-i-gg' aûgkut ilanka maligcugyaaqluki nacikenka."
Maaten-gguq wavet meciknauraa imna
qetunraa.
Utercami nutaan tua kenuggluni, *shampoo*-rluni, {nel'arluteng}
quyam ugaan'.

***

121
Nutaan tuani
qasgimi,
aûgkut
murilketallrulliniameng angutet,
qavangartaqata-gguq tauna tan'gaurluq
quuyuarturluni pagkut
tangvaurluki iqutmun
kamilarquratullruuq, ûgayarluni.
122
Tua-i-llu-gguq tua-i wayaumariami
v̇aken iquat ullagluku qeckaan
imkut pagkut nakacuut
kallagqurluteng ayagluteng iqutmun
kassuamiki-llu-gguq
tuavet aciatnun
qeckaq'erluni tus'arrluni tuavet.
Mecungpiatullruuq taûgaam-gguq tuatnaaqami.
123
Nutaan
tuani
taun' piyaurcami, ayagayaurcami, nutaan makut maa-i
qanrutkelallri.
124
Makut-llu-gguq maa-i unguvalriarraat, kaviaret uliiq-ll' iternaurtut,
"Aa!
Uum, ukugnek uum atiin pikitaanga!"
Tuamte-llu-gguq maklak iterlun' pinaurtuq,
"Uum-wa
pim atiin
kukgarkanek cikiqiinga."

when she packed water, she came upon this nice-looking boy
    sobbing at intervals.
She asked, "Why are you crying?"
"Because I wanted to go along with my companions."
It is said, when she got a better view of him,
she saw that it was her son.
When she got home she groomed herself, shampooed her hair {laughter}
on account of being so happy.

***

121
Now going back to [a scene in] the
qasgiq,
since the
men in the past were very observant,
it is said, when they got ready to go to bed, that boy
would look up smiling
watching the bladders from one end to the other
while removing his boots and undressing.
122
And then, when he was undressed,
he would go to the end and when he jumped up,
those bladders
would make rattling noise from one end to the other
and after he went around them
he would jump down and land
right under them.
However, when he did that he would be soaking wet.
123
Finally,
when
the boy was able to travel around and hunt, he talked
about these things.
124
He said, these living things, the red fox, and white fox would enter,
"Ah!
this one, the father of this one has given me this!"
Furthermore, a bearded seal would enter and say,
"This one,
so-and-so's father,
has given me a harpoon."

125
Tamakut tamaa-i tangvagluki qasgim iluani waten wangkucicetun
    yuuluteng tau͡gaam.
Makut-llu-gguq-am yuut
tuutarrarluteng aqumganaurtut, cunawa-gguq asveret.
Makut-wa imkut kumelgulriit,
neresciqelgulriit,
issurit useqnaaraat-llu.
126
Tauna tua tamaaggun makut maa-i inerquuteput alaillruut.
Tan'gaurluum taum
qalarutekluki nalqiggluki-llu. Au͡gna-ll' ava-i cali elitaqluku
mer'utii,
kelqutaa.
Tua-i tuaten pitauq.

***

127
Arnaucuaq:
Au͡gna cali qanrutkenritellra qanrutekciqaqa.
Tauna tua ava-i qanrutekngalkii, ciutaicuama tang.
128
Tamaani-gguq tamaa-i
ayagangluni imarpigmi piami...
Ayuqenrilameng tamaani
uitallrani-am ilaita
imkulalliniat
tua-i-gg' nakukerrlugluku piaqluku.
Ilaita tau͡gken naklekluku.
Tamaa-i
qanellratun
ayangami
tanglallinii tamakut taqukat.
129
Tua-am cali una,
tamakut-gguq tamaa-i,
waten-llu nutegluki piyuitellruameng tamatum
nalliini narulkarluki tau͡gaam,
tamakut-gguq imkut
uumikestek'lallni
akngirtengnaqluki narulkarnaurai.
Tuaten-am tua-i qanrutekluku.

344

125
Those the boy observed in the [undersea] *qasgiq* were perceived as
    humans like us by him.
And some of these "people"
seated there had labrets, and were actually walruses.
And ones that always scratched themselves,
the ones with lice,
were the adult and young spotted seals.
126
That is how, through him, some of our proscriptions came to be known.
That boy
talked about them and explained them. I recognize that one
about his water supply,
how it was provided for him.
So, that's how long it is.

***

127
Mike:
I am going to say some of what he overlooked.
Notice I have a hearing problem so he might have talked about them.
128
It is said that at the time
when he started to hunt on the ocean...
You know [seals] are all different
and when he was there [in the undersea *qasgiq*] some of them
used to do things to him,
you know, pick on him.
However, others felt compassion for him.
When
he started hunting
he saw
those very seals.
129
Also,
in those days
they never shot seals with guns
but harpooned them.
Those that
used to pick on him,
he would harpoon trying to hurt them as much as possible.
That's what they used to say.

Taugken-gguq makut
naklekestni
cali tua-i
akngirtellerkait umyuaqluku
narulkaraqluki mianikluki.

130
Tua-i-ll' tua
tamaa-i ayallrata kinguani-am
tamana-gguq nakaciuryaraat cali ilacuarallruuq yaani iquani.

131
Tamaani-gguq ayallermeggni waten qavartaraqameng
tua-i curulugkaitaqluteng
pilallruut.
Cali-llu meqsugaqluteng, merkaunateng.

132
Tua-i-gguq taum kinguakun
waten nalugaqameng,
nalullrem kinguani,
melgitulqait imkut
tamaa-i anluat.
Mernek ayaulluteng-am
can'ggarnek-llu ayaulluteng tamaa-i piyaurtellruut.
Tuaten tua tangvallruunga.
Tua-i-gguq atakumi melgiraqluki taukut nakacuut.
Tamaa-i-gguq tamana tuatnayaurtelqaat
taum tua-i ayallrem kinguakun.
Meqsughiteng pilallrulliniata
tamaa-i kingunipailegmeng
curulugkaunateng tuaten.

133
Augna cal ava-i ilaqerqa aug'umek
neq'angamkug-wa.
Tua-i.

However, regarding the ones
that had shown compassion towards him,
he would
think of the agony he would cause them
and so he harpooned them very carefully.
130
Subsequent
to that boy's journey,
toward the end of the Bladder Festival some additions were made to
    the [*Nalugyaraq*] ceremony.
131
They say that at the time they [the boy and the bladders] were on
    their journey and they stopped to overnight,
they didn't have any
grass for bedding.
They also became thirsty and had no water to drink.
132
So ever since then
when they pushed the bladders under the ice,
after that ceremony,
they provided fresh water [for the bladders]
through that hole in the ice.
The people started taking water along
and some grass for bedding.
That is what I observed.
During the evening [of the ceremony] they provided water for the
    bladders.
After that boys journey,
they started to follow that tradition,
since they [the bladders] would be thirsty
and would have no grass for bedding
before they reached their destination.
133
That is my addition to the story,
now that I've remembered it.
That's all.

Photo from Jesuit Oregon Province Archives, Gonzaga University, negative number 504.12.

WAR AND PEACE

"She went out and looked around and saw a heavy vapor rising from the qasgiq. She saw the vapor was different, being unlike ordinary smoke...[It] was the blood from their killing one another."
—*Arnaucuaq,* "How War Began" (Orr and Orr 1995: 281)

"For this purpose this drum was intended. If we use this drum, we shall love our neighbors, no longer killing one another, and this one here, this drum, shall sever us from the action of our perpetual self-slaughter."
—*Arnaucuaq,* "The Boy Who Made Peace"

Kevgiq 'The Messenger Feast'

The conflict *Arnaucuaq* refers to in the following story was known as the War of the Eye. It occurred in the first two decades of the nineteenth century, before the first Russians reached the Nushagak and Kuskokwim region, and involved virtually the entire Yup'ik area in a bloody and exhausting internecine conflict. An ethnohistorical overview of the war is given by Oswalt (1990: 40-42) and narrative accounts are found in numerous tales, among which are Mike Angaiak's story *"Qaill' Anguyiim Ayagniucia*: How War Began" (Orr and Orr 1995: 272-285), Charlie Pleasant's *"Ciuqliq Yupiit Anguyallrat*: The First Eskimo War," and *"Kusquqvagmi Callullrat*: Ambush on the Kuskokwim" (Tennant and Bitar 1981: 15-17, 35-39). Here is a summary:

Two boys were throwing darts at a target in the *qasgiq* and one of the boys made a wild throw, striking out his companion's eye. Had the father of the injured boy been content with an eye for an eye, the matter might have ended there, but he struck out both eyes of the offender in retaliation. The two fathers fought and were both killed, but the feud spread to kinsmen and neighbors, then to neighboring villages, and finally throughout the Yup'ik area.

The ensuing war was cruelly genocidal, pitting one region against the other. Oswalt states that the conflict began in the lower Yukon and then spread north and south (Oswalt 1990: 40). According to *Qaluyaarmiut* elders, the *Qaluyaarmiut* were allied with the *Nunivaarmiut* (Nunivak Island) and the *Qissunamiut* (Chevak) and *Naparyaarmiut* (Hooper Bay) against the *Kuigpagmiut* (Yukon people). A favorite tactic was to go into an enemy village undetected at night, block up the entrance to the *qasgiq* so there was no escape, and then rain fire and arrows down on the occupants. It was customary to slaughter all the males (including boys) but one; this one survivor would have his ear sliced off as a graphic demonstration that he might have been killed but was spared so that he might tell the tale. Women and perhaps young children were taken captive. Given the *Yupiit* reputation for nonviolence, the war was extraordinarily brutal. E.W. Nelson heard tales of southerners decapitating their enemies and impaling the heads on stakes with arrows stuck through the noses (reported in Fitzhugh and Kaplan 1982: 222). Or at Mud Creek, on the Kuskokwim near Kalskag, so many warriors were slain that the blood reached the midpoint of the blades of kayak paddles that were dipped into the water at the battle scene (Oswalt 1990: 41). *Kevgiq* 'The Messenger Feast,' the origins of which *Arnaucuaq* explains in his story, presumably ended the War of the Eye and brought peace again to the region:

Instead of being wary and mistrustful,
they hunted
for all kinds of animals and caribou
in the wilderness
for their food
and did not dread anything, nor were they afraid at last to gather
    them.
With what they caught,
they invited other villages
and fed them,
gathering food for that purpose,
at that time when they began to have Messenger Feasts.

    Kevgiq, as opposed to the *Nakaciuryaraq* 'the Bladder Festival' and *Elriq* 'the Feast of the Dead,' had a primary social character and was one of the most widespread of traditional ceremonials in Alaska, having been celebrated in a variety of ways among the Inupiat and Yupiit. It was an intervillage event, lasting several days, and involved masked dancing and the often lavish exchange of gifts, food and provisions between villages. According to Lantis, *Kevgiq* was "essentially a promotional scheme to help one man (or a few men) maintain his social position or achieve a higher one" (Lantis 1946: 188). It was part of the winter cycle of ceremonials, occurring sometime after *Nakaciuryaraq* 'Bladder Festival.' Although particulars differed from region to region, there were certain essential features characterizing *Kevgiq,* at least among the Central Yup'ik. The following is a summary from Curtis (1930), Lantis (1946, 1947) and Fienup-Riordan (1994):
    The *Kevgiq* was initiated when the men of one *qasgiq* sent a *kevgaq* 'messenger' (or two), who bore a ceremonial staff, often a stick decorated with bands of red ocher, and delivered a memorized list of articles to the *qasgimiut* '*qasgiq* dwellers' of another village. If the invited guests reciprocated with a list of the articles and provisions they desired, then the feast was on, since it was possible for a community to decline an invitation to a *Kevgiq* feast if it was thought that it might be too difficult a matter to obtain the requested goods (although in doing so they lost face). Preparations for the upcoming feast might take months, even years, as the requests

in the exchange were often difficult to satisfy, and people made it a point to request items, for instance foods, that were not easily obtained. Lantis notes that among the items exchanged were dried walrus skins, coils of rawhide rope, even kayaks, all articles of considerable value that required ample time and energy to obtain (Lantis 1946: 191). When the time came to hold the feast, the guest village traveled *en masse* to the host village, and over a period of several days, in the midst of feasting, singing, dancing, and considerable teasing, the two communities vied to outdo one another in the giving of gifts and provisions. Although the rivalry was bounded by good humor, it was considered an embarrassment to be outdone in generosity, and failure to come up with a requested gift, be it a difficult-to-obtain food or an item of value, was a cause of shame and ridicule.

It is evident that underlying the *Kevgiq* was a strong current of competition and intervillage rivalry. As Fienup-Riordan states, *Kevgiq* was framed in terminology and symbolism that was warlike and aggressive. The hosts were referred to as *inglut* 'enemies, adversaries,' and the guests were *curukat* 'attackers.' When the guests traveled to the host village for the feast, the verb describing this action was *curukarluteng* 'attacking, challenging.' Messengers and guests took care to arrive at nightfall, thus simulating the nighttime raids of wartime. During the festivities, there was a great deal of ritual teasing and ridicule. On the first night, as the guests feasted, the hosts sang *nernerrlugcetaat* 'songs of indigestion,' mocking and teasing songs that exposed the misdeeds of certain guests to public laughter. Many of the exchanges were between *ilurat* 'cross-cousins,' who were charged with the task of exposing one another's foibles and misdeeds, often in the context of fun and humor, but frequently with a pungency and edge that was discomforting. The objects of ridicule were expected to maintain calm and composure in the face of attempts to rile them; to do otherwise would only provoke more of the same (Fienup-Riordan 1994: 324-348).

Arnaucuaq's conclusion, that *Kevgiq* was a sublimation of the uncontrolled and destructive aggression that led to the intervillage wars of the last century, replacing physical aggression with controlled ritual competition, provides a background and context to the ceremony and is an excellent illustration of the fit between ritual and narrative. The boy's address in the *qasgiq* in the eighth section is a superb example of Yup'ik oratory. This story was recorded in the late 1980s for an audience of middle grade students at the Paul T. Albert Memorial School.

The two stories following "The Boy Who Made Peace" deal with the exploits of *Apanuugpak*, a legendary warrior who took part in these intervillage wars. He was famous for his boldness, courage, and an especially loud and intimidating voice which he projected before him when launching an attack. To most traditional *Qaluyaarmiut*, the stories about him are not legends in the Euro-American sense, that is, stories composed of a core of fact embellished by deeds and exploits of dubious historicity. Rather, they are viewed as credible accounts about actual people and events and have the same status as personal narratives. Note that both *Paningayak*'s and *Qulvarkaq*'s narratives begin as ordinary narratives do, without any special frames or literary introductions. Like "*Ciuliaqatuk*: The Ancestor," the fragmentary account of *Qaluyaarmiut* beginnings, there is a concern with facts, the narrative reconstruction of incidents, people and places, which constitute the oral documentation of the past. Both these stories were recorded some time in the mid to late 1980s. The audience was a group of high school students of the Paul T. Albert Memorial School.

Tununermiut at *kalukaq* 'feast' with goods to be distributed, *Tununeq*, circa 1980. Left to right, *Nanurrualek*, Rita Angaiak (in the dark-colored parka, kneeling and facing the camera); *Ayaprun*, Josephine Tom (face partially concealed); *Inuguarpak*, Eva Panruk; *Teksik*, Matilda Flynn; *Uyuruciaq*, Cecelia James; *Paningayak*, Medina Flynn; *Arnaqulluk*, Martha Flynn; *Kumangulria*, Louise Kanrilak; *Inuk*, Rosalie Kanrilak; *Panigpiaq*, Bertha Kanrilak Ohman; *Nalugalria*, Clara Aluska. Photo by Andrew J. Chikoyak.

TAN'GURRAAM ANGUYAVKANRILLRA

Arnaucuaq Tununermiu

***

1
Waniwa tamaani ak'a
avani
yuut
anguyatullruut
nutgunateng
urluvernek taŭgaam caskurluteng.
Tamatum nalliini ca nurniimi Kass'aq-llu nurniimi
watqapik camek kass'allamek atuyuitellruut.
2
Waniw' qanemciqatartua uumek
wii neq'akurallemnek, niitlemnek.
3
Tamaani
qagkut
Hooper Bay-rmiut wall'u makumiut—
qagaa-i Kuigpagmiunek niitelartuci qagaani Yukon-am qaŭg'um
    Kuigpiim yuinek—
tamaa-i inglukulluteng waten anguyagluteng tamaani pitullrulliniut,
waten kiagmi taŭgaam.
4
Tua-llu cat iliitni-am
anguyalliniut nani qagaani nunat
iliitni Kuigpagmiut,
tua makumiunek ceńarmiunek ingluluteng.
5
Tua-i taukut Kuigpagmiut
ingluteng
tua cirlakluki nangllinikait.
Uumek-gguq
angutmek
ilangqelliniut

354

THE BOY WHO MADE PEACE

Mike Angaiak of Tununak

***

1
In those times,
a long time ago,
people
fought
without guns,
using bows as weapons instead.
Because in those days the white man was hardly even around,
and they never, never used *kass'aq* things.
2
I am going to tell you a story here
about what I remember about what I heard.
3
In those times
those[1]
Hooper Bay people out there or people from here—
you've heard of the Yukon people out there, about the Yukon people
    upriver—
at that time they were enemies and they used to fight,
but only in the summer time [with the Yukon people].
4
So one time
they fought out there in one of those villages
on the Yukon;
they were fighting with the coastal people around here.
5
Those Yukon people
overcame their enemies
and evidently wasted them.
They had
this man
among them

waten irniangyuunani.
Maa-i yuut ayuqenritut ilait irniangesciigatetuut.
Mikelngurmek waten tangerciigatetuut tayim' pisqumallermegteggun.
6
Tua-llu tuqurqellermeggni tuani,
ukuk anngaqelriik
kingumek uitatqallinilukek,
tauk' anngaqlutek.
7
Tua-ll'-am tauna ingluita

Ciquyaq, Bob Charlie, circa 1980. Photo by Andrew J. Chikoyak.

who apparently couldn't have any children.
People are not all alike; some can't have children.
They can't bring forth children as expected.
6
So then, while they were slaughtering them,
they saved these two brothers
for last;
those two were an older brother and his younger brother.
7
And when their enemies

anngaa tauna piamegteggu,
kemga man'a
waten
unatmeggnek waten piqtaalliniluku, kemga tauna
taum anngaan.
8
Tuaten-am pirraarluku
qanlliniut,
"Una tang wani cakaunrilnguq!
Caungaituq una."
Egmian tuqutelliniluku.
Taukuk tua-i waten usvingelriarulutek elpecicetun waten
apqiitnek usvinglutek waten
miketkacaganrirlutek.
9
Tua-ll'-am taun' uyuraa cali tuaten
kemga tamana
cali taucetun anngaatun
waten kemga man'a nunurarraarluku qanlliniut,
"Aling uumi-llu wani tuqutellerkaani qununaqsaaqvaa!
Una tang wani tuqutellerkaa
tuqucunaicaaqvagta!
Kemga man'a
assirpagta!
Una tang wani,
nalirpeci-qa tayima
teguluku anglicarluku
piyunritaa?"
10
Aren taum tua-i
nukalpiam, taum angutem,
irniangyuilami,
pilliniuq, "Ataki wiinga-qa
pikumku,
qaill' ayuqa?"
Tua-i
taumun
pivkalliniat
angutet iliitnun.
11
Tua-i teguluku utrutliniluku nunameggnun tamaavet.

went to that elder brother,
they examined him several times with their hands,
doing like so
on the flesh
of that elder brother.[2]
8
Having done so,
they said,
"Look, this one here is good for nothing!
This one won't be of any use."
They killed him immediately.[3]
These two were at the point of acquiring sense, like you guys,
getting what they call understanding,[4]
no longer being so small.
9
Then again [they did] the same thing with that younger brother,
feeling that flesh of his
just as they had done with his elder brother,
and having squeezed and examined his flesh thus, they said,
"*Aling*, this guy here, to kill him would be such a waste!
Behold him here, the idea of killing him,
oh, he ought not to be killed!
His flesh here,
how good it is!
Behold him here,
which one of you
would want to take him
and raise him?"
10
Aren, that
great hunter, that man,
because he couldn't have any children,
said, "Now then, if I
were to take him,
how would it be?"
Then
they
let him
take him.
11
So taking him he returned with him to their own village.

***

12
Cunawa-gguq imna tauna taum tua-i anglicallinikii
taum angutem
taukuni nunani.
13
Kiituani angturringelliniuq.
Waten angturringartellrani,
cali tua-i murilkelluku, murilkelliniluku,
ukunun nunalgutmeggnun
qaillun pinayukluku
tua-i-gg' tamaa-i inglukluteng ayuqngameng.
14
Maa-i mikelnguut makut
waten cukanrilnguut piyaurtellrat. Tua-i pivakarluni
angturrian
qayinariaku-llu
taum atiin qayilliniluku,
aulukestiin taum.
15
Cali tua tuaten ayuqengraan,
tua-i cali murilkelluku
ukunun ilainun
waten
qaillun
pinayukluku waten nunalgutkevkenaku,
piamegteggu.
16
Tua-i-llu cam iliini
nantellrani tayima, ak'a
qavciulluku aūgkut
piyaaqelliniat.
Aren taum tua-i ellangartellermini qasgimun itqerrluni qanerluni tuaten
pilliniuq,
"Arenqiapaa ak'a-llu pillrulliat!"
Maaten tua pilliniuq tua waten pivkenaku tua-i
piyaaqerraarluku taq'ertellinilriit.
17
Tua-i-llu
tamaa-i
atii, tauna-gg' tua-i aulukestii, umyuarteqenglliniuq
waten mernungluni cumikurallminek,

360

***

12
Indeed, they say, that man evidently raised
the boy
in that village there.
13
Finally he began to grow up.
Thus when he began to grow up,
he [the man who was raising him], kept a close eye on him,
thinking
that their fellow villagers
might do him harm because they were enemies.
14
Children, in general,
are slow in getting started.[5] Time passed,
and when he had grown up,
and it was time to make a kayak for him,
that father of his, his guardian,
made a kayak for him.
15
Moreover, even though he was grown up,
he kept an eye on him
in case
one of those people
there
might do him harm, since he was not from their village,
since [he feared] they might get him.
16
Then one day
when he [the foster-father] was off somewhere,
a gang of them
tried to get him.
Aren, when he [the foster-father] realized this, he rushed into the
    qasgiq as he was saying,
"*Arenqiapaa*! Oh my gosh, maybe they already got him!"
He found out that they had tried to get him,
but, when they heard him [coming in], they stopped all of a sudden.
17
So then
his father,
his guardian, began to think of
how he was getting tired of continually watching him,

nunainun taũgaam uterrluku pikan
assinrunayukluku.
Tamaa-i-llu
maligut'langluni qayarluni qayillruani taum aulukesteḿi.

18
Tua-i keltelnguluni tauna atii,
tauna-gg' tua-i anglicartii.

***

19
Tua-i-llu pivakarluni taum tua qanrutlinia, "Alingnaqvaa!
Waniwa-qa kingunerpenun
utercuumiituten?
Tua-i tang wii cumikelngukemken.
Ukut wani nunat
nunalgutkenrilamegteggen
kelnariut
waten nallumni qaillun pinayukluten.
Waten pillerkan una qununaqsaaquq.
Tua-i-qa nunavnun uterrluten

362

thinking that it would be better
if he would return to his own village.
At that time
the boy began to accompany him in his own kayak since his
    guardian had made him one.
18
So that father of his, the one who raised him,
was getting tired of having to be on his guard.

***

19
So then one day he told him, "*Alingnaqvaa*! Oh goodness me,
wouldn't you want to go back
to where you came from?
I am worn out from watching you.
Because the ones here
are not your fellow villagers,
they must always be watched now
lest they do something to you without me knowing it.
I hate to see something like this happen to you.
Shouldn't you go back to your own village

Left to right are *Tumailnguq,* Mike Albert; *Cakataar,* Jack Angaiak; *Tumailnguq,*
Dick Lincoln; *Uqamailnguq,* Augustine Heavy; and *Arnaucuaq,* Mike Angaiak,
Tununeq, circa 1980. Photo by Andrew J. Chikoyak.

uitayugnganrituten?"
20
Taum tua-i pillinia, "Tua-i-wa pisqumakuvnga
tua piyallilrianga tuaten."
"Ataki,
nunavnun taũgaam uterrluten
pikuvet assinruyartuq."
Nutaan uptelliniluku
taum
anglicartiin.
21
Tua-ll' pillinia, "Kitaki,
ayagniartuten erenrani ayagyaqunak!
Unukan taũgaam ayagniartuten. Erenrani ayagyaaqekuvet
tayima aipaagni kingunerpeggun maligciiqelliatgen."
Tua-gg' waten tamakut alerquasteteng maligngallruamegteki waten
atateng qanellrit,
maligtaquluki pitullruameng. Tua-i-'m tuaten
piarkaurtelliniuq tauna tan'gaurluq.

***

22
Tua-lli pivakarluni tua-i unugngan ayalliniluni taum tua-i
anglicarteñi pisquuciatun.
Tua-i unugngan ayalliniluni kinguneni nallunrilamiki taukut nunat,
tuavet ayagluni.
Ceñarmiunguuq-gguq tauna, Kuigpagmek tamaa-i
taukuk tegualqaak tauna apqiitnek,
tuqutevkenaku teguluku,
anglicallruluku tua-i tan'gurraq tauna.

23
Tua-i nunaminun tuavet tekitelliniuq.

***

24
Tua-i-llu uksurluni.
Uksullrani tauna tan'gurraq
calingelliniuq
waten qasgimi, qasgimi taũgaam calitullruameng,
cauyamek, cauyacuarmek
calilliniluni.

and remain there?"
20
Then he answered him, "If that is what you want of me,
I suppose I could do that."
"Well then,
If you return to your own village,
it would be better."
Finally that foster parent
of his
got him ready.
21
So he said to him, "*Kitaki*! All right,
you can go, but don't go during the day!
You should only go at night. If you go during the day,
they might come after you, following you."
Since they always heeded those who gave advice, like
what their fathers said,
since they were accustomed to obey, thus
that boy had to do that.

***

22
So one day he left at night as his
foster parent had advised him.
He went at night and since he knew where his home was,
he went there.
It is said that he was one of the people who had inhabited the coast
and was taken by those two from the Yukon,
being what is called a captive,
and that boy was captured without being killed,
and raised by his captors.
23
So he got there to his own village.

***

24
Then winter came.
When winter came,
the boy began to work
in the *qasgiq*, since they only worked in the *qasgiq*,
making
a drum, a small drum.

365

25
Tamatum-gguq nalliini kevgiyuitellruut, yurayuitellruut
waten taũgaam tua-i anguyagyarturluteng nunanun
ayagaqluteng.

26
Tuamte-ll' taun' cauyaq taqngamiu,
muragamek tuamte-ll' calilliniluni. (Man'a maa-i
elitaqciqngatarci
piinanerpeceñi; uani agayuvigmi ilii qancuaqautekillruuq.)
27
Tua-llu
muragaq
calillinia.[a]
Pikna kangra uitermek
mingulliniluku imumek kavirlimek.
Uiterret tayim' imkut kavirliugut.
Man'a-llu qukaa minguunaku
cali taqliniluku.
28
Tuamte-ll' taqngamiu,
tamana
qatellria,
imkut allgiaraat,
teqsuqrit—icigg imkut allgiaraat teqsuqrit tak'lalriit—
kangrat-am qivyurrarnek
elliqervikaqluki kapusvikliniluku.
29
Taukut-llu nunalgutain aptelaryaaqelliniat,
"Qaillun umyuarteqluten
tamakunek calisit?"
Taum-llu kiuyuunaki
qaillun-llu qanrucuunaki.
Tauna tan'gaurluq
ellminek umyuangluni
tuaten tua-i
calilliniluni.
30
Tua-i-llu kiagluni.
Kiakartelluku
waten iliit,
yun'erraullgutmi, pillinia

25
At that time, it is said, they didn't have messenger feasts and they
    didn't have dances,
but only went to other villages
to fight battles.
26
Now then, when he was done with the drum,
he again set to work on a piece of wood. (You will probably
recognize this
as we go along; some of it was told at the Church down there.[6])
27
So then
he worked
on the wood.
The top
he painted with red ochre.
Ochres, *uiterret*, are red.
He left the middle without paint
and then finished.
28
Moreover, when he was done with it,
[he took] that
white part and
[from] tails of
an old-squaw duck—you know the tails of old-squaw ducks are long—
he took those and put downy feathers on the tips of them,
sticking them in[to the unpainted part].
29
And his fellow villagers would ask him,
"What are you thinking of
as you make those?"
And he never answered them
and didn't say anything.
That boy
came up with
that idea on his own
and worked on it like that.
30
Then it was summer.
In the early summer
the boy said to one of them,
who was a young man like himself

(Taukut tua-i nunat camiungullrit wiinga
niitellrunritanka)
tua tuavet unayaqlinia, "Ataki-qaa
taukunun
maligcunritarpenga ayakuma?"
31
Taum tua pillinia,
"Tua-i-wa maligeskilaken pisqumakuvnga."

***

32
Tua-i kiagngan nutaan ayallinilutek
maliklutek
tuavet tua nunanun Kuigpagmun, qagaani nunat
qagkut im' naliitnun.
33
Ayaglutek anguarlutek (levaaryugnaunatek)
qayakun. Tauna-llu
caliallni cauyacuaq tauna-llu muragaq
ayaullukek.

***

34
Maaten-gguq tua tuavet tekitelliniuk,
waten-am cali erenrani
tuavet iluvallerkartek piamegen'gu ununercirlutek,
kuigata uatiinun uavet pilutek pilliniuk
uitavkenateng
taukut nunat!
35
Tua-i-llu
unugngan
itrallinilutek
ikavet-llu kuigem akianun,
qasgim akianun,
mayullinilutek.
Tua tuantellinilutek unugpak.
36
Tua-ll' errluni.
Erteqerluni atam, erteqertelluku,
makut alakellinilukek
taukuk qayak.

(I didn't hear where that
village was),
asking him to come along, saying, "*Ataki,*
when I leave,
wouldn't you like to come with me?"
31
That [companion of his] replied,
"I shall accompany you if you want me to."

***

32
So sometime during the summer they went
together
to that place, to one
of those villages out there on the Yukon.
33
They left paddling (definitely not using an outboard motor)
by kayak. And
he brought along
that little drum he made and that piece of wood.

***

34
Then they reached that place,
and because they were worried about
going into that village during the day, they waited for night,
and landing downriver from their [enemies] village, lo and behold, they
saw that the people of that village
were [not retiring for the night, but were] restless and moving about!
35
So then
when it got dark,
they moved upriver
and crossed over
to the bank across from the *qasgiq,*
and went up onto the bank.
They stayed there all night.
36
Then daylight came.
As daylight came, just when dawn arrived,
these [villagers] noticed
those two kayaks.

37
Tua-i-llu
maaten-gguq murilkelluki pilliniuk
tua-am
anguyagyarturluteng
ayakunaluteng tamaa-i
uptengllinilriit waten nunanun,
tamakut nunat allat tuqurqelluki waten pinaluki,
anguyagluki.
38
Iliit tailliniluni,
taingami pillinia,
"Waqaa,
calutek
maavet maani waten pillinicetek?"
39
Taum-am
tuaten qanrucani
tauna cauyacuar teguqerluku,
an'arrluku
qaillun-llu qanerpegnani kaugtuaqalliniluku.
40
Tua kaugtuaqerraarluku qayaminun iterrluku.
Tauna-ll' arvirluni qasgimun tayim' itliniluni.
41
Uitavkenateng tua-i kangarluteng agkut qasgiluteng tuaten.
Tua-i-ll' piqerluni anngami tuamte-ll'
maa-i tailliniluni ketiignun piami pilliniuq,
"Ikegkut qasgimiut qanertiita, atanrata,
arviisqaatek.
Calutek, qaillun pilutek,
pillertek nallunricugaat."

42
Nutaan tuaten qanerngan
tua-i arvirluku maliggluku,
arvillinilutek qasgim-ll' uavet ketiinun qayatek mayurrlukek.
43
Tua-i-ll' tagngamek
taum tua-i aipaan
cauyaq tauna
cali-ll' tauna muragaq caliallni teguluku

37
So then,
upon observing them, those two saw
that
they were preparing
to go to war,
getting ready to go to a village
so that they could kill off those other villagers,
waging war against them.
38
One of them came over
and when he came he said to the boy,
"*Waqaa*,
what are you two
doing here?"
39
When he
said that to him,
the boy took his little drum
and drew it out,
and without saying anything, he beat it a few times.
40
After beating it for a minute he put it back in his kayak.
Then the man went across to the *qasgiq* and went in.
41
Those across there were restless and walking about, and some were
        going into the *qasgiq*.
Then after a while the same man came out,
and when he got below them he said to the two of them,
"The speaker of that *qasgiq* across there, their leader,
wants you to come across.
They want to know
what the two of you are doing and what you're up to."
42
When he said that,
they went across with him,
going across and pulling their kayaks up in front of the *qasgiq*.
43
Then when they went up,
that one
took the drum,
as well as the wooden staff he had worked on,

371

tag'llinilutek qasgimun.

***

44
Tua-i-llu
iterlutek.
Iterluni kiarqurallinikii, kiarquralliniluku man' qasgiq.
Tua-i makut tangvallragni imkurluteng
nalluyurnaqluteng makut
angutet qaũgkut-llu tan'gurraat egkumi uitalriit.
45
Uivurluku pillinia imna tua ua-i
tauna anglicartellra
tuanlluni!
46
Iterluni taum
elitaqa'arrluku
taum tua-i pilliniluku,
taum anglicartellran,
"Waqaa,
cunawa-am elpenguuten!
Camek waniw' ircaqungqercit?
Cassurluten tang tua maavet maa-i
taillinisit?"
47
Tua-i-llu tauna
kanavet qasgim natranun
nacitain akuliitnun
muragaq napartelliniluku.
Tauna-ll' cauyacuar call'[b] tua tegumiaqluku.
48
Tua-i aptellinia taum, "Caluten taukuk
maavet taicikek?"
Tua-ll' tauna cauyaq teguamiu
kaugtuaqalliniluku, kaugtuarluku,
pillinia, "Una waniwa cauyaq
waniwa niitarci ava-i.
Man'a-gg' call' kaugtuutaa maa-i.
Una cauyaq
mat'umek
mimermek piinani qaillun calisciigatuq."
Kaugtuaqalliniluku.

372

and together they went up to the *qasgiq*.

***

44
So then
they entered.
Entering, he [the boy] glanced about him, looking around the *qasgiq*.
When they stared at him, it was as though
these men and the boys in the back
made him feel unwelcome.
45
He looked all around the place, and there he was by the exit,
the one who had raised him!
He was there!
46
He went in and that one,
the one who raised him,
recognized him
and said to him,
" *Waqaa*,
so it is you?
Wow, what do you have for a heart?[7]
For what purpose
did you come here?"
47
Then he took that
piece of wood
and stuck it on the floor of the *qasgiq*
between the floor planks.
He held onto that little drum.
48
Then that one asked him, "Why
did you bring those here?"
So then when he took that drum,
he beat it for a minute, beating it,
and said to him, "You just heard
this drum here.
Now here is its drumstick.
This drum,
without
this stick cannot work."
He beat it for a moment.

49
Tua-ll' pilliniuq,
"Uum wanigg' cauyam
kangia waniwa elpeceńun qanrutkeqatarqa.
Una tang waniwa cauyaq
kangingqelria kenkutmek,
ilaliurutmek!
50
Cali nerulluni camek umyuarteqevkenani
kangingqertuq una waniw'."
Cauyaq una kaugtuaqaqluku.
"Cali-llu
nunat allat waten aqvaluki nunaniryugtelluki uum waniwa
piarkaukai.
Tua-i tuaten
una waniw' cauyaq tuaten ayuquq, umyuartequsngauq.
Uuggun cauyakun wangkuta
ilaput kenekluki
tuqurqutevkenata
pikumta, uum waniwa
tamana kepsaraa wangkutnek tuqurququrallerput, uum waniw' cauyam."
51
Tuamte-ll' tauna muragaq ullagluku
man'a kangra
uitermek mingulek kavirlimek
pillinia, "Tua-i tang waniw' wangkuta maani yugni waniw'
    ayuqucirput tangrrarci!
Kesianek aunralriakut nunam qaingani
waten anguyagaqamta; anguyagaqavci
waten ilaci nunam qainganun aunralartuq; maa-i tang man'
    kavircelnguq!" Uiteq tua tamana
tuaten-am kangililliniluku.
52
Tua-i-llu tamana
qatellria
tuamte-ll' pillinia,
"Man'a tang maa-i qatellria, minguilnguq tangrrarci!
Nunam qainga uksuraqami qatrituuq
camek tunguuralriamek catairulluni.
Maa-i tang man' uksuq;
uksuulria!"

49
Then he said,
"I'm going to explain the meaning
of this drum here to you.
You see, this drum
symbolizes love
and cooperation with one another!
50
Moreover, to share with one another without thinking ill,
this is what this drum represents."
He would beat it every now and then.
"And again,
this one here shall bring different villages together
and give them joy.
For this purpose
this drum was intended.
If we use this drum,
we shall love our neighbors,
no longer killing one another,
and this one here,
this drum, shall sever us from the action of our perpetual self-slaughter."
51
Next he went to that wooden staff,
whose top was dyed
with red ochre
and spoke of it, "Behold, you see then how we, the people, are!
We are constantly bleeding on the surface of this land
when we wage war; when you wage war,
some of you bleed on the surface of the land; behold this part that is
     red!" Thus he designated a meaning
for that red ochre.

52
So then
he next spoke of that
white part,[8]
"Behold this white part, the part you see that isn't painted!
When winter covers the land, it becomes white
and dark spots are absent.
Behold, this represents winter;
it is winter!

53
Tuamte-ll' tamakut
imkut allgiaraat
teqsuqrit kapusngalriit pillinii,
"Makut-llu tang maa-i
pitarkat
nunam qaingani amllertut.
Piciatun pektellriit
wangkuta unakluki,
tuqulluki.
Arca yugnek
tuqurqiviiqnata, makut taũgaam ungungssit pektellriit
wangkuta tuqulluki.
Nutaan-llu tuqucimarikumteki
nutaan
quyurrluki,
uuggun waniw' cauyaq aturluku.
Quyurcirraarluta nunat kelegluki allat
nerevkaqumteki nerulluki, nutaan-lli
assirpaa!
Maa-i makut tuaten kangingqertut."
54
Tua-i tamakunek qanerturautellinii.
55
Piqerluteng ukut nepaunateng qasgiq-llu nepaunani.

***

56
Tua-i-ll' piqerluni
tauna tua-i anglicartellra qanlliniuq,
"Alingnaqvaa-ll'
elpeni!
Ilumun-lli aũg'umi
piciqsuuminaqsaaqvaa wangkuta tuaten piyaureskumta!
Ilumun yuullgutput
waten unguviit man'a arca nanilicarpiiqnaku!
Ilumun taũgaam una cauyaq aturluku
tuaten
kenkulluta ilaliurulluta pitukumta
assirpaa-ll' nutaan, assiryarpaa!"
57
Aren imkut qasgimiut

53

Then again he took
those tail feathers of old-squaw ducks
that were stuck in [the staff] and spoke of them,
"Behold the wild game here,
which abounds
on the surface of the land.
All kinds that move about
we catch
and kill.
We must stop killing people
and kill the animals which move about
instead.
At last when we have killed [the animals],
then
gather [the people] together,
using this drum.
After we have invited and assembled the other villages,
if we share our food and feast with them, this is
indeed a very good thing!
This is what they signify."

54

So he spoke to them of these things.

55

All of a sudden they were silent and the *qasgiq* was without sound.

***

56

So then it happened
that the one who raised him said,
"Bless
you!
Indeed that
is something greatly to be desired should we begin to act thus!
Indeed we have to stop
cutting short the lives of our fellow men!
Indeed we should only use this drum
thus
and love and cooperate with one another;
now that is a very good thing, that would be very good!"

57

Aren, those in the *qasgiq*

tuaten tua qan'ngartelliniut tauna qanerngan
ilaseng. "Ataki tang wangkuta
tamana anguyak taqluku waten taũgaam cauyaq aturluku
piyaureskumta nutaan
assirciqlinivaa!"
58
Tua-i
nutaan tuaten piarkaurtelliniata
tua-i nutaan
utertelliniuk.

***

59
Tua-i-gguq taum tan'gaurluum
umyuangluni kia-llu qanruteksaunaku.
Tamaa-i

began to talk like that because of what
their kinsman had said. "We should
stop that fighting and instead start using the drum,
and if we finally started to do so,
that would indeed be very good!"
58
So
when at last they were going to do that,
they returned
home.

***

59
It is said that boy
came up with the idea without anyone telling him.
At that time

tuaten-gguq cunaw' tua umyuarteqluni taukugnek tua calillrullinilria.
60
Taum-gguq tua-i qanemciullermini
taum anguyagyaraq man' ak'a
avani, ilalkucaraq,
taum tua taqevkalqaa.
61
Man'a taũgaam yuraryaraq
nutaan piciryaraqsagulluku
waten
taum tua qanellratun.
Waten maaken keltevkenateng,
canek
yuilqumek ungungssinek piciatun tuntunek
nutaan pissurluteng
neqkameggnek
camek-llu umyuarrluuqertevkenateng alingevkenateng-llu quyurrluki
nutaan.
Tamaa-i tamakut unangkengateng cali nunanun allanun
waten aqvaluki,
nerulluki,
neruyutkameggnek tamaa-i piyaurrluteng,
tua tamaa Kevgiryaurrluteng.
62
Tamaani-gguq kevgiyuitellruut
tamatum nalliini.
Waten taũgaam tua-i inglukulluteng
nunalgutkenrilnguut anguyaulluteng
pitullruluteng. Tua-i-gguq taum
man'a anguyagyaraq
tua taqevkalqaa.
63
Tauna yun'erraq
umyuartulliniami
tua tuaten cal' caliluki taukut.
Tua-i-gguq ayagneqluku
anguyayuirulluteng kevgirluteng taũgaam waten nunanun allanun
aqvaluki
yuraryaurtellruut.
64
Tuaten tua-i
waniw' taktaluku

he evidently made those two, having thought about that.
60
It was said that he, when this story occurred,
brought to an end
the fighting, the torturing,
which took place a long time ago.
61
However, this dancing
became a tradition
according
to what he said.
Instead of being wary and mistrustful,
they hunted
for all kinds of animals and caribou
in the wilderness
for their food
and did not dread anything, nor were they afraid at last to gather them.
With what they caught,
they invited other villages
and fed them,
gathering food for that purpose,
and at this time they began to have Messenger Feasts.

62
Back then [before this time] they never invited
other villages to come over.
Instead those from different villages
were enemies and would customarily
wage war. So that boy, it is said,
brought an end
to such warfare.
63
That young person
because he was wise
worked like that preparing those two things.
So beginning from that time
they stopped waging war, and instead sent invitations to other
    villages to have them come over
and dance.
64
This is
the length

aũgna ava-i tuaten qanemciq
qanemciuguq.

***

65
Tua-llu
up'nerkaq
pilillruut ua-i agayuvigmi
tanglaraci.

66
Cauyaq aũgna-gg' muragaq
mat'um maa-i qanemcim ugna ua-i
qanemcilqa. Ugkut ua-i agayuvigmi tangtukci
kangikai aũgna ava-i qanemciqa, ugkut ua-i
agayuvigmi itrutellrit.

67
Waten una umyuarkiulluku tayima,
uum wani tayim' Agayutem
umyuarkitellrungataa assilriamek ikayuutekamek
tuaggun tua-i
cauyakun waten Kevgikun maaggun,
anglaniluteng cali-llu ilateng kenekluki canek cikirturluki ikayurluki.
Ilait imkut ak'a avani neqmek amllermek
piyuitellruameng tamakut tuaten cali
pisciigalnguut arcaqerluki angutailnguut cal' kevgirqameng cali ilakluki
   tamaa-i
maligutenrilengraata neqkanek cali
aruqetullrukait tamana tamaa-i.

***

68
Tua-i aũgna ava-i iquklituq
qanemciqa.

382

of the story
just told.

***

65
So then
last spring
they made what you see
in the Church.[9]
66
The drum and that stick
down there figure in this story
which I just told. The ones you see down there in the Church,
[they] symbolize this story, the ones which they
brought into the Church.
67
Thus he was inspired
by God,
who seems to have given him intentions to work good
through these,
through the drum and through the Messenger Feasts,
[through] their having fun and loving others enough to give them
      things to help them out.
In those days some of them didn't get a lot of food and
when they had Messenger Feasts they would especially give to those
who couldn't hunt or had no providers, including them
in the distribution of food
even if they didn't come to the dance.

***

68
So it has come to an end,
this story of mine.

APANUUGPAK ANGUYAGMI

Qulvarkaq Tununermiu

***

1
Tua-i-wa wiinga tang tua-i una Apanuugpak kaumanrilkeka cakneq.
Tua-i taũgaam uumiku tayima qanemcisqekuvcia qanemciyarturciqua
   Apaqassugarmek taũgaam,
taum wani
Apanuugpiim ciungani
yuurtellermek.
2
Tua-llu ukut Apanuugpiinkut ikaken ika-i Engelumiunek,
   nunallret quliitni ikegkut,
nunallret.
Nunallernek ika-i pilarait.
Ikegkut-gguq ika-i nunallret
Engelumiungullruut
taukut Apanuugpiinkut Panik-llu Pangalgalria-llu nunallrat.
Umkumiut kiatiini imna kanaryaraq,
Apanuugpiim ika-i ikna
nunallra.
4
Tauna tua-i
Apanuugpak
waten pitgutqata'arqami-gguq maaggun naqugtelartuq
imarnillugaaraagnek-llu all'uni.
Tua-i-gguq taũgken pitgutellmi taktaciatun imarnillugaagnek aturluni
anguyaulluni.
Ak'a tamaani nutegmek nallullermeggni
urluvernek taũgaam caskirluteng
pitgaquluki yuut tuqurqelallruit.

384

APANUUGPAK DURING THE WAR

Bob Hooper of Tununak

***

1
I don't know *Apanuugpak* all that well.
But if you ask me to come and tell a story about *Apaqassugaq*,
    I will come and tell about him instead,
the one
who was born
before *Apanuugpak*.
2
So *Apanuugpak* and the others [were] at *Engelumiut* across there,
    above the deserted village, across there
at the old village.
They call that *Nunallret*.
That old village across there
is where the village of *Engelumiut* was
and that is where *Apanuugpak, Panik* and *Pangalgalria* lived.
Behind *Umkumiut*, where the trail leads down [to the ocean beach],
that is where *Apanuugpak*
once lived.
4
That
Apanuugpak,
when he was about to shoot an arrow, would put a belt on around here
and put on seal-gut raingear.
All through the time that he was engaged in war, shooting arrows, he
would wear his shabby old raingear.
As they didn't know anything about guns a long time ago,
they used bows and arrows as weapons
to slaughter people.

***

5
Caqerluteng ayalliniluteng avavet
yaatmun curugluteng.
Curuuciinateng-gga tua ellmegteggun ayagluteng.
Taukuuluteng tua-i anguyaggsuutet pingayun;
Apanuugpak,
Panik,
una-gg' iliit
Pangalgalria.
6
Tua-i taukut cali ciunrit,
ciunrita atrit nunat nalluanka.
7
Kuigkun tua-i tamaaggun asgulliniluteng.
Tua-i asgurluteng.
8
Asguinanermeggni taukugnek yun'erragnek tekicameng
maligglukek.
9
(Tua-i niigartellemtun maa-i qanemciqatartua wii-llu ukvekevkenaki
     tangvallrunrilamki.
Tua-i taũgaam ciutegma imagkenek waniw' qanemcitamci.)
10
Taukugnek qayagnek maligtelliniluteng.
Tua-i paangriinanermeggni
aipaan pillinia,
"Camiut negaatnun napteqatartutek!"
Tua-i paangriinanermeggni
cingik ingna tekicarturluku.
Cingik taun' igvaumaalliniat tua nunarrluut-gguq tuar agkut.
Aren tua-i taqerrluteng ameltunritlian-llu tamana,
erinam engelqaqngaku agkut nunat,
qacigarrluteng tua-i.

12
Pugtaqalliniluteng.
13
Tua-i-ll' pugtaqertelluki imkut qayat tamakut
up'ngelliniluteng tua-i.
Ulyugluni-gguq man'a.
Ulmek tua-i tekiucugpagluki.

***

5

It happened once that they left
going that way, on a raid.
Well, they weren't exactly going on a raid, but left on a whim.
It was these three lethal weapons;[1]
Apanuugpak,
Panik,
and their partner
Pangalgalria.
6

As for that place to which they were heading,
I can't remember the name of that village.
7

They evidently went upriver,
going against the current of that river.
8

As they went against the current they came across two young men
and pursued them.
9

(I am going to tell the story as I heard it, although I don't believe
    it because I didn't actually obverse them.
I am only telling you what I heard with my ears.)
10

They pursued those two kayaks.
As they paddled along with their double-bladed paddles,
his partner said to him,
"You are going to get trapped in some village's snare!"
As they paddled along with their double-bladed paddles,
they were approaching a point over there.
As they slowly went around that point, all those houses across there
    came into view.
Aren, they suddenly stopped, perhaps because that river wasn't wide,
and also because that village was within voice shot,
and they relaxed.
12

Then they were just floating, not moving.
13

As they were sitting there afloat, [the men in] those kayaks
started to get ready.
The tide, it was said, was coming in.
The tide was coming in strong.

14
Aren tamakut imkut
qayat pugtertellriit tuaten
pitegcauteteng qisraksuarait katagturluki pillratni, caqerluni imna
Apanuugpak murilkevkenani, umyugaa tua qamna qamerrlugluni,
murilkevkenani piinanermini piqalliniuq
iliit una Panik
qisraksuarnek tamakunek pugtalrianek avurturalria anguarluni
    ullakaniqaqluki.

15
Taum tua-i Apanuugpiim anguyaggsuutngungermi umyugaa
    alingluni pillermini
tauna tua tangrramiu
qamenritellranek uum
pilliniluni,
umyugaa qamna
qamenriqertelliniluni. Alingevkenani una
Panigtaak
tamakunek qisraksuarnek
pillinilria. Tua-llu-gguq taum Apanuugpiim aptellinia,
"Aling, cakarpeneg-mi tanem tua tamakunek quyurciurcit?"
Tua-llu-gguq
taum Paniim kiulliniluku,
"Makut icigg' tua-i
caliaqellrat taqesciigatyagarluteng ayuqelalriit.
Wanigga tua-i tamakut taqesciigatellrat
umyuaqluku
avurturaranka."

***

16
Aling tua tamaani piinanermeggni
taum imum
Pangalgalriim qanrutlinia tauna
Apanuugpak
(tuqluutengqerrlutek tua-i piamek
uumek)
tuqlullinia,
"Tugulullraa,
erinan-ggem anguyagpenun alikniaqaat.
Qaku wanigga anteqataraqsiu erinan?"

388

14

Aren, so those
[other] kayaks were floating down,
and when [the men in them] were dropping off their wooden
    containers for arrowheads,[2] it was then that
Apanuugpak, who was preoccupied, feeling somewhat dismayed,
and not paying attention, noticed
their comrade, *Panik,*
was collecting those floating wooden containers, paddling right up
    to them.

15

That *Apanuugpak,* even though he was a lethal weapon, was afraid
but when he saw that he [Panik],
was not daunted or dismayed,
all of a sudden
his mind
was no longer downcast either. Not being afraid,
the one named *Panik*
was gathering up arrowhead
containers. Then, it was said, that *Apanuugpak* asked him,
"*Aling,* what are you collecting those for?"
And then
Panik answered him,
"You know,
it takes a long time to make one of these.
Considering
how hard they are to finish,
I'm gathering them up."[3]

***

16

Aling, so while they were there,
that one,
Pangalgalria, spoke to that
Apanuugpak[4]
(since they called each other
this)
calling him,
"*Tugulullraa,*[5]
they say that your enemies are afraid of your voice.
When are you going to let your voice out?"

Aren, taum Apanuupiim-am tauna Pangalgalria kiulliniluku,
atataarqu pinariksaitniluku.

17
Aling aren tua-i-gguq tang man'a asgulirnerat tua-i pugtertellria,
   qayaurrluni avavet.

18
Tua-i makut tekiucugciungartaqateng
anguarluteng tua qimakaniraqluteng.
Ellait-gguq taugken tua-i tamakut anguyameng maani uqratni
   uitiimeng tua tekicugciurluteng piurallratni
qaciggluteng tekiucugciurpegnateng.

19
Taukut-gguq tua-i
ilangqellinilriit
Ukinqucugpalegmek.
Tauna-gguq tua-i
qayaan ingna ciungani ukinqucua amirkamek tua-i amituuq, patuluku.
Tauna tua-i
Ukinqucugpalek aanangqelliniami aanii-gguq tua-i cenirtaalria maani.
Tua
nangerrluni tua kangarluni,

Covering an *angyapik* 'skin boat' frame, 1948. Photo from Jesuit Oregon
Province Archives, Gonzaga University, negative number 506.09.

Aren, that *Apanuugpak*[6] answered *Pangalgalria*,
saying in a while, that it wasn't time yet.
17
Aling, it was said that the area downstream was filled with floating
    kayaks all the way across.
18
When the incoming tide got to them [the enemy],
they would paddle and retreat a bit.
Since, however, they [the three men] were on the lee side of their
    adversaries, whereas the enemy were being carried along
    with the incoming tide,
the incoming tide didn't present them with any problems since it
    wasn't carrying them along.[7]
19
It was said that the enemy
had *Ukinqucugpalek*[8]
with them.
It is said that the hole
on the prow of his kayak was covered with a single young bearded
    seal skin.[9]
Since that
Ukinqucugpalek still had his mother, she was walking back and
    forth [along the shore].

ceńirtellinilria taum wani
Ukinqucugpalgem aanii.
Tua-ll' tua erinani anlluku alerquciaraluni,
tauna im' Ukinqucugpalek
atraqertelliniluni kayimqerluk' kinguneni anguarluni-ll' tua ketmun
    ayagturaqerluni,
aren pitangyussiyaagpakaami tua ketvaaraqerluni, maani taukut
    qayat pingayun ciuqratni,
aren qaillun piqallermini paluarturlulliniluni!

20
Palucan tua qallarvallrani Apanuugpiim tamakut nagiiquyani
    teguluki qapengtelliniluku.
Qapengteqerluku akitmiaqerluteng taukut imkut
nagiiquyain kangrit pekangruyagluteng tua tayima kit'elliniluteng.
Cama'anlengraan mer'em aciani narulkarluku-am tua-i tauna,
Ukinqucugpalek tauna,
nall'arrluku.
Aanii-gguq-wa paugna ceńirtaalria.[a]
Qayaq tua tamana palungqaqaan
taum imum Pangalgalriim tuqlulliniluku, "Tugulullraqa,
erinan-ggem anguyagpenun alikniaqaat!"
Tua-llu-gguq nutaan
kiulliniluku tua-i nutaan maa-i pinariyaaqniluku.

21
Apanuugpiim taum anguarutni taman' tegulliniluku
qanrullukek tumemikun, kingunermikun, maligcesqelluni.
22
Tua-i-ll' im' Apanuugpak
tamaani
mikurqaaraat taukut
tungiitnun erinani,
erinani, anlluku tuaten
curukalliniluk' taukut imkut qayarugaat. Aren erinani-gguq ancaku
    qayat imkut
avegyartulliniluteng, qukvirluteng.
Erinani tua aturluku paungelliniluni
taukut qayat tungiitnun.
23
Tua-i-gguq makut maa-i ayangarcan ava-i, maliggluku-ll' taukuk
    ilagken,

392

She
would suddenly stand up and pace around,
going from here to there,
Ukinqucugpalek's mother would.
Then she called out, giving him directions,
and that *Ukinqucugpalek*
suddenly pushed off and rushed down, rowing toward the deep water,
heading toward the deeper water right in front of the three kayaks,
 and since he really wanted to get him [*Apanuugpak*],
aren, the poor guy did something all of a sudden and capsized!
20
When he capsized and bubbles were rising to the surface,
 Apanuugpak took his spear with a wooden throwing device
 and speared him.
After he threw the spear, it stuck fast and the butt of the spear
 moved to and fro and then sank.
Even though he was under water he speared and struck
that *Ukinqucugpalek*,
hitting him right on the mark.
His mother, it was said, was up there on shore pacing around.
Just after that kayak had capsized,
Pangalgalria called to him, "*Tugulullraqa*,
I heard your enemies are afraid of your voice!"
And then *Apanuugpak*
answered that the time had come at last.
21
Apanuugpak took his paddle
and told them to follow along in his wake.
22
Then *Apanuugpak*
let out his voice
in
the direction of
the swarm [of enemies]
and hurled himself against that multitude of kayaks. *Aren*, when he
 let out his voice, all those kayaks
started to divide, parting and pulling back.
While projecting his voice outward he paddled
in the direction of those kayaks.
23
When he started to go his companions followed him,
and they would be saying

393

qanaallininaurtut
anirtima-gguq tang at' ukut
alingararanripakartut
Apanuugpak-gguq-am una ilakelliniamegteggu!
24
Aren tua-i anqertelliniluteng tamakut imkut qayarugaat kuigem iluani
　　uitalriit
avavet yaatiitnun,
avavet-gga tua-i amalirneratnun anqerrluni.
25
Tua-llu tua-i
tamakut imkut

"Patriarch of Kashunak in a loon skin parka, 1928." Photo from Jesuit Oregon Province Archives, Gonzaga University, negative number 504.06.

that since they had *Apanuugpak* with them,
it was no wonder they
were fearless!

24
Aren, that host of kayaks that was in the river quickly took off
to some place yonder, beyond them,
somewhere over there on the other side of them.

25
Then
that great host

Ussugan, Oscar Usugan, and *qayaq*, *Tununeq*, circa 1980. Photo by Andrew J.
Chikoyak.

qayarugaat
qungalliniluteng tuavet nunanun.
Qungagluteng taguriita
akiatnun ika-i (aling canimetlinivakar!)
kuigem akianun ikavet carr'ilqerrarmun mayurluteng,
aren tuani tua-i
atakuyarcilliniluteng.
26
Tua-llu-gguq iliit anqertelliniuq cameg' aũg'umek (aling,
    nalluyagulluki-'m tuaten!)
canek taukunek anqerrulluni pilliniuq ellait makucinek aturaitniluki.

27
Tua-llu-gguq-am taum
Apanuugpiim taukut atkuni qayaminek anlluki manilliniluki.
Maaten-gguq tang imkug' ilagken tangrrakek taukut atkui
qimugkauyaraat, imkut anenerrayagaat, tua-i
ang'uranerait. Tamakunek-gguq-am qimugkauyarnek
    atkungqellinil' taun' Apanuugpak.
(Tang ucurnaitetaacia tua niicukngarci! {qanemcista engelartuq}
28
Aling tua-i qanemciurarqamek imkuk Apac'inkuk una-ll'
    Nengqerralriim atii tayima
anglanarquk. Iliini tua-i iilektiirangnaurtuk.)

***

29
Tua-i pilnguameng
taukut tua qaill' pivkenaki
ullakengateng.
Cali tua-i ayallruameng uterquralliniluteng-am tua tamaaggun
    tumllermegteggun unaggun
ceñakun,
imarpigkun.
Tua-i unugaqateng qavartaqa'aqluteng.
30
Tua-ll' tua-i
kingunilluteng tua-i ikavet Engelumiunun.
Aren tamaani (nalluyagucillrulliniunga)
utertevkenateng
unugngan,
tauna ilasek Pangalgalria-gguq una

of kayaks
retreated to their village.
When they retreated further up
over there on the other side (*aling*, how close they were [to each other]!),
the three of them went up to the other side of the river to a clearing
and waited there
for evening to come.
26
Then one of [the enemy] suddenly rushed out [of one of the houses]
    with something (*aling*, I'm forgetting some!),
suddenly rushed out with something and said that they themselves
    didn't have that kind of clothing [like *Apanuugpak*'s].
27
It was said that
Apanuugpak had taken out his parka from his kayak and displayed it.
Then his companions saw, lo and behold, that his parka was made
out of little puppies, ones that were a little bigger than
newborns! *Apanuugpak* had parkas made out those puppies.
(See how he's not especially praiseworthy, the one you want to hear
    about! {narrator laughs} [10]
28
Aling, when *Apac'iq* and the father of *Nengqerralria* would tell stories,
they were very entertaining. Sometimes they would utter their
    astonishment.)

***

29
Time wore on
and they left the ones they had encountered
without doing anything to them.
Furthermore, having journeyed away from home, they returned via
    the same route that they had come by,
down there by the shore,
along the ocean.
They would camp whenever night fell.
30
And so
they arrived at *Engelumiut* across there.
Aren, at that time (I forgot [to mention this])
prior to returning home,
when night fell,
they let their companion, *Pangalgalria*,[11]

unaggun en'akun qaúgyam qaingakun aqvaqurcetliniluku tua-i
    amlliraullri aúgkut
cuqluki.
31
Ercan tua tamakunek iillayugluteng tuani tua-i
taukut nunat
aciatni.
32
Maaten-gguq tua-i
tamakut imkut amlliraullri,
tutmallri cuqtait, imkuk tua paangrutek
akuliigni tua
nelqaqsalriamek nurturlutek.
Paangrutet atam imkut
tak'ut, yagenrek tua-i malruk
anguarutngulutek.
Waten atunem
mulelget
(mulget-qa nalluaci imkut yaani nuugani anguarutet
piit?)
tamakut tamaa-i paangrutnek piaqait.
33
Tua-llu tua-i
utertekuggluteng
piinanermeggni
tamana imna
taukut unuucateng, qavarngariata ikegkut,
arvirluteng
qayanek tua-i tamaaken
tegulautelliniluteng qayateng cimirluki.
Mat'umek-gguq tua-i Apanuugpak tauna qayaqegtaarmek mat'umek
    tan'germi,
qayaqegtaarmek tua tegulluni
qayarkaminek pilliniluni.
34
Tauna-gguq taúgken Pangalgalriartaak
qayat makut-am tua naru'urluki ceńirtelliniluki.
Tua-i-ll' tamatumek qatkacaganrilengraan qayamek tegucami
tegutelliniluni tauna imna
Pangalgalriartaak.
35
Panik tua-ll' tauna tua qanrutkeksaunaku pilaraat,

run on the sand bar, on top of the sand and
would measure his strides.

31
When daylight came they were amazed [upon seeing]
that place below
the village.
32
They saw
those strides he made
and measured his steps; behold, double-bladed oars
were a little short,
but almost fit in between them.
Atam, those double-bladed paddles
are long. Paddles measure
two arms length.
Those ones
with blades
(do you know those blades on the end of oars,
on the end?)
they call those double-bladed oars.
33
So then
while
they were thinking of going home,
as soon as
night came upon them, when everyone seemed to be asleep over
across there,
they crossed over
and took kayaks,
exchanging their own kayaks for some others.
It was said that while it was dark *Apanuugpak* took this very nice kayak;
he took a very nice kayak
for himself.[12]
34
But of the three, the one who was named *Pangalgalria*
went over the kayaks, sniffing them.
And when he chose one,
the one who was named *Pangalgalria*
took a kayak that wasn't particularly white.
35
They didn't talk about *Panik*,

taukuk taũgaam tua-i.
36
Tua-i-ll' qayarluteng uterrluteng
ercateng.
Maaten-ggur' imna tanqigian piut
Apanuugpak tauna qayamek tamatumek tegutellinilria
urasqalegmek, qayavialugmek tua-i tegutellrullinilria, {qanemcista
    engelartuq}
tan'germi.
37
Ii-i, assinqurrarmek pingnaqsaaqluni.
38
Aling tua-i tauna Pangalgalria tauna qanemyuugautekliniluku!
39
Tua-i
qaill' pivkenateng tua-i anguyaggsuutngungermeng tua taukut.
Taukut tua-i anguyaggsuuterrlainaugut Pangalgalria,
Apanuugpak, Panik-gga.
Utertelliniluteng tua-i ikavet Engelumiunun.

***

40
Tua-i-ll'
taukuk Pangalgalriinkug' Apanuugpak-llu tekicamek
(qanemcima aũgkut ilait qeckaraluk' qanemcilliniunga)
tekicamek
ikani ika-i angullugaraurrlutek
Pangalgalria-llu.
Tutgaranglutek-llu. Tutgarangamek
Apanuugpak tauna
tuqluqngesqelluku taumek tutgariinek.
41
(Qaillun ima tanem tuqluutii tamana ayuqellria?
Tua-i tang ata nalluyaguskeka
tua-i tamarkeggenka. Tua-i tang qanemcinek-llu
neq'ayugteqsunrilama,
uguan' qellugtem.) {qanemcista engelartuq}
42
Tua-i-ll' tauna imna Apanuugpiim
tauna Tugulullrani
tuqlullinia tauna
Pangalgalria.

but only about those two.
36
And so they returned home by kayak
when daylight came upon them.
They noted, when it finally got light enough,
that the kayak which *Apanuugpak* had taken
was smeared with clay, that it was a shabby old kayak, which he
    had taken {narrator laughs}
in the dark.
37
Yes, he had tried in vain to get the best one.
38
Aling, how he grumbled about *Pangalgalria*!
39
Yet
although they were warriors, they didn't attack that village.
All of them were warriors, *Pangalgalria*,
Apanuugpak, and *Panik*.
They returned over across there to *Engelumiut* .

***

40
When
those two, *Pangalgalria* and *Apanuugpak*
(I guess I'm skipping some parts of my story)
when they went home,
they eventually became old men, across there,
he and *Pangalgalria*.
And they had grandchildren. When they had grandchildren,
Apanuugpak
was asked to chose a sobriquet for his grandchild.
41
(Now, what did he nickname him?
You see, I forgot
both of them. I can't remember
stories
on account of [my mind] being so decrepit.) {narrator laughs}
42
Then *Apanuugpak*
called out to *Pangalgalria*,
his
Tugululler.

Tua-ll' tua-i ciunran taum
tua-i pillinia
ellii tua-i
tuqluutekaitniluni
callerminek-llu unguvallermini neq'anaitniluni.

43
Tua-ll' tua-i Apanuugpiim pillinia
tuqluutekaitenritniluku tuqluqngesqelluku tutgaraanek.

44
Tua-ll' tua-i taum wani Pangalgalriim pillinia tauna Apanuugpak
waniwa
ellii tuqluqengqatarniluni.
Tua-ll' tuqlulliniuq, "Wayassaagaucestekaqa,[b]
Makut Maani Pillinruataqengraata!"
Taum tua-i
Apanuugpiim tuqluqngan
eng'aluggluni tua tunutelliniluku.
45
Aling, tua-i tang qanemcikaqa man' patagmek taqelria.
Tua-i waten waniwa amllertaluku
niitellruaqa
tauna.
46
Tua-i-llu-qa!

And his respondent, *Pangalgalria*,
answered him
that he
couldn't think of a sobriquet for his grandson
because he couldn't recall anything noteworthy that he himself,
    [*Pangalgalria*], had ever done while he was alive.[13]
43
And then *Apanuugpak* chided him
that indeed *Pangalgalria* didn't lack a name with which to nickname
    his grandchild.
44
Then *Pangalgalria* told *Apanuugpak*
that
he was now going to make a sobriquet.
Then he nicknamed him, "The one who will rob, pillage and plunder
people for me, although they think they may know more!"
Then
Apanuugpak, when he said that,
just muttered "*Enga!*" and turned away.
45
Aling, this story is quickly over.
That is how long it was
when I heard
that one.
46
That's it!

APANUUGPAK

Paningayak Tununermiu

***

1
Apanuugpak taun' tan'gurrauluni ayagluni,
waten tan'gurraarauluni,
elliraurtellinilria, angayuqaak tamarmek tuqulutek.
Tua-lli-wa-gguq tua-i taukut
ilain,
tua-w' yuut,
nakukuraurlungraatni-ll' akiqayuilkai.
Caluki-ll' kiulerluki-ll' piyuunaki
umyuarteqluni anglirikuni
akinaullerkani amlleran.

Paningayak, Medina Flynn, cutting, braiding, and drying herring, *Tununeq,*
1958. Photo by Christine Heller, courtesy of the Anchorage Museum of History
and Art B91.11.390.

APANUUGPAK

Medina Flynn of Tununak

***

1

When *Apanuugpak* was a young boy,
just a little boy,
he became an orphan, both of his parents having died.
And it was said that although those around
him,
the people,
picked on him and tormented him, he never fought back.
He never yelled back at them,
thinking when he grew up
there would be time enough for revenge.

Qaluyaarmiut on roof of school in *Tununeq*, circa 1931. Photo from Jesuit Oregon Province Archives, Gonzaga University, negative number 504.32.

2
Tua-ll' akiqayuunaki yuuguralliniluni tua pingraatni ilangciksaunaki.
Tua-ll' aipangluni Pangalgalriamek,
wa-gguq uumek Pangalgalriamek.
Tuqluullutek tua tangrrucamek Turulullramegnek,
Turulumegnek.
3
Tua-i tangrrucamek Turuluqlutek tua-i
ellmegnek tuqluucilutek.
Ilikurlutek tua-i piuralliniaqelriik
waten yuut
nalluatni.
Tua-w' ellmegnek ayuqucirtuaguraullutek aipartek
uumek alarrluni piaqan
aipaagnek qanrutaqluku.
Tauna angayuqangqerrsaaqluni Pangalgalriamek pilallrat Apanuugpiim
taum aipaa.
4
Tua-i-ll' caqerlutek anguaralutek ayaganglutek.
Anglirinragen'gun-llu anguyangluni,
imkunek
iciw' ingluitnek.
Agken anguyiit pavaggun tekitaqluteng.
5
Apanuugpiim qanrutliniluku tauna
apeqni Turulullrani,
"Kitaki,
waniwa anguyiungeqatartukuk.
Waten yuut nalluatni taũgaam elissarraarlunuk
elisngarikumegnuk anguyiungniartukuk."
6
Yuut nalluatni aqvaqurlutek-ll' ayagaqlutek,
aqvaqurlutek tua yaaqliqlutek, amaqliqlutek ipesngallutek.
Tua-i-ll' piuraqerlutek
tua-i imna igvaartarkaureskan arulairlutek.
Tua-i tamaa-i igvarqan taum aipaan pitgaruaraqluku.
Pitgaqsaunaku
taũgaam tua pitgaruaraqluku.
Pitgarqani-gguq tua-i narulkausnguarnaurtuq
kiituan' tua-i cayugnairutuk.

2
And so he lived without fighting back even though they did things to him.
Then *Pangalgalria* became his partner,
the so-called *Pangalgalria*.
When they saw each other they called one another *Turuluk*,
having nicknamed one another *Turuluq*.
3
They called each other *Turuluq* when they met,
conferring sobriquets on one another.
Without the knowledge of the people,
they remained
comrades.
They constantly taught one another and whenever one
made a mistake,
the other would tell him.
Apanuugpak's partner, the one they called *Pangalgalria*,
had parents.
4
Then one day they began to travel about by paddling [kayaks].
By the time they were old enough, war had begun;
you know,
[they had] enemies.
Their enemies arrived from way over across there, from inland.
5
Apanuugpak told the one
he nicknamed '*Turuluk*,'
"*Kitaki*,
we are now going to begin to contend with our enemies.
But we must first learn without the people knowing about it,
and when we become adept, we will fight our enemies."
6
Unbeknownst to the people, they would travel around by running,
running along side by side, alongside of one another but concealed
    from each other by a barrier of land which separated them.
Then all of a sudden they would stop
just before the other one came into view.
When the other one came into view, his partner would pretend to
    shoot him with an arrow.
He didn't really shoot him,
just pretended to shoot him with an arrow.
Whenever one shot, the other would pretend to fall down,
so soon they acquired considerable skill and prowess.

7
Tuamte-llu qayatek
mayurrluki
kuigem ceńiinun, mayurrlutek waten tua aqumgaurlutek,
pinauraa-gguq taum Apanuugpiim, "Kitaki,
anguyagtanguq!"
Anguyagtailnguq-wa-gguq.
Pileryauskunek qayakeg' imkuk tamaavet kuigaarmun akagarciiquk,
   akaucirlutek,
uitaurarraarlutek. Tua-i alqunarmek pileryaullutek
ataucikun kuigmun uyangarrlutek.
Uyangareskunek-llu tua-i piuraqerlutek ayaglutek, anguyiqnguarlutek.

8
Tua-i yuut nalluatni tamaani elissarturlutek.

***

9
Tua-i-ll' anguyiurluteng,
anguyiulliniluteng.
Nunanun taukunun naspaalutek ayaglutek,
iliklutek.
Unugpak ayallinilriik
tua-i-ll' tamaavet
kuigem iluanun itramek, qayatek tua-i itrullukek natmun maavet,
   atrarlutek unavet ceńamun kellucillinilutek.
10
Qayaq tua-i unuakumi
cetuluni igvarqan pitgaraqluku wall' uniurcuunaku
egmian tua-i paluartaqluni.
Tua-i nutaan tuatnangamek
yulkit'langlutek.
Yulkitaqagnek
tamakut anguyaita-am
pileryautaqlukek.
Pileryautaqatek tua-i qimagaqlutek.

11
Tua-i kiituani tua-i tauna Apanuugpak erinialanguq.
Qayagpagnaurtuq, "Apanuugpiim piciqaaci!"
Tauna Turuluni qanruqaarluku,
tua-i Apanuugpaurrluni ellminek.

7

Furthermore, they would bring
their kayaks up
onto the beach, bringing them up and sitting in them,
and *Apanuugpak* would say to him, "*Kitaki*,
enemies are here!"
But there were really no enemies.
They would suddenly slide their kayaks down to the stream, sliding
    on rollers
after having waited there. They would hastily launch their kayaks
down into the river together.
And when they launched their kayaks from the shore of the river,
    they would go, pretending to encounter enemies.

8

They were teaching themselves without the knowledge of the people.

***

9

So then war came;
they apparently were at war.
They went to that village to try out,
being allied partners.
They journeyed all night
and then they got there,
and entering that river they brought their kayaks up and waited,
    going down there onto the beach to be on the lookout.

10

During the morning, whenever a kayak heading downriver appeared,
they would shoot arrows at it and since they never missed,
it would capsize immediately.
When they began to do that,
their presence became known by the
noises they made.
Whenever those two made noises that could be detected,
the enemy warriors would
attack them.
Whenever they attacked them, they would retreat.

11

Soon *Apanuugpak* began to shout.
He would shout, "*Apanuugpak*'s going to get you!"
after telling his *Turuluq*
that he named himself *Apanuugpak*.

12
Tua-i taugken pileryaucaaqekatni
anguyani tamakut tua-i nangluki,
anguyatek tauna-ll' aipani-llu
elissallruamek tua-i
tamaani
yuut nalluatni,
elissarlutek tua-i elissarlutek anguyiungengata ilatek.

***

13
Tua-i caqerluni
ayallermegni imarpigkun
Eqtarmiut ketiitnun (nantat-llu tayim' taukut Eqtarmiut?)
maaten tua-i ellangelliniut tua-i qayat kassugutkacagarlukek.
14
Tua-ll' taum tua-i
Pangalgalriim pillinia, "Aling aren, Turulu,
qaillun-kiq maa-i makut anguyiit aneniarceńuk?
Anviilnguut-llu!"
15
Tua-i-ll'
pillinia,
"Qaill' alinguten-qaa? Wiinga tang alingenrilngua!"
Tauna tua-i aiparrii alingyaaqluni.
16
Anguarutni eggluku ayalliniuq ikegkut tua-i
yugugaat tua arcaqerluki tumekluki.
Tua-i-ll' tauna tamaani tamakut yuut qukaamegenki erinani
    antelliniluku.
17
Tua-i
qayagpalliniluni
tuamte-ll' inglua anguarluku.
Kingyalliniuq tauna tua Pangalgalriartaa maaken mermek pilria,
"Qaill' calriaten taryumek neqnialngurmek tamatumek taryuturcit?
Alingevkenak! Alingnarqenritut!"
Naugga-gguq qayat makut tua-i elaqliryaggluteng.

18
Matartelliniluni Apanuugpak.

410

12
But when they tried to attack him,
he would finish off his enemies,
he and his partner,
because they had taught themselves how
back then
without the people knowing,
having taught themselves how when the hostilities with their
    enemies had begun.

***

13
One day
when they traveled on the ocean
to *Eqtaq* (wherever *Eqtaq* is)
they realized they were completely surrounded by kayaks.
14
And so *Pangalgalria*
said to [*Apanuugpak*], "*Aling aren, Turulu,*
I wonder how we will get past these warriors?
There is no way out!"
15
So he
answered to him,
"Why, are you scared? Look, I'm not scared!"
His partner was apparently afraid.
16
With one powerful stroke of his paddle he headed toward the other side
where the people were most concentrated.
When they got to the middle of those people he let out a shout.

17
He
yelled
and again he thrust with a powerful stroke on the other side.
When he glanced back the one who was named *Pangalgalria* was
    drinking water from there.[1]
"Why are you drinking that repulsive salt water?
Don't be afraid! There is no cause to be afraid!"
Yet it was said that the kayaks were all crammed together side by side.
18
Then *Apanuugpak* undressed.

Aipani pillinia ellii pisqevkenaku;
ayuqelisqevkenani ayakatarniluni kingunemikun taũgaam
  maligcesqelluni.
Piuralliniluni qayagpagaqluni,
"Erinaka, erinaluryaka, anguyiit alikekiit!",
tuarpiaq-gguq ing' ciunrat qukviryartullermeggni. "Un'a-'m-taq
Apanuugpauguq?
Un'a-am cunaw' Apanuugpaungami uluryararanripakalria!"

19
Aren tua-i-am tamakut tua-i nanglliniluki tua-i tamalkuita
anguyatek,
anguyagugatek mallraulutek taũgken!

***

20
Tua-i nutaan ayallinilutek. Tua-i-am anguyagnek
tekicagnek pilliniut Eqtarmiut
kiturviilnguut calukek kituuciitnek.
"Eqtarmiut-wa taukut qavanertulliniameng kiturcetellriit."

21
Tua-i ayallinilutek tua-i.
22
Tua-i-llu-ggur-am taukut tua-i ciunekek
kiturluki ayaglutek.
Mat'umek-gguq ilangqertuk
Capenruilngurmek—Capenruilnguunricaaquq
Apanuugpiim-gguq Capenruilnguurtellrua—ilanglutek naken-llu
  tayim' yugmek piak.
23
Taum tua-i naspaavkaraqluku Apanuugpiim
qairet kangritgun aqvaqurcetaarluku.
Tua-i-gguq piqarraallermini
kit'laryaaquq nug'aqluni. Tua-i-ll' piuraqerluni
kuik tamana naspaavkalliniluku-am Apanuugpiim.
Kuik tamana qer'aqertelliniluku aqvaqurluni qairet kangritgun
  tutmarluni
aren tus'arrluni-llu-gguq!
Tua-i tuani tua pian nutaan Capenruilnguurrluk',
Capenruilngurmek acirluku.

412

He directed his partner not to do the same,
telling him not to follow suit, but told him to follow along in his wake.
He shouted as he went,
"My voice, my mighty voice, the enemy fears it!",
as the ones in front of them began to part and draw back. "Now that
    one down there,
is that *Apanuugpak?*
So that's why that one down there is so dauntless, because it is
    Apanuugpak!"
19
Aren, so they finished off all their
enemies,
their many and numerous enemies, although they were only two of them.

***

20
Then they went on their way. When they arrived from having been
with the enemy,
they were asked how they managed to pass by the impassable
    village of *Eqtaq*.
"Since the people of *Eqtaq* evidently sleep late, they let us pass by."
21
And so they left.
22
And so it is said that they continued on their way,
passing by the one that was in their path.
They had *Capenruilnguq*
with them—actually *Capenruilnguq* wasn't his name;
it was *Apanuugpak* who named him *Capenruilnguq*—and where they
    got him is not known.
23
Apanuugpak had him try
to run along on the crest of the waves.
When he first tried to do it, it was said
he would sink and then come up again. Then one day
Apanuugpak had him try the river.
He ran across the river, striding lightly along the crest of the waves;
aren, it is said he got to the other side!
After he did that, he called him *Capenruilnguq*,
giving him the name of *Capenruilnguq*.[2]

24

Tuamte-llu-gguq-am pivakarluteng tauna tua-i Capenruilnguq
pillinia, kitak, kuiggacuayaarkun tamaaggun asguusqelluku,
elkek tua-i
maani utaqaciqniluku
anguyagnek tangerqan utercesqelluku.
Tua-i-am ayalliniluni tauna kuiggacuayaaq tamana nequturiinarluni.
Tua-i-ll' kiituani-gguq man' tan'geriuq.
Tua uterrnariani utertelliniluni nequturian.
25
Cunawa-gguq tua-i nevum aciakun camaggun ayangellinilria.
Utercami tua-i Apanuugpak pilliniluni (tauna-w' tuunrangayaulliami)
pillinia, "Waqaa, camek-qa alangruqanrituten?"
"Camek-wa alangrukaunrilan alangrunrilngua nevum aciakun
    ayangelliniama."
Pillinia, "Tua-i, tua-i!"

***

26
Aren, tua-i-gguq tauna Apanuugpak yugnek
amllernek tuquciuq, Apanuugpiinkuk Pangalgalria-llu.
27
Tua-i yuut nalluatni elissallruamek elitkacagaamek
yugugaungraata anguyait pingraata
tua cavkarngaunatek. Qaingak-wa-gguq tua-i pitegcautnguyaaqelria
amta-llu-gguq tua-i piyuunatek.
Tua-i-ll' anguyiit pellukata
Apanuugpak imna matarciiqelliniuq
matareskuni-llu ungulerqurluni tua cairluni.
Ungulerquqan
pitegcautet imkut cingilgit kaimluteng unavet acianun.
Tauna-ll' tua-i aipani cal' tuaten tua pivkaraqluku.
Kingunrit tuaten mamluteng tamakut pitegcautet
(tauna-w' angalkuulliami)
avurluki-gguq taugken [qanerlutek], "Taqumauralriit makut
    pegcunaitai."

24

Then again one day he told *Capenruilnguq*
to follow this little river upstream
and to return when he saw enemies,
telling him that the two of them
would wait there for him.
As he was going along, that little river began to get wider.
Then it began to get dark.
Since it got wider and wider, he returned when it was time to go back.

25

Apparently, it is said that he had been going underneath the ground.
When he got back *Apanuugpak* said—maybe because he was a
    tuunrangayaq, a spirit [man][3]—
he said to him, "*Waqaa*, did you see anything unusual?"
"Because I was beginning to go underneath the ground, I didn't
    see anything since there was nothing to see."
He said to him, "There, there, [just as I thought]!"[4]

***

26

Aren, it is said that *Apanuugpak*, together with *Pangalgalria*,
killed a lot of people.

27

It was because of the fact that they practiced without the people
    knowing and had become experts,
and although there would be a whole host of enemy warriors,
they couldn't touch them. Even though they would be covered with
    arrows,
they couldn't be killed.
When the enemy warriors had gone away,
Apanuugpak would undress,
and as he undressed he would shake everything lose.
When he shook himself,
the arrow heads would fall to the ground.
He would let his partner do the same.
The places where the arrows had lodged would heal as they dropped
(maybe because he was an *angalkuq*, a shaman)
and then they would collect them, saying, "The ones that are already
    made ought not be wasted."

***

28

Tua-i-ll' caqerluku tua-i taum, taukut iliita,
tuaten-am tua qainga pitegcautngurrluni,
qamiqurranun-gguq taugken tucuunateng,
pilliniat taukut anguyain ilaita,
"Qaillun augna Apanuugpak qaingqelalriim
pitegcautet amllerpakangraata
cayuit'larpakartak, augkuk?"
Tua-llu-gguq kingyarluni piuq,
"Apanuugpak pitgaqungerpeceñi pitgaquvkarngaituq.
Eqtarmiut qapilaallritnun tutmalartut cingilgit!"

29

Tuaten tua-i imna Apanuugpak,
tuaten tua-i caperrsagulluku tamakut anguyain.
Tua-i tuaten
piaqameng kassugucaaqaqatni
erinani antaqaku anguyai tamakut tua-i tayim'
qanerluteng tuaten, "Una-am cunaw' Apanuugpaulria!"

Qaluyaarmiut slaughtering reindeer. Photo from Jesuit Oregon Province Archives, Gonzaga University, negative number 506.01.

***

28

Then one day one of them
did the same thing, shooting arrows all over his body,
but none of them landed on his head,
and one of the warriors said to him,
"How is it that with *Apanuugpak*'s body,
that although arrows rain down upon them,
those two never come to any harm?"
And then he cast a glance back over his shoulder and said,
"Although you may shower *Apanuugpak* with arrows, he's not
    going to permit you to shoot him.
All the arrowheads land on the empty mussel shells of *Eqtaq*!"[5]
29

Thus it was with *Apanuugpak*,
and thus it was that his enemies were unable to vanquish him.
Thus it was
that when they tried to no avail to block him,
when he let out his voice, his enemies would
say, "So, this is *Apanuugpak*!"

Tua-i qukvirluki unilluki ayagaqluni.

30
Tuaten tua piaqateng Apanuugpak tauna quyinruyugluni yugnek
  tuqurqiaqluni.
Tua-i tuani tuaten qanrutkelaqiit. Kiituan'-gguq tua piniarutuq
piniarucami tuaten
ayagassiyaanrirluni.

***

31
Tua-i-ll'-am
ayagpakarluni taukunun tua nunanun tekitelliniluni unugmi
iliitnun tua qasegpakayallraam-gguq, tua qasegpallraam
elaqlianun taumun nerpall'ermun itqataralliniluni.
Itqataraami pilliniuq... (Waten-gguq, naparyat iciw' imkut
  naparyangqetullruut nepiit.
Aren tangellrunrilkeci-wa. {qanemcista engelartuq} Nel'itullrulriit
  naparyalegnek waten
akiqliqluki muraganek-llu
pagkut pirraarluki ukut-llu
nutaan muraganek qanirturluki,
qanirluki.
Canegnek-llu tupigluteng
pagaavet elliurturluki tamakut muragat
patuurluki.
Nutaan patuurarraarluki nevirluki
nevunek tua nevupignek, mat'umek nevupiamek.
Qaingit-llu nevirluki egalirluki pikaggun
nem,
nem tamatum
pianek cikumek.
Cikut-wa egalrit
kaminiarit'laameng uruyuinaki.
Tuaten tua-i nengqetullratni.)...naparyaq una, kiani-wa-gguq tamana
yualuq piirraq,
taqukat imkut iruita yualuit,
uyamigugarnek-gguq tua-i uyamigugarnek agailria ikna-wa-gguq
  cali akiqlia cal' tuaten tua-i.

They'd part to get out of his way, and he'd pass right through them
    leaving them behind.
30
Thus is was that whenever they did that, he would kill people,
    wanting to be exalted above everybody else.
That's what they said about him. Finally, it is said, he began to
    grow old and weak
and since he was more feeble,
he didn't venture out so much.

***

31
And so
once as he traveled on he came to this village at night,
and next to a great big *qasgiq* was a very large house which he very
stealthily entered.
As he was slowly stealing in he saw...(it is said, that it was like this, you
    know, those foundation poles, which sod houses used to have.
Aren, you haven't seen one. {narrator laughs} They used to make
    houses and put two foundation poles
across from each other,
and after putting the wood on them, they then put split logs
slanted up there
side by side.
And making grass mats,
they covered those split logs
up there.
After covering them they put soil on them,
genuine dirt, real soil.
And put soil on the top and put a
window up there on the house,
with
ice.
Their windows were ice
and since they didn't have stoves they never melted.
Thus it was when they used to have sod houses.)...there was a pole
    here, and back in there
[on the line of sinew between the poles] was braided sinew,
sinew from the legs of those seals.
It is said there were a lot of necklaces hanging there [and the poles]
    across from it were the same.

32
Imumek-gguq tua-i itqata'arluni, pugqata'aryaaqaqan mikelnguq im'
    qalrillagnaurtuq
tua-i-gguq tua murukarluni. Tua-i-ll' tua piuraqerluni
tuatnainanrani
qamna angulluat iliit pillinilria, "I!
Qalrillagavakarta! Qalrillagaviiqnak!
Apanuugpiim piciqaaten!" Niicugnistekluku cama-i amigmi!

33
Tua-i taukut ilangcivkenak'. Amiat-gguq-am taũgaam tua-i avirluku
    tua-i pengegnairluku,
amiat imna tua-i anesciigaliluki.
Tua-i
pirraarluki
qasgimun mayuqatarallinilutek.
Mayuqatarlutek uyangtelliniak qasgi tauna
qilumek,
taqukat qiluitnek,
egalengqellinilria.
Allegluku, alkarluku
qinertelliniuk qavalriit.
34
Tamakut tamaa-i
angutet kiarquralliniluki, tua-i kiarqurluki.
Ellaita caskuitnek
Pangalgalria qup'agluni
taggliniluni tua ellimerrani.
Amiat avirluku qavaatni, avirraarluku, amiigirraarluki
tamakunek yuut imkut kapulliniluki tua-i, kapurluki qavaatni
    tuqurqelluki, caskuitnek, tegutnek.
Kapurluki tua qasgi taman' yuilliniluku qaillun-llu
    nep'ngarcaaqeng'ermeng anqercaaqeng'ermeng amigteng
    caviilan anevkenateng,
anesciiganateng.
Nutaan tua-i
ellaseng man'a piirucan,
tamakut imkut angutet nangengata, nen'un cali iterlutek tuqutaqluki
    angutet.

35
Tua-i pilliniluki yuut tamakut,

32

As he was slowly sneaking in, when he was about to crawl out and
     emerge from the tunnel entrance, a child suddenly began to cry
and he ducked back into the entrance. And as
he did that,
one of the old men inside said, "*I!*[6]
Why does he keep crying out! Stop crying out!
Apanuugpak will get you!" It was he who was the very one who
     was listening to him down there by the entrance!

33

He didn't do anything to them. But he made sure that their door
     was securely covered
so that they couldn't escape through the door.
Then,
having done that,
they slowly started climbing up onto the *qasgiq*,
slowly going up, and then peered down. That *qasgiq*
had a gut window,
a seal-gut
window.
Tearing it, making a small tear,
they peered down into [the *qasgiq*] and saw them sleeping.

34

They kept looking at
all those men, observing them.
Pangalgalria came up,
bearing their enemies' weapons on his shoulder,
as he was told to do.
They blocked their door while they slept, and after covering it, after
     making sure they couldn't go out,
he stabbed those people, killing them one after the other using their
     own barbed harpoons as they slept.
Stabbing them, he decimated the people in the *qasgiq*, and
     although they had started to raise the alarm and tried to go
     out, the door was blocked
and there was no escape.
Finally
when it was quiet around them,
and those men were finished off, they went into the other houses
     and killed the men.

35

Then he said to all those people,

"Ataucimek angutmek
yirluci, anerteqelrialirluci,
tua-i kinguveruarpeceńun qanemcikestaitnayuklua pinritamken elpet,
pinritamegten."

36
Tua-i-gguq ataucirrarmek qanemcikescecirluki
tamakut qasgimiut taq'aqait,
taq'aqakek taukuk.
Allat-gguq taugken anguyagyaaqurluquneng
elkenka ilikenrilkek
tua-i nangluki tua anguyiit
tuqulluki.
37
Avaken ayagluni elissallruami, usvituriuraami
elissarluni,
tua elitkacagarlutek tauna-llu Turuluni-ll', Turulullraminek-llu
pilaqengani
elissarluku tauna.
38
Aling cunawa-gguq tamakut
anguyiit nang'arkakek,
yuuk,
taukuk yuug' malruk.[a]
Ukinqucugpalgenkut-llu tamakut.
39
Elitnaurat iliit aptuq:
"Kina-llu? Kitumek ima tanem pilaqiit?"
40
Tauna tua-i-am iliit
keggasgirluku
yuut iliit,
anguyiit iliit.
Pilliniluku, "Kinguverpet ateqniaraatgen, Keggasgilnguarauluten
tuaten yuugi, Keggasgilnguarauluten!"
Tua-i Keggasgilnguarmek acirluku.
41
Aciatgu-ll' tua-i tamakut maa-i tayim' niitelalriakut Keggasgilnguarmek.
Tamaa-i tamakut anguyiim
keggasgillran kinguliarat.
Keggasgilnguarmek acirluku tauna tua-i.

"I am leaving only
one man alive from amongst you
because I thought there might not be anyone left to tell your
    descendants about me; I'm sparing you,
we are not touching you."[7]
36
It was said that they used to leave at least one [survivor]
from amongst those *qasgimiut,* those *qasgiq* dwellers, to tell the tale
when they finished them off.
But it is said that whenever those other unfortunate warriors fought,
the ones who were not *Apanuugpak*'s allies,
they just finished their enemies off,
killing them all off.
37
Because from the time when he was first able to understand,
he learned,
they both learned [how to fight], and he taught his *Turuluk,*
the one he called his *Turuluk.*

38
Aling, incredible as it was, it is said that those
warriors
were finished off
by those two people,
[including] *Ukinqucugpalek* and those with him.[8]
39
One of the students asks:
Who else? Now what do they call him?
40
They removed the shoulder blade
of one of the people,
of one of the enemy.
He said to him, "So that your descendants may be named after you,
    live without a shoulder blade, that you may be known as
    Keggasgilnguar."[9]
He gave him the name of *Keggasgilnguar.*
41
Because they gave him that name, we hear the name *Keggasgilnguar.*
These are the descendants
of the one whose shoulder blade was removed during the war.
They gave him the name of *Keggasgilnguar.*

Tua-i Keggasgilnguarmek niitelartukut yugmek,
taum tua-i Apanuugpiim Keggasgilngualiari.

***

42
Tauna tua-i angun
caperrnarqelliniami.
Elliraurrluni, mikcuayagauluni elliraurrluni,
ellminek tua-i anangnaqu'urluni anagluni.
43
Aling tua-i-gguq tua-i tuquan nutaan,
tua-i caviirucami
angulkacagaami,
tua-i anguyiit tamakut
tamarluteng tua tayim' maliggluku tamarluteng.
44
Qagken-gguq alarutellruut tamakut tamaa-i anguyait,
qagaaken
yaaqvanek,
taillruut natmun maavet.
Anguyiit maa-i nunallrit makut
qertuk'acagarnaurtut. Yaani-llu wangkuta nunallemteñi, nunalput
ingkut Cicingmiuni, ingricualleraag' ingkuk
aciagni,
nunallret qertuluteng,
tua-i taukut cal' anguyiit nunallrit.

So we hear of a person named *Keggasgilnguar,*
and *Apanuugpak* was the reason for the name of *Keggasgilnguar.*

***

42
[All this happened] because that man
was invincible.
He had become an orphan, becoming an orphan at a very young age,
and trying to make it on his own, he survived.
43
Aling, so it was said that when he was so old
and was unable to do anything
and died,
those wars
all disappeared with him.
44
It is said that their enemies came from up there,
from way out there
far away,
and they came to someplace around here.
Today the sites where they fought
are on very high ground. And over there where we once lived, at
    our former village of *Cicingmiut*,[10] below those two hills
over there
is an old village on elevated ground;
that is also a village where there were warriors.

Tununeq gravesite with the personal possessions of the deceased, 1927. Photo from the Geist Collection, courtesy of the Anchorage Museum of History and Art B92.33.49.

PAMALIRUGMIUT
'THE LAND OF THE DEAD'

"When death came to her she lost consciousness for a time; then she was awakened by someone shaking her, saying, "Get up, do not sleep; you are dead."

—unnamed Yup'ik storyteller
from Andreivsky on the lower Yukon (Nelson 1899: 488)

In Memoriam: *Elriq* 'The Great Feast For The Dead'

At death, the shades of the deceased journeyed to two principal places. Suicides and those who met a violent death or died of starvation went to a land in the sky where they lived in abundance and happiness.[1] Most others went to another land beneath the surface of the earth, a land quite like their former existence on earth, a place where they experienced neither torment nor bliss, but encountered the same material needs that they knew on earth (Nelson 1899: 423). For this reason, they were still dependent on the living for the satisfaction of these. Those who died without close relatives to provide for them, or those who were disliked enough so no one would want to honor their memory, were believed to suffer great privation in the afterlife.

Two great ceremonies, both mortuary feasts, were principally concerned with provisioning and honoring the dead. The first of these was *Merr'aq*, the annual Feast for the Dead, which was celebrated each year on *Qaluyaaq* just after the *Nakaciuryaraq* 'The Bladder Festival.' The other was *Elriq*, the Great Feast for the Dead, the timing of which varied, but occurred during the winter ceremonial cycle (Fienup-Riordan 1994: 299-302). Of the two, *Elriq* was the more elaborate (involving the most sumptuous giving of gifts, clothing, utility items and food) of all Yupiit ceremonials, rivaling the Northwest Coast potlatches in the extent to which wealth was redistributed. According to Nelson (1899: 366-379), whose account of the Razbinsky Great Festival which he witnessed in January of 1880 is the most thorough and detailed eyewitness ethnographic account we have of *Elriq*, thousands of pounds of game food and hundreds and hundreds of dollars (in 1880 values) were involved in the distribution. Preparation for the event was a collaborative effort of several families who had lost a close relative and who were obliged by custom to give a memorial feast in honor of the deceased, thereby providing for his needs. It involved years of work and

---

1. Rasmussen (1929: 74) records a similar and no doubt related belief among the Iglulik Eskimos of the Eastern Arctic. Suicides, the greater shamans, women dying in childbirth, those who died violently at the hands of their fellow men, and all those who perish by drowning go up into the land of the dead in the sky to live with *Tarqip Inua*, the Moon Spirit.

saving in order to accumulate sufficient goods to distribute. Indeed, so extensive was the gift-giving that upon the conclusion of the feast individuals and families were left impoverished in all things except for prestige. Fortunately, the system of ceremonial distribution was reciprocal and the givers could expect to be recipients of other distributions for some time to come.

When the feast givers had gathered sufficient goods for the distribution, a time for the ceremony was fixed. *Elriq* was a regional affair, and guests came from distant villages. Since these visitors could not be expected to reciprocate, they were required to present gifts to the host village, and in return received a greater quantity of goods in the distribution. Also, invitation stakes, which were slender wooden rods with red marking and an image emblematic of the deceased, were planted before the grave sites of the deceased being honored. These, along with songs of invitation, invited the deceased to return to the village and *qasgiq* to be commemorated and to receive sustenance for the necessities of life in the abode of the dead. Lamps were lit in the *qasgiq*, each one representative of a shade being feasted, and these lit the way of the dead as they returned to the world of the their kinsmen and fellow villagers.

It was believed that the shades of the dead gathered in the firepit of the *qasgiq*, and for the duration of the ceremonies they remained there, at the gravesites, and upon occasion even entered into the *qasgiq* itself, mingling with the people inside to participate in the dancing and feasting. In two ways especially were the dead commemorated and provisioned by the living. Whenever food was presented to the namesakes (those who were still living and who had the name of the deceased and as a consequence bore a special spiritual relationship to the deceased), small portions of food and libations of water were cast into the firepit. Thereby, it was believed, the shades partook of the spiritual essence of the food, receiving it in far greater amount than the minuscule portions being presented. Secondly, in the distribution of goods, the namesakes were presented with gifts of apparel, often to the extent of receiving a full wardrobe of clothing. In this way were the dead clothed and fed. It was presumed that upon the conclusion of *Elriq*, the Great Feast for the Dead, the needs of the deceased for whom the feast was given would be fully met and there would be no further need for additional mortuary feasts.

The following two stories involve people who return from the dead and appear among the living. In the first, the shade of a girl finds herself in the midst of a feast, presumably *Merr'aq*, the annual mortuary feast. While others receive offerings in abundance, she, because her family is absent, gets nothing; hence, she is despondent. This agrees with what he know of the custom of mortuary feasting among the Yupiit. Those to whom no food offerings are made, whose namesakes receive no gift of clothing, suffer privation in the land of the dead.

In the second story, told as well by *Cakataar*, the father of *Tengesqauktar* and his wife and daughter return from the land of the dead (see the story "*Tengesqauktar*" for more information). The description of their daughter is very typical of the dead. Her face is invisible, hidden behind a veil of hair covering her face. Later on her father reveals that she has no eyes. Recall also the representation of the deceased wife in the story "*Qavcik*"; although her husband attempts to get a glimpse of her, she hides her face from her husband's gaze. The dead often appear under this guise: faceless, eyeless, invisible, isolate.

Numerous literary and mythological traditions attest to the belief that blindness, immobility, and invisibility are associated with the passage between the worlds. The Inuit and Yup'ik shaman is bound with cords before he makes his extraordinary journey to the moon or the world beneath the sea. Tiresias, the Theban prophet who sees into the secrets of the past, present and future, is blind and must be led about by a boy. The gifted boy in the Grimm's fairy tale, in order to penetrate to the splendorous underworld of the twelve dancing princesses, must feign unconsciousness and cloak himself with the mantle of invisibility. On the other hand, the dead too, as we see in the story above, are severely proscribed. The dead of Erebus flit about Odysseus as impotent phantoms, unable to speak or communicate until they are given fresh blood to drink. Dante's dead in *The Inferno* are able to prophesy about the future, but they are oddly ignorant of the present and must rely on the recently dead to bring them up to date. In the Yupiit stories, the dead are often invisible, mute and dependent on the living for basic necessities of life. As in many traditions, they depend on the living to summon them into incarnate existence, just as the living depend on them for guidance and inspiration when they are summoned.

Qaluyaarmiut. Tununeq, 1934. Photo from Jesuit Oregon Province Archives, Gonzaga University, negative number 504.10.

TUQUMARRAARLUNI UTERTELLEQ

Cakataar Tununermiu

***

1
Taukut nunat
nunaulriit,
nunaullinilriit,
nani ak'a, ak'a tamaani
nunat
tua waten wangkucicetun nunauluteng.
2
Cali tua-i
maa-i wangkuta ilaput
tua tuquaqelriit,
tuquaqata-ll' qungilluki;
tamakut cali augkut ciuliaput tuatnaut.
Nasaurluut,
mikelnguut,
tan'gurraat, aanat, aatat, apa'urluut tua-i ayuqluteng tuquuraraqluteng
maa-i arulaiyuunateng piciryaraqluku ukanirpak.

3
Taukut tua nunat
waten tua uitallinilriit.
Tua ilangarcugaqameng ilangartaqluteng piciatun
nasaurlurnek,
tan'gurraat,
yuunriraqluteng,
aanat,
aatat
apa'urluut-llu.
Taukut tua-i.
4
Tua-i-llu
tua-i iliit tuaten nasaurluq waten yuunrilliniluni,

432

ONE WHO CAME BACK FROM THE LAND OF THE DEAD

Jack Angaiak of Tununak

***

1
There
was a settlement,
apparently a village,
somewhere a long, long time ago,
a village
which was like ours.
2
And
nowadays when someone in our community
dies,
after dying, we bury them;
the same happened to our ancestors.
Young girls,
children,
young boys, mothers, fathers, grandfathers are all the same
    in that they occasionally die
as they always have from time immemorial to the present.
3
That village
was like any other village.
Whenever the time came for any of them to depart,
either young girls,
young boys,
mothers,
fathers,
or grandfathers,
they would cease living.
So it was with them.
4
And so then
one of the young girls evidently died,

tua-i yuunrian
qungitelliniluku.
5
Tua-i-llu
tamaani tua-i,
ellarramini,
tamakuni tua tuqullerni uitaluni!
6
Tua-i makut ilai
imkuraqluteng,
aturarkait,[a]
pilugugkait,
pilugungaqluteng
assilrianek.
Atkungaqluteng-llu cali assilrianek
tua-i tuqumalriit tamakut.
7
Ellii-gguq tang taugken
aturat
piciatun, piluguut atkuut-llu tekicuunaku
piuralliniaqelria.
Ukuk tua pilugullraaraagni ak'allaurrlutek atu'urqekek atkullraarani-llu.

Children at *Tununeq*, 1927. Second from right is *Qilangaq*, Jojean Charlie. Photo
from the Geist Collection, Anchorage Museum of History and Art B92.33.41.

and when she died
they buried her.
5
And
there she was,
in the land
of the dead!
6
Those with her
were receiving
gifts of clothing
and skin boots for future use;
they were acquiring
very nice skin boots.
Those who had died
were also receiving beautiful parkas.
7
But it was said that she herself
got
nothing
as she stayed there,
neither different kinds of clothing, nor skin boots or parkas.
She was still wearing her old skin boots and parka.[1]

8
Tua-i nayirnek taũgaam pilugungqetullrulriit
tengmiat-llu piciatun, tuntut, kanaqliit, qanganaat
tamaa-i aturaqtullrukait.
9
Tua-i tuatnalliniaqelria tauna.
Ilai makut nunaniryugnaurtut tua-i waten,
nunaniryugluteng cam iliikun tua.
Ellii tang taũgken tua tuaten avuliuquratulliniluni.
10
Icigg' maa-i kalukarqelriit maa-i; nerevkariaqelriit kanan' *hall*-ami
qagkut ilaput.
Quyurrluteng-llu nerervagluteng, nerluteng.
Nerluteng tua-i imkut mikelngurtuumarmeng
aatat aanat-llu
(elpeci-llu cali),
ayagyuat ilagaulluteng,
pilalriit neqnek ayuqenrilngurnek.
Tua-i-llu piinanratni waten,[b]
tua-i tuatnallinilriit
ellait-llu elliin ilai,
makut
tuqullret [ilagaulluteng],
qasgiq taũgaam uitayaraqellruamegteggu.

***

Tua-i ilani makut ayagngata tuavet
ellii-ll' itliniluni.
Iterngami tua-i
ellii cali ilagaulluni tuaten tua-i elpecicetun.
Aqumluni
maavet tua-i ilami akuliitnun.[c]
Piurallinii
imkut makut, unkut-gguq-gga natermi
waten tamakurmiut tuqumanrilnguut
kangalriit
tua-i nunaniryugluteng. Makut-gguq-gga cali aqumgalriit ellait,
tuqullerni.
Aqumgalriit ilai nunaniryugluteng,
aturaqegciluteng,
atkukegciluteng,
pilugukegciluteng.

8
They only used hair seals for skin boots;
different kinds of birds, reindeer, muskrats, and squirrels,
were used for other clothing.
9
That was what was happening to her.
Those others with her would be happy,
would rejoice occasionally.
Nevertheless, she continued to remain amongst them.
10
You know, nowadays they hold feasts; some of us out there
would let people eat down there at the community hall.[2]
They would gather and have a great feast and eat.
They would eat along with their children;
mothers and fathers,
and young people all participated,
(just like you do);
they ate all different kinds of food.
And so while they were doing this,[3]
they did that [held a feast].
They, the ones with her,
those
who had also died [were there],
since the *qasgiq* was where they used to gather.

***

So when the others with her went in there,
she also went in.
When she entered,
she mingled with them, like [you do] yourselves.
She sat down
there among them.
She saw they
were the ones who were dead, and those down there on the floor
moving about
were the people who were not dead,
enjoying themselves very much. It was said that these, who were dead,
were sitting there.
The ones sitting with her were happy;
they were wearing nice new clothes,
nice new parkas,
nice new skin boots,

Tua-i nunaniryugluteng tangvallrat.
Ellii-gguq tang taũgken ukut aturallraaraũrlui ukut tua-i ak'allauluteng
ilamitun ayuqevkenani.
12
Neqnek ayuqenrilngurnek itrutellriit
tamaavet qasgimun,
itrulluteng neqnek.
13
Tua-i-gg' nalluvkenaki unkut una-i yuut.
Kiarquryaaqelliniuq-gguq:
ilai tayima; aanii,
atii
ilai-llu cali nakmiin, anelgutai cataunateng tayima.
14
Makut-gguq tang taũgken maa-i,
makut ilain
aanait, atait, uyurait, anngait una-i-gguq alqait-llu
avuliulluteng nunaniryugluteng tua-i
pilriit.

15
Makut-llu tamaa-i aqumgalriit
tangvallrani tua-i ellarriini
nunaniryugngurluteng-gguq. Ellii-gguq nunaniryugciigatellruuq
      taum nalliini.
16
Tua-i-llu-gguq
tamaaken kanaken qantanek
imalegnek neqnek aruqelliniluteng,
ukut tangssukngai.
17
Qantanek-gguq tamarmeng[d]
tua-i tegumiangqellruut,
tegumiarluteng. Elliin-llu-gguq qantarluni—
muragnek atam qantangqetullruut.
Aruqellinilriit. Ellii-llu-gguq qantaa tauna imiyuunaku makut aruqellriit.
Ilain-gguq tang taũgken qantait
imirturluki tua-i
tamakunek neqnek piuralliniaqekait.
Ayuqevkenateng,
neqnek ayuqenrilngurnek.

and they seemed so happy.
But she herself, it was said, was wearing her same old clothes,
not at all like her companions.
12
They brought various kinds of food
into that *qasgiq,*
bringing in food with them.
13
She recognized those people down there.
She glanced around, it was said,
and saw that her family was absent; her mother,
her father,
her other close relatives and her siblings were not there.
14
But then it was said that her companions,
those in her own group,
their mothers, their fathers, their younger siblings, their older sisters
    were down there,
mingling and
enjoying themselves.
15
And these ones here who were sitting down,
she perceived them
as being cheerful. Yet she herself, it was said, could not feel happy
    at that time.
16
And then
the ones whom she was watching
distributed food from bowls down there
which were filled with food.
17
It is said that they were[4]
all holding bowls,
grasping them. And she herself had a bowl.
(They used to have wooden bowls.)
They were distributing food. Those who were passing out food
    didn't fill her bowl.
But her companions' bowls, it was said,
were being filled
with that food.
There were all different kinds,
[and they were being served] with different kinds of food.

18
Qantaa tua caqerluni
iliita—
tangviarrluut nallunritlikci, taqukat imkut
uquit egellret tangviarrlugnek pitukait—
qantaũrlua tua tauna
tangviarrluarmek imiqallinikiit
pivakarluteng.

19
Tua-i-llu cali piinanermini,
tua-i-gg' piinanermeggni,
kemkuinermek cali tua-i
ek'arcilliniluni iliit.

20
Tua-i tuatnaluteng.
Tua-i taqluteng
nangucameng.

***

21
Tua-i-llu
tuani tua aqumgaurarraarluni taqngata
anlliniluni,
atakumi-gguq
taũgaam.
An'uq-gguq^e
qasgim elaturraanun, kenurrarluni—atam uqunek avani
    kenurrangqetullruut-llu qasgit elaturrait.
Kenurrarluni. Tua-i atam kenurram
acian unavet, talinranun,
acianun waten aqumqalliniluni.

22
Tua-i aqumgaluni uitauralliniluni tua-i anglaninrilami,
aliayugngami
ilamitun nunaniryugpegnani.

23
Neq'aqalliniluku qantani imna unitelliniluku qamavet qasgimun.
Tua-i-llu neq'aqerngamiu aqvaluku.
Iteryaaqelliniuq tua-i-gguq imkut tayim' ilai cataunateng-gguq tua-i!
Tua-i imkut ilai cataunateng tua-i!
Anelkirtellrunrilnganateng-llu-gguq tua-i,
taukut.

18
Then it happened
that one of them put into her bowl—
you probably know what a strip of seal blubber is, the seal blubber from
which the oil has been rendered; they call it *tangviarrluk*[5]—
they put a bit of rendered seal blubber
into her poor bowl
after some time had passed.
19
And then after she was there for a while,
well after they were there for a while,
one of them put a
bit of meat in.
20
That's what they did.
When they had run out of food,
they were done.

***

21
And so
when they were finished, having sat there for a while,
she went out,
only
it was at night time.
She went out[6]
into the *qasgiq*'s entryway, where there was a lamp— you see, in
        those day there used to be oil lamps in the entryways of the *qasgiq*s.
It had a lamp. And there under
the lamp, where it cast a shadow,
she sat down.
22
She sat down and stayed there because she was unhappy
and lonely,
and not cheerful like the rest.
23
She suddenly remembered her bowl, which she had left inside the *qasgiq*.
Having remembered it, she went to get it.
She entered, but, alas, those others who were with her were gone!
Her companions were gone!
It seemed as though no one had left
(although they were gone).

441

24
Tua teguluku
anngami tuavet tua-i
kenurram talinranun kanavet-am aqumqalliniluni.
Tua-i uitaurluni tua-i.
25
Tua-i-ll' uitainanrani,
qasgimek kiaken
yulkitliniluni anelriamek—
amiigit atam takratullruut,
tamakut amiigit.
Tua-i-ll' anluni maa-i pillinia
angutngullinilria man'a, tua imna aataurtellria.
Maa-i tua-i
nallaiqerluku
piqalriim pilliniuq, "Waq' ataki!
Waq' atak!" Wavet tua elitaqluku. Taum elitaqa'arrluku,
"Waq' ataki!
Waniwa qaill' pilriaten waniw' alaicit?"

Tumailnguq, Mike Albert, circa 1980. Photo by Andrew J. Chikoyak.

24
So she took it,
and went out
and sat down in the penumbra of the lamp.
There she remained.
25
As she stayed there,
from inside the *qasgiq*
came the sound of someone coming out—
you see, those entryways
used to be kind of long.
He came out and she saw
that it was a man, a man in his prime.
When he
got to where she was,
he said, "What do we have here!
What is this!" He recognized her there. Having recognized her, [he said],
"Well,
how is it that you are now visible?"

Uqamailnguq, Augustine Heavy, circa 1980. Photo by Andrew J. Chikoyak.

26
Tua-i
qaillun kiutii nalluaqa taum tua-i, kiullra.
Aling arenqiapaa-ll' tua-i!
Imna una tuqulleq,
tuqullruluni tua nasaurluq, nasaurluullruuq-gguq tauna arnaq.
Taugaam elpecicetun tua nasaurluuluni.
27
Kenurram talinrani tua uitaurluni.
Tua-ll' pillinia,
"Kitaki uitavkenak angayuqaagpenun agutnaamken!"
Aaniinun atiinun-llu.
28
Tua-i teguluku
anucamiu tuavet tua [agulluku]—nalluvkenaku-llu-gguq elliin tua
taukut nunani nunakngamiki,
yuum taum tua tuqullrem.
Agulluku.

***

29
Tua-i itrucani, itrulluku taum,
itrucani tua taukuk angayuqaak alangaarlutek tua-i uunguciilkarrlutek
tua-i,
alqunamek tangerrngamegnegu taun' panigtek,
imna una tuqulleq.
Tua-i cavkenani
yuuluni tua-i.
30
Taugaam-gguq tua-i aturai ukut tua-i imkurluteng,
ak'alliluteng,
tamarmeng aturai.
31
Tua-i arenqianaku, tua-i arenqianatek taukuk tua-i angayuqaak.
Tua-i piinanermeggni taukut tua nallunriqertelliniluki
nunat qasgimiut-llu.
32
Tua-i-ll' angalkut iliit[f]
ellimeqlirilliniluni
tauna tua-i,
ama-i nem'eggni uitalria,
matarrluku

26
I
don't know what her reply was.
Aling arenqiapaa! Oh my goodness!
That dead one,
the girl who had died, it was said that she was a young girl.
She was only a girl like yourselves.
27
She was sitting in the shadow of a lamp.
Then he said to her,
"*Kitaki*, don't sit there, let me take you to your parents!"
[He was going to take her] to her mother and father.
28
He took her
and when he took her he brought her there—she knew him because
    she was from the same village,
that dead [girl] was.
He brought her over.

***

29
When he took her in, when that one brought her in,
when he took her in, her parents were surprised and confused
because they saw their daughter unexpectedly,
the one who had died.
She was alive and
there was nothing wrong with her.

30
But it was said that her clothes were like so,
old and worn,
all of her clothes.
31
They were thankful for her; her parents were very thankful.
After a while that village learned about them,
about her and those in the *qasgiq*.
32
And then one
of the shamans,
directed them,
while she was staying over there at their house,
to remove her clothes

teq'umek...
(Atam tequutengqetullruut
tuknilrianek.
Atam *clorox*-aartun ayuqut
tamakut teq'ut tuknirilriit.
Atam assigtangqetullruut angtuarrarnek.
Ca uquq,
uquq uitangaunani qaimi.
Maani uquurciiqsaaqluni
yuum aturai, ervikuneng tamatumun teq'umun
tuknirilriamun aũg'arciqut waten-ll' ellirluteng.
Atam tua-i tamana
aũgkurluut calissuutellrat. Taqukat-llu cali ervigaqamegteki
assiriqapiarluki tua taq'aqluki
pitullruluki.
Cangaunateng-llu.
Wangkuta-ll' tamakunek qayat...
qayat-llu amirkait, amirkat, tungunqut tuavet kenicitullruluki ekluki.
Keniq'apiarluteng-llu ciilerqaarluteng.

Mellgar (Apac'iq), Jimmy Short; *Uliggaq*, Susie Angaiak; *Ayaginar (Acac'iq)*, Maggie Short; *Nauliar,* Rosalie Hooper; *Maklak*, Edward Hooper (child in front of mother); Maggie Sipary; *Asgulria*, John Hooper; and George and David Sipary. *Tununeq*. Photo from Jesuit Oregon Province Archives, Gonzaga University, negative number 504.22.

and with urine...
(You see, they used to have urine,
which was potent,
similar to Clorox,
a strong and potent urine.
They used to have big containers.
For example, oil
wouldn't permanently stain clothing.
Oil may be spilled
on someone's clothing, but if they were washed in urine,
in the strong kind, it would come off and become [clean] like this.
You see, that
was what they used, those poor people. Again, whenever they
      would wash sealskins
they would come out very nice;
that's what they did.
And they wouldn't be ruined.
And we, [in making] kayaks,

Wangkuta-llu
tamaaken liqneritnek
aaqessaatullruukut, *gum*-aqluki,
tamakut
ig'aqluki.
Yuk cangaituq nerlang'ermi, tamakunek-llu nerngermi cangaunani,
ik'iqerrngaunani-llu.
Tuaten tua ayuqetullruut.)
...pillinia
matarrluku
tamakucimun teq'umun
eruusqelluku, ervuqaasqelluku— ervuqeryaraq nallunriskessi.
Ervuqerluni wall' maqiluni cali tua-i erurnarqelarait.
Taũgaam tamakucimek piluku erusqelluku qainga,
ervuqaasqelluku, nutaan ervuqarraarluku aturaasqelluku.

33
Tuatnalliniluku tua-i angayuqaagken
angalkum taum alerquangateng
erurluku, ervuqerluku
tauna tua-i.
34
Tua-i-gguq
cavkenani assirluni tua-i; cangatevkenani wangkucicetun;
    elpecicetun ayuqluni
piluni, tauna tua-i.

***

35
Tua-i-gguq taumek qanemcillruuq.
Cunawa-gguq tamaa-i
nasaurluq taun' qanemcillinilria—
(Icigg' maa-i wangkuta
kanavet kalukarqata neryarturaqellriakut.
Ilaput-llu piyuunateng tayima; taiyuunateng
wall'u tapirraucuunateng neqrarnek.)
—waten-gguq
kalukarqata
ilagautetuyaaqetulliniut
imkut

would soak the young bearded seal skins which we used for the
     kayaks in it.
They would become soft and pliable after they were stiff.
And we used to
take those [dried] scrapings [from the inside of the skin]
and chew them like gum,
swallowing
them.
Even though a person ate from that nothing would happen,
and he wouldn't get sick.
That is how they were.)
...he gave instructions
that her clothes were to be removed
and she was to be washed in that kind of urine,
telling her to bathe—you know what *ervuqeryaraq* is,
that is, to wash or to take a bath.[7]
They were told to use only that kind in washing her body,
and after bathing she was to put on her clothes.
33
That's what her parents did,
because those were the instructions that the shaman gave,
that is, to wash and bathe
her in urine.
34
It was said
there was nothing wrong with her; she was fine like us; she was like
     yourselves,
that one there.

***

35
So, it was said, she related that story.
And so apparently that young girl
actually told a story about how—
(You know, nowadays we
go down there to eat when they have feasts;
some of us don't participate and some of us don't come
or share and provide food.)
—when they had feasts
like this,
those
who had died

maa-i tuqullret. Icigg' qungitelaqput;
tua-i-ll' tangyuunaki.
Ilagautetuyaaqetulliniaqut-gguq
wangkuta-gguq taũgaam tangerciigatetulliniaqaput.
Ilagarluta-gguq
nertuyaaqelliniaqut
wangkuta-gguq taũgaam tangyuitaput.
36
Cali-llu-gguq naugga avani
yuk tuquaqan,
uum yuum irniaminun aciutaqkii.
Tua-i taungurrluni ateqsagulluku tuqullrem atra, wall' arnassagaq,
    wall' angukar,
wall' angutngurtellria, nasaurluq, tan'gurraq
tuatnaaqan, tuquaqan.
37
Tua-i-gguq tamaa-i tamakut naugga ilaita tamaani
tauna tan'gurraq,
taum
qetunrarmi atra,
qantamek tua, apqiitnek imaqegcaqerluku payugtetukii neqkaanek.
Wall'u-gguq
iliini pilugugkaagnek-gguq piluguliluku taum arnam
tauna tua-i
atra irniami
pilugkit'laqii.
Wall'-llu-gguq iliin' cali
atkuliluku
cali taum
panimi, qetunrarmi,
aatami,g
aanami
atrit.
Atkuliluki-ll' cali,
tauna tua cikiqluki nutaranek atkunga'artelluku,
tamaani-gguq pitullruit.
38
Cuna-gguq tamaa-i
tuaten atrit
tun'aqaceteng atkugkilluki, pilugugkilluki, nerevkarluki neqnek,
cuna-gguq tua tuavet tua tuqullermun
tut'elallinilriit tamakut.

evidently used to come and join in. You know, we bury them;
then we don't see them anymore.
She said they evidently joined in;
however, we couldn't see them.
She said they joined us
and would eat,
but that we never saw them.
36
Moreover, it was said that
whenever a person died,
some person would give the name of the deceased to his child.
Therefore, when that happened, when someone died,
that child acquired the dead person's name, whether it be an old
    woman or an old man,
or a man in his prime, a young girl, or a young boy.[8]
37
For instance, a man who'd lost his son
would bring his son's namesake
something to eat in a bowl,
because it was for the sake of
his son's name;
or at times
a woman would make a pair of skin boots
for the one
who had her child's name
and present them to him.
Or sometimes
one would
make a parka
for her daughter's, or her son's,
or her father's,
or her mother's
namesakes.
They would also make parkas for them,
that is when they presented them with new clothes;
that is how they did it.
38
So apparently
when they
gave their namesakes parkas, skin boots, food to eat,
apparently those things were conveyed
to the one who had died.

Tua-i-gguq tuatnatulliniut-gguq tua maani
wangkuta.
Ila'urluitni wangkuta maa-i
tuatnayuilngukut ilaput
nerevkariluteng pilangraata!
39
Ilaketuyaaqelliniaqaput-gguq tua-i
callemteńun, pillemteńun, anglanillemteńun.
40
Tuaten tua-i
qanemcillrullinilria tauna tua-i, qanemciurayagallrullinilria nasaurluq.
Tuaten-gguq tua etetulliniukut tua-i.
41
Wangkuta-gguq taŭgaam tangyuitelliniaqaput.
Tamaa-i-gguq wangkuta tamakunun maligucunrilngurni—ilaput
    icigg' maligucuilnguut—
wall' ilagaucuilnguut
cuna-gguq tamaa-i tamakut ilagaucuilnguut
tua-i tayim' cataunateng taukuni
yuk.
Alianarqelliniuq-gguq cataitaqata ilani, aanani, aatani,
alqani uyurani-ll'.
Tamakut-gguq ilai nunaniryullruut taum nalliini,
tangaaluki aanani, aatani,
uyurani
alqani-llu.
Tua-i-gguq etetulliniukut tuaten.

42
Anirtima
wii cal' Kuigpagmi,
Kuigpagmi cal' qanqauteqallruanga
aŭg'um angukaraurtellriim.
Qanqauteqallruanga-am tua carrarmek tua-i waniwa-ll'-am
    nalluyagucuunaku.
43
Tua-i-gg' tuaten waniw'
tuaten tua iquklitellria. Ilii tua pinricaaqsugnarqaqa, pinrilkekag tua.
Tang akaurcan nalluyagupakaamku.

That is how it is with us
today.
Alas, some of us, poor things,
we do not participate
even though they have feasts!
39
It is said that they evidently join us
in our work, in our activities and in our festivities.
40
That is
what that one recounted; that is how that young girl told the story.
That is what apparently happens to us.
41
But, it is said, we never see them.
So for those of us who do not follow—you know, those among us
    who do not get involved—
or participate,
apparently for those who do not participate,
they are not there with them,
with that person.
It is a very sad affair when their families are not there, that is, one's
    mother, one's father,
one's older sister, and one's younger sibling.
Her companions were happy back then,
seeing their mothers, their fathers,
their younger siblings,
and their older sisters.
That, it is said, is what happens to us.
42
No wonder then
when I was at the Yukon,
at the Yukon he also told me about this,
this old man did.
He told me a little bit about it, and I have not forgotten it.

43
This is
the end of it. I probably didn't tell all of it, I know I didn't.
You see it's been so long and I have started to forget the story.

TENGESQAUKTARAAM ATII

Cakataar Tununermiu

***

1
Camek atak piqaalta?
Im' taũgaam Tengesqauktaraam taũgaam atiinek pikuma.
Cali tua
qanemcikellratun niicugniurallemtun piciqaqa; ilii tayim' piksaiciiqaqa.

2
Taum tua Tengesqauktaraam atii...
Ikani ika-i
Qanrangami
tuqullrulriik [Tengesqauktaraam] angayuqaak.
3
Tua-i-ll' waten
kiugna Cakcaaq,
yungqerturatullruut atam makut carvat
qaũgkut kiatmun qavani.
School-arvingvailgata
yungqerrluteng qaũgkut.
4
Tuaten tua-i Cakcaarmiut yungqellratni,
cikuluni.
5
Tua-i-ll' cikulnguuraqanrakun
piinanratni
ikamraq,
ikamrak-gga, tekitellinilria ikamralugpianek ikamrarluteng.
6
Tauna tua-i Tengesqauktaraam angayuqaak,
aatii aanii-llu
una-gg' cali
paniak,
pingayuuluteng;

454

THE FATHER OF TENGESQAUKTAR

Jack Angaiak of Tununak

***

1
What shall we do now?
I'm going to do "The Father of *Tengesqauktar*."
Moreover,
I'm going to tell it the way it was told, the way I heard it; I'll
    probably not tell it all.
2
That *Tengesqauktar*'s father...
Over there
at *Qanrangaq*,
his [*Tengesqauktar*'s] parents died.
3
So it was like this:
inland *Cakcaaq*,
and other streams and tributaries used to have people living around them,
upriver there in the inland areas.
At the time before schools came,
there were people up there.
4
Once there were people at *Cakcaaq*,
[the land and river] froze up.
5
So then it had been frozen for a while,
and after some time,
a dogsled
arrived, their sled being a freight sled.
6
It was the parents of *Tengesqauktar*,
his father and mother
along with their
daughter,
there were three of them;

tekitellinilriit imkut tuqullret.
Tua yuuluteng, tua-i yuuluteng wangkucicetun tua-i!

***

7
Tua-i tuavet nem'un itlinilriit.
Taukut cakneq nemiut alangaarluteng imkunek taukunek
    tuqullernek.
Taugkun-gguq yuuluteng tua-i,
cavkenateng tua-i waten yugtun ayuqluteng!
8
Iillayugluteng taukut.
9
Cali tua-i qanaangraan una atiit qanyuunateng,
kiuyuunaku.
Tua-i-gga
tuqullruata,
tuqullruluteng tua piata.
10
Tua-i-gguq taukut
taum
umyugait nalluvkenaki.
Umyuarteqellrit qanyuilengraata nalluvkenaki,
taum tua-i angutem.
11
Pillinikai
qanraqami kiugaqluni pilaasqelluni.
Cangaitniluki.
Qanernanrirngaitniluki-llu.
Cangaitniluki waniwa.
12
Tuaten-gguq tua qanaalluki, qanaaskai.
Nalluvkenaki umyarteqellrit taukut,
imkut taukut tuqullret.
Tauna taugaam nasaurluq,
irniarak,
maliak
waten kegginaa-gguq cataunani.
13
Nuyai maani waten
aqevlaluteng kegginaani.
Kegginaan tua-i capluku, kegginaa tangrrumavkenani.

the ones who had died had arrived.
Yet they were people, they were people like us!

***

7
They entered his house.
The people in the house were astonished at these people
    who had died.
But they were alive;
nothing was wrong with them and they were people like us!
8
They were utterly amazed by them.
9
Although *Tengesqauktar*'s father was talking, they didn't speak,
they didn't answer him.
It was because
they had died,
because they were dead.
10
It was said this [dead] person
knew
what the people were thinking;
that man
knew their thoughts even though they didn't say anything.
11
He told them
to answer him when he talked.
He said nothing would happen to them.
And they wouldn't lose their [power of] speech.[1]
He said nothing would happen to them now.
12
He talked to them in that fashion, he was talking to them [thus].
The people who had died
knew what they were thinking.
This girl, however,
their child,
the one who accompanied them,
her face was not visible.
13
Her hair was
dangling in front of her face.
Her face was covered, her face could not be seen.

Tua-i uitaurallinilria tauna.

***

14
Tua-i taum atii
qanlliniuq
tua-i waniwa
utercugngayaaqniluteng,
wangkucicetun waten yuurrluteng,
wangkutnun yuucimteńun,
utercugngarpagyaaqniluteng.
15
Taũgaam
piyugngang'ermeng
waniw' tua uitaniluteng.
Tauna tua-i panini pillinia,
apertullinia
uumun taũgaam waniw' nuqniluteng.
16
Tua-i-gguq-gga
waten
uterrluteng

She did not move at all.[2]

***

14
So the girls father
said
that
they could come back
and become alive, just like us,
returning to our way of life,
and that they could come back quite easily.
15
But
even though they could,
they said they were staying [where they were, amongst the dead].
Concerning that daughter of his,
he pointed out
it was she who was holding them back.
16
He said it was because
if they did
return again [to the world of the living],

Carriralria, Peter Aluska, *Tununeq,* 1958. Photo by Christine Heller, courtesy of the Anchorage Museum of History and Art B91.11.423.

wangkutnun yuucimteńun pikuneng,
tauna-gguq tuani
paniak
ilaminek waten nasaurluullgutminek
aquigaqata-llu
ayuqnialarciqngan
ellaicetun piyugyaaqluni,
ilagarciigaciiqngalamiki-gguq.
17
Cali-llu-gguq ilain
imkurciqngatgu,
tua-i-gg' alikluku tatamurratekluku.
(Cat-kiq tayim' piatgu?)
Tua-i-gguq-gga
iingirarallrulliniatgu
tua-i taumun kalivvluteng.
Ayuqnialarciqngan-gguq
waten ilagaulluni waten nasaurlurnun
aquigaqata.
Tua-i taun' pisciigalutekniluku.
Yuurcugngayaaqniluteng ellaicetun.
18
Tua-i taukut
nemiut taukut itellrita
nerevkalliniluk' tua-i.
Nerluteng tua-i.
Tua-i-llu
nernermek tua taqngameng pilliniuq,
tua-i taun' qanlliniuq,
atiit
quyaluni cakneq, "Quyanaqvaa-ll' tua-i cakneq
nerevkarluta
elluarrluta ciuniuqevcikut,
elluarrluta!
Elpeci-ll' maa-i cangaituci.
Cakanirngaituq man' yuucirci
yuugurallerci-ll' cangaituq.
19
Cakanirngaituci!
Ik'iqerrngaunaci-llu!"

if they did come back to our world,
when the young girls of her age group
played,
then that
daughter of their's
would envy them and want to be like them;
she would yearn in vain to be like them,
since, he said, she would probably be unable to join them.
17
Moreover, he said, her playmates
would react to her
and would be frightened and be startled by her.
(I wonder what they meant?)
He said it was because
something had removed her eyes,
and they were held back on account of that.
He said, she would envy the girls
who were the same age as she was
whenever they played.
That was their reason for not coming back.
Yet they would be able to become living people again and be like them.
18
So the
people in the household
fed the intruders.
Then they ate.
And so
when they were done eating
that man, their father,
said
he was very grateful, "Thank you very much
for letting us eat;
you received us well,
very well.
Nothing will happen to you now;
your lives will not change and
your way of life will not change.
19
Nothing will change!
And you will not get sick!"[3]

***

20
Waniwa tua-i qanlliniuq
upagniluteng
nunakegtaarkameggnun
assilriamun,
elluarrluteng uitallerkameggnun
upagniluteng.
Piqaa,
Cakcaam-qa kangiani nallunritarci Qasginguaq?
Tanglararci waten penguq
neglirnermi?
Tua-i taun' Qasginguamek pitukengaat.
Tuavet-gguq tua-i upagtut
elluarrluteng uitallerkameggnun.
Tuaten tua-i qanaallinilria
atii tauna.
21
Tua-i-llu
quyavikliniluki tua-i taukut.
Anluteng tua ayakatarniluteng tua waniw'
nunakameggnun.
Anngameng tua-i
ava-i Cakcaakun ayangartelliniut.
Cakcaaq asgurluku.
22
Aling tua-i-gguq tang tua-i
tayim' ayalriit.
Taukut-llu-gguq imkut tua-i
itervikellri yuut
qanellratun cavkenateng.
Qanaayaaqelriameng-llu qanernanrirpegnateng.
Cavkenateng ayuquciat tua-i cakanirpegnani.
Tuaten tua-i
taumek qanemciuraqalriim taumek
tuaten tua-i taktaluku
taqellrukii.
Tua uitayaaqelrianga-llu cali,
cali qanernayukluku,
tua-i tayim' taqluku
tuaten.

***

20
And then he said
they were moving
to a better place to live,
saying that they were relocating
to a good place
where they would live comfortably.
What is it called now?
Do you know that place *Qasginguaq*, at the source of the *Cakcaaq*?
Have you seen the berm
on the north side?
They call that berm *Qasginguaq*.
They were moving to that place
where they would live comfortably.
That's what [*Tengesqauktar's*] father
said.
21
And so
he thanked those people.
They went out and said they were going
to their future home.
When they went out,
they started on their way over yonder along the *Cakcaaq*,
heading upstream on the *Cakcaaq*.
22
Aling, so it was said
they left.
And as for these people
upon whom they had intruded,
nothing happened to them, just as he had said.
And although they talked, they didn't lose their speech.
They stayed the way they were, without alteration.
The person
who told this story
made it that long
and concluded.
I stayed a while longer,
thinking he might tell some more
but he ended it
this way.

23
Tua-llu!
Waten tua taktaaqa.

***

24
Cingarkaq: (mumigcista)
Aũg'umek apnaluten.
Alangrut-qa qanaataqatki qanernanrilartut akwarpak akwanun?
25
Cakataar:
Tuaten-ggem tua-i qanqautellrukiingaa,
aũg'um angutem iliini,[a]
waten kiumraluki
pillerkaat.
Tuaten-am tua-i qanqallrulria.
26
Cingarkaq:
Qanyuirulluteng?
27
Cakataar:
Ii-i!
Tuaten-am tua-i.

Iraluq, Bernadette Agimuk, jigging for tomcod near *Tununeq*. Photo from Jesuit Oregon Province Archives, Gonzaga University, negative number 504.23.

23
So then!
I'm making it this long.

***

24
Eliza Orr: (translator)
I want to ask you about something.
If somebody talks to a ghost, do they stop talking forever and ever?
25
Jack Angaiak:
According to what
one of the men told me,
this is the way
to react to them [by not talking].
That is what he said.
26
Eliza Orr:
They would stop talking?
27
Jack Angaiak:
Yes!
Just like that.

Fishing for tomcod at the foot of the cliffs near *Tununeq*. Photo from Jesuit
Oregon Province Archives, Gonzaga University, negative number 504.18.

28
Cingarkaq:
Assiringairulluteng?
Qanyuirulluteng?
29
Cakataar:
Naam', pillilriit-gga taum tua-i assiringaitellilria tua tuaten,
tuaten pilria.
30
Cuniq:
Tamana-gg'-am tamaa-i
waten yuunrilngurmun,
alangrumun,
qaneryaraq
tua-i
una
qanaangraan
alangruq
tua-am inerquutekluku.
Inerquutnguluku wiinga niitelallruaqa
kiumrasqevkenaku.
31
Taũgaam tua-i umyuakun ugg'un
kiumrang'ermi cavkenani.
Una waniwa
waten kiumrakuni,
tauna-gguq
qanaalleq
yuk
qanernanrituuq.
Tuaten-am tua-i
niitetullruaqa tamana
kiumasqevkenaku.
32
Waten
aũgna uum qanemcillra
qanaangermi
cavkenani qanernanrirnaunani
nalqigulluku taum piani.
Tuaten tua-i ayuquq.

28
Eliza Orr:
They would never recover their speech?
They would stop talking?
29
Jack Angaiak:
I don't know; perhaps it's that way and one would not get better
if that happens.
30
Jents Flynn:
Well,
when a dead person,
a ghost speaks,
the rule
is that
even though it is talking,
there is a prohibition against talking to
that
ghost;
I heard there is a prohibition
against responding to it.
31
But nothing will come of it if one responds
with just his thought alone.
It is said that if a person
here
replies,
that person
who talks
will lose the power of speech.
Thus, according
to what I used to hear,
one should not answer.
32
However,
according to that story he just told,
even though one spoke,
his power of speech was unaffected
since that [ghost] clarified the matter for him.
It is like that.

Canaar, Peter Post, and family, 1930s. Photo from Jesuit Oregon Province Archives, Gonzaga University, negative number 504.19.

ANGALKUT
'SHAMANS'

*"Then I sought solitude, and here I soon became very melancholy.
I would sometimes fall to weeping, and feel unhappy without
knowing why. Then, for no reason, all would suddenly be changed,
and I felt a great, inexplicable joy, a joy so powerful that I could
not restrain it, but had to break into song, a mighty song, with only
room for the one word: joy, joy!"*

— Aua, an Iglulik shaman,
as told to Knud Rasmussen
(Rasmussen 1929: 118-119)

Shamans

One aspect of shamanism has been often misrepresented: its practices and beliefs, rather than being a manifestation of the purely exotic and archaic, express certain authentic themes that cut across all religions, cultures and historical periods. As Eliade (1964) tells us in *Shamanism: Archaic Techniques of Ecstasy*, the shaman above all is adept in the techniques of spiritual ecstasy; he is able to traverse the different planes that separate the sacred and the profane. He is the very essence of the religious life, able to experience the eternal, changeless and irreducibly real amidst the chaos and suffering of the moment. Although the shaman is often portrayed as a charlatan who finds his cultural niche and an outlet for his psychosis preying on the pious imagination, in fact he is a bona fide religious figure, akin to the mystic or the saint. He is variously a healer, a medium, a magician, occasionally a celebrant, but in all these his unique qualification is that he possesses the ability to transcend the bonds of body and sense, to assume a purely spiritual being and thereby journey into the beyond to communicate with the world of spirits.

Death and resurrection are common metaphors in shamanic initiations. In order to communicate with the spirits, an aspirant must die and return to life again (Eliade 1964), thereby becoming a spirit himself. Among the Iglulik as described by Rasmussen, the initiation of the shaman begins with the procurement of his *qaumanεq*, his special "lighting" and "enlightenment," which enables him to see the secret world that only the spiritually adept can know. But before he can acquire his familiar spirits, the shaman's stock-in-trade, he must first see himself as a skeleton, divested of all perishable substance. Hawkes (1916: 129) and Lantis (1950: 312) report similar initiation motifs in Labrador and East Greenland respectively. Lantis says that in the case of the East Greenlandic shaman, Ajukutoq, the aspirant is devoured by a great white bear, and the bear then regurgitates the bones, which are re-fleshed and re-animated. This experience of the disarticulation and re-animation of the skeleton is practically universal in shamanic initiation rites (Eliade 1964), for among hunting and gathering people the bones are the element of the physical entity that symbolize enduring, changeless nature. It is the bones of game animals, for example, that are preserved and buried in a consecrated place in order to assure the reincarnation and return of the animal to the hunter. In obtaining this vision of himself as a skeleton, every bone of which he must be able to name in the special shaman's language, the shaman undergoes, at least metaphorically, a death and resurrection experience, being transformed into a spirit. He has annulled death and the frailties of his corporeal existence and is once again able to ascend to the celestial regions or to descend to the infernal regions (Eliade 1964; Rasmussen 1929: 109-114).

Much less is known of Yup'ik shamanism than of shamanism among the Inuit, largely because of the work of Rasmussen, who attained a remarkable knowledge of his subjects. But we do know that Yupiit and Inuit shamans engaged in many of the same activities: healing, divination, weather conjuration, exorcism of ghosts and malevolent spirits, descents to the underworld, and ascents to the sky and moon. Whether such shamanic journeys took place in the flesh, or occurred only in the spirit while the shaman was away from his body, is a moot point; all participants believed that in either case the journey was authentic (Lantis 1950: 316). Yupiit shamans, like their Inuit counterparts, performed their seances in a state of semi-nudity in the dark with lamps extinguished, with gut-skin parka and dog-skin mittens, a type of shaman's costume, often bound with cords. Finally, in Yupiit and Inuit shamanism the selection, training and initiation of shamans seems to have been quite similar. By all accounts the aspirant was prone to introversion and melancholia, even occasional bouts of dementia, and spent much time alone in the wilderness. In the Eastern Arctic shamanism was a deliberate choice of aspirants who sought out solitude and mortification, whereas in the Western Arctic one was "chosen" by the spirits (Lantis 1950:313), often against one's will, although one could not refuse the summons, which by some accounts could be terrifying. This has led to much speculation about the personality type of the shaman and the origin of the ecstatic trance. Lantis (1950: 317) viewed the shaman's experience as a controlled schizophrenic state, in the service of the organized system of religious beliefs of the community. Eliade, on the other hand, maintained that the difficulties involved in the mastery of the craft, the apparent prestige of the shaman in many communities, and, most importantly, the fact that the shaman attains his position not because he was sick but because he was able to cure himself of his sickness argues against the thesis of psychopathy (Eliade 1964: 24-30).

In the following stories, we encounter shamans engaged in activities that are typically associated with shamanism: healing, shamanic competition and cursing, and exorcism. In *Angutet Pingayun* a shaman who is being vexed summons his familiar spirit, a *neqleq*, a white-fronted goose. It was the possession of familiar spirits that enabled a shaman to practice his craft and perform his wondrous feats, and practically any creature could serve as a familiar: foxes, bears, wolverines, dogs, sharks, mountain spirits, moon spirits, the dead, sea scorpions (Rasmussen 1929, 1931); dogs, walrus, half-people, half-birds, fish, mosquitoes, ghosts, dwarfs (Lantis 1946). In *Arnaq Irniani-llu* a shaman performs another familiar task, exorcising the malevolent ghost of a woman. Souls are volatile entities, particularly vulnerable and dangerous during rites of passage and times of life crises; people must be especially careful not to offend or damage animal or human souls for fear of retribution. A mother dies in childbirth and is buried with her live infant; she subsequently returns in a rage to seek revenge. In this story we encounter the familiar Yup'ik motif of the "lesser shaman" (see *Tuunrangayiim Iteryaaqellra* [Orr and Orr 1995: 187], or the first part of the Bladder Boy story in *Nakaciuryaraq cali-llu Tan'gurraq Uitalleq Taqukani* in this volume). Whereas shamans of greater repute prove insufficient to the task, a lesser shaman of no repute is selected and accomplishes what none of the others can do. In *Callartellria Angun* a shaman is cursed and made wretchedly ill by a rival; we glimpse the sometimes intense rivalry that existed between shamans and occasionally erupted in supernatural duels. In this story we encounter a shaman who is able to separate spirit and body, to exist temporarily in a disembodied state, this being the purpose of the shaman's self-induced ecstasy. Finally, in *Illugngali* and *Tengesqauktar*, we encounter two shamans, one a reckless daredevil and the other a healer, both of whom are essentially benevolent, using their supernatural powers to do good and refraining from using it to curse or seek revenge against enemies.

With the advent of Christianity and the subsequent devaluation of shamanism, a great deal of valuable information on the subject has been lost. For a very long time many people were reluctant to discuss the tabooed subject. Nowadays, although elders may be willing to talk about it, much is unknown because the generation of elders who observed shamanistic performances did so in their youth and may not have fully understood what they observed. Consequently, the narrative record is considerably diminished, and although in these stories there is mention of shamans as performers of marvelous feats, there is little about the cosmology and theology that underlies the rich religious complex of shamanism and makes it intelligible to contemporary thought.

ARNAQ IRNIANI-LLU

Cakataar Tununermiu

***

1
Ii-i, tua-i waniwa
niitellruaramtun qanrutkeqatarqa tua imna pisqellren tua,
niitellruaramtun.
2
Waniwa qanqatartua, qanemcikqatarqa niicugniurallemkun.
3
Qanemcikestiin qanemcikurallrani tauna niicugniurallrukeka
qaillun-llu ayagnirpegnaku camek.
4
Taugaam qanellrulria tauna niicugnilqa taukut nunat,
nunat taukut tua aperluki.

***

5
Tua-i-llu tauna
nunat taukut iliit, arnat,
makut qingatulit,
iliit qingarluni.
6
Tua-i-llu
anenariani tauna qingaa
anlliniluni.
7
Tua-i naugga avani irnicurlagluki,
yuungcaristetaitellrani
qanlallrulriit, tuaten tua-i apquciqellrukiit; irnicurlagluni tuquaqluni,
aunrarluni-gg' tua pilallilria.
8
Tuaten tua-i taun' irnilria
irnicurlagluni tua-i
tuqullinilria.

MOTHER AND HER CHILD

Jack Angaiak of Tununak

***

1
Yes, now
I'm going to recount the story you wanted, as I heard it,
the way I heard it.
2
Now I'm going to talk; I'm going to tell it the way I heard it.
3
When the storyteller told the story I listened to,
he didn't introduce it with anything.[1]
4
But the one I listened to spoke of a certain village;
he mentioned a certain village.

***

5
So then
one of the villagers, one of the women
of child bearing age
was pregnant.
6
And then
when the time came for the baby to be born,
it arrived.
7
They spoke of complications in those days during childbirth,
back when there were no doctors,
as one of the causes of death in childbirth,
most likely from bleeding.
8
Thus the one who gave birth
had complications during childbirth
and she died.

475

9
Irniacuayagii-ll' tauna tua mikluni
tua-i anenerraaraami.
10
Tua-i-llu
tua-i tauna
aanii [tuquan],
aaniinun
tauna mikelnguq—
aling tua tegunritliniamegteggu-am—
aaniinun qumiliutelliniluku, atkungqerturatullruameng
aũgkut.
Qumiliulluku,
iluanun atkuin qemaggluku
qungitelliniluku
tauna
arnaq.
11
Tua-i-llu
piavet tua-i
tagulluku
qungilluku, qaillun ellamun pilliatni,
ellamun
pillikiit, qerratarrluku acia.
12
Qungilluku tua-i eggluku tauna-ll' mikelnguq tua-i,
mikelngucuayagaq, tua-i neplirluni
atkuin iluatni.
13
Tua-i-llu
taum kinguakun ernerni-ll' tayim' qavcini uitaat tamakut,
taukurmiut,
tua-i upagauralliniluteng
up'nerkillerkameggnun. Tua-i-llu
tua-i tuanlluteng
up'nerkillerkameggni, tua nangluteng
tamaavet ellilliniluteng.

***

14
Tua-i-llu
qakuan tayima

9
And that little baby of hers was tiny,
since it was newly born.
10
So then
when
that little child's mother [died]—
aling, because they didn't take it and keep it—
[they took the child]
to its mother
and put it [in its mother's parka],
since those people always had those parkas.
They put the child inside,
placing it inside her parka
and they buried
that
woman.
11
And
they
brought her up there
and buried her, and since they probably placed her outside,
they might have placed her
above the ground.[2]
12
So they put her in [a box], burying her and that little child;
that tiny child was making noise
inside her parka.
13
After
that incident, those people stayed there for some time,
those people from thereabouts,
and then they started moving away
to their spring camp. So
they stayed there
at their spring camp, and there was nobody left behind,
all having gone [to their spring camp].

***

14
Then
some time later

477

malruulutek taukuk
aqvaillinilutek
tan'gurraak.
15
Qamigautegnek-gguq ikamrirlutek
taukut tua-i nunameng tungiitnun
ayaglutek, ernerpak tua ayaglutek.
16
Tua-i yaaqsinritlian unugpailgatek tekicarturlutek taukunun
nunanun
yuirutlernun.
17
Tua-i-llu
yaa-i canimelliqerluk' pilliniuk
paũgkut elivret tanglliniik, pilliniik,
pingna-gguq icivaq imumi
qungitellrat,
qungitellrani yuk paũgna
qungum mengliini utertaarturalria.
Tua-i pava-i tua-i!
Tuavet tua nunanun tekicamek pilliniak
tunumingqellinilria
pamani!
Waten tua-i
tunumigluku atkumi iluatgun
utertaarturluni, pilliniak-gguq imna, imna-gguq tua tauna icivaq tuqulleq,
utertaarturluni qungumi mengliini.
18
Tua-i taukuk arenqialamek
mayurrvigmun
mayurlutek.
19
Tua-i-llu
tauna-gguq mayurrvik tua-i,
alailameng makut qulinrin akuliitgun
pilliniak:
pia-i!
Piuraqerluni man'a
taillinilun', atralliniluni
ullaglukek, tua-i maa-i tailuni tua-i!
20
Tua-i-ll'

a couple
of boys
went to get some things.
15
Using a *qamigaun*, a low kayak sled,[3]
those two traveled on and on all day long
in the direction of their home.
16
Perhaps because it wasn't far away, they were about to reach that village,
which was deserted,
before nightfall.
17
So then
when they got closer they looked
up there where the grave markers were and saw
the one they had buried
not long ago,
up there where she had been buried,
pacing back and forth next to the coffin.
So there she was!
When they got to that village they saw
that she was carrying someone on her back
up there!
She was carrying it like this,
on her back inside her parka;
they realized that it was the one who died not long ago,
pacing back and forth, back and forth, next to her coffin.
18
So because those two were spooked,
they climbed into
an elevated food cache.
19
And
because that elevated food cache
had cracks between the [planks],
they looked
and there she was!
Soon she
was approaching them, coming down,
drawing near them! There she was, coming towards them!
20
Then

tayima tekilluni.
Pilliniag-am una-i
waten cali nacitet qelpaussuarallritgun
tangerrluku una-i mayurrviim aciani.
Imna-ggur' man'a icivaq tua-i
tuqulleq!
Tunumiayagarluni-gguq
mikelngurmek.
21
Taugaam-gguq
kegginaa-gg' tua cataunani;
nuyaminek waten pimaluni, nuyain capluku.
Kegginaa alaitevkenani.

she got there.
Again they saw her down there,
through the cracks on the floor planks,
underneath the elevated food cache.
It was the one who
had died not long ago!
They say she was carrying a little child
on her back.
21
But, it is said,
her face wasn't visible;
she was using her hair like this, [using] her hair to cover it.
Her face wasn't visible.

Cakataar, Jack Angaiak, circa 1980. Photo by Andrew J. Chikoyak.

22
Aren tua-i qaillun pillerkailamek uitaurallermegni, tuaken
    neqsaaglutek-gguq piamek,
waken tua-i
neqnek qillertaanek
aipaan
waten tua teguqaucecuaqerluni neqkuinrayagarmek
tamaaggun tua-i
ig'arcetliniluku.
Igceskiini-llu camna migpallarrluni.
23
Tua-i-llu-gguq camna qanertuq,
"Arenqiapaa! Cat ukut?"
Aren quyaluni cakneq tua-i tauna
taukunek neqnek, neqrugarnek,
cikiucirminek!
24
Tua-ll'-am tuaten qanerngan tangengnaqu'urluku
tamaaggun qulinerrarkun tangrraa
imkut-gguq waten neqkuinermek teguqautellni kana-i.
Aren imkut-gguq tua-i ukut
amllertaciluteng kana-i tusngalriit kanani!
25
Aren quyaluni tua-i!
Tua-i-llu teguluki kana-i
anlliniluni,
qungum tungiinun pava-i ayagturalliniluni taukut tegumiaqluki
neqrugaat. Carrarmek ig'arceciyaaqluni!
Tamaa-i aviukaqniluki pitullruut atam, aviukaqluteng
neqkuinrayagarnek.
Wiinga-ll' tangvatullruanka.
26
Tua-i-ll' qungum amatiinun tua-i,
tekicamiu qunguni tauna,
tekicamiu amatiikun uivluni pilriim tua-i-ll' tamarluni tayima.

***

27
Tua-i tamarngan
tua-i up'arrlutek, uplutek.
Qamigautek tua tauk' pilukek,
ayallinilutek tua-i aqvaqurlutek.

22
Aren, since they didn't know what to do while they were there,
    because they were getting food from there,
one of the two
took a tiny bit of food
from a bundle of food
there
and dropped it
through [a crack] there.
When he dropped it, it made a loud thump down there.
23
So then, it is said that the one down there exclaimed,
"*Arenqiapaa*! Oh my goodness, what are these?"
Aren, she was very grateful
about that food, about that big bundle of food,
for having given her some!
24
So then, when she said that, he kept trying to see her
through those cracks and saw
that the little pinch of food which he had taken was down there.
Aren, there it was down there,
a goodly amount, lying down there!
25
Aren, she was grateful!
So then she took it
and left,
heading for the grave up there, holding on to that
big bundle of food. Yet he had dropped just a pinch!
In those days they said they used to give food offerings, offering
tiny amounts of food.
And I used to watch them.
26
So then when she got to the other side of the grave,
when she got to her coffin,
she went around to the other side and disappeared.

***

27
So when she disappeared,
they quickly got ready, preparing to go.
They took that *qamigaun*, that low kayak sled
and left running.

28
Tua-i kingyaraqlutek tua-i
piamek,
tua-i-gga uluryayugngamek.
Ayainanragni-gguq pilliniuk,
kingyalliniuk,
pama-i-gguq
alaillinilria
kingunragnek!
29
Tua-i-gguq aqvaqulriik. Tuatnangraagnek-gguq imna
tauna canimelliinarluni, angungiinarlukek,
cukanrulliniami tua tauna.
Arenqialami-gguq anguarkaurcatek
caviggangqelliniami aipaak,
qaillun pillerkailamek,
tauna tua, arulairlutek, caviggani
aipaan
man'a tua qanikcaq,
waten tua kingunertek qanikcaq man'a,
pilalliniluku.
Pilaggaarluku tua-i cali ayallinilutek
kingyaraqluku.
30
Tua-i-llu maa-i yaaqsinriqerluni tamana-gguq tekisngatqerluku
arulailliniluni.

31
Ukatmun-gguq tua-i ayagyaaqnaurtuq tua-i tauna.
Tua-i-llu-gguq ak'akik' yaaqsigiqerluni cali uterrluni cali avatmun cali
    ayagnaurtuq waten.
Ak'anun
tamana kepesciiganaku.
32
Pellaluni-llu-gguq-am tayima.
Tayima tua-i. Akaurteqanrakun kingyalliniug-am uka-i.

33
Taugaam-gguq alarutlermini
imum cukanqelluku.
Cukanruluni
piluni, cukarikanirluni.

28
They kept on looking back
because
they were afraid of her.
As they went on
they looked back
and there she was;
she had appeared
behind them!
29
So, it was said, they ran. Even so,
she was getting closer and closer and overtaking them
because she was apparently faster.
It was obvious that she was going to overtake them,
and since one of them had a knife
and because he was scared and they didn't know what else to do,
they stopped, and taking his knife,
that one
cut into the snow,
making a line in the snow
right behind them.
After cutting it, again they took off,
glancing back every once in a while.[4]
30
So then when she wasn't far off, just when it seemed that she had
    reached that line,
she stopped.
31
She would try to go this way.
And then, it was said, she would go a long way and would go back
    again and try the other way.
For a long time
she couldn't cut through that line.
32
And then she disappeared.
Time passed. After a long while they looked back and there she was,
    coming towards them.
33
But, it is said that when she appeared,
she was faster than before.
She had picked up speed
and was approaching faster than before.

34
Tua-i-ll'-am cali
arenqiarucameg-am tua-i anguarkaurcatek
tuatnalliniluk' tua-i ceterluku.
35
Tekicamiu-am tamana tua-i taum
arulailliniluni.
Tua-i-ggur-am tuaten ayagnaurtuq tua-i tayima.
Cali-ll' tumllermikun cali tua-i ayagluni cali tua-i.
Tua-i-'m kepesciiganaku.
36
Tua-i-llu tayim' pellaluni.
Pellaqerluni, tua-i waten kingyarturaamek,
ak'anivkenani
imum tua-i-gg' cukanqelluku alarulluni-am tua maa-i.
37
Cali-am tua alarutellria-am cukarikanirluni!
38
Tuatnaaqlutek.
Tua-i tamana qaritekaqluku tauǧaam-gguq tua cukariinarluni
angullrak.

***

39
Tuatnaluku-ll'-am tua-i. Tuatnarraarluku tua ayaglutek tayima-am tua.
Nunanun-llu tekillutek
taukunun tua-i.
Qanrutliniluki-ll' tua-i qanemcilluki
taukut.

40
Tua-i qanrucaiceteng imkut,
nunat taukut up'nerkillerni uitalriit
qasgimun tua-i agurallinilriit, qasgimun tua-i, qakemkut.
Yugtairulluni qasgimun tauǧaam quyurrluteng.
41
Tua-i taman' agiirrluni tua-i.
Anenermek-llu taqluteng
tekiteqataan tua.
Imumek tua-i yugyagluni qasgim ilua tua-i.

34

So then again
because they were scared and since she was going to catch up with them,
as before, they made a mark.[5]

35

When she got to that mark,
she stopped.
Then she proceeded as she had done previously.
Again she went back the way she had before.
And again she couldn't cut through it.

36

So then she disappeared.
She disappeared and they kept on looking back,
and it didn't take long
before she was coming up on them, even faster.

37

Again she was coming up on them, even faster and faster!

38

As before, they kept doing that.
And that would slow her down, but it was said that she kept getting
     faster and faster
at catching up to them.

***

39

They did that again [making a mark]. Having done that, they went on
     and as before she disappeared.
They got to the village,
to that one.
And then they told
the village people the story.

40

As soon as they were told,
the ones who were staying at the spring camp,
all those out there, went to the *qasgiq*.
There were no people outside, but all had congregated in the *qasgiq*.

41

That one, she, was approaching.
They stopped going out
because she was about to arrive.
Thus the *qasgiq* was full of people.

***

42
Tua-i uitainanratni
cakma tua-i amigkun itliniluni.
(Pugyarangqetuameng
qasgit
avani.)
43
Tua-i piinanermeggni nuggliniluni.
Nug'uq-gguq, puggliniuq-gguq—
maatekaarluku taum tua waten pillrua—
imna-ggur' una tua-i icivaq tuqulleq!
44
Tua-i taũgaam tua-i
carayauluni alikluku tua, alingnaqluni tua-i.
Kegginaa taũgaam tua-i alaitevkenani
nuyain capumaluku.
45
Tauna-llu tua-i atiik,
tua-i-gg' atiik tauna,
yuut keluatnun iirluku
maancetevkenaku.
Kitumeg' ima tanem tauna pilaqiit?
Aterpagtelaqiit
kitum atiinek?
46
Macian:
Qam'ulriim atiinek!
47
Cakataar:
Ai!
48
Macian:
Qam'ulriim atiinek.
49
Cakataar:
Aa-a, tauna tua-i umyuaqela'arqa.
50
Waken-gguq
caniqamek
ayagluku
kiarciiqaa waten

***

42
While they stayed there,
she came in through the entry way out there.
(In those days
the *qasgiqs* had
underground entrances.)
43
Soon afterwards she began to rise up [from the underground entry].
When she rose up, when she emerged—
she was up to here according to the one who told this story—[6]
it was she, the one who died not too long ago!
44
But
she was a ghost and they were afraid of her since she was terrifying!
Her hair, however, concealed her face,
which wasn't visible.
45
As for the father,
as for the father there,
they hid him behind the people
instead of letting him be here [in the front].
Now what did they call him?
What name did they give him,
what's-his-name's father?
46
Mathias James:
Qam'ulria's father!
47
Jack Angaiak:
What!
48
Mathias James:
Qam'ulria's father!
49
Jack Angaiak:
Oh yes, that's the one I'm thinking of.
50
Starting here from
the corner,
it is said,
she would look for him, like this,

uivluki yugugaat makut,
qasgim iluanlengraata, canimelengraata.
Tua-i-gguq uiveciqai. Tua-i-llu nallii tekiskuniu
arulairluni,
Qam'ulriim atiinek yuaraluni,
tauna tua-i irniacuayagami
(Qam'ulriarullinilriim atiinek).
Nallii tekiskuniu arulairluni, arulaiquni-gguq qanerciqliniuq,
uum-gguq tang taugken nallii catangqerrluni.
Tua-i nallunricaaqluku-am
cali-ll' tua kiturluku.

51
Tua-i-gguq tang tekitaqamiu tua-i,
tua-i uum nallii catangqerrninauraa.
Tua-i
nallunricaaqluku.
52
Taum tua-i niicugniurallma pianga,
angalkut-gguq-gga cali makut
tua-i arenqialnguut,
angarvauluteng
ilait.
53
Tamaa-i tua alingluteng tua casciiganaku.
(Piciullilria-ll' tayim', tua-gg' niitellemtun qanemcikqata'arqa.)
    Angalkuq-gguq una
maaken teguluku atrarcaaqnauraat
tagqertaqluni-gguq kelutmun.
Tauna tua alikluku tua-i.
54
Allanek maaken angalkunek piiyaaqaqluteng;
tua-i angalkurluut imkut tua-i
tagqertaqluteng tua-i
alingkacagarluteng.

***

55
Tua-i-llu
iliit piinanermini, imkutangqertuq—
waten-gga tua-i wanigg' qanerturalrianga niicugniurallemtun—
angalkurrartangqertuq-gguq angalkukeggneruvkenani-llu-gguq

going around [scanning] all these people,
even though they were inside the *qasgiq*, even though they were close by.
She would scan all around [the room]. When she got to where he was,
she would stop,
searching for *Qam'ulria*'s father,
the father
of her little child (who was evidently *Qam'ulria*).
When she came to the spot where he was, she stopped; when she
     stopped, she would say to herself,
"But look, there's something here!"
She sensed something there,
but kept passing him by.
51
It is said that whenever she got to him,
she would say that there was something there.
So
she sensed him somehow.
52
The one from whom I heard this told me
that there were shamans there
and some of those incredibly
strong shamans
were among them.
53
At that time however, they were afraid and couldn't do anything to her.
(Maybe it's true; I'm going to tell it the way I heard it.) They would
     take a shaman, it is said,
from here and they would pull him down;
he would just run back up again.[7]
They were afraid of that one.
54
They would try another shaman, but to no avail.
Those poor shamans
would just run back up,
being terrified.

***

55
So then,
while this was happening, there was one amongst them—
here I am telling it the way I heard it—
there was a lesser shaman, it is said, who wasn't much of a shaman,

491

tuunriyuunani-llu-gguq tamakucicetun
tauna, taũgaam-gguq tua-i imuuluni
tua-i-gg' angapengyar,
pikeggneruvkenani
tauna.
56
Tua-i caqerluku tua-i taum tauna tua pilliniluku.
Aa, qessaqeryugnaitelliniuq!
57
Tua-i piatni taũgaam matartelliniluni.
Tua-i aturairluni.
Taũgaam tua-i pilu'ugluni.
Kaumaterluni—kaumatengqetullruameng-llu—
kaumaterluni-llu qimugtegnek kaumategnek,
all'uni taukugnek tua-i.
58
Aa, tuani ima tanem tuan' pugumallermini
maatekaarluni,
maavet-gguq nuglaryaaquq; waten amllilaryaaquq
waten-llu-gguq pikan
irua pinvulluni.
Nugesciigaqu'urluni, nugesciiganani
maavet wangkuta tutmaqngamteńun.
59
Tua-i piyaaqaqami tua-i pinvutaqluni,
mayurciigaqu'urluni.
60
Taum tua-i ullagluku
tuatnallrani,
man'a qengmiumalliniamiu,
pillinia
avitekanicuaqaasqelluku qaruqurluku tua-i.
Piyaaqengraani tua-i kan'a ciumuarluni,
taum atiinek
yuarluni.
Tua-i kat'um tua qaruqurluku taum tua-i avitekaniqaasqelluni tua.
Tua-i piinanermini iruk imkuk kalevtellinilukek tua
    pingnatugaarturluni.
Alingyugnaunani; aliksugnaunaku tauna!

61
Tua-i piinanermini tua-i

and that one didn't conjure like the others,
but was something like a useless
shaman,
not being
much good at all.
56
So then at last someone chose him.
Oh, he didn't refuse!
57
Only when they chose him did he undress.
He removed his clothes.
However, he put on his skin boots.
He put on mittens—since they used to have mittens—
putting on mittens which were made of dog-skin,
putting those on.
58
Oh yes, at that time when she had emerged,
being this far out [up to her waist],
she tried to come up; she tried to step up
and whenever she did that,
her leg would go through.
She couldn't climb up; she couldn't
climb up to the level we walk on.[8]
59
When she tried, she'd go right through;
she couldn't raise herself up at time.
60
He [the shaman] went to her
while she was trying that
and since she was flush against the frame of the underground entrance,
he told her
to move a little and make room, trying to coax her.
Although he tried she persisted in what she was doing,
looking for that child's
father.
So the one down there keep trying to persuade her to move a little
and make room.
He slipped his legs down [into the passage way] and kept trying to
force himself [between her and the edge].
He wasn't the least bit afraid; he wasn't afraid of her at all!
61
After a while,

nutaan tua-i camavet tut'elliami tua taqluni tua-i wani mengliini.

62

Piyaaqekiini tua-i ciumuarluni.
Tua-ll' tua-i caqerluni pillinia,
"Tua-i ciumuarpakalriaten
tegustekagpet wanigg' teguqataraagten!
Pistekagpet piqataraagten, wanigg' teguqataraagten!"
Tua-i-llu-gguq tauna piuraqerluni carayak tauna, carayaurtellria,
     nanikuangartelliniluni.

63

Nanikuangarrluni tua-i!

64

Piuraqerluni-ll' tua-i ayumian tua pillinia, "Tua-i teguagten!
Peggngairutaagten!"
Qamyartuaralliniluni.
Qamqerluni-ll' camna, tauna tua-i
qalrillalliniluni, cungiallalliniluni.

65

(Cungiallalleq nallunritan? {Iliit mikelnguut piluku})
Tuatnalliniluni.
Aren tua-i-llu-gguq imna tua-i cungiallagaqluni!

66

Waten-gguq tua
taukuk
kitngiallrak, pektellrak alaunani.

67

Cungiallaka'aqluni tua erinii imna tua-i
acitmun taũgaam tayim' umingurcartulliniluni.
Kiituani-gguq tua tayima tua-i
tamartuq.

68

Qalrillakaqluni tua.

69

Nutaan tua-i caarkaunriami taunall'er tua mayurluni
aturaaralliniluni tua-i.
Tua-i-gguq cavkenateng tua-i nutaan petengluteng tua-i.

perhaps when he finally touched the ground, he stopped right up
   against her.[9]
62
He tried to push her but she persisted.
After a while he said to her,
"Because you're being so obstinate,
the two [familiar spirits] who are going to take you are about to take
   you away![10]
The two who are going to deal with you are about to take you away!"
At last that ghost, the one who had become a ghost, got desperate.
63
She became desperate!
64
After a short while he said to her, "They've got you!
They won't let you go!"
She began to gradually sink into the ground.[11]
Just when she disappeared,
she suddenly started to wail, started to whimper.
65
(Do you know what it means to 'cungiallak'? {addressing one of the
   children})
That's what she did.
Aren, that one would whimper!
66
It is said it was like such,[12]
that
the sound of their footfalls and their walking about was audible.
67
As she kept on whimpering, her voice began to recede
and gradually became inaudible.
Then finally
it was gone.
68
She kept wailing now and then.
69
When finally that good old guy didn't have anything more to do,
he came up and started to get dressed.
So then, it is said, since nothing happened to them, they finally relaxed,
   moving about in the *qasgiq*.

***

70

Tuaten tang tua-i taum qanemcikellrukii waten wanigg' taktaluku,
niicugniurallrukeka. Tayim' iqungqerrsaaqellilria.
Kia imum, nallunrilkuvciu iqua,
pinritelqa pikuvciu.
Tuaten tua-i niicugniurallruaqa taun' qanemcikestii.

71

Ullakanirluku
iquklitevsiarru!

***

72

Macian:
Augna avani pinritellren qanemcikqata'arqa.
Tauna tuani
angalkuangssagaq tauna nengaugitaulliniluni,
Nengaugitaq tauna Qissunamiu; Qissunamiungullrulliniuq tua tauna.

73

Uani-gguq amiigem
mengliini tua-i tauna uitauratuuq.

74

Tua-gguq natetmun-llu
natmun-llu tua-i
piyuunani tua uantaqelria. Tamakut-am tamaa-i
taukurmiut
nunalgutkenrilamegteggu-am tua-i ilait-am tua-i
pimiukluku waten,
tua-i-gg'
pitullinikiit, pitullrullinikiit
tauna.

75

Tamaani ima tanem
tuani qimaglutek nunanun tekicartulriik, taukuk tekiteqatallragni,
taukut tua-i nunat tekicartullratni imumek tua-i kev'tullinilriit.

76

Tua-i-'m qaillukuarlutek-qa tua-i mis'arcan-qa tamana nutaan
tuavet nug'lliniuk nunanun tua taukunun,
taukuk qimalriik.

77

Tua-i tuani tua-i

***

70
That is how long he made it,
the one whom I listened to. Maybe it has an ending.
Whoever knows the ending
should tell what I missed.
That is how I heard the storyteller.
71
Come closer and
tell the rest of it![13]

***

72
Mathias James:
I'm going to tell the part you missed.
That one there,
that poor shaman, was apparently an in-law,[14]
an in-law from *Qissunaq*, he was apparently from *Qissunaq*.
73
It is said that his usual place was
by the door.
74
He didn't sit anywhere else,
anywhere else,
but always stayed there. And those
who lived in that village,
some of them, because he wasn't from
their place,
would, you know,
ignore him, would disdain
that one.
75
Oh yes, at that time
when those two were fleeing to the village and were about to get there,
that village they were just getting to would evidently lift off of the
        ground.[15]
76
They did something [to it?] and when it momentarily landed they finally
stepped onto that village,
those two who were fleeing.
77
In that place

arenqialluggluteng,
makut angalkut piyaaqsaaqelliniluki, cal' tua taukut.
Imna-gguq-gga uitaurarqellria,
tauna tua-i nengaugitaq.
78
Tua-i-llu
piatni-gga tua qessaqeryugnaunani nangertelliniluni, pilliniluni
nutaan pinarqellria
kan'a
pinritellratnek.

Traditional grave. Photo from Jesuit Oregon Province Archives, Gonzaga
University, negative number 504.16.

they were having a hard time
and those people tried in vain to get the shamans to do something.
And it is said that guy, that in-law,
was just sitting there,
78
So then
when they chose him, he stood up without refusing and asked
why indeed weren't they attending
to that one down there
who needed to be dealt with.

79
Tua-i
tuani tua-i
taum tua
qiiviarturluni-gga tua-i ekengnaqu'urallrulliniuq tua tuani
tauna tua.
Tuaten tua-i
angalkukeggnerunrilngermi tauna,
taum-gguq tua-i
nunat taukut augiutellrui nengaugitam taum Qissunamium.
80
Pilliniluku, "Ayautnamken!
Wiinga ayautnamken!"
Tua-i tegussuutegmikun tamaani
tegulug'.
Aren tuani tua-i
ayautellerminiu tua-i
camaggun tua pellugyartuutelliniluku tua-i tayima tua-i
avavet
qasgim egkuanun kumlalengraan tua-i!
81
Tuani-llu tua-i
tekitellermini tauna tua-i ayauqaarluku
urr'arrlirluni tua
nuggliuq tua-i
urr'aqegtaarmek tua-i urr'arrlirluni tua-i, cai tua-i tamarmeng tua-i.
82
Nuyai-llu-gg' pillilriit. {Qanemcista engelartuq}
Tuaten tua-i.
83
Augna ava-i pinritellra tua qanrutkeqa'arqa.

***

84
Cakataar:
Ii-i, tauna tua-i
taum qanemcikestiin qanemcikellrani
tamakut-gguq tegussuutellget angalkut,
avnernek pitukait tamakut
carayagnek tegussuutet.
Avnernek pitukait.

500

79
So
at that time
he
kept wiggling and continued to try to squeeze in there,
that one [did].
Like such,
even though he wasn't worth much as a shaman,
that in-law from *Qissunaq*
removed her from their village.
80
He said to her, "Let me take you away!
Let me take you away!"[16]
Using his two familiar spirits
he took her.
Aren, when he
took her away,
he cast her away underneath the floor[17]
over there,
through the back wall of the *qasgiq* even though it was frozen!
81
When he
arrived after taking her away,
he was covered with white clay
when he came up;
he was covered with white clay, very nice white clay, his entire body.
82
I guess his hair too. {Qanemcista engelartuq}
Like that.
83
I just told what he missed.

***

84
Jack Angaiak:
Yes, when
that storyteller told the story, he said
those familiar spirits used by shamans
were called *'avneret,'*
those familiar spirits who take ghosts away.
They called them *'avneret.'*

85
Avenruniluki piaqekait tamakut angalkut tegussuutait.

***

86
Arnaucuaq:
Arnar' aũgna
niitellemni
pillruat,
taum-gguq tua-i
mikelnguum
tuqullrani tua-i tupaggluku
pilqaa.
Qungitellratni tuani
taum taun' mikelnguq
(qel'kenricuktallinikiit!)
aaniinun tua qumiliulluku qungilluku.
Tuaten tua qanrutkelaraat taumun
mikelngurmun-gga tua-i tupaggluku-gguq
tuqumallranek,
qiagurallermini,
qiallermini-gg' pillilria.
Aũgna cali ava-i
qanrutkenritellra qanrutkaqa.

85
They said that they were called '*avneret,*' the ones that those shamans
used to take ghosts away.

***

86
Mike Angaiak:
The way I heard it,
they said
that
when she died
that child
awakened
that woman.
When they buried her,
they put that child
(they should have kept the child!)
inside its mother's parka and buried her.
That's what they say about it,
that that child woke her
from the dead
as it cried,
perhaps when it cried.
I also told
what he didn't tell.

TENGESQAUKTAR

Cakataar Tununermiu

***

1
Wiinga
aũg'umek
imumek niitelallerpeceńek
tua niitlemtun qanruteksugyaaqaqa tauna imna Tengesqauktarmek
     pilaqengaat, ukut nallunritaat.
Uniurrluku taũgaam
wii ilii piciqngataqa.[a]
Qanemcikqaqeryugyaaqaqa tauna.
2
Maa-i makut Niugtarmiut atam ilaita
nauvikaat makut
Tengesqauktar tauna.
Waniwa una nallunritaqa
ciuliaqaa.
Nuyarralgem-qa irniaqaaten? Ii-i, tua-i tauna.
Ciuliaqan Tengesqauktar, angalkuq.
3
Tang miknani aanairutellruluni, tuqullrulutek
angayuqaak mikteyagarluni.
Tang umyuartuyagarluni-ll' cal' tauna
pillinilria,
yuk tauna.
4
Ikani ika-i...Qanngaramek niitelartuci?
Niicuituci? Tang maa-i makut nallunritarkaci.
Tuqullrulutek taukuk angayuqaak
taum tua-i Tengesqauktaraam.
Atqenricaaqaa-gguq una Tengesqauktar
taũgaam angturrinermikun ateqsagulluku.
Tua-w' angalkuungami tengqanqeggsuliullrulliniami angalkuullermini
     tauna.

504

TENGESQAUKTAR

Jack Angaiak of Tununak

***

1
I
want to tell one [story]
that you [elders present] have already heard,
telling it as I heard it, about the one they called *Tengesqauktar*, who is
    known to these elders present.
It may seem, however, that
I omit part of the story.
I would like to tell a little bit about it.
2
Some of these people from *Niugtaq*
are descendants
of that *Tengesqauktar.*
I know that he
is her ancestor.[1]
Are you the child of *Nuyarralek,* Mark Tom? Yes, that one.
He's your ancestor, a shaman.
3
See, he lost his mother when he was little;
both of his parents died when he was still tiny.
You know, he was also a very precocious
little
child.
4
[This happened] across there... Have you heard of *Qanngaraq?*
Never heard of it? You know, these are things you should all know.
Those parents of
Tengesqauktar had died.
They say that *Tengesqauktar* was not his given name,
but he acquired that name as he grew older.
Because he apparently liked to use his shamanistic powers to move
    about freely through space, [he was called] that.

5

Tauna tua-i
waten niitlemtun tua-i qanrutkeqata'rqa.
Taukuk angayuqaak
waten apqucim tuskek—
apqucitulliniameng avani tua-i.
Waten-gguq wani akuliigni uitallruuq
aatami aanami-llu.
Atii-ll' tauna angalkuuluni.
Tua-i-ll' tua-i assiirucami nallunrilamiu taum atiin,
atii cauyarrangqetuuq-gguq, atii,
tamaa-i tuunrissuukaraminek.
Tua-i tauna
qetunrani tauna,
Tengesqauktar,
curillinikii cauyaminek.

6

Tua-i-gguq aanii una inangqaluni waten.
Miktelliniami,
taunayagaq tan'gurraq,
taũgaam umyuartuyagalliniluni.

7

Maa-i makut ilait umyuartuyagartut atam
elpeci,
mikngalngerpeci.
Tuaten yugni ayuqukut.

8

Tua-lli-gga nallullinikek ukuk, angayuqaak-gguq ukuk aatii aanii-ll'
peknanrirlutek,
inangqaurangllinilriik.
Aamatullruameng miktellermeggni aanameggnek taũgaam aamaaratullruameng,
camek piyuunateng.
Tua-i aamaryungaqami aanaminek waken aamalallinilria.

9

Tua-i-llu tua piinanermini
aanani una allakliniluku.
Pillinia-gguq anernerunani
tegg'illiniluni; aatani-llu-gguq cali pillinia cal' tuaten.
Nutaan-gguq nallunrirluku tua-i
aanaminek tua-i
tuqullrungraan nalluamiu
tua-i aamalallinilria, nerlallinilria,
tauna tua-i.

5
So I am
going to tell it the way I heard it.
Those parents of his
had an ailment fall upon them—
because they got sick back then [just as they do now].
It was said that he was there between them,
between his father and mother.
His father was a shaman too.
Because his father knew he was getting worse,
he had a little drum, his father [did],
which he used for summoning his familiar spirits back then.
And so
he placed that son of his,
Tengesqauktar,
on that drum.
6
And so, it is said, his mother was lying down like this.
Although he was little,
that little guy,
he was an intelligent little boy.
7
Some of you here are bright
little ones as well,
although you may look small.
We people are like that.
8
But he was unaware that his parents, his father and mother,
were no longer moving at all,
but were just lying there.
When the children were small they were breast-fed by their mothers
and given nothing else.
So when he wanted milk, he would suckle at his mother's breast.
9
After a while
he noticed something different about his mother.
He found out she wasn't breathing
and had hardened; he also noticed his father was like that.
At last he realized what had happened,
that although his mother
had already died, since he hadn't known it,
he had continued to suckle her, nursing
at her breast.

10
Tua-i-am umyuangami,
umyuarteqngarcami [anlliniluni].
Taūgaam qakmaggun elagyarluteng. Atam elagyangqetullruut
neqivignek,
nevunek tua-i nevut taūgaam pikellruamegteggu.

***

11
Tua-i
uitayuumiilami tuani
akuliigni,
anllinilria.
An'uq-gguq tua-i
qanikcanglliniluni man'a,
tauna tua-i tan'gurracuayagaq,
taukut taūgaam tua neqet
umyuaqluki.
12
Tua-i anngami
tauna tua-i elagyarteng,
waten neqivigteng,
ullalliniluku.
Tekitellinia tua-i. Atam tuskataitellruuq *plywood*-artaitellruluni-llu.

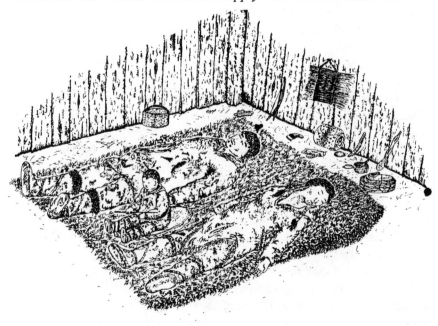

508

10
And so when the realization dawned on him,
because he had begun to figure things out, [he went out],
since they had a storage place outside. You see, they used to have
partially underground food caches
made out of sod, because sod was all they had.

***

11
Because
he no longer wished to stay there
between the two of them,
he went out.
They say that
when that tiny little boy went out,
there was snow on the ground
and he was thinking only about
that food.
12
So when he went out
he headed for
their *elagyaq,*
where they stored their food.
He reached it. You see, there was no lumber or plywood then.

Atam elagyat
amiigit kumlangaqameng [tegg'ituut].
Nevumek qag'umek qagaa-i nunapigmek,
waten eliqluku
kiilluku-llu
patukiutullruit
assircaarluki.
Tamakucinek patuluni.
13
Tua-i ullagluku tekicamiu,
tua-i kiitengnaqliniluku
tua mik'lami arturluku
tua-i.
Tua-i nequturiuraan,
itrarkaurcami,
itliniluni tuavet. Itertuq-gguq
neqet tua-i makut amllerrluteng tua-i.
Tua-i-ll' neqet qaingatnun
aqumelliniluni.
Tua-i maaken piyunarquralrianek
nerangnatugaaralliniluni.
14
Cunawa-gguq imna,
uumirpak,
taun' tan'gurrayagaq,
tamaani tua-i uitauralliniaqelria
elagyami neqet qaingatni.
Tua-i neryungaqami maaken
piluni neraqcaararaqluni.
Tua-i neruraami kaigyugnaunani qerrucuunaku-llu. Tua
   qerrutelaryaaqellikii-gg' tayima.

***

16
Tua-i-llu
uitaaqellria. Tua caqerluni tua erucit iliitni
qakemna
elatii cavallartelliniluni,
qakma-gguq tua-i.
Niicugniurarak-gguq malruulutek
qanaaguralriik
qakma
tekitellinilriik taukuk.

When the doors of the *elagyaq*s
get cold, [they freeze up].
From sod on the tundra out there
they cut out the door pattern,
peeling off [the layer of sod],
and made covers for the entrance,
doing everything carefully.
That's the kind of door it had.
13
He approached it and upon reaching it,
he tried to pry it off,
but being so small, he had great difficulty
with it.
As the opening gradually widened,
enabling him to enter,
he went in. They say when he entered
there was plenty of food in there.
And so he sat down
on top of the food.
Then from among those that were easy to obtain
he scrounged up something to eat.
14
Amazingly,
for several days
that little boy
remained there
in the *elagyaq* on top of the food.
Whenever he wanted to eat something from there,
he did the very best he could to feed himself.
Because he continued to eat, he didn't go hungry or get cold. He
    might very well have gotten cold.

***

16
And so
he stayed there. It happened that one day
something outside
in the immediate area [of the *elagyaq*] made a sudden noise;
something, it was said, was out there.
As he listened he heard two [people]
who had just arrived
talking
out there.

511

17
Tua-i-ll' piuraqerlutek
uaggun, tamaaggun tua qelpiin,
igvalliniuk
tan'gurraak malruk,
imkuk tua angturrilutek
pilriik.
Tua tekitellinilriik kiavet tua tanglliniluku tauna,
taunayagaq,
tan'gurra'ar.
18
Tua-i tangerrngamegnegu
aren nakleksugnaunaku!
Aren kenkenritlinikiik
taunayagaq!
Aren kenkevkenaku, eq'ukluku tua-i!
19
Aling arenqiapaa-ll' taukugni! Waten-llu pilliniluku
neqet qunguurrniluki!
(Una-qa qunguurtellra nallunritarci?
Aren nalluksi-gga!
Icigg' makut maa-i tuquaqelriit.
Tuqunitukput cali-ll'
qungitniluki.)
Tamaa-i qunguurrluku-gguq, neqet quinakluki.
Wall' anerteq'eūrluryaaquq!
20
Tua-i alingellinilria.
Tua-ll' aipaan tua-i kenkevkenaku pillerminiu.
(Camek piagu tayima?
Wall'u-qa cikuliurutmek pia?)
Kiavet urniutelliniluku.
Aren tua-i alingallalliniluni, tua alingkacagaūrlurluni!
Tua kenkevkenaku taukuk.
Tua-i piyaaqerraarluku tua pivkenaku.
Neqet taukut qunguurrniluk' tegucunaitniluki, quinakluki. Tua-i
    wall' anerteq'eūrluryaaquq!
Unitelliniluk' tua tayima, tua-i
nepairutlinilutek.
Tua-i-am kinguagni uitauralliniaqellria tua-i.
Tua-i unuutaqani tua-i qava'urluraqluni taūgaam.
Taūgaam-gguq tamaaken
neru'urluni tua piyunarqelrianek neqet qaingatni tua uitiimi.

17
Just then,
because the door was partially open,
two boys,
a couple of teenagers,
came
into view.
They arrived and saw him in there,
that little guy,
the little boy.
18
When they saw him,
aren, they didn't feel any compassion for him!
Aren, they apparently didn't like him,
that little one!
Aren, they despised and scorned him!
19
Aling, how could those two feel that way! Then they said
that the food had turned into a grave!
(Do you know what it means to become a grave?
Aren, you don't know!
You know, nowadays people die;
we talk about them dying and also
we talk about burying them.)
They said that it had turned into a grave and they found the food repulsive.
Yet that poor boy was alive!
20
So he was afraid.
One of them didn't like him and was about to do something to him.
(What was it that he used?
Maybe it was an ice pick?)
He aimed it toward the boy.
Aren, he got scared; the poor thing was terrified!
Those two didn't like him.
At first they meant to hurt him, but they didn't.
They said the food had turned into a grave, preventing them from taking
     any since they were repulsed by it. Yet the poor boy was alive.
So they left him and
it became quiet.
So after that he remained there.
However, the poor thing would go to sleep when night fell.
Since he was sitting on top of the food,
he continued to eat what was easy to obtain.

***

22
Tua-i-llu
piinanermini
qakemna-am yulkitliniuq qakma,
qakma tua-i.
(Icigg' qanikcaq man'a
tutmalriani qalriuraurarqelria.
Nem'elngurni-ll' qakma waten man'a qiaryigquratullruameng
qanikcamun waten tutmalriani,
tutmarqateng.)
23
Tua piinanrani
qakemna qanertuq uaken,
"Waq' atak tua-i, canrituq-qa tua-i?" Aling nallunritlinikiit taukut,
taukuk-wa tua qanemcikellrulliagnegu.

24
Tua erinii qakemna angutngurrluni.
Tua-ll' tua-i ua-i uyangtelliniuq ugna
yuk, angun,
angutngurtelliniluni,
"Waq' atak, canrituq-qa tua-i?" Tua-i elliin uavet
tangvaagayagalliniluku. Aling tua-ll' pillinia, "Tua-i canritliniuten tua-i."
Alingcetaaryugnaunaku taukugtun.
25
Tua-i pillinia, "Aling tua-i caksaitelliniuten!"
Tua-ll' pillinia, "Waniwa-qa
tegukumken caciqa?
Wall' ima-qa
wanigg' tegukumken,
anakuvet..."
(Icigg' naugg' maa-i
ilait—nalluaci—
aatateng aanateng-llu unitengaqekait.
Aatateng aanateng-llu cakev[kenaki] imutun tua-i
angturriaqameng
pegtelaqait, pegtellriatun ayuqait. Tanglartua-ll' wii tua taũgaam
akultuut.)
Pillinia, "Wall' ima-qa
angturrikuvet,
piyaureskuvet,
anakuvet,

***

22
Sometime
later
there were human sounds again
out there.
(You know, the snow
when it is stepped on makes a certain sound.
When one is inside the house, [one can hear] crunching sounds
when the snow is stepped on,
when they step on it.)
23
After a while
someone out there by the exit spoke.
"Well now, is he doing all right?" *Aling*, they apparently knew he was
    there,
since perhaps the other two told about him.
24
The voice outside was that of an older man.
Then a person peered in at the exit,
a man,
an older man.
" *Waqaa*, is he doing all right?" The little boy was
staring at him. *Aling*, then he said to him, "So you are doing all right."
He didn't try to frighten him like those other two.
25
So the man said, "*Aling*, so evidently nothing has happened to you."
And then he said to him, "How would it be
if I were to take you?
What
if I were to take you,
and you were to become self-sufficient and independent..."
(You know, nowadays
some people—you don't know this—
are beginning to abandon their mothers and fathers.
They are indifferent to their fathers and mothers
when they grow up;
they separate from them as though they were letting them go. I see
    that happening, but not often.)
He said to him, "What if
if you were to grow up,
if you were to become capable,
if you were to become self-sufficient and independent,

uniciiqngatarpenga
ilangcivkenii."
26
Aren tua-i umyuamikun tua umyuarteqliniuq, "Aren tua-i tegukuvnga
wanigg' tua-i
unisngaitamken piyuumaringerma." Umyuarteqyagalliniluni tua
    qaillun-llu qanqeryugnaunani.
27
Tua-ll' pillinia tua-i elliin teguyugluku
tuatnaarkaungraani.
Aling aren tua-i quyalun'. Teguamiu tua-i taum angutem,
wavet tua-i ek'arrluku
utrutlinikii
nunameggnun
tuavet tua-i.
Taukuk tua-i uitallinilutek alingcetaartellrek.
Aren tua-i taukuk irniangyuitellinilutek,
taukuk nulirqelriik.

***

29
Tua-i-llu
anglicalliniluku,
waten mikellrani elpecicetun,
taukuk.
Tua-i aanakluku aanii aatakluku-ll' tua aataksagulluku
angun aanii-ll' aanaksagulluku.
Auluku'uralliniluku
kiituan angturriuq elpecicetun.
30
Aren tua-i umyuaran taukuk
alingcetaartellregni malruk,
umyuarani uitalutek.
Taukuk-llu cali,
angun tauna tegustellni cali-ll' arnaq,
taukuk cali,
cali tua-i umyuarani uitalutek.
Akinauqeryugyaaqlukek
anglicartegni
elluarrluni.
31
Tua-i piinanermini,
angturriqerluni
516

you might leave me
and forget all about me."
26
Aren, then he thought to himself, "*Aren*, if you take me
now,
I won't leave you even if I were to become self-sufficient." The little
    boy was thinking this, but without uttering a word.
27
The man said he wanted to take him
even though he might do that [eventually leave him].
Aling aren, the boy was happy. After that man took him,
he put him in [the sled] here
and took him home
to his village
there
where those two that frightened him lived.
Aren, that couple couldn't bear any children of their own,
that man and his wife.

***

29
And so
that couple
raised him,
when he was little like you.
So he acquired the woman for his mother
and the man for his father.
They took care of him
and then at last he grew up like you.
30
Aren, those two
who had terrorized him
were always in his thoughts.
And those other two,
that man and the woman who had taken him in,
preoccupied
his thoughts also.
He wanted to repay
those two who had so generously
raised him.
31
Then later on
when he got older

angalkuurtenglliniluni. Angalkum tua pulaluku
atii taun' angalkuungami.

32

Taukuk tua-i
angturriami
angayuqaagni, angayuqaqenricaaqekegni-llu
tua-i piyaurcami auluklinikek
unicugnaunakek.
(Maa-i icigg' pilaqaitkut
aataput aanaput-llu
takaqesqelluki, kenkesqelluki.
Tang tua-i tauna ayuqellra,
taum.
Keneklukek yuuluni takaqlukek.)
Akinaurlukek tua pingnatugluni cangnatullermikun,
neqsullermikun.
Qacigcetengnaqlukek, una angun
tuatnallinilria.
Tua-i umyuarani tuanlluni
naklekellni.

33

Cali taukuk yuuk malruk alingcetaartellregni,
tua-i umyuarteqluni waten,
"Aling naũgg'un-kiq wanigg' akinauqerlakek ukuk
    alingcetaartellregka?"[b]
Iqlutmun umyuarteqsugnaunani
taukuk angalkuurcami.
Ik'imek-llu
angalkumikun piyugnaunakek taukuk
taũgaam naũgg'un tua ikayuqeryugyaaqlukek.

***

34

Tua-i piinanrani
taum aipaan,
waten aipanglliniami cali-ll' irniangluni …
(Maa-i icigg' makut mikelnguut nangteqaqelriit. Nangteqaqata-llu
    wall' assiirtaqata uavet
clinic-aanun maa-i piyaureskait.
Clinic-at angalkuurrluteng,
angalkuksagulluki.
Tamakut avani angalkut
clinic-aaqetullruit.

518

he started to become a shaman. The shamanistic powers possessed him
because his father was a shaman.

32
As for those two,
his parents, although they weren't actually his parents,
once he had grown up,
he took care of them when he became capable of doing so
and did not abandon them.
(Nowadays, you know, they instruct us
to respect and to love
our fathers and mothers.
Look, he was like
that;
he loved them and respected them.)
He repaid them by trying to do things, by getting things and getting
food.
This man made sure they were free of labor;
he did it that way.
[Their] act of compassion for him
was always in his mind.

33
Also, concerning those two people that terrified him,
he was thinking thus,
"*Aling*, I wonder how I should repay those two that frightened me?"
He wasn't thinking maliciously.
Since he had become a shaman,
he didn't do bad things to those two
and never used his shamanistic powers against them,
but wondered how he might help them instead.

***

34
So then time passed
and one of the two,
because he had married and also had a child ...
(Nowadays, you know, the children get sick and when illness strikes
    them they take them down by the river
to the clinic.
The clinic is like a shaman,
having become their medicine man.
In those days the shamans
were like the clinic.

Assiitaqameng angalkunun pitullruit
yuut;
aataurtengraata, aanaurtengraata,
piipicuaraungraata-ll' mikelnguut, tua-i *clinic*-aqluki.
Tua-i wanigg' umyuaqetuaqa tamana.)
35
... piinanrani taum tua-i aipaan
alingcetaartellran
ellii tua caulliniluku
irniani tauna tua-i assinrilnguq
piyugngakaku
tua-i qaillukuaqaasqelluku, wanigg' kaigavikniluku.
Aling tua-i-gguq tang quyaq'apiarallrulria!
Angalkuuluni tang taugken!
Tang iqlutmun umyuarteqsugnaunani ik'imek-llu umyuarteqsugnaunani.
36
Tua-i tauna
irniara
tuunramikun calillinikii
kituggluku nangtequtii,
tuunramikun.
Assiriluni-llu tauna
irniara.
Nutaan-gguq tuatniin umyugaa imna tua-i nutaan assiriqerrluni taum
    tungiinun, akinaurluku tua-i.
37
Taugaam-gguq cal' aipaanek,
cali tua-i aipaanek umyuarrliqluni
akinauqeryugyaaqluku naugg'un tayima assilriamek.
38
Tua-i-ll'-am piinanrani aipaan
pillinia,
tua-i-am tuatraarpiaq
kaigavikluku. Kaigavikniluku pituit
waten irniateng
angalkumun piaqamegteki.
39
Tua-i-llu
taum tua-i quyaqerluni-am tua-i Tengesqauktaraam,
Tengesqauktararkam,
tua-i-am taun' mikelnguq angalkumikun calilliniluku,
yuungcarluku.
Nangtequtii alaitenrilengraan tuunramikun taugaam caliluku,

When people were ill, they were taken
to the shaman.
Whether they were fathers and mothers,
or even little babies and children, they would go to the clinic.
So then, that's how I think of that.)
35
… sometime later one of the two
who had scared him
came to him;
he begged him to try to do something immediately,
if he were able,
for his sick child.
Aling, it is said that he was so very happy!
Behold, this despite the fact that he was a shaman!
He didn't harbor evil thoughts or have bad intentions towards him.
36
And so he worked on
that child,
using his familiar spirit,
healing his ailment
with his helping spirit.
He cured that
child of his.
Finally, it is said, because he did that, his mind improved towards the
    one he repaid.
37
However, in regard to the other one,
he still felt anxious about the other one,
wanting to repay him somehow with good.
38
So then it happened sometime later the other one
went to him
just as the first one had
and implored him for help. They say they beg them
like this when their children
are brought to the shaman.
39
And so
that *Tengesqauktar*, the one who was to be called *Tengesqauktar*, was so
happy.
Then with his shamanistic powers he worked on the child
and treated him.
Although his ailment wasn't visible, he nevertheless worked on him

kituggluku, tumarrluku, ayaggluku. {engelartuq qanemcista}
Tua-i-ll'-am piuraqerluni taun' assirilliniluni.
Aren assirian-gguq im' nutaan tua-i akinaurlukek tamaaggun tua-i,
nunaniryugtellukek taukuk!

40
Nutaan-gguq tua-i
umyugaa assiriluni.
Iqlutmun umyuarteqsugnaunakek.
Iqlutmun akinauryugnaunakek.
Tang angalkuuyaaqetacia taum!
41
Maa-i qaneryaraq aturluku-am taum Tengesqauktaraam

Ayaprun, James Sipary, and *Aparuk,* Joe Terchik. Photo from Jesuit Oregon
Province Archives, negative number 506.04.

using his familiar spirit,
healing him, fixing him and removing the affliction. {narrator laughs}
And then shortly afterwards that one was cured.
Aren, since he was cured, it was said that he had finally repaid
    them both in the same vein,
having made them both happy.
40
So finally, it is said
his mind was better.[2]
Neither did he think evil of them
nor did he repay them with evil.
See what kind of a shaman he was!
41
That *Tengesqauktar* followed the traditional teachings and advice

taukuk
alingcetaartellregni
tuatnallrullinikek
assillrakun.
Tuatnalliniaqekek!^c Icigg' maa-i wangkuta
alerquumayaaqaqkaitkut agayuvigmi.
Qanrut'laryaaqekaitkut tang
agayuvigmi-llu tamakucitgun tamaa-i
ilaput naklekluki pisqelluki-llu
akinauqsaunaki-ll' pilaasqelluki.
Tauna tua-i cangallrunritlinilria-am.
Nallunringkuvciki atam makut qaneryararraat ilait elitaq'laryaraci.
Alerqularyaaqellinikaitkut wangkuta agayuvigmi
taũgaam wangkurluut ilaitni
imutun caqiryugtukut
yugni.
Yugni tuatnatulliniukut.
Wat'-llu yupiim mat'um qaneryaraanek cali alerquangraitkut cali
elluarrluta yuullerkamteñek
tuaten cali tua-i caqiryullemta navgutulliniakut.
Murilkurlua piurangua.
Ayuqluta nasaurlurni [tan'gurrarni-llu] ayuqluteng ellarpallraam iluani.
Ilii-am taũgken maligutellria,
imutun tumkelilriatun ayagciqliniuq,
paallautekani makut
uniurqaqluki waten.

***

42
Tuaten tua-i ayuqelalliniuq. Tauna tua-i
angalkur-am
tuaten tua-i ayuqellinilria.
43
Niicuitaqa taun' Tengesqauktar ikiuluku, angalkuni
ikiuluki atullrit.
Wanigg' niigarteqaqsaitaqa.
Elluarrluni taũgaam
angalkuullni tamana aturngatellrullinia.
44
Tua-i tuaten-qa pitaqerqa?

in dealing with those two
who had frightened him,
dealing with them
benevolently.
That is how he treated them! You know, nowadays
they instruct and advise us at the church.
Look, they keep trying to admonish us,
exhorting us in various ways
to treat others with compassion.
exhorting us not to take revenge.
[Our traditional teachings are] no different.
See, if you become knowledgeable, you'll recognize some of these
    traditional teachings.
They regularly instruct and teach us in church,
but, alas, some of us
tend to go astray.
That's
human nature.[3]
Moreover, although they instruct us in the traditional Yup'ik teachings,
which instruct us to live a good life,
we tend to go astray and this is what leads to our ruination.
I am now beginning to be observant [of these things].
It is the same for all of us, with [all] boys and girls throughout the
    whole world.
However, for the one who does heed this,
it is as though he were walking along a good trail,
avoiding whatever
hindrances and temptations there may be.

***

42
That was the way he was;
that shaman
was like that.
43
I never heard of *Tengesqauktar* being a bad shaman,
of his misusing his powers.
[To this day] I have never heard of it.
On the contrary,
he used his shamanistic powers for the good.
44
Well, is this how far I go?

ILLUGNGALI

Cakataar Tununermiu

***

1
Cali
niitetuarci-llu-qa cali Illugngali?
2
Ca? {eskuularaq aptuq}
3
Illugngali!

***

4
Cali-gg' tauna angun cali Illugngali.
Illugngalimek aprumalalria.
5
Asriq.
Asriuluni.
6
Asriq-qa nallunritaci?
7
Yaa! {eskuularaq kiuguq}
8
Ii-i, tamakuciq.
9
Angungssagaq tua-i asriuluni, tauna
Illugngali; Illugngalimek aterluni.
10
Angalkut-gguq tua-i cali imkut
angalkut, nallunrilkeci angalkut niitetukci.
Tukninengqetullruut atam,
tamakut tukninerluteng.
Makucetun
ski-doo-ciicetun levaacetun-llu tukninruaqluteng
angalkut ilait. {qanemcilria engelartuq}

526

ILLUGNGALI

Jack Angaiak of Tununak

***

1
Now then,
did you ever hear about *Illugngali?*
2
Who? {student asks the question}
3
Illugngali!

***

4
Well, there was this man named *Illugngali.*
He was called *Illugngali.*
5
A naughty and audacious one.
He was a naughty and audacious one.
6
Do you know what *asriq* means?
7
Yeah! {students reply}
8
Yes, [one of] that kind.
9
This little old man was reckless and mischievous, this[1]
Illugngali; his name was *Illugngali.*
10
And you know, those
shamans, you know the shamans that you've heard about.
Well, they used to have more powerful ones;
they had more powerful ones.
Just like, for example, these
ski-doos and outboard motors, some of the shamans
would be more powerful. {narrator laughs}

11
Tua-i-gguq tamakucit
taum angalkum ca, Illugngalim tamakucirpallraat tuknilriit,
tua-i arcaqerluki-gguq tua-i kenkenripallaarluki
akusrarutekvallaarnaurai.

12
Tamakut-llu-gguq tua-i
angalkut tuknilriit
Illugngali capeqluku tua qaill' pisciiganaku.

13
Qaillun-llu-gguq tamakut pisciiganaku
Illugngali.
Tamakut tamaa-i angalkullret
arenqiatut;
yuut alikellruit avani pirpakekacagarluki.
Wa-gguq umyuarrlugciullerkarteng alikluku {qanemcista engelartuq}
tamakut.

14
Tuani-llu-gguq taum anglanitekaqekai tamakut
angalkut. Makut-gguq tang taugken
angalkukeggnerunrilnguut, pikeggnerunrilnguut,
tua-i kenekluki cakneq tua-i caqaqauvkenaki.
Tuaten tua-i pillrullinilria.

15
Tua-i
kenkekacagarluki,
caqeryaaqevkenaki naklekuraqapiarluki.

***

16
Tua-i-llu-ggur-am
piinanrani waten ayallratni,
ilai-gguq
kinguani alangrulliniluteng
unugmi,
carayiim piyarpiarluki.
Carayagmek alingallagluteng.
Tua piyarpialliniluki carayiim tuani
kingunratni alingevkarluki.

17
Tua-i-llu-gguq
Illugngaliq ayaumaluni.

11
So it was said that *Illugngali* would
especially dislike those kinds of shamans,
those big powerful ones,
and would fool around with them more.
12
And it was said that those
shamans who were powerful
couldn't do anything to *Illugngali.*
13
So it was said of *Illugngali*,
they couldn't do anything to him.
Those former shamans
were too much;
people were afraid of them back then and they held them in awe.
This was because they feared the evil {narrator laughs}
they could do.
14
They say he would have fun at the expense of those
shamans. However, he liked
the lesser shamans who didn't amount to much,
and wouldn't let anything happen to them.
That was how he was.
15
In fact
he loved them very much
and tried not to do anything to them, feeling charitable toward them.

***

16
One day, they say,
while he was away,
his family,
in his absence, evidently was haunted
at night;
a ghost almost got them.
They were startled by a ghost.
The ghost almost got them while
he and others were gone and frightened them.
17
So, they said,
Illugngali was away.

18
Ayainanrani,
tekican tekipailgan pilliniak taukuk
malruk,
inerqulliniak,
"Imna ata tekiskan,
qanrucaqunategu!
Tua-i-am piciquq." Nallunrilamegteggu taukut ilain, nulirran.
"Tua-i-am piciquq. Angu qanrucaqunaku!"

19
Pilliniluku carayagmun piyarpiarniluteng.
Tua-i-llu-gguq-am qanertuq,
"Eqnarivakar! Alingcetaariqtarluteng!"

20
Naugg' wangkuta maa-i una-i kankut qunguput
kristanek taugaam pingqelalriit.
Tamaani tang taugken yuut,
tamaani avani
yuut tuqullret
piciatun,
piciatun wa-gguq alailucirluki
pitullrukait
ikamranek
murak-llu naparrluku
nutegnek,
egatnek,
urluvernek,
tua-i piciatun, cautaitnek
kenurraitnek-llu tamaa-i alail[ucirluki]. Waten piaqluki "alailucirluki."
Kristamek-llu caunateng yullret naugg' pitullrukait.
Imkucicetun unkut-llu kristarrlainaurruteng maa-i.
Tamakut tang taugken piciatun
tuqullret
tuquaqata piciatun tamaa-i wa-gguq alairucirluki.
21
Illugngali-am tua tauna anlliniluni anngami-ll' muragmek tegulluni
tuaten tua-i tuqumalriit
qunguitnun ayalliniluni.
Tekicamiki-gguq,
kaulliniluki caqutait-llu tamakut.
Kaugtuarluki ceńirtelliniluki. {engelarluteng}

530

18
He was still gone
and on his return, before he came back she [*Illugngali*'s wife] said to
     those
two [children],
warning them,[2]
"When he arrives,
don't tell him!
He'll do something," because his wife and his family knew him.
"He'll do something. Don't, don't tell him!"
19
Nevertheless, he was told that a ghost almost got them.
So then he said,
"Damn it! How dare they scare them!"
20
You know nowadays our graves down there
only have crosses.
But in those days
back then,
people used different things
to mark the dead people,
different things to show where they were;
they did it
with sleds,
and upright pieces of wood,
guns,
cooking pots,
bows,
and all kinds of their possessions,
and also lamps. They said this was "making them visible."
They didn't use any crosses for the dead.
For instance, those down there now are all marked with crosses.[3]
The earlier ones, however, used various things
to mark the dead.
When they died, variouis things were used to show their location.
21
That *Illugngali* went out and once outside he took a piece of wood
     with him
and went to graves of the dead.
It was said that when he reached them,
he beat those grave boxes of theirs.
He went to each one, beating on them. {laughter}

22
Tua tuqumalriit, qanaaluni-gguq tuaten,
"Ciiqtaq unuk alingcetaariqtarceci?" {engelarluteng}
23
Tua-i-am
taukut pilliniut,
"Aling, ciin tanem tua-i, inerqullruat-ggem tanem,
uitaciqenrilan-am!"
24
Tua-i-gguq tauna asriullruuq.
25
Tua-i-llu
tua-i atrarluni nangucami kaugtuararkairucami. {engelarluteng}

26
Atrarluni tua-i.
Tua-i-gguq kinguakun nutaan
imkuryaaqluni assiircaaqluni.
Tamana-gguq tua cangimikenritaa,
kaugtuallni tuqumalrianek,
kaũg'agallni.

Children swimming in the Bering Sea. Photo from Jesuit Oregon Province
Archives, negative number 506.03.

22
To the dead there, he would say,
"Why the hell did you scare them last night?" {laughter}
23
They [the family]
said to him [child],
"*Aling*, why ever did you tell? I thought they warned him,
because he would react."[4]
24
They say that he was bold and mischievous.
25
Then
he went back down when he was done, because he ran out of graves to
        beat. {laughter}
26
So he went down.
Then they say that afterwards
something happened and he got sick for a while.[5]
So he didn't want any more of that,
his beating of the dead,
his heavy beating of them.

***

27

Kinguani-gguq tua assiiterrlugyaaqluni taugken-ggur-am assiriluni.
28

Tua piurainanermini-am tua-i tuqunariani tuqulliniluni.
29

Tua tuqulliniluni tuqunariani eggluku-ll'-am tua tuaten.
30

Kegga-i-gguq tua tuqumalria. Tua-i-gguq piinanermeggni
naken—aquigaqelriaci maa-i aquitullrulriit waten elpecicetun
    angtalriani.
Aquitullruut angqerluteng.

31

Arnat, nasaurluut tan'gurraat-llu avukluteng tua-i neplirluteng
atakuarmi waten angqatullruut.
Akusraruciqluku.

32

Yaaqsinrilkiini-am tua aquilliniluteng.
Taum tua tuqullruluni Illugngali tuqumallrani.
Qunguan yaatiini aquilliniluteng.
33

Tua-i-llu-gguq piuraqerluni tuaken tua caqugkenek
aquilriit-am nunullinii. {engelarluteng}

34

Tua-i-gguq tuqullrem!
Nunullinii!
"Eqnarqut qakemkut!
Ayagluci aquiyarturci!" {engelarluteng}
35

Taugken-ggur-am
tuqullruluni-gguq tang taugken.
36

Qaillurluq taun' ayuqa?
37

Tua-i-ggur-am alingallagaluteng ayagarqelliniluteng
tua tamakut. {engelarluteng}
38

Cunawa-gguq im', cunawa-gguq-gguq
tua mengliini

***

27
After that he got a little sick; however, he got well.
28
Time passed, and when his time had come to die, he died.
29
So he died when his time came, and they took care of the body.
30
The dead one, it was said, was outside.[6] So then, it was said, as time
    passed for them—
[you know how] you play nowadays and they used to play like you,
    being of that age.
Somewhere out there they used to play ball.
31
The women, the girls, and the boys would play together with a lot of
    boisterously,
playing ball in the evening.
That was their way of playful recreation.
32
Where they played wasn't far from him,
from *Illugngali* who had died.
They apparently played next to his grave.
33
Then, it was said that after this had been going on for a while, from his
    coffin
he scolded the kids who were playing. {laughter}
34
The dead one!
He evidently scolded them!
"Damn you out there!
Go away to play!" {laughter}
35
Yet the fact of the matter was
that he had died!
36
How the heck did he get to be that way?
37
So then those kids got scared and started
to run away. {laughter}
38
For that reason, it was said,
they couldn't play

aquisciiganateng. Menglemini-gguq-am tua-i aquigaqata
nunurnaurai.
39
Qaillun taun'? Wall'u-qa tuqunguallruuq? Qaill' pia?

***

40
Tua-i-llu piinanermini alangrukenglliniluku
caaqameng; payugtellriit alangrukaqluku
Illugngali tauna.
41
Taugken-gguq tamakut alangrullret cayuunateng.
Tua-i-am piinanratni
alangruullrani angalkumun pivkalliniluku.
42
Tua-i-llu angalkum taum tua-i
tuunramikun
cakma qasgimi tegulliniluku elaturrami.
43
Tua-i-ll' waten pillinia alangruugurallranek tua-i.
Tua-i cakma tua-i.
44
Tua-i-llu qasgimiut pilliniat,
"Aling tauna
cali alangruuciquq!
Iivkarluku piu, iivkaqiu!"
45
Tua-i-llu-ggur-am cakemna carayak qanertuq,
"Iqluuq! {engelarluteng}
Iivkaryaqunii!" {engelarluteng}
46
Aling nekanaqvagta taun' yuk tuqulleq!
Tua-ll' qasgimiut pilliniat qamkut,
"Iqluuq!
Alangruuciqur-am cali.
Iivkaqiu iivkanritevkenaku!"
47
Tua-i-llu-gguq-am cakemna, "Iqluuq! {engelarluteng}
Iivkaryaqunii!" {engelarluteng}
48
Tua-i cakma
tua-ll' tua pilliniat,

next to him. Whenever they played around him,
he would scold them.
39
How was that? Maybe he pretended to die? What was it with him?

***

40
And then after a while he began to appear to them
occasionally; the ones who brought gifts of food would see
Illugngali.
41
But then nothing happened to the ones who saw him.
So eventually when he did that,
when he did appear, they had a shaman deal with him.
42
So the shaman, using his
power,
took him out there into the storm-shed.
43
He asked him why he kept on appearing.
That's what went on [in the storm-shed].
44
Then the people in the *qasgiq* said to the shaman,
"*Aling*, he will
appear again!
Therefore exorcise him, cast him down!"[7]
45
And then the ghost out there said,
"Don't listen to that! {laughter}
Don't cast me down!" {laughter}
46
Aling, that dead person is really a nuisance!
Those people inside the *qasgiq* said to shaman,
"Don't listen to him!
He'll appear again!
Exorcise him, cast him down without fail!"
47
Then the one out there: "Don't listen to that! {laughter}
Don't exorcise me!" {laughter}
48
He was out there
and they said to the shaman,

"Aling tua-i iqluuq. Cali piciquq!
Cali pilarciquq! Iivkaqiu!"
49
Tua-i-llu-ggur-am cakemna,
"Iqluuq; iivkaryaqunii!
Eqnarqut qamkuqtat!" Ayumian-ggur-am nunullinii qamkut
    qasgimiut carayiim.
"Eqnarqut qamkuqtat! {engelarluteng}
Iivkakunavakarqelriit,
nugkuma-ata!" {engelarluteng}
50
Tua-i-gguq
tua-i nunuqengluni qamkunek.
51
Tua-i iivkallrunritaat-gguq. Tua-ll' tua pillinia
nutaan
wanigga
alangruularniluni irniani taũgaam
tanglasssaagarluki, tangerrsungamiki
tanglassaagalarniluki.
52
Tua-i tua wanigg' ayakatarniluni nunakaminun.
Tayima natmun nunakaminun ayakatarta.
Ayakatarniluni wanigg' tua-i alangruunqigngaitniluni.
53
Una-gg'-am wanigg' carayak qanaaluni tua-i.
Tua-i-llu-ggur-am tua tayima qanellni aturluku tua-i taum kinguakun
    alangruunqigtevkenani.
54
Tuaten tua-i tua iquklitellruuq. Tua-i-gguq tauna Illugngaliq asriullruuq.

***

55
Cali anguyiim nalliini tuani malirqeralriit
ilakluku.
Tua-ll' naugg'
makunek maani ingrinek tanglalriaci kiugumek,
ul'aqami meq tekitaqluni.
Waten-llu ayuqluni, teggalquq.
Yuk tua tuavet,
yugmek malirqalriit angutet, angutet,

"*Aling*, don't listen to him! He'll do it again!
He will do it again! Cast him down!"
49
And so the other one out there said,
"Don't listen to that; don't cast me down!
Damn those in there!" The ghost began to upbraid the ones inside the
    qasgiq.
"Damn those in there! {laughter}
Since they've been talking about exorcism,
I should come up from below!" {laughter}
50
So it was said
he upbraided those inside.
51
They say that they didn't cast him down. *Illugngali* finally said to
the shaman
right then and there
that he was never going to appear again, since he had only been trying
to see his own children, because he had been wanting to see them,
    he had been trying to do that.
52
Now he said that he was going to depart for his future abode.
He was finally leaving to wherever his future home would be.
He said he was leaving now and would never be seen again.
53
That ghost there was saying that.
And it was just as he said; he was never seen after that.

54
That's was how it ended. That *Illugngali* was an audacious and
    mischievous one.

***

55
Again during the time of war they were in pursuit [of an enemy];
he [*Illugngali*] was one of those in pursuit.
And so
you see these hills here, the ones back away from the river,
when the tide comes in, it would reach that far.
It looks like this, the rock.
A person went there,
someone the men were chasing, as men did

anguyakutellermeggni.
56
Tamatum nalliini tua yuullrullinilria Illugngali.
Tamakucimun-llu itqerrluku,
teggalqum waten
akuliignun kiavet.
57
Tua-i
ullagciiganaku alikluku.
Igvaqussuaralria taum tua-i pitgaqeryugluku. {engelarluteng}
Pitgaqeryugluku.
Tua-i qaill' pisciiganaku.

58
Illugngali-ggur' taun' iliit.
Tua-i qaill' pisciigalamegteggu,
Illugngali pilliniat,
"Illugngaliiq,
kiugna pisciigalkengarput,
asriuguten,
asriuguten
pisciigatevkenaku,
piqerru
asriutacirpetun!" {engelarluteng}
59
Illugngali-ggur-am uitaurqili
qaneqsaunani.
Tua-i-ll' pilliniat tua pisciigatqerluku kia-i ingna
asriutaciatun pisqelluku elliinek.
60
Tua-i piuraqerluni Illugngali matarqenga'artelliniuq,
kiagmi tamaani pillrulliniami.
Ketiini-gguq-gga taun'
kan'a teggalquq
mermi pugumauralria.
61
Illugngali matarrayagarluni tua-i
atralliniluni-am.
Mermun-llu tua tekicami angllulliniluni.
62
Tayim'-am tua cataunani
piuraqerluni teggalqum cam' amatiikun kana-i pugumaalliniuq. {engelarluteng}

when they had enemies.
56
Illugngali was living during that time.
The person dashed into one of those,
into the cleft of the rock
back there.[8]
57
So
they were afraid to go to him.
Every time someone peered in, that person would shoot an arrow at
    him. {laughter}
He kept shooting every time.
So there was nothing they could do.
58
Illugngali, as was said, was one of them.
So when they couldn't do anything more,
they said to *Illugngali,*
"*Illugngali,*
we can't get to that one in there.
You are bold
and mischievous.
It's no big deal for you
as you are so audacious.
Get him!" {laughter}
59
Illugngali just stood there
without saying anything.
So they told him, since they couldn't, to get the one in there by himself,
by means of his audacity.
60
After a while *Illugngali* began to undress
since this happened during the summer.
Down there below him, it was said, there was
this rock
sticking up out of the water.
61
Illugngali went down
completely naked.
When he got to the water he dived in.
62
Then he was gone and
after a while he slowly appeared behind a rock. {laughter}

Pugngami tua tauna teggalquq
tunuani uitaqerluni,
mengliikun igvalliniuq, waten tua piluku.
Ping'um-llu tua tangerqaani
pitgarluku. Pitgaryaaqekiini urluvermek anglluq'alliniluni.
Pitegcaun-llu-gguq ayagarrluni.
63
Tua-ll'-am cali akiakun alaiqata'artuq.
Tua-i-am ping'um pitgalliniluku pitgaani anglluq'alliniluni.

Nuyarralek, Mark Tom; and *Curiralria*, Lucy Tom, circa 1980. Photo by
Andrew J. Chikoyak.

When he appeared he was
now behind that rock and
peered out along the side, like this.
When the one up there suddenly saw him,
he shot an arrow at him. When he shot at him with his bow and arrow,
    he quickly ducked into the water
as an arrow whizzed by. {laughter}
63
Then once more he slowly started to peer over across from him.
Then the one up there shot an arrow at him, and when he shot he
    quickly ducked under.

Cunawa-ggur' im' Illugngali
pugglerkartungnaluni. {engelarluteng}
64
Tua-i ping'um-gguq-am keluqlian iirumalriim pitgaryaaqnauraa.
Tua-i-llu-ggur-am piuraqerluni qanertuq,
"Pitegcautairutqatartuq! Pitegcautairutqatartuq!" {engelarluteng}
65
Ik'atak tauna ca, yungssagaq! {engelarluteng}
Tua-i tayima!
Piuraqerluni-am tua
pug'uq kana-i.
Tua-i-llu-gguq ping'um pitgarluku pitgaani-llu aviarrluni-am
    anglluq'erluni.
Pugngami pileryalliniuq,
"Pitegcautairutuq! Pitegcautairutuq!" {engelarluteng}
66
Aren nutaan-gguq imkut angutet
ullagarrluku teguqalliniluku tauna!
67
Tua-i-ggur-am tua-i asriutacirmitun tua-i
unakevkarluku.
68
Aren nutaan-ggur-am im' Illugngalilkuk
taum kinguakun
aren ilani-llu-gguq cakenripalla'arluki.
Nutaan cakenripalla'arluki tua-i imkurluki
umyuaqellrani qaingatni man' uitaluni. {engelarluteng}
69
Tua-i-ggur-am tuatnallruuq. {qanemcilria engelartuq}
70
Tua-i-gguq tua Illugngaliq tuaten tua-i assiitellruuq.

71
Tua-i allat maa-i kinguakun tuatnayuunani
tuaten tua-i asriullermitun.
Taugken-gguq tua tamakut angalkut pikeggnerunrilnguutnaklekellrui.
Tua-llu-gguq tamakut-gguq tang tukninrit,
angalkut tukninrit,
tua naklekenripalla'arluki nutaan tua-i,
cakenripalla'arluki tamakunun nutaan asriullni aturaqluku
    cakneq. {qanemcilria engelartuq}

And so it happened that *Illugngali*
kept on popping up here and there. {laughter}
64
The one up there who was hiding would try to shoot.
Then after a while *Illugngali* said,
"His arrows are almost gone! His arrows are almost gone!" {laughter}
65
He was so bad, that darn person! {laughter}
So it went!
After a while
he appeared down there.
Then the one up there shot at him, and when he shot at him he
    dodged and ducked under water.
When he appeared he quickly said,
"He's out of arrows! He's out of arrows!" {laughter}
66
Aren, finally those men
rushed up to him and grabbed him!
67
It was said he used his audacity to
capture him.
68
Aren, finally after that
that darn *Illugngali*,
aren, was even more disrespectful toward everyone.
He was even more disrespectful toward everyone;
it was as though in his thoughts he was above them all. {laughter}
69
It was said that that was what he did. {narrator laughs}
70
It was said that *Illugngali* was like that, mischievous and audacious
    like that.
71
Thereafter there was no one like that,
who was as reckless and mischievous.
But he pitied those shamans who weren't as powerful as others.
Yet, it was said, those who were stronger,
the stronger shamans,
he didn't especially pity them
nor especially care for them, but vented his naughtiness and audacity
    on them. {narrator laughs}

CALLARTELLRIA ANGUN
Cakataar Tununermiu

***

1
Tua-i taukut
ilakelriit
uitalriit
allamek-llu ilaunateng yugmek.
Tauna
aanaluteng tauna-gg' paniak ataucirraq,
ataucirrauluni.
2
Tua-i-llu tauna atii kiagmi
qayani akiviggluku
uqrani
caliurallrani.
Qayaq tauna tekilluni
qayarpall'er.

***

3
Uitainanrani,
agiirtellinilria
qayarpall'er
yugluni malrugnek.
4
Tua-i tangvakalliniluku taum angutem
tua-i.
Tua-lli-gga-gguq uka-i agiirtellria kana-i-llu-gguq
ketiinun arulairluni.
Ketiinun-gguq arulairtuq
angun-gguq una
ciungani
ingna-gguq cali arnaq cali
kinguani.
Qayarpall'er tamana angluni!

546

THE SCABBY MAN
Jack Angaiak of Tununak

***

1
There was this
family
that lived
with no other people among them.
That family
had a mother and one daughter,
just one daughter.
2
And so that father of hers, during the summer,
with his kayak leaning on its side,
was busy working
on the lee side of it.
Then a kayak came,
a huge kayak.[1]

***

3
While he was doing that,[2]
a huge kayak
approached
with two people in it.
4
So that man stared at it for a
moment.
And they say that it was approaching down there,
stopping there below him.
It stopped below him,
and they say there was a man
in the front
and a woman also
in the back.
That kayak was huge!

547

5
Kan'a-gguq-gga
waten tua pillruluku,
kan'a-gguq-gga cali
qukaagni
cali qayam painga taũgaam-gguq patumaluni.
6
Patumaluni tua-i
qillrucimaluni avatii.
Tua-i-ll' taggluku.
7
Tua-i tauna
angun taman' tailliniluni.
Tua-i-ll' wanigg' tekitelliniluni mengliinun tekicamiu waten tua-i
   aqumelliniluni tauna.
Mengliinun.
8
Tua-i-ll' tua-i
ilangcivkenaku tua piurluku.
Piurainanrani taum angutem
pillinia
wanigg' tua-i
kaigavikluku wanigg' tua-i ullagyaaqniluku,
kaigaviksaaqniluku pania
tua-i-gg' anirtuqernayukluku,
tauna tua-i angalkuulliniami.
Tua uitauraqarraarluni atralliniluni.
9
Tekitaa-gguq tauna
qukaani—tauna qayaq pingayunek-gguq taman' qayaq pailuni—
una-ll' tua qillrucimalun' umcigingaluku.
Angilluku,
angiqaarluku,
ugg'un tua callarrluku waten mak'arrluku.
Mak'arrluku, makluku
uyangtelliniuq
waten-gguq tua nasaurluq
qayam iluani tua tuani
tuqumaluni
uitalria!
10
Tua-ll' imu' tep'ngelliniluni-gguq tua-i tauna!

5
Down there
it was like this,
and down there
between them, mid-deck,
was another hole, but it was closed.[3]
6
It was closed;
it was tied shut.
So they hauled it up.
7
So that
man there arrived,
and then having arrived, he went up right next to him; he sat down
    like this right next to him.
Right next to him.
8
So then
he didn't pay any attention to him [the visitor].
After a while that man
spoke to him,
saying that
he had come to him to request a favor,
asking him whether
he might save his daughter,
since evidently he was a shaman.
So, having stayed there a while, he went down.
9
He got there, it was said, and there
in the middle—it was a three-hole kayak—
it was lashed down, tightly shut.
Untying it,
having untied it,
he uncovered it there after quickly setting it upright.
Quickly setting it upright, setting it upright,
he peered down,
and there, they say,
was a young girl,
there inside that kayak,
dead!
10
So then, they say, she had begun to stink!

Tepiinek narluni imumek anllullallrani.
Narngami-llu
tua-i ayagartellin' qamavet qamiqurranun.
11
Tua-i qaill' pivkenaku arenqiatellinian.
Narumayunaitellinian patuluku.
Ilungulluku piaku,
egmian taum tua-i tamana atrarrluku.
Aren eklutek tua qaill' piqerpegnatek qanerpegnani-ll' taun'
    ayallinilutek tua.
12
Tua-i tauna
tuqurqiutekliniluku tuaten
yugnek,
tauna tua-i
panigtek tuqumalria ak'allaq!

Man with a dried seal skin. Photo from Jesuit Oregon Province Archives, Gonzaga University, negative number 504.15.

He got a whiff of the stench when it rushed out.
And when he smelled it,
it rushed inside into his head.
11
He didn't do anything to her because she was hopeless.
Since the stench was insufferable, he closed the hole.
When he told him [the visitor], he was all in a huff
and pushed that [kayak] down right away.
Aren, without further ado or without saying anything, they got into it
    and left.
12
Thus they
used her to kill
people one after the other,
[using] that one,
their daughter, who had been dead a long time!

***

13
Tua-i-llu tagngami tuavet tauna angun
aqumelriim, piyaaqelriim ayagciiganani tamana
narumallra.
Qamiqurrani taũgaam tua uitaluni.
Cunagga-gguq uumirpak
qaillukuaryaaqaqelria.
Qaillun piluni tamana
ayagtengnaqsaaqaqkii!
14
Assirisciiganani taũgaam-gguq piuraqerluni ikiurrngiinangluni.
Tua-i ikiurrngiinarluni tua-i.
Piuraqerluni-ll' tua-i
imkurluni qainga callartengluni.

15
Arungluni.
Cali
tamakut,
cani tamakut canek,
piciatun
iinruyaaqluki makunek canek.
Iinruyaaqluki aren tua-i arcariluni tua-i imna qainga.

***

16
Tua-i-llu arenqialami tua-i waten ayuqluni uitangaitelliniami
ayalliniluni.
Yuilqumlluni tua-i yuilqumi tua-i
uitaluni.
17
Tua-i nunanun tekitelliniluni ayagpakarluni.
Tekicami-ll' tua-i angalkuungami,
tauna tua-i
imkuni,
qantarkuq,
ellarramini tua tauna amini
keggavet tua unilluku.
18
Tua-i itliniluni qasgimun.

***

13

And when that man went back up
and sat down, what he was smelling
wouldn't go away.
It just stayed in his head.
And from then on
he tried all sorts of different things.
How he tried to
remove it!
14
He couldn't get well, but instead kept getting worse.
He got worse.
After a while
something began to happen and he began to get sores on the surface
    of his body.
15
He began to rot.
And
as for those,
those [sores] of his,
he tried all sorts of different things on them,
trying to cure them with these [medicines];
he tried to cure them but his body got worse.

***

16
So then, because he was uncomfortable and wasn't going to live like that,
he departed.
He was in the wilderness, remaining
in the wilderness.
17
He came to a village after wandering about.
And when he arrived, since he was a shaman,
he left his skin,
what was
for him
his bodily raiment,[4]
there outside.
18
Then he went into the *qasgiq*.

Aren tuatnaami tua qinuiteqalliniluni man' ayuqucia tua-i!
Qinuinani tua-i uitalliniluni.
Tua-i yuut, angutet, iterluteng.
Tua-i iterpakarluni iliit qanertuq,
"Aling keggna keggani tang
qantarkuq tua keggna
yuan atak tayima alliu!
Arenqialnguq tang
waten ayuqsunailnguq!"

19
Tua-i
niiteng'ermi,
cangallagpegnani
tua-i acuumiicaaqngamiu tua tauna
kumlaan ca man' nangteqellra.
20
Tua-i uitalliniluni.
Tua uitainanrani alla cali angun tauna
iterngami qanlliniuq,
"Aling, ampi atak keggna
tayima pikestiin
qantarkuq,
qantarkuq keggna
alliu,
piliu!
Waten ayuqsunaipakartuq."
21
Aren tua-i -ll'-am tua-i pillagpegnani uitalliniluni tua
arenqialan-gguq-gga atuyunailan, atuyunaicaaqngan tua.
22
Tua-i-ll'
piinanrani cali pulenglluni pian,
arenqialami ellii piatni piyaaqngatni,
anlliniluni.
Anngami tangrraa tua.
Tua-i-gguq ac'unaicaaqluni tua-i
tauna.

23
Tua-i arenqialan-gguq nagguirngailan,
tua-i atelliniluku tua tauna

Aren, when he did that his whole being was suddenly serene and
    peaceful!
He calmly remained there.
People, men, came in.
After several of them had entered, one of them said,
"*Aling*, that one out there,
that bodily raiment out there,
the owner should put it on!
It's really a bother
and shouldn't be like this!
19
So
even though he heard that,
he didn't do anything different
because he really didn't want to put that on
since that sickness of his itched.
20
He just stayed put.
While he was there another man
upon entering said,
"*Aling*, quickly now, that one out there,
that bodily raiment,   ·
that physical being out there,
let its possessor
put it on,
do something!
It shouldn't have to be like this."
21
But again he didn't move and stayed there because, it was said, it was
    impossible to wear, because it shouldn't have to be worn.
22
And so
when this occurred again while he was there, because they were
addressing themselves to him, because it was really him to whom they
    were speaking,
he went out.
When he went out he saw it.
That one
oughtn't to be worn.
23
So because it couldn't be otherwise,
he put that on,

ayuqucillni.
Tua-i-llu-gguq-am assiinani tua kirciurluni canek qainga man'a.
Tua-i-am tuantesciigalami-gguq,
taukut tuani avulirciigalamiki,
ayalliniluni-am tua yuilqumun.

***

24
Ayagngami tua-i,
nani
tamaani tua yuilqumtaqelria.
25
Arcariluni taũgaam tua-i taman' qainga.
26
Tua-i-llu
ayainanermini nunanun tekitelliniuq.
Tekitelliniuq nunanun tua-i yuunateng.
Piyaaqai tamakut yuunateng tua-i.
27
Tua-i qasgimun itliniluni,
itrami tua kiavet...
(Naugga egkuit net nalluaci?
Egkuit?
Yaa-i tang ingna!
Qasgiukuni amiik
kiugna-wa
pagkuciit egkuitnek piaqait
makut-gga caniqerrit
maa-i.)
Waten tua-i
qasgim egkuanun kiavet aqumelliniluni
taunaũrluq tua-i.
28
Tua-i aqumngami tua-i,
umyuarteqliniuq,
"Aling qaillun atak waniw' piqerlua assiriqerlii tua waniwa?
Qaillun waniw' pikuma tua-i utumarcarcia?"
Iluteqem tua tekitelliniluku waten uitaurallrani, uitaurallrani.
Tua-i tekicani tua-i tuan' qialliniluni.
29
Tua-i qiagaqelria tua-i.

[returning] to the way he was.
And it was, they say, terrible; his body was burning.
Then, since he couldn't remain there,
because he couldn't be among them,
he left for the wilderness.

***

24
When he left,
he was staying
somewhere there in the wilderness.
25
His body only got worse.
26
So then,
while he traveled on, he came to a village;
he came to a village which had no people.
He saw that there were no people.
27
So he went into a *qasgiq*,
and when he entered he went all the way in...
(Are you familiar with the *egkuit* of a house?
Their back walls?
See that one over there!
If it were a *qasgiq*, the door,
and that one in the back,
those kinds would be their back walls
and these here
would be their sides.)
Like so,
that poor man
sat next to the back wall of the *qasgiq*.
28
So when he sat down
he thought,
"*Aling*, what can I do to get better now?
What must I do to become well?
Sorrow came over him while he was there, while he was there.
When it came over him he cried there.
29
He cried and cried.

***

30
Tua-i-ll' piinanrani,
qianginanrani,
qakma tua-i cavallartelliniluni
ellatii.[a]

31
Tua-i cavallartengraan-llu tua-i ilangcivkenaku tua-i qiaguralliniluni.
Piuraqerluni cakma-gguq!
Amiigmek
imkurluni.
Icigg' cat imkut kekiungqitalriit nallunrilkeci maa-i
qalriuraqelriit waten
passitaqameng.

32
Cali ak'a tamaani
tuqullret wiinga-ll' tangtullrukenka yuut tuquaqata,
acia qerratarrluku waten ellitullrukait.
Cetamanek waten naparyirluku

558

***

30
So then after a while,
while he was crying,
something out there moved,
just outside.
31
Even though it made a move he didn't pay attention to it and kept on
    crying.
In a short time there it was!
It was doing like this,
coming from the door.
You know, those creaking noises, you know how
they squeak like this
when they are crushed.
32
Also, a long time ago,
the dead whom I used to see whenever people died,
these they placed raised above the ground.
Using four posts,

Herring fishing near *Tununeq,* circa 1980. The rocky point at left is *Uyaqurruam
Nuuga.* Photo by Andrew J. Chikoyak.

qaingatnun-llu elliluku,
nayuutevkenakek ellami maani;
wa-gguq citaat.
Caqutait
citaitnek pitullrukait tuaten tua-i.
Ilait-llu nayuulluki ilait-llu tuaten tua-i.
Imkut-gguq ellami tua-i
waten taũgaam alaunatek.
33
Atam-gguq piqalliniuq
amiigkun tamakut,
tua tuqumalria,
tauna tua tuqulleq,
tuqumalria tua-i
itliniluni tamakunek-gguq imirluteng waten-gguq
pitaurluteng waten tua-i ukuit.
34
Tua-i kinguanek itliniami maaggun ayalliniluni
waten tamaaggun
yaatiinun-llu arulairluni.
Aren tua-i-gguq imkut
allat it'ngut.
Maavet ayagluteng waten tua-i
ayagturalriit
uavet tua-ll' amiik tekicamegteggu-am cali,
tamana muirngan,
cali tua-i tuaten
yaatiinun tuaten-gguq-am tua-i yaaqliqu'urluteng.
Tamakut tua-i yuuvkenateng-llu
tuaten tua-i caqutet, yuut caqutait.
35
Taqeqaqsaunani-llu-gguq tua qialria. Qiayuumiirucuitellinivaa tanem
    taumi qiaguralriami;
iluteqairucuitellinivaa.
36
Tua-i muirluku.
Tua-i muirngan,
piuraqerluni iliit,
tamakucit, ug' uanelnguq
qanlliniuq,
"Aling, qaillun tua-i waniwa tang
qayagaurpakaavkut,

and putting [the grave box] on it,
they placed it above ground instead of burying it;
this is what they called a grave box.
Their containers
which they used [to bury them in] they called "grave boxes".
They buried some of them like that.
Those kind were above ground and,
like this, were visible.
33
See, he realized
that those things were at the door,
the dead,
one who had died,
one who was dead
was entering, filling [the space of the *qasgiq*] like this,
being about yea high off the ground![5]
34
So when it entered behind him it went this way,
that way
and stopped near him.
Aren, all the others
started to file in!
Going here, they continued
to go like this
and when they got to the door,
having filled that [side of the *qasgiq*] up to the entrance,
they began again like that,
filing one after the other to the other side and did the same.
Those were not people but
coffins, containers for people.
35
And he was, they say, crying without stopping. The one who was
    crying sure never wanted to stop crying;
he never wanted to stop sobbing.
36
So they filled it [the *qasgiq*].
Then when it was filled,
just then one of them,
one of those, the one who was by the door,
said,
"*Aling*, because you have been
calling us,

arenqialan tua uitaviirucamta,
qayagaurpakaavkut,
waniwa tua-i aren uitasciigaliamta tailriakut ullakemteggen.
37
Ca pitekluku tua-i
qayagaurpakarcikut?
Ca pitekluku taisqevvakarcikut?"
38
Tua-i nutaan taqluni
tua-i qanlliniluni
ca pitkevkenaku
qaini man'a pitekluku wanigg' tua-i
nunaniryunritniluni cakneq.

***

39
Tua-ll' tua-i pilliniuq, Aa, cunagga-gguq tua tamana pitekluku.
    Tauna-gguq imkut iliit
yaassiit tuqumalriit iliit qanaaluni taūgken tua yugtaunani.
40
Tua-ll' tua pilliniuq, qanlliniur-am ugna,
kanavet atrartesqelluku
matarrluku.
41
Tua-i pisqeńgani-am taklartelliniuq atrarluni matarrluni.
Tua-i-ll' nutaan
nangertelliniuq;
angutnguluni, tua angutngurrluni, angukaraurluuluni
tailuni-ll' uka-i.

42
Tua-i-llu-gguq iquanek ayagluku maaken
it'gai paingartelliniluki.
Keggagceńani-gguq imna camna ulua.
43
Qainga man'a tua tamalkuan mayurqurallinikii.
Pillinia-gguq
ulurpakayallrii anqetaalria naugg' qimugtet tangvalaqeci
pairtura'arqata; tuaten-gguq tua-i
ayuqluni
taum tuani,
cam taum pairtiin.

because it has become impossible for us to ignore,
because you have been calling us,
because we couldn't stay away, we have come here, we have come to you.
37
For what reason have you been
calling us?
For what reason have you been telling us to come?"
38
So he finally stopped
and said
that it was for no other reason
than this body of his,
saying he wasn't happy at all.

***

39
So then he said, Ah, so he said that it was on account of that. And one
    of those
boxes, one of the dead was talking, although there was no person.
40
Then it, the one by the door, told him
to go down there
with all his clothes off.
41
Then since he evidently told him to lie down, he went down and
    removed his clothes.
Then finally
he [the one in the coffin] stood up;
it was a man, an older man, an old man
who came over.
42
So then, it was said, beginning from his extremity here,
it began to lick his toes.
His tongue down there, they say, was rough.[6]
43
He worked his way up along his entire body.
He noticed
his long tongue going in and out, like the dogs you see
when they lick; it was, they say, just
like that,
that one there,
that thing that was licking him.

44
Tua-i qainga man' tamalkuan
paiqii tua-i yaavet,
wavet tua-i qainga tamalkuan.
Kingunra-gguq tuaten tua waten mamluni tuaten.
45
Imna callarteqapiaralleq
tua-i mamluni waten ellirluni.
Tua-i-ll'
pilliniluku tua-i taqniluku.
46
Tuavet-llu-gguq-am tua-i yaassiigminun tua-i
piluni.
Tua-i-llu-gguq
piameng ciumek taukuk itrallrek, uaken-gguq-am ayagnirluteng,
cetamanek ipigluteng
uvaaluteng imkut-gguq-am
muragglainaat.
Taŭgaam-gguq tua-i neplirluteng
qalriuraluteng
tamakut.
47
Anngelliniut-ggur-am
tua-i-gguq-am makut nangciit.
Nangengata-llu-gg'-am cali tua-i yaaken ayagluni,
una-i-gguq caqtaarturluteng taŭgken tua uvaaluteng caqutnguluteng.

***

48
Anngelliniut-ggur-am tua-i
tua-i-llu-gguq catairulluteng.
49
Tua-i catairucata tua-i, nutaan catairucata, qaini tamana tangrraa:
qainga-gguq tua man' askacagarluni tua waten mamumaluni
    cataunani tua-i.
Aturani-gguq tangrrai taukut tua-i ac'unaunateng tua-i arenqianateng.
50
Arenqialami-gguq tua-i
anlliniluni
tua matarmi.
Anngami kiartelliniluni.

44
He licked his entire body from here
to there,
all of his body here.
It was said that the parts he had finished [licking] were thus made whole.
45
What was very scabby and sore-infested
healed and became like this.
So then
he said that he was done with him.
46
Then, it was said, he went back
into his box.
And
the ones that had come in first, starting there at the door,
were rocking from side to side
on four legs,
all wooden.
Yet, it was said, they were noisy
and squeaky,
those.
47
So they filed out
as though they were towing each other.
And when these were done, again starting from over there,
[those] down there began moving, yet they were just containers,
    rocking from side to side.

***

48
They began to go out
and then were gone.
49
Then when they were gone, when they were finally gone, he looked
    at his body;
his body was very nice, healed like this, with nothing on it.
He looked at his clothes there, which were impossible to wear.
50
Because he felt uneasy [about his clothes],
he went out
naked.
When he went out he looked around.

51
Kiarcami tua-i
pilliniuq ingna qer'at,
mayurrvik.
Mayurrvingqetulriit ak'a tamaani
qertukayagluteng.
Ugkut ua-i
Qull'inkut pingqertut.
Kat'umek kana-i
ellivimeggnek.
Waten-am qertutullruut atam canek imitulqait.
52
Tua-ll' mayullinilun' tamaaggun
tuaggun.
Mayurrvigmek imkucimek cali ellivignek elliviksaguskemteñek
    wangkuta.
Wiinga-llu tangerrsugnaitetullruluki tua tamaani.
Canek ta͡ugaam tua-i
muragnek pingqetullruluteng.
53
Itliniuq-gguq.
Itrami patuirluku kiartellinia.
Neqet
amiit tamaa-i missuuget,
imkut tua missuullret.
Missuullernek wangkuta maa-i qemagquriaqelriakut.
Tamakut-llu tamaa-i ak'a neqet,
neqet qeltaitnek,
qeciirluki missuulitullrulriit.
Mecungcugnaunaki-am mer'em-llu piyugnaunaki.
Umciggluki cali mingeqluki
pitullruluki.
Mermi-ll' uitang'ermeng iterngaunaki.
Arnat tamaa-i caliallrit.
54
Tamakuciq
agalria.
Tegungamiu tua-i
una painga angilluku
callarrluku
pillinia aturat,
tamaa-i

51
When he looked around,
over there he saw a fish rack,
an elevated cache.
They had elevated caches a long time ago,
which were very high.
[Like] the ones down there where
Qull'ik's family has one;
that's their food cache
down there.
They used to be high and they would fill them with things.
52
And so he went up through there
by that way.
[It was] like that elevated food cache, the kind we use as food caches
now.
As for myself, I was prevented from seeing them back then.[7]
But [now]
they have only wood.
53
He went in.
When he went in, opening it, he looked around.
There were
fish skin sacks,
you know, those sacks.
We save gunny sacks nowadays.
Way back then, they would
skin the fish
and use those skins for making storage sacks.
They were water proof; water wouldn't get to them.
They used to sew them
tightly.
And even if they were in the water the water would not go in.
That was the women's work.
54
One of those
were hanging.
When he took it,
he untied the mouth,
opened it
and saw clothes,
clothes

567

aturat,
aturanek imarluni.
55
Tua-i iquklilluni
aturanek taukunek at'uq.
Qerrulliignek-llu
piluguugnek-llu
tua-i tegutelliniluni
aturkagminek at'ellinilukek tua tamalkuita.
Tua-i qaqilluni.
56
Tamaa-i
ak'a tamaani
nallukeci tua-i, nallukeci maa-i nalluvallaaqeci.
Elriqatarqameng-gguq
quyurtetullruut
aklunek.
Piliameggnek, qerrullignek piliameggnek,
atkugnek cali piliameggnek
quyurrluteng yugnek aruqutkameggnek.
Wa-gguq elriqatarqameng.

57
Qayuqegglinek atkuliluteng,
kanaqlagnek atkuliluteng,
piciatun tua makunek atkuliuraqluteng.
Tuaten tua-i at'elliniluni.

***

58
Ac'ami nutaan tua-i
kingutmun
ayalliniluni.
Tua-i nunaniryugluni ayuqucia man'a.
59
Nunaniryugluni tua-i.
60
Tua-i-llu
nunaminun tua tekilluni uitaviminun.
61
Tua-i uksuarpak.

there;
it was filled with clothes.
55
From head to toe
he put on those clothes.
Pants,
boots,
he took them
and put them all on to wear.
He had a complete outfit.
56
Those times back then,
back long ago,
you don't know anything about it, you know absolutely nothing about
    it, especially nowadays.
It was said that when they were going to celebrate *Elriq*, a Memorial
    Feast for the Dead,
they would gather together
clothes.
All the stuff they made, the pants which they made,
and the parkas that they made,
all these they would assemble together to distribute to the people.
This was when they got ready for the Memorial Feast.
57
They made tundra hare parkas,
they made muskrat parkas
they made parkas of all kinds.
He donned the clothes.

***

58
When he finally got dressed,
he headed
home.
He was in high spirits.
59
He was exultant.
60
And so
he arrived at his village, his own place of residence.
61
He stayed throughout the fall.

Tauna-llu tua-i
aipani
waten amirkamek kiagmi waten
amirkaq kenilluku
cetuanek-llu
kevirkainek egaaruluki ungirqelluku tauna.
Mingeqluku-ll' umciggluku.
62
Tua-i kiagpak kiagiluni
uksuan-llu
taukunun ayagluni.
63
Taukut nunait nallunrilamiki,
ikamrarragnun ekluku tamana.

***

64
Tekitai-gguq
elrillinilriit,
tamaa-i tamakucirluteng.
65
Aren tua-i-gguq imkut angutet
kipucugyaaqelliniaqekiit taun', piyugyaaqelliniaqekiit ucia.
Niicuunaki tua-i
pilliniaqekai.
66
Tua-ll'-am qasgimi waten uitallermini
iliit-am tua piyugyaaqellrani tua ilangcivkenaku.
Nutaan tua angutet quyungqallratni pillinii,
qanrutlinii
wanigg' qanqatarniluni tua-i wanigg' tua nutaan.
67
Kiak
arenqiatellermini nanikuallermini,
kiak,
tua-i aturanek yaaken mayurrviim iluanek
at'ellruniluni.
Waniwa-qa
tayima iliit paqriciqallrunritellranek
caarayain ilaitnek.
68
Tua-i iliit

And that one,
his wife,
had a young bearded seal,
a young bearded seal which she had [skinned], soaked
and stuffed with cooked
belukha whale, first having soaked and softened it.
Then it was sewed up tightly.[8]
62
So he remained there all summer
and when winter came
he went to them.[9]
63
Because he knew about their village,
he put that poke into the sled.

***

64
When he got to them, it was said,
they were having a Memorial Feast for the dead,
doing the sort of thing [they did] back then.
65
Aren, it was said those men
kept on wanting to buy that one, were really wanting his cargo.[10]
He didn't
listen to them.
66
And so when he was in the *qasgiq,*
one of them wanted it but he ignored him.
Finally when the men were together he spoke to them,
telling them
that he was finally going to talk.
67
He told them that
during the previous summer,
when he was uncomfortable and in desperate straits,
he said that he had taken clothes from inside an elevated cache
and had worn them.
[And he wanted to know] right now
if anyone of them had missed anything
from among their things.
68
Then one of them,

tua nepaircameng, nepaiteqapiga'arrluteng tua qasgim ilua uitaqalliniuq.
Piuraqerluni angutet iliit qanlliniuq,
"Wii tang tua waniwa
tua-i caarayaggama ilaitnek paqriciyaaqellrulrianga tua tayim' naugga
    cataicullrulrianga."
69
Tua-ll' pillinia,
"Allam pillrunritai; wiinga pillruanka."
70
Tua-i cunawa taum qelgaari.
Tua-ll' pillinia,
"Kegga-i keggna ucika taumek navertanka ucika; tua kegga-i pikiu."
71
Tua-i quyaqakacagarluni tua tauna,
aruqutaminek cetuanek
taumek tua-i.

***

72
Tuaten tua tauna pitaluku waten iquklilluku tua qanemcitullrukiit.

when they became quiet, it being absolutely quiet in the *qasgiq*,
and time having passed, one of the men said,
"I right here
have missed some of my things, I have missed them and I don't know
    where they are."
69
So then he said to him,
"No one else did it, I did it!"
70
Apparently that was what he had saved up.
Then he said to him,
"I'll trade my load out there for it; you can have it."
71
That one was very, very thankful
about the belukha he would be receiving
from him.

***

72
That's the extent of that story they used to tell.

ANGUTET PINGAYUN

Cuniq Tununermiu

***

1
Tua-llu tua-i waniwa
ayagnirluku.
1
Ukut
angutet pingayun,
angutnginarauluteng avani Caninermi,
yaatmurtellinilriit,
Caninermi avani.
2
Tua-llu amavet
Cal'itlermun tekilluteng,
Cal'itmiunun tekilluteng.
Yuirutellrulliniluteng
taukut
nunat.
Yuit natmun pivimeggnun cali upagallrullinilriit.
Tua-i yuitqapiggluteng taukut nunat.
Tua-i
arivamalartuq Cal'itmiunek amkunek.
3
Tua-i tuavet arulairluteng
waten atakuyartumi.
Tua-llu
maqililuteng
waten uksuarmi, uksuaryartumi
makut yaqulget, tengmiat uterqaqellrata tamaa-i nalliini.
4
Tua-i
maqililuteng, tua maqiluteng tua-i anglaniluteng.
Tua-i-ll' imumek tua taqluteng kan'a kenillrat qamluni.
Tua maqilnguqerrluteng piameng

THREE MEN

Jents Flynn of Tununak

***

1
And now to
begin the story.
1
These
three men,
who were just ordinary men from the lower coast,
traveled yonder,
along *Canineq*, the lower coast.
2
Then they arrived over there at
what was once *Cal'in*,
reaching the village of *Cal'itmiut*.
There were no people left in
that
village.
Its residents had already migrated somewhere to their winter homes.
There was absolutely nobody in that village.
And
that place was called *Cal'itmiut*.
3
So they stopped there
sometime at dusk.
And then
they made a fire bath;
this happened in early fall
at the time geese and ducks migrated south.
4
So
they made a fire bath, took a bath and enjoyed themselves.
And so they finished when their fire burned out.
Having had enough of the fire bath,

tauna tua iliik
ukalirnermi tallirpim tungiini
uitalria
ukuk-wa ilak ika-i akiani.
5
Tua-i
ina'artelliniluni, tua ina'arrluni, tua kelutmun ina'arrluni.
Tua-i-llu tua inangqainanermini
qavaqalliniluni.
Tua-i egaleq-llu pikna tua pika-i paturraunani.
6
Makut,
egalret
waten unugmi
patuitesqumayuitetuit. Inerquutauluni tauna tua-i
egalrem patuitlerkaa unugmi yungqerrluni qavaquni
taugaam pikailkuni
muraggarmek cani'irrvikluku
tua-i patunguaqerarkauluku.
Tuaten cali qaneryaraulria inerquutnguluni.

[they relaxed] with one of them
staying
here towards the right side
and the other two there on the other side.
5
And so the one alone lay down to sleep facing away from the middle.
And while he was lying down,
he fell asleep.
And the window up there had no cover of any sort.
6
They always wanted
some sort of cover
for the windows
during the night. It is a rule that
the window must be covered during the night when anyone is sleeping,
but if it happens to have no cover,
a piece of wood can be laid crosswise
and be used as a cover for the window.
That is one of the rules.

Men with *qalut* 'dip nets' and a woman with a *qiluq* 'seal intestine' to use for waterproof garments. Photo from Jesuit Oregon Province Archives, Gonzaga University, negative number 506.02.

***

7

Tua-llu tua-i tauna imna una
wanelnguq
qaini pacetengan
tupalliniuq.
Tupagngami
makcaaqelriim
umyugaa taũgaam makluni pek'artevkenani-ll' tua-i.
Pekcesciiganani.

8

Tua-i asqigmi igvaumalukek ikegkuk akiqliigni inangqiimi
tanglliniak
cali tua-i ika-i inangqalutek kegginakek-llu alaunatek.
9
Uitaqanrakun
qakemkut
qasgim qaingani
yugtangqellinilria qakemna.
Qan'ataarturalriit, qanerturalriit
niitengllinii qakma.
10
Qanerturalriit qakemkut
tua-i-w' yugpallaralriit qakemkut amlleriinarluteng taũgaam.
11
Tua-llu iliit
qanlliniuq qakemna, "Aling
imna imumi-lli
utaqakngamteñi
tekicuipagta!"
Nerinilluteng qanaaluteng
tekitellerkaanek tauna ilaseng.
12
Tua-llu tua-i
piinanermeggni,
tua makcesciiganani-ll' tauna tua-i.
13
Ilak-wa cali ikegkuk tua-i ika-i maaten
tauna tua-i
allakarrarmi uitalria
yupiunritlinilria

***

7
The man who was sleeping
here on the right side
woke up
when he got chilled.
He woke up
and attempted to get up,
but his mind was the only part that would function; he himself was
    unable to stir.
He was totally incapable of movement.
8
Since he was lying down at a good vantage point, on the opposite side,
he could see his two partners lying down
with their faces clearly visible to him.
9
While he was lying there,
he realized that
there were people outside
on top of the *qasgiq.*
He could hear them
talking back and forth with each other outside.
10
The talking out there
and the human noises just kept multiplying.
11
And one of them
out there said, "*Aling,*
where is that person
we are waiting for!
When is he going to get here!"
Their conversation was about how impatient they were
waiting around for the arrival of one of their own people.
12
And so
as time went on,
that one still could not get up at all.
13
Unlike his two partners over there,
that one
who was by himself
was not an ordinary person,

angalkuuluni taũgaam pillinilria
tauna.
14
Maaten tua-i
angalkumikun
ilagni
pilliniak
elliitun tua-i
uitallinilriik ika-i pekcesciiganatek tupaumang'ermek.

***

15
Tua qakemkut tua qan'ataarluteng nerinilluteng tua-i.

16
Tua-llu
iliit qakma qanertuq uka-i-gguq alarutuq.
Tua-i
qakma
tekitniluku.
Tua-llu tuaten tua piata
piuraqerluteng qanlliniut
kepqenga'artelliniut
uyangcestekaatnek,
uyangtarkamek waten taukut yuut uyanglluki
egalerkun.
17
Tua-i qakma tua-i
pikaiturluteng tua-i-ll' pikangluteng tua-i pakma
iliit uyangteqatarluni.

***

18
Tua-i ima murilkellinii tua-i niicugniurluki.
Tua-ll' pika-i uyangcartulliniuq,
uyangtelliniuq
yuk pikna
angun.
Kegginaa tua qiuk'acagarluni tua-i
tangniinani tua-i kegginaa qiuluni!
19
Uyangqarraarluni-llu pika-i

but was a shaman
instead.
14
And then he found out
through his shamanistic power
that his
companions,
as was the case with him,
were also unable to move even though they were awake.

***

15
The people outside were talking back and forth with each other,
    waiting impatiently.
16
And then
one of them outside said that someone was approaching.
Then
he said
he had arrived out there.
When that occurred,
shortly afterwards they said
they needed
someone to peer inside,
someone to peer down at the people inside
through the window.
17
For a while nobody would volunteer,
then one of them up there did offer
to peer inside at the people.

***

18
The shaman inside was listening to them carefully.
And then there he was up there beginning to look in;
the person up there,
a man,
peered down.
His face was very blue,
unsightly because it was blue![1]
19
After he peered down from up there,

581

makluni.
Ilagni
ikavet tua-i tanglliniak
kegginaūrlukek tua qiuk'acagarlutek,
qiulutek.
20
Tua-i-ll' makluni pika-i.
21
Qanerluteng,
"Tava-qaa! Tava-qaa!" Tava-qaaraluteng
unakellerkameggnek.
22
Tuamta-llu cali alla
uyangcesqelluku.

***

23
Tua-ll' uyangtelliniuq tangvallinia pikavet
kegginaa qakik'acagarluni, tua-i qakirpak, tua kegginaa!
Ila'urluugni-am tanglliniak
kegginakek tua qatkacagarlutek, qakilutek.
24
Tua-i-llu makluni.
Makcan tua-i
qanlliniut
tua-i kankuk
ilak
piciunrirnilukek,
kan'a
taūgaam atauciq,
pingayuak,
tua-i unakumaqatanricukluku.
25
Maaten tua-i ila'urluugni tanglliniak,
pilliniak,
ak'a tua-i
yuunrillrullinilriik.
Ellii taūgaam tua-i unguvaluni.
26
Tua-i caperrsualuteng
qakemkut.

he stood up.
Then the shaman looked over across
at his two partners
whose poor faces were very, very
blue.
20
So the one up there had gotten up.
21
The ones outside were saying,
" I doubt it! I doubt it!" expressing doubt
about their ability to get the man inside.
22
Once again they told someone else
to peer down.

***

23
As he peered down the man below observed
that his face was very white, absolutely white!
Again he looked over at his poor partners and saw
that their faces were just as white, just as pale.
24
Then the man up there stood up.
When he got up,
he said that
the two down there,
his [the shaman's] partners,
were no longer alive,
but the one [the shaman]
down there,
the third one,
they were uncertain whether or not they could get him.
25
Then the shaman looked over at his poor partners
and saw that they were
already
dead.
Only he was alive.
26
The ones outside
were beginning to feel challenged.

27
Tuamta-ll' tua-i
uyangcesqelluku ilaseng.
Uyangtelliniuq.
Yuk pikna tangllinia
kegginaa tua tunguk'acagarluni, tua tungulriaruluni.
Ilagni-am tanglliniak ikavet
kegginakek tua tungurpak tua tungulutek.
Tua-i-llu makluni.
Makcami tua qanerluni,
"Kan'a kanani iliik
pimaqatanrilngatuq tua kana-i."

***

28
Nutaan
umyuarteqem tekitellinia, tauna imna inangqalria,
angalkuq.
Tua-llu tua-i
makut pissuukarani yurvirluki
piurallinii.
Tua-llu tua-i uumek
pissuutmi iliitnek—
makut
tengmiat, yaqulget makut tamarmeng tengmiat,
piurteqarraallermeggni tamaani—
tuqumalriaqerraakacagiit una umyugaanun kanalliniluni;
tengmiani tamalkurmeng
tuquqerraakacagalleq una tengmiaq,
yaqulek.
29
Tua-i nutaan
tuqlulliniluku tauna
taisqelluku.
30
Tua-i ak'anun pivkenani
tua-ll' imumek
qalrialriamek
niitelliniuq.
Pilliniuq
maa-i tekitellinilria
imna tua-i yaqulget iliit.

27
Then again
they told one of them to peer in.
He peered down.
The shaman inside saw
that his face was very black, that it was black.
So he looked over at his partners
and their faces were pitch black.
Then [the one that was peering down] stood up.
When he got up he said,
"Their partner down there
is not going to be caught."

***

28
Finally
an idea came to that one lying there,
to the shaman.
Then
he examined the magical paraphernalia
he usually used.
Then
through one of his powers—
these
geese, all geese around here,
back when they first came into existence—
the very first one of them to die came to his mind;
of all the geese,
the very first goose that died,
that bird [came to his mind].
29
Then finally
he called on that goose
to come.
30
It wasn't long
before he heard
one of them
honking.
He noticed that
the one goose
that he called for arrived.

Wangkuta
neqlermek arivatukvut,
neqleq,
yaqulget iliit;
erinii ciilertekacagarluku tua-i.
31
Aren tua-i imkut taukut
yugugaat uitalriit
aren uitanriqertelliniluteng maa-i; pagaa-i tua-i
anllugneratni
egilraluni.
Nepelkitaqami erinii ciilkacagarluni tua-i ciilerrluni piaqluni.

***

32
Aren tua-i qan'ngartelliniut qakemkut, "Arenqiapaa!
Picurlakatartukut uitayunaituq!
Amci ayagnariaci!
Arenqiatuq, kan'a pimanrituq tua unakumanrituq!"

Drying salmon. Photo from Jesuit Oregon Province Archives, Gonzaga University, negative number 506.07.

We
call it *neqleq,*
the white-fronted goose;
it was one of those birds;
its voice was very dry and crackly.
31
Aren, suddenly all those
people who were up there
became very restless;
up above them it was
flying around [The goose had a face on its chest].[2]
Whenever it made a sound its voice would be very crackly.

***

32
Aren, they started saying out there, "*Arenqiapaa*! Oh my goodness!
We're going to be in trouble and shouldn't be here!
Hurry up, it's time for all of you to go!
Arenqiatuq! Oh dear, that one down there won't be gotten; he won't
   be caught!"

33
Aren tuaten qanqertelluku,
aren tem'illalliniluteng qakemkut,
tua tem'irrluni neplirluteng tuaten,
qalriallgutkevkenateng,
tengmiat qalrialuteng tua-i,
tem'irrluni taũgaam
qakemna.
34
Tua-i tusruirucarturluni,
tua-i tayim' tusruirulluni.

***

35
Tua-i caarkaicunga'arcan man'a umyuartequrallni,
nutaan tua-i qaillukuaqcarluni ellminek
natii imna tua pek'arcecani
pekngiinarluni tua-i kiituani tua-i pekluni maktuq.
Makcami tua nangerrluni akluluni
ilagni taukuk tua-i pilliniak tua tuqumalutek.
36
Tua-i
nani uitavigkailagnek
tuani tua-i quyurrlukek qasgim iluani
tua uitavkalliniak.
Amiigak taũgaam una
camun piciatun
melqulegmun-llu itlerkaa tauna qasgiq
piciatun
umyuaqluku tua muragnek
kevilliniluku, tua qalliqurluki tua umciggluku tua amiik tauna tua
    kevirluku.
Egaleq-llu pikna cali patuluku umciggluku.
37
Tua-i ilagni taukuk tua-i
arenqiacaaqlukek.

***

40
Tamaa-i,
waniw'
iquklicaaquq taũgaam uumek iquliqaqata'arqa

33
Aren, once that was said
they made rumbling noises outside,
making thundering sounds
using various goose calls,
honking,
making rumbling noises
outside.
34
Then it started getting calm,
and then became peaceful.

***

35
When the shaman had no more worries,
he tried to help himself
and when he made a part of his body move
other parts followed until he sat up.
Getting up, he stood and dressed
and saw that his partners were indeed dead.
36
Because
they had no other place to be,
he laid them side by side in the *qasgiq*
and left them there.
Thinking [to prevent] fur bearing animals
or anything else
from going inside,
he packed logs into the entrance way,
lying them on top of each other
until nothing could get inside.
And the window up there he covered up tightly.

37
He felt for his partners,
but there was nothing that could be done about it.

***

40
This story is supposed to be over now,
but I am going to elaborate
on the rule

tamakut inerquutaatnek.
41
Waten
inerquutauguq
qaneryarangqerrluni-llu.
Tengmiat-gguq,
makut yaqulget,
uterteqatarqameng, utertaqameng
taquaricuitut; tamaani taquarkartelartut.

42
Tua-i
yuut imkut
angutet[a]
nani uitaurayuitellruameng ayagaurluteng qavartaquluteng yuut
    angutet pitullruameng.
Tamaa-i qanirtuun:
43
Una wani
nem'i qavaquni,
qavaqataquni kiirrarmi,
egalra patusqumarrlainarluku
tua-i-gguq uyangtellerkani
umyuaqluku,
aũg'utun qanllemtun.
44
Cali tuamta-llu yuilqumi
yuk mer'ilkuni
mermek tua-i nuuqilluni maani mararrlainarmi qavartaqataquni—
qayat aklungqetullruut qaqimaluteng,
negcikcuarluteng, tallirpacuarluteng muraggarmek,
iqua negcikcuarauluni tamaa-i calissuukaraqluki qayam—
tua-llu tua qavaqataquni mer'unani,
tamana tua-i tallirpacuarani wavet mengleminun
kangra nuagarqaarluku nuaminek
kapuarrluku.
Tua-i tauna
nuani meqluku.
Tua-i tauna qanirtuutnguluni tamaa-i.
Cat makut qanirtuutengssaaraat nalluaci
tua maa-i.
Taũgaam maa-i ayagniuteqataraci

that is relevant to it.
41
So this is a rule;
it is also
an adage.
They say that geese,
these birds,
when they are about to migrate south, when they return to the south,
they never go without provisions; that's when they accumulate their
    provisions.
42
And
so
men
were never idle anywhere, were always on the move, were camping
    overnight as men did then.
And this is the rule:
43
When one
sleeps in a house,
whenever he's going to sleep alone,
he must always cover the window,
thinking
about what could peer in at him,
just as I mentioned before.
44
Moreover, in the wilderness
if a person is out of fresh water and in
need of some and is about to spend the night in a lowland marsh—[3]
the kayaks had all the necessary tools
including gaffs, wooden arm extenders
with a small hook at one end, which were tools for the kayak—
then when he was about to go to sleep without a water supply,
he would take his arm extender, put it here next to him
and after wetting the tip with his saliva,
he poked it into the ground.
That saliva there
would represent his water supply.
That is a long practiced precautionary measure.
You people don't know about these various precautionary measures
these days.
But now you are beginning to,

taqenrilkuvci waten.
38
Tua-i augna tauna imna
kiimelami
kingunerminun uterrluni.
Tua tekilluni taukuk-llu ilagni qanemciklukuk tua-i.
39
Tua-i una wani qanemcika
ava-i iuklitaqa.

***

45
Cingarkaq:
Apnaluten.
Ciin-gguq mer'itlerkaatnek wani
pia?
46
Cuniq:
Ai?
47
Cingarkaq:
Ciin-gguq mengqerrarkauga
inareskuni?
48
Cuniq:
Tua-i-gguq
tauna meq,
nuaminek mel'iqerluni, mer'itevkenani.
Mer'ilkuni
mer'irnayukluni-gguq. Una cali
qanemcitangqertuq,
una mer'irluku. Meq man'a qanemcitangqertuq cali.
Tua-i tauna nuani
meqluku.
Tua-i-gguq mer'irnayukluni.
Inerquutangqertuq una wani.

49
Tua-i ava-i
qanrutamken aug'umek.
Taugaam qanemciksungramku qanemcingiinaryuumiitua
tauna meq pitekluku.

as long as you continue these recording sessions.
38
And since that man
was alone,
he returned to his village.
When he reached it he told about his two partners.
39
And now my story
has come to an end.

***

45
Eliza Orr:
I wanted to ask you.
Why is he worried about his not having
fresh water?
46
Jents:
What?
47
Eliza Orr:
Why does he have to have fresh water
when he goes to bed?
48
Jents:
It is said
that
for his supply of water he used his own saliva; so he didn't go without
    water.
If he doesn't have a supply of fresh water,
it is said that his bodily fluids might be removed from him. And this too
has a story,
this removal of bodily fluids. Fresh water has its story, too.
So he used his saliva to represents his
supply of fresh water,
because he thought his bodily fluids might be removed otherwise.
So that's the rule for this.
49
I just
told you that one.
Even though I want to tell the story, I don't want to elaborate anymore
on this story about fresh water.

Notes to the Stories

Iingilnguq Tunutellgek-llu — The Blind Boy And The Two Arctic Loons
Pages 6-25

1. A short version from the Eastern Canadian Arctic is given below for purposes of comparison (from Nungak and Arima 1969: 49-51):

LUMAAQ

Story by Aisa Qupiqrualuk

These people—a woman with a son who is blind and also a daughter—these are being come upon by a bear. When the bear peels through where the window used to be [the heavy ice pane having melted and fallen in], the mother of the blind boy is telling him to shoot it with a bow and arrow. Though blind, he is strong enough; so he shoots. And his mother is lying already, saying, since they had a dog called Uuka, "You shot Uuka." She lies, but the blind boy hears the animal hit by his shooting and says, "It sounds as if I shot some beast." His mother still replies, "No, no. You shot Uuka." Since the bear dies afar off, his mother and sister will leave him behind because they want the food all to themselves. When it is almost spring, they leave the blind boy behind in the old snowhouse. His sister will save him by stealing.

Thus the boy is left in the old abandoned snowhouse. Having shot the bear, he is being forsaken by his mother because he is blind. But he is fed by his sister. Loving her blind brother, she used to bring him some of her food inside her parka. She was feeding her brother with stolen food without getting found out by her mother. He was now in an old snowhouse without a roof [the spring warmth having melted and collapsed the dome]. "My brother, good dog meat, " she always said. Wanting to regain his sight, he will have his eyes opened since he wanted them opened.

Blind, abandoned by his mother and left behind in the old snowhouse, he is continually seeking to be given sight. So, since he is in an old snowhouse without a roof, he calls to the loon, and the loon comes. The loon wants to lead him to the water, and the boy is led there. When they arrive, the loon says, "Dive down. When you are dying, suffocating and dying, I will bring you up to the surface." And so he dives underwater. When he moves because he is choking because of lack of breath, he is brought up. Then the loon says, "What do you see?" The boy says, "I see light." The loons speaks again, "But indeed! Move only when you are suffocating and dying," and he makes him dive for a second time. The boy moves again because he is choking, and when he is brought up, the loon asks again, "What do you see?" The boy answers, "I see land, but not very clearly." The loon says again, "But indeed! Move only when you are dying of suffocation," and he makes him dive a third time. Because he is dying of suffocation, the boy moves once more, and when he is brought up, the loon asks again, "What do you see?" The boy says, "Far away there on the side of that hill I see a lemming going into his hole." Thus the boy is made to see by the loon and is now back to normal.

Then, since he had regained his sight, he was providing for his mother and sister with game, with tomcods and sculpins. As he was doing so, there were some white whales in close beside the land, and he wanted to harpoon them. To brace against the line, he says to his mother, "When I harpoon, we will brace against the line together. You will be behind me, so tie the line around your waist when I harpoon." And then when he harpoons, just as he is about to pull back against the line, he lets go of it without pulling at all. Hence his mother, because she is tied around the middle, starts running towards the water and plunges under. As she goes under, she says, *"Lumaa, lumaa, lumaa, lumaa,"* and also, "If only I could squeeze the water out of my skin on top of that hill, *lumaa.*" These sounds were repeated over and over again as she surfaced with the white whales. Here are the words the boy spoke when his mother plunged underwater: "My mother's hood has become a fish's tail, *iya, iyaa.*" So he said as his mother dove down.

Note: Hawkes gives a version, perhaps from Atlantic Labrador, in which the cry '*lumaa*' is explained as the last part of *irngnialuma*, translated as "My son did it" (1916: 158).

In a Labrador variant of this story (Rink 1875), the grandmother is the boy's antagonist. She meets her demise in much the same way, except instead of white whales (belukhas), it is a herd of narwhals which passes by, and it is a narwhal which the grandmother becomes.

Nelson Graburn, professor of anthropology at Berkeley, who speaks Inuktitut, says that in the version with which he is familiar, the refrain is '*lumaa.*' He says that it is one of the rare words in Inuktitut which begins with the [l] sound, a clear indication that it comes from a name or an irregular formation. *Levaa* (the refrain from Andy Charlie's Yup'ik version) and *lumaa* are of course phonemically very close and may derive from the same proto word: [v] and [m] are both labials and since there is no schwa [e] in Inuktitut, the [e] in the vicinity of an [m] or a [v] would be a [u]. Franz Boas records another version of the same story from the Central Eskimo; the refrain in this version is *"Louk! Louk!"* Again, the presence of the [l] and [u] segments (a labial like [v]) suggests a common linguistic origin (Boas 1888: 218).

Pat Afcan, originally from the Yukon, is familiar with at least two versions of this story among the *Kuigpagmiut* 'Yukon dwellers.' The grandmother is the food provider who denies sustenance to her grandson. In one version, the boy is blind from birth; in another she makes him blind by rubbing ashes in his eyes.

2. Actually, he says literally *umyugaa navgualuku pisqevkenaku* 'don't break his mind,' which we translate variously as 'to destroy or shatter one's peace of mind' or 'perturb.' Thoughts, according to the traditional way of thinking, are powerful; bad thoughts can have far-reaching consequences, breaking another's mind and resulting in illness, a mishap or lack of success in hunting. In the Yup'ik way of thinking, the barrier between mind and matter is more fluid than in traditional Western metaphysics. Ann Fienup-Riordan, working extensively with Yup'ik elders, sums up the traditional Yup'ik attitude with the metaphor of boundaries and passages: bad thoughts, disrespectful attitudes and behavior, rule-breaking and disregard for the proscriptions of the elders have the effect of clearing a pathway for illness and misfortune while obstructing the pathway of the game to the hunter (Fienup-Riordan 1994). Conversely, good thoughts, respect for elders, and adherence to the rules of culturally sanctioned behavior will ward off sickness and misfortune and clear a way for the animals. The good will and good thoughts of others, especially elders, is essential for success in the hunt. Elders repeatedly admonish students to obey their teachers and parents, to avoid conflict, and to deflect and neutralize anger with good thoughts and non-resistance.

3. In our version the loon is a *tunutellek* 'arctic loon' (*Gavia arctica*); among the *Kuigpagmiut*, according to Pat Afcan, it is a *tuullek* 'common loon' (*Gavia immer*). In Krauss's Eyak version, this species of loon cannot be pinpointed from the Eyak word (*Yehs*), but Krauss believes it most probably is a common loon (*Gavia immer*). In the Eastern Inuit version we have obtained (see notes), the loon is a *tuulliq*, which is most likely a common loon (*Gavia immer*).

4. The rule or prohibition he refers to is the most fundamental requirement of human society, the requirement that parents and grandparents love, protect and nurture their offspring and keep them from harm. In Yup'ik society the giving of food is the most visible expression of parental solicitude. Whereas men go out into the wilderness to hunt and bring back game to the village, women generally do the cutting, butchering, storing, preparing and cooking. Children receive food from their mothers and grandmothers and are expected to ask for food when they are hungry and never to take food without permission. Mothers and grandmothers are then expected to provide cooked or prepared food. In giving ashes, which are a type of anti-food, the useless end-product of cooking, she is guilty of the worst form of parental neglect, a refusal to provide her offspring with real food.

5. In Yup'ik the expression used is '*iigminek qakemkugnek.*' *Qakem-* is a demonstrative pronoun referring to something 'outside' obscured from the field of his vision. The Yup'ik phraseology is precise and apt. The ashes cover his vision and blind him, making everything 'outside' his field of vision and external to him.

6. *Quaq* and *qaqauraurlutek* 'making *quaq-quaq* noises' are onomatopoeic words that represent the sound of loons. English words representing waterfowl noises, like 'quacking,' 'honking' and 'cackling,' hardly approximate the sound an Arctic loon makes, which ranges from a haunting, other-worldly wail to a mundane *quaq-quaq*.

7. In Yup'ik stories, a small amount of food offered to a spirit or other-worldly being becomes a larger amount when it is received. Thus, a pinch of dried fish

becomes a bundle of dried fish. Furthermore, such offerings are always recognized and sufficiently recompensed, as this story illustrates.

8. When asked to comment on the meaning of this saying, Theresa Hooper and Rose Charlie explained that it was related to the ability of animals in stories to assume human characteristics, like the power of speech. The beneficiary of the animal's supernatural assistance is directed to cast a look backward on parting, thus ascertaining that his supernatural helper was indeed an animal.

Consider also the following, commentary by Pauline Akaran of Kotlik in *Agayuliyararput* "Our Way of Making Prayer":

> They say the stories they tell are accounts of what our ancestors experienced long ago. I, too, heard stories in those days, and if any person came into the house while the narration was about to end, when the story ended and the late arrival was leaving, they would tell him, "When you go outside, look back a few steps away from the house if you are curious to see whether or not I am a person." When they left and finally looked back, they would see that had been in an animal's den (Meade 1996: 39).

9. One should be considerate of the feelings of another. In traditional Yup'ik society, respect for others, for animals and for the spirit world, is a cardinal virtue.

10. We asked Andy Charlie about the meaning of *levaa* or *levaaq* in this context. He said that it referred to an *inqun*, pet name or special cooing term for a child which she gave to her grandson, and had no particular meaning. We cannot determine the base in question, whether it is *levaa* or *levaaq*. In modern Yup'ik *levaaq* means 'outboard motor.' It is true that the grandson in his kayak propels her through the water, but we are unable to establish any deep or distant connection between *levaaq* 'outboard motor' and *levaa* (or *levaaq*), the nickname she gives to her grandson. See footnote 1 for a further explanation and a possible Inuit correspondence.

11. See footnotes 1 and 10.

12. Literally 'because the making of mistakes is a part of us.' He means that making mistakes is part of life, i.e., 'To err is human.'

13. Literally 'live trying to show yourself,' but we believe he means by this that one should live in such as way as to reveal one's 'true' self as opposed to the superficial self which is subject to distorting passions.

14. The implication is that they are going the wrong way in life, not just living a variant lifestyle.

15. Literally 'However, as they try to tell us nowadays, try to live without changing back and forth.'

Qavcik — Wolverine
Pages 32-61

a. Ciumek: Tamaani tamaa-i kanaranek qantullrulriit kanarat, yuk taun' tuquaqan, kanarat-gguq naacirturluki erenret talliman...

b. Una *line*-aq ciuqlia-llu *line*-aq aug̃'allruuk qanemcista alarcan. Elliluku-llu qanemcistem elliciqngalkiinun. Piqapiarallra manimauq kana-i:

Taitesqurallni cakaniqeryugnaunaku, tua-i-gg'
qungvagyugyaaqelria cakneq taumek nuliallminek cakneq,
taq'ercugnaunaku-am tungcirturalliniluku.

Tua-i taum pivakarluni angutem taum qamuutallrem
aqumlelliniuq. "Aa-rra..." Aa-a, tuani ima tam tuani angun qanlalria, "Ampi
    tua-i ayagceskuk, tumkarpuk amna atuyunairceciiqan!"
Tamaa-i tumkamegnek
qungvagyugluni taun'
qamuutalria
piyaaqluni. Taum tua-i ayagcessngaunakek tauna nuliani
    taiteqarraarumavkenaku.

"Aa-rra-rra rraa!" tauna imna
qamuutalleq pilliniuq, "Aa-rra-rra-rraa! Aling, arenqiapaa-ll' ..."

    c. Ciumek qanellruuq 'ikamratek' taũgaam cimillruaput.
    d. Ciumek qanellruuq 'caucatni' taũgaam cimillruaput.
    e. Ciumek qanellruuq 'kingunerluni' taũgaam cimillruaput.

1. *Puyangun*'s prefatory remark is in response to a discussion of the essential difference between *qulirat* and *qanemcit*. Her story begins with a very typical story frame and would seem to be a clear example of that type of proto-fictional genre, a type of *märchen*, which other elders have identified as a *quliraq*.

2. In times past, something, either bladders or skins, of the first kill, whether edible or not (mice, muskrats, and other small mammals), was preserved and then brought to the *qasgiq* to be commemorated during the *Nakaciuryaraq* 'Bladder Festival' (Fienup-Riordan 1994: 269; Curtis 1930: 61) or in a first catch ceremony (Oswalt 1990: 32). Even today, people enjoy having feasts for any first *pitaq* 'catch' such as a boy's first ptarmigan or duck, or a girl's picking her first berry. Although not obligatory, it is considered an occasion to demonstrate affection for a child. Thus, the parents in this story must have indeed loved their child very much.

These first-catch ceremonies must be distinguished from an *uqiquq*, in which the first spring catch of a *tungunquq* 'bearded seal' by any hunter is distributed among the women of the village who are not consanguineous kin of the hunter.

3. The following is a brief summary of traditional *Qaluyaarmiut* funerary practices, taken from *Boundaries and Passages*. At death the corpse was prepared as if for a long journey. It was dressed, placed in a sitting position, and provisioned with food and clothing for its journey to the land of the dead, a lamp being placed beside the corpse to light its way. The body was removed from the family dwelling through the sky window or through a hole opened in the wall specifically for that purpose; in any case, it never exited the dwelling through the passageway normally used by the living. This happened preferably on the same day as the death occurred. Then the body was carried around the sky window from east to west, being placed on each of the corners and in the center, and on the way to the gravesite,

which was usually contiguous to the village. The mourners stopped with the body five times, commemorating the ritual numbers of four and five and the ritual steps of the shade's journey to the land of the dead, four for a woman and five for a man. At the gravesite the body was placed in a shallow, circular grave, or on the ground, and covered with rocks or drift logs to prevent scavenging; however, by the late nineteenth century this method was replaced by the use of grave boxes, which were often set on raised posts above the ground. All those articles and possessions which were essentially associated with the deceased—pots, pans, ladles, kettles and buckets for a woman, hunting equipment, tools and weapons for a man—were attached to upright planks and poles set in the ground. These were visibly displayed, marking the grave and the person as well as serving as utensils for the shade in the land of the dead. Before leaving the gravesite, relatives burned morsels of food in a fire kept burning by the grave and sprinkled fresh water as further provisions for the journey, then they circled the grave, again from east to west, and returned to their homes, often by a different route to confuse the shade. On the way they cut across their path with a knife, or sprinkled ashes, thus preventing the return of the shade.

The entire village was restricted from certain activities from the moment of the announcement of death until the corpse was put in the grave. Fires were extinguished, buckets were emptied to prevent ritual pollution, no food was cooked, nor could tools, weapons or sharp objects be used, since it was believed that these might injure the shades of the dead or sever the trail that the deceased was following to the land of the dead. These same restrictions applied to the close relatives of the deceased for a full five days. At the end of the five day mourning period, the immediate relatives appeared belted about the waists and marked with ashes, further precautions to insure social invisibility and to prevent their being noticed by *Ellam Iinga* 'the eye of awareness, of the universe, of the weather.' Certain restrictions might apply for up to an entire year. For twenty days members of the family might abstain from sexual activity and the eating of fresh food, and for a year they went about belted and hooded, unable to hang out clothes, to wash, to cut hair or to change clothing. The summer following the death of the spouse, a woman could not pick berries and a man was restricted in his hunting and fishing activities (Fienup-Riordan 1994: 213-240).

4. It is said that the spirits of the dead linger for a year. Close relatives observe mourning for a year and then a memorial feast is given in honor of the deceased. At the end of the year, the spirit of the deceased completely withdraws. We do not know why the man, who we presume to be the wolf who was curled up at her gravesite, is so apprehensive about losing the trail. We believe they are journeying to the abode of the dead and are under some kind of ritual restraint.

5. This and the preceding line were moved because the narrator made a performance error. We rearranged it the way we believe the narrator intended it. For purposes of accuracy, the original is given below:

> He continued to insist on her return even though he was appalled
>> by that dead wife of his;
> he didn't stop, but kept telling him to give her back.
> After this went on for a while, the man who was pulling the sled

suddenly sat down. "*Aa-rra...*" Oh yes, that man would say,

"Hurry up and let us go; you're going to let our trail become unusable!"
He was worried
about their trail,
that one who was pulling the sled
would say. But he would not let them leave without first getting
    his wife back.
"*Aa-rra-rra-rraa*" the one who was pulling
sighed in frustration, "*Aa-rra-rra-rraa! Aling,* you are..."

6. See footnote 11 in "*Anngaqelriik*: The Two Brothers" about wolverines.

7. Yup'ik storytellers typically insert disclaimers at the beginning and ending of their stories, downplaying their narrative competence, suggesting that someone else may remember more. Then too, if there are other elders present, this is the time when someone else may tell the narrator what has been left out.

Anngaqelriik — The Two Brothers
Pages 68-93

a. Cimillruaput qanenqigtellra 'ellmegnek' qanellni kituggngapakaagu.

b. Ciumek qanellruuq 'aqvataql...tua-i-gg' ayagaqamek pitaqlutek' taũgaam cimillruarput.

c. Ciumek qanellruuq 'Tua-ll'-am caqerluni' taũgaam uumek cimillruarput.

d. Ciumek qanellruuq 'Aiparmi, taum-llu-gguq kegginalgem, kegginalek man' navgurluku' taũgaam cimillruarput.

e. Alarrluni ayagnillra cimillruaput. Ciumek qanellruuq 'Tua-i-gguq qavciit makut maa-i...qavciurrluni tuani...'

1. Eliza Orr believes *uivvaarturluni* 'going round and round' is somewhat generic, not specifying whether she was coming down in tight, fast circles, that is, 'twirling,' or descending in slower, wider circles, that is, 'spiraling.' We asked Mike Angaiak to specify in detail the manner of her descent and he said that he was simply using the word *uivvaarturluni* as he heard it and could not specify further.

The descent and ascent of the sky woman is a common motif in Yup'ik stories. See "*Ciknalleq Nuliaq*: The Jealous Wife" in the present volume and "*Tutgara'urluq Siimarmek Kegginalek:* The Stone-faced Girl" (Meade 1996: 163-165).

2. *Keniq* is the lap or apron part of clothing. For example, in the *Nakaciuryaraq* 'Bladder Festival,' in one of the concluding dances, the women do *ingulaq*, a slow, swaying dance holding the skirts of their *qasperet* 'outer parka cover' as though they could enfold something inside. This is referred to as *kenirmigluku* 'cupping the skirt of the dress.' In the descent of the sky woman, she is holding the skirt of her *qaspeq* in just this way, grasping the hem and creating a pouch in the fold in which something might be carried.

Significantly, Raven in the *Qaluyaaq* 'Nelson Island' creation story directs his daughter, who seems to have a human form, to go outside their dwelling and to place fine soil in the fold of her *qaspeq* and to fling it in the direction of *Qaluyaaq*. This soil then became the land mass of *Qaluyaaq* . In the *Nunivaaq* creation story the woman who descends from the sky with soil in her cupped skirt creates the first land from this soil.

3. They are weathered in and unable to return to their home. In the *Nunivaaq* version of the story, the two brothers are at sea, in a kayak, on ice floes. In the coastal regions of Alaska, this could also be understood as meaning that their return is along a water route, either by sea or by river, and until the wind abates, the water is too rough for travel. The land she creates from the pouch of her *qaspeq* will be the means by which they can return.

4. His proposal and her acceptance seem very non-committal. This, however, is standard for a marriage proposal in the traditional stories. In Yup'ik culture, requests and replies are quite often put very indirectly, perhaps to save face in the event of refusal.

5. The woven grass mats were curtains which partitioned a room and were also used to cover the earthen and split log walls. Presumably, she is digging in the earth at the perimeter of the house, at the base of the wall.

6. The word for this in the original Yup'ik is *kegginalek*, which literally means 'one with a face,' but is a common word in *Tununeq* for *uluaq* 'a semi-circular woman's knife.'

7. Wolverines are solitary predators with a reputation for ferocity, tenacity and guile. They were a common totemic animal, since it was believed that by possessing a part or a likeness of a wolverine some of the qualities of the animal, such as exceptional skill in hunting, would be communicated to the possessor. Nelson describes the wolverine thus:

> The Wolverine is one of the most detested animals found in all the fur country. Its life is a continual warfare against all living things, and every man's hand is against it. They invariably steal the bait from traps whenever they have the opportunity, and very rarely do they get caught. Should they find an animal in the trap they make short work of it, and in Northern Alaska, as elsewhere in the fur country, they sometimes take up a line of traps so persistently that the hunter is forced to abandon it and look for a new route. They frequently follow a sledge party in the interior for days, visiting every camp as soon as it is abandoned, in order to pick up the scraps left, and anything left in a tree for safe-keeping is sure to be destroyed if the Wolverine can get at it (Fitzhugh and Kaplan 1982:106).

Traditionally wolverine pelts were highly prized, not only for their beauty but also for their talismanic virtue. For example, old men on Nunivak told Margaret Lantis that one wolverine skin would fetch 20 caribou skins in trade with inland people (Lantis 1946: 170). Nowadays wolverine pelts, which are rare and extremely expensive, are used in ruffs. Wolverine ruffs have the unique quality of not frosting or collecting moisture, making them ideal protection against facial frostbite. Yup'ik women sew a strip of wolverine between wolf and usually beaver to make their ruffs, folding back the fluffy wolf part of the ruff, so the long white-gray of the wolf is showing out and the wolverine part of the ruff is against the face, thus combining elegance with utility.

8. He is indicating his storytelling partner Jents Flynn sitting beside him.

Negairpak — Big Spider
Pages 98-127

a. Aurrnguarluni pillruuq.

b. Alarrluni ayagnillra cimillruaput. Ciumek qanellruuq: Tua-i-llu-gguq / ayagaqluni-gguq.

c. Alarrluni ayagnillra cimillruaput. Ciumek qanellruuq: ceñami.

d. Unatni arulalluki pekcessngualqaa neqa.

e. Iqelquugni quletmun mayurrngualqaak imarpik kevegluku.

f. Ciumek qanellruuq 'nayurtii taum, taukuk' taũgaam cimillruarput.

g. It'gani kitngigaa.

h. Unatminun elliluki.

1. The narrator mimics crawling.

2. Here she uses English 'reindeer,' but the original in Yup'ik was probably *tuntuq*, which designated caribou.

3. Since she isn't sure whether the audience, composed of children, will understand the Yup'ik word, she repeats it in English. She does this quite often.

4. Although a woman was an integral part of the hunting partnership with her husband and could, by following the prescribed rules, favorably influence his fortune and prowess in the hunting, unmarried men were advised that intimate contact with women could impair their effectiveness as hunters. Unmarried men were advised to never look a woman squarely in the face, to always pass a female upwind to avoid possible contamination from her 'bad' air, and, when they were sitting or lying down, to avoid being stepped over by a woman (Fienup-Riordan 1994:166-169). This may suggest that Spider's son is having a liaison with the woman and that his hunting virtue is ruined.

5. The Yup'ik word is *nacarrlugteqluni*, which consists of the base *nacar-* and the postbases *-rrlug-* (<*-rrlugte-*, 'to be afflicted in one's N or in respect to N, to have bad N') and *-teqe-*'to be affected in some sense with regard to one's N or one's V-ing' is an example of an idiom. Literally it might mean 'he's got his hood on improperly.' But it is not the hood that is afflicting him. The image here is of one sitting alone with his hood pulled down to hide his face, afflicted with gloomy thoughts on account of some private grief. Children, when they are *luqsangqaluteng* 'they are in a state of sulking' (<*luqsa-* (root: emontional) 'to sulk, withdraw in fit of pique' and *-ngqa-* 'to be in a state of V') will often pull their hoods or hats down to partially conceal the face, assume a withdrawn and introverted posture, and refuse to communicate. This is a message to others that they wish to be left alone. Typically, Yup'ik adults will ignore them or attempt to humor them.

6. She moved her hands up and down to simulate the movement of a flounder.

7. This is the normal position when there are two passengers traveling together in a kayak.

8. The figure of the shabbily attired hunter appears at strategic moments in Yup'ik texts to inform or rescue the protagonists. Although seemingly worthless, he may possess extraordinary abilities or hold the key to the protagonists' release. For example, in the *qulireq* of Mary Kokrak (Woodbury 1984), there are four

brothers and a sister living in isolation, and one day the youngest inexplicably disappears. They have no clue to his whereabouts and fate, and they resign themselves to hopelessness until one day a worthless looking man appears to tell them that their youngest brother is being held prisoner and tortured by villagers upriver. The shabby hunter is described thus (also see *"Qellugtellria Nukalpiaq*: The Deformed Hunter" in the second volume or Edward Curtis's "The Flounder Spirit" (1930: 80-82) for a similar description):

Without warning,
there came from that slough
an ugly, ugly kayak!

A kayak so miserable
that both ends were pointed upwards.
A very ugly old kayak!

And in it,
coming downstream in a friendly manner,
was a very ugly man.

At each stroke of his paddle,
his old kayak yawed;
that is how miserable it was! (Woodbury 1984: 74-75)

Ordinarily, the worth of a hunter is reflected in his attire, his equipment and deportment. If he appears shabby and loose-ended to the animals, if he is not squared away and alert, a respecter of traditional warnings and rules, with all his equipment in order, he will appear strangely distorted and askew to them, and they will not allow themselves to be captured, on the presumption that he is not worthy. But in the case of the shabby hunter in the narratives above, two constants hold: he appears *deus ex machina* to extract the protagonists from a hopeless situation, and his looks belie his worth.

9. The narrator mimes the man's actions. He licked the tips of his little fingers and then placed his hands in front of him with his little fingers extended. As he raises his hands up, he magically lifts the ocean by its edge. This is also a stylized gesture to influence the weather. For instance, in the story *"Ellam Irniara*: The Child of Ella" recorded in *Agayuliyararput 'Our Way of Making Prayer,'* Mary Mike, the narrator, comes upon a strange transparent egg on the tundra. It is the child of *Ella*, the Spirit of the Weather, having dropped out of the sky, and to prevent the Spirit of the Weather from weeping, that is, raining, her grandmother wets the tips of her little fingers and "lifts" the weather to prevent if from getting bad (Meade and Fienup-Riordan 1996: 179).

10. The narrator pretends to kick the rock.

11. She pretends to put the little balls of dirt on the palm of her hand.

12. According to another *Qaluyaarmiut* account, the mosquitoes were created by Raven when he became drowsy and wanted to wake himself up (see *"Ciuliaqatuk:* The Ancestor" in the present volume).

Uqurilria Neviarcaq — The Obese Girl
Pages 132-177
    a. Naninaku qaneryaraa 'tanem'.
    b. Nuyangqerrluteng cungua-llu ilakluku.
    c. Ciutait cingikeggluteng.

    1. The sinew of larger mammals is removed from the legs, along the backbone and elsewhere and then the strands are separated and dried. After they are dried, the separate strands are twisted back together to form thread. It is extremely tough and durable. Nowadays dental floss is used instead.
    2. The narrator added this after having told the story.
    3. On the open tundra there is no shelter from the wind, which on *Qaluyaaq* 'Nelson Island' and along the Bering Straits can reach gale or hurricane force. During the winter, overland travelers must keep a cautious eye on the weather. People are advised to carry a shovel and tarpaulin, with which they can construct a snow shelter, either by digging a small snow cave into a drift or by digging down into the packed snow and erecting a tarpaulin tent roof with the shovel as a pole. Nevertheless, wind chill factors can plunge in gale force winds to well below minus 80 degrees. At these temperatures, exposed flesh freezes almost instantly and even with appropriate winter clothing, a person in the open has a greatly diminished chance of survival after a few hours. Even in a snow cave or shelter, hypothermia and death can occur after a day or two.
    People are admonished never to construct their snow cave or shelter on the lee side of a drift, since in a full blown arctic blizzard tons of snow can build up into a new drift in a relatively short while, burying and suffocating the occupants. Moreover, people are advised to set up a marker or pole where they construct a snow shelter so searchers will be able to locate their remains.
    The *Yupiit*, who have never built igloos, lack the sophisticated snowhouse technology that is found among the *Inuit* of the Central and Eastern Arctic. Therefore, the best protection against storms and exposure is caution; people are admonished to be perpetually vigilant and at the first sign of an approaching storm to head for a safe haven. Experienced hunters and travelers have a profound respect for the weather and take few unnecessary chances.
    4. An example of onomatopoeia, not unlike the English 'crunch,' only more voiceless and more like the natural sound. On *Qaluyaaq* and much of the Bering coast the wind packs the snow, making overland travel in the winter easier. It is not usually necessary to follow trails, and travelers, whether on foot, with dogs and sled, or on snowmachine, may move freely over much of the surface of the land. Further inland, especially in the boreal forest of the interior where there is little wind, the dry, fluffy snow piles up several feet deep, and travelers are compelled to use snowshoes or to stick to broken and packed trails, since dogs or snowmachines become bogged down and stuck in the deep snow.
    5. *Tan'gerpiit* 'crowberries' (*Empetrum nigrum*) are harvested in the fall. When the snow finally comes, the berries from the previous year are frozen and preserved underneath the blanket of snow until next spring, when they are still edible.

6. The Yup'ik here is *akikeqatarniluku* 'they said they would have her for payment, reciprocation, etc' (<*aki-* 'other side, payment, exchange, etc.' + *-ke-* 'to have as one's N'). The concept of sacrifice as it was known, for instance, in Biblical or Greco-Roman societies — that is, the giving of the blood, flesh or life of an animal or person to a deity or supernatural entity as a form of offering or payment — was unknown among the *Yupiit* and indeed most Eskimo peoples. However, the Siberian Yupik did on rare occasion sacrifice dogs in accord with the practice of other northeastern Siberian peoples (Serov in Fitzhugh and Crowell 1988: 252), and the *Alutiiq*, or Koniag Eskimos, killed slaves as a mark of grief as the funeral of eminent people (Lantis 1947: 9).

The *Yupiit* in their rites and ceremonies do make various kinds of offerings or exchanges. For instance, in *Elriq* 'Memorial Feast for the Dead,' small symbolic offerings and libations of drink and food are given to the shades of the dead (Nelson 1899: 363-379). We know also that food might be presented as a raised offering (*nalug-* 'to hoist, to raise'), perhaps to spirits, or cardinal directions, or perhaps to *Ellam Yua* 'the owner of the weather or universe' in *Nakaciuryaraq* 'the Bladder Festival' (Orr and Orr 1995: 162-163). The smoke of plants might be presented as an incense offering to the animal souls which inhabited the seal bladders (Nelson 1899: 379-393). Animal guardians or spirits might be presented with offering of food (*aviukarte-* 'to make a food offering') left at their dens or territories (Orr and Orr 1995: 100-101). Or small symbolic offerings of food, for instance dried fish, may be left behind as a gesture of gratitude for mice when their underground caches of roots (*utngungssaq** 'tuber of mare's-tail plant' (*Hippurus vulgaris*), *iitaq* 'tall cottongrass' (*Eriohorum angustifolium*), *negaasek* 'type of edible roots') are taken by women in the fall (*elingra-* (root:emotional) 'gratitude, grateful'). But the idea of blood as a spiritually potent substance, the quintessence of life which is sacrificed to a deity or numen ("for the blood is the life thereof" (Leviticus 17: 14)), thereby restoring spiritual life and placating the invisible powers, is not present among the *Yupiit*. An individual may jeopardize his relationship with animals or the invisible powers by the breaking of rules or taboos, but ordinarily confession is sufficient in times of stress, and there is no requirement or even notion of the sacrifice as recompense. Indeed, to our knowledge, there is no word for sacrifice in the Yup'ik language. The concept of sacrifice, as it is translated in the Yup'ik Moravian Bible, is found twice in one verse in Hebrews 7: 27, first as *erenret tamaitni ekuagalriacetun* 'daily need to offer sacrifice,' where the base is *ekua-* 'to burn' (i.e. *ekuagarkaq* 'something to be burned, animal for sacrifice', which undoubtedly came from missionary interpretations of the Bible and not from actual Yup'ik practices), and afterwards as *ellminek cikiutlermini* 'when he offered himself as a sacrifice' (<*cikiun* 'gift').

7. Perhaps they call her this because the sound of the name is very guttural and raspy, simulating the sound of her voice.

8. She is in the *elaturraq* 'the outer porch or entry way'; the other villagers are in their homes and perhaps some may be in the *qasgiq*.

Ciknalleq Nuliaq — The Jealous Wife
Pages 182-209

a. Qantam imaanek tegusnguarluni elliqeringuallruuk.

b. Ciumek qanellruuq 'anqataamek' taũgaam uumek cimillruarput 'anngami.'

1. He took a pinch of food from his bowl and made an offering, placing it on the ground.

2. On *Qaluyaaq* the snow starts to melt at the end of April and early May.

3. *Yupiit* invariably express revulsion at the thought of having to marry one's relatives. The Yup'ik kinship system is similar to the Iroquois system; thus the Yupiit place more restrictions on who one may marry than Euro-Americans customarily do. Young people often complain that they cannot marry anyone in their village because they are all related. Cousins who from the Euro-American point of view are distant and many times removed may be considered relatives and thus ineligible as marriage partners. Relative and first cousin marriages among the Yupiit were not permitted, unlike the Netsilik of Central Canada, who according to Balikci had a preference for marrying relatives (Balikci 1970: 94-95).

Ciuliaqatuk — The Ancestor
Pages 216-257

1. He is probably referring to one of the translators, who is a Caucasian. Both translators for several weeks prior to this storytelling session had been after some of the elders to tell some traditional Raven stories. Many elders, like Jents, expressed a reluctance to tell Raven stories. It is important to note that these stories were told in the Tununak Catholic Church. The Jesuit priest, who enthusiastically supported our efforts, was present.

2. Literally 'the one who left me behind.' The Yup'ik term is *uniste-* 'the one who leaves behind,' referring to a deceased parent. Certain terms designating close kinship have poetic and figurative connotations; a child can be referred to as *avaqutaqa*, a word closely related to *avayaqa* 'my branch,' or as *yuk'a* 'my person, my possession.'

3. *Aayaarrluk* designates an area on the tundra contiguous to ponds where the thickly matted heather, roots and soil of the tundra, has pockets of water underneath. Walking on *aayaarrluk* is like walking on a waterbed or a trampoline; it ripples and waves underneath. So the land in the first stages of creation was like freshly formed sea ice, solid enough to walk on but not yet rigid or brittle.

4. *Engelullugaq* is a fishcamp four to five miles beyond *Tununeq*, going northeast along the coast. It was occasionally used by people from *Niugtaq* 'Newtok' as a subsistence camp during the herring run. Other than that, it is deserted. There is a large boulder along the shore with curious indentations or markings on the topside resembling raven footprints. People say these come from Raven's daughter telling story-knife stories while he was away; she was lonely thinking about him so she drew his footprints.

5. According to Jack Angaiak he is chipping away at ice, perhaps attempting to make a spring.

6. This means 'the wife and her husband' or 'married couple.'

7. This means literally 'ice that was chipped away.' *Cikuliurun* is a device for working on ice, for instance an ice pick.

8. A girl's first menstruation was a time of strict seclusion and social isolation. For five days she had to remain outside in a small hut or in a separate section of the sod house behind a woven grass partition. She was required to use a separate entrance from the rest of the household, could not work on raw skins or eat raw or fresh foods. In addition, she wore old clothes, went about with her head bowed and her gaze averted from others, and wore thumbless mittens (reminiscent of the thumbless hands on ceremonial masks, suggesting an impaired grasp and escapement of game). At the end of her ritual seclusion, she was considered a woman, although further restrictions applied for as long as a year. Any contact with a menstruating woman, even to the point of being exposed to her air downwind, was considered polluting; it was offensive to the animals and could cause a man to lose his virtue in hunting (Fienup-Riordan 1994: 160-163).

9. He is referring to the rite of first menstrual seclusion.

10. They would drive a stick into the earth, testing for red ochre beneath the surface. Forcing the stick deep below the surface, they would draw it out and if the tip were red, they would know there was red ochre underneath and would therefore dig all around the testing hole.

11. He means he will excerpt a fragment from another Raven story.

12. Perhaps to prevent the escape of the woman.

13. This is perhaps to indicate that when he went down he was still a man wearing white-soled boots.

14. This means literally 'the one with former story-knife pictures.' See Note 4.

15. See Note 7.

16. 'Imitation boat' or 'toy boat,' a place name in the area he is referring to.

17. Herring fish, which migrate to *Qalayaaq* in late May and early June and which are then harvested in large quantities and dried, are the staple food of the *Qaluyaarmiut*.

18. Oil is rendered by cutting the blubber of a seal into strips. Ordinarily, the oil is rendered by allowing the blubber to sit at room temperature for one to two weeks, thus providing seal oil which has a rich and slightly aged taste and aroma. The rendered part of blubber is called *tangviarrluk* and is enjoyed without cooking as an accompaniment to dried fish or meat, and can be boiled and enjoyed as is. However, when oil is needed quickly, the blubber can be fried. In the latter case, the oil is bland and heavy, and to certain palettes, less desirable.

19. The translators had been asking certain elders to tell Raven stories for some time. A common excuse for not doing so was that no one felt entirely in command of the material; that is, the people we asked claimed that they only knew parts of the Raven narratives. We suggested that they tell the stories in a group, pooling their memories and recollections. After considerable prodding, they agreed, and this narrative is the outcome.

20. The story he is referring to is "*Tulukaruk Iqlungarli*: The Lying Raven," narrated by Theresa Hooper of *Tununeq* and published in the first volume of

Qanemcikarluni Tekitnarqelartuq. It is a humorous account of Raven's stroll along the beach and his encounters with various animals, whom he tries to trick but who in the end actually get the better of him. According to Rita Blumenstein, originally from Tununak, Raven's adventures along the beach form an open-ended narrative which can be supplemented with numerous episodes and can take up to four days to tell.

21. He uses the Yup'ik word *quliraq* which we sometimes translate as 'traditional story.'

Tulukaruller — The Mischievous Raven
Pages 258-271

a. Ciumek qanellruuq 'cikinrilkumken' tau͡gaam uumek cimillruarput 'cikinrilkuvnga.'

b. Ellminek alartellni kitugcaku, una *line*-aq nugtartellruaput.

1. Along the Bering Sea coast, this is the most probable place to find food.

2. *Akutaq*, commonly called 'Eskimo ice cream' is a mixture of fat, *naunrat* 'salmonberries' (actually, cloudberries (*Rubus chamaemorus*)), and *tan'gerpiit* 'crowberries' (*Empetrum nigrum*). Each family has a slightly different recipe and way of making *akutaq*. Here is *Ackiar*'s, Theresa Hooper's, recipe: Using a very large stainless steel mixing bowl, mix about two cups of Crisco, a half cup of evaporated milk and a cup of sugar. Roll up your sleeves, wash your hands, and then for about ten minutes whip it until the mixture is light and frothy. Then add about a quart of cloudberries and whip some more. Finally add a quart of crowberries and whip them in too. To top it all off, mix in a cup or two of *puyuruat* 'nagoonberries' (*Rubus arcticus*), an extremely delicious and flavorful kind of berry which is relatively difficult to find and which tastes like the finest distillation of black raspberries. Serve semi-frozen and follow up with hot tea. This makes enough *akutaq* for family and drop-in guests for a few days.

The orange cloudberries have an extremely tart and sour taste, a cross between raspberries and lemons. The crowberries are sweet, juicy and crunchy, like small grapes. They pop in one's mouth. The combination of tastes and textures — tart and sweet, sugary and fatty, smooth and crunchy — results in a remarkable culinary delight which is also rich in vitamin C, fats and carbohydrates.

3. This is the hoarse croak of a raven.

4. *Katngite-* is a finger gesture of insult or contempt. In the *Yup'ik Eskimo Dictionary* (Jacobson 1984) it is described thus: 'to hook one's curled index finger under someone's nose and push upward.' Among the *Qaluyaarmiut*, it is done with the middle finger; one places one's middle finger on the tip of the nose of the one whom he wishes to insult and pushes. It is a gesture of extreme contempt. Interestingly, among the *Sivuqaghmiit*, the Siberian Eskimo of St. Lawrence Island, there is a similar gesture: one licks one's index finger and quickly draws it underneath the nose of the one whom he wishes to offend.

5. He corrected himself, so we moved the order of this line.

Nakaciuryaraq Cali-llu Tan'gurraq Uitalleq Taqukani —
The Bladder Festival And The Boy Who Lived With The Seals
Pages 278-347

1. *Nunakauyarmiut* 'Toksook Bay elders' told Ann Fienup-Riordan that the seal was anointed with water on five points (the mouth, two front flippers and the two back flippers), which she notes also parallels the five drinks given to the boy who went to live with the seals (Fienup-Riordan 1994: 96). A paraphrase of *Nunakauyarmiu* elder Paul John's story of "The Boy Who Went to Live With the Seals" is given in *The Nelson Island Eskimo* (Fienup-Riordan 1983: 177-181).

The Yup'ik word *Nuqarrluk* uses for 'receive' is *ciuniur-* and can mean 'to receive as a guest, to greet, to welcome.' It is not necessarily used here in a poetic or special way, since one may also *ciuniur-* 'receive' inanimate objects, like a package. However, in the context above, *taqukat elluarrluki ciuniulallruit arnaita* 'their women received them and took care of them properly' can also be understood as 'their woman welcomed them as guests and took care of them properly.'

2. In *Cevv'arnaq* 'Chefornak' *maklak* is the word for bearded seal (*Erignathus barbatus*). This is the word found in most Central Yup'ik dialects to designate a bearded seal (<Proto-Eskimo *maklag* 'bearded seal'). However, on *Qaluyaaq* there is no such word other than in the form of a proper name (although the *Qaluyaarmiut* are familiar with this word to designate a bearded seal). Rather, a bearded seal is a *tungunquq* (<*tungu-* 'to be black' + *-quq* 'one that is V,' or 'black spot,' 'bearded seal'; < Proto-Eskimo *tungu-* 'be dark blue'). In fact, some of the *Qaluyaarmiut* words to designate certain animals differ from those of their neighbors. Perhaps this is the effect of a naming taboo, since the bearded seal, being of such cultural and economic importance, may merit name avoidance. But also there is the matter of the loss of the original Yup'ik word for the brown bear (*Ursus arctos*). In many regions the word *taqukaq* designates a brown bear (<Proto-Yupik *taqukaq* 'brown bear'). On *Qaluyaaq, taqukaq* is the generic name for seal; the word for brown bear is *ungungssiq* (<Proto-Yupik *ungungssiq* 'animal'), which can either refer to 'bear' in particular or 'animal' in general. There seems to have been a bear-naming taboo operating in Yup'ik culture, which meant that another word was appropriated to refer to bears. Quite possibly, this has set off a linguistic chain reaction, rearranging the relationship of designators to designees.

3. Originally, men took firebaths or saunas together in the *qasgiq*. With the demise of the *qasgiq* as a functioning institution in the village community, people began building small saunas, called *maqiviit* 'bathing places' and sometimes called *qasgit*, near their houses. Now these *maqiviit* are the domain of the extended or nuclear family, although friends and relatives frequently take sweatbaths together. The stove in the heat room of the *maqivik* is usually a converted 55-gallon drum covered with volcanic rocks to retain heat. Originally, when men took sweatbaths in the *qasgiq*, a fire was built in the firepit in the center of the floor. When only embers were left, they covered the sky window, thus creating intense heat in the *qasgiq*. *Nuqarrluk* is referring to the transition from communal sweatbaths in the community *qasgiq* to the present custom of taking sweatbaths in the family *maqivik*, a process that occurred in two generations' time.

4. Note that he uses the demonstrative pronoun and adverb *kankut kana-i* 'those ones down there' (< *kan-* 'the one down toward the river, or down below (restricted)'). At the time of narration, he was in *Negeqliq* 'St. Mary's' on the Yukon; *Calitmiut* is approximately 100 miles southwest. One might expect him to use either the extended or the obscured terms *unkumiut* or *camkumiut*. On the other hand, if he is using his place of origin as his psychological reference point in the narration, then *kankumiut* might be the expected paradigmatic selection, since along the flat coastal plain where the *Caninermiut* live, villages are visible from long distances. Yup'ik allows for this kind of topographical subtlety and fine-tuning. See Note 1 to "The Boy Who Made Peace."

5. *Ikiituk* 'wild celery' (*Angelica ludica*), which people gather in the early summer when it first matures; otherwise, it dries and grows bitter-tasting quickly. Picked at the right time, it has a sweet, crisp taste, not unlike domestic celery, only more pronounced and distinctive. People eat it uncooked with seal oil, or it can be mixed and boiled with *quagcit* 'sourdock' (*Rumex arcticus*) and, along with sugar and seal oil, made into a vegetable *akutaq*. By late summer, the wild celery is completely dried. The desiccated stalks were used for ritual purposes, principally, for smoking, purification and incensing. Hunters fumigated their bodies with the smoke of wild celery before going hunting since it was thought that the sea animals were attracted to the smell of the land (Meade 1996: 91). Fienup-Riordan suggests (from Oswalt) that the wild celery may be associated with the ancestral spirits in the Yup'ik mythico-religious system (Meade 1996: 280).

6. In Yup'ik dancing the men usually kneel or sit in the foreground and the women stand in semi-circular formation behind them. While the women dance, their feet are stationary and all movement is from the knees upward. They sway their upper bodies, moving the arms and head in gracefully stylized motions, often pantomiming the story of the song, all the while bending the knees slightly to the rhythm of the drums. All dancers, women and men, move in unison. Men, particularly younger men, tend to enact the motions of the dance with great vigor and agility, whereas the women are inclined to move with fluidity and grace. Dances begin in slower motion; with each repetition the tempo builds until the dancers are required to move in a kind of near frenzy, with great exertion and considerable haste in order to keep up with the beat of the drums. Drums are the only musical instruments used, and only men are drummers. Generally, only the men sing.

7. This is the *kangaciqaq*, a ceremonial staff which has bundles of wild celery and Labrador tea lashed onto the end. During the *Nakaciuryaraq* the *kangaciqaq* is set upright in the *qasgiq*. It is treated as a sentient being and offerings of food are presented to it during the ceremony (Fienup-Riordan 1994: 287-288).

8. This is the climax of the ceremony. With the bladders being released into the sea, they had returned the animal souls once again to the sea. If they had been properly and respectfully treated, the same souls might be encountered again in the hunt. Fienup-Riordan makes the point that the Yupiit view the universe of souls of humankind and sea mammals (and perhaps all creatures) as finite; consequently, to assure continuation of the species, re-cycling is necessary. In ceremonies such as *Nakaciuryaraq* and the tradition of naming children after the deceased, people

play an important and necessary role in the renewal of life (Fienup-Riordan 1983: 189-235).

9. He means this in the sense that Yup'ik society is rapidly changing, traditions, knowledge and language are being lost, and the elders, as tradition bearers, are not doing what needs to be done to preserve these. Formal schooling for many *Yupiit* began in the 1930s and thereafter. For many of the older people alive in rural Alaska today, the dominant institution involved in rural education was the Bureau of Indian Affairs. Although there were individual exceptions, the policy of the Bureau of Indian Affairs until the late 1960s was cultural and linguistic assimilation. Native parents were encouraged to delegate the education of their children to the teachers and bureaucrats, who for the most part were non-Native and in many cases believed that their mission was to "Americanize" Eskimo, Indian and Aleut children. Parents were often discouraged from speaking their native language to their children and in many subtle ways were led to accept the idea that Native American cultures and languages were doomed to extinction.

The late 1960s brought a gradual revision in pedagogical and social policy concerning Native Americans. Bilingual education and the policy of encouraging the use and maintenance of Native American languages and traditions became the official policy of the Bureau of Indian Affairs and the State of Alaska schools which served Alaska Natives. This policy of tolerance also ushered in a period of rapid demographic and social change. Cultural and social barriers that had previously maintained distinctiveness in Alaska Native communities were removed. Intermarriage, integration, new economic opportunities, upward social mobility, television, travel, the ever increasing immigration of non-Natives to rural Alaska, all accelerated assimilation and the replacement of Alaska Native languages by English. This period when native languages were officially accepted for the first time was the very period when most Alaska Native languages accelerated their march to extinction, as though there were a sort of dread inevitability to language loss, in spite of all the best intentions. By the 1980s, only Central Yup'ik and Siberian Yupik were viable in the sense that significant numbers of the young spoke them as a first language, and even these two languages are hardly secure.

10. 'Cross-cousin.' The person asking the question in the audience is a cross-cousin of the narrator.

11. Yup'ik ceremonies were held mostly in the winter and usually in the evening. The following passage from Mircea Eliade's classic study on shamanism may provide an explanation:

> The peoples of North Asia conceive the otherworld as an inverted image of this world. Everything takes place as it does here, but in the reverse. When it is day on earth, it is night in the beyond (this is why festivals of the dead are held after sunset; that is when they wake and begin their day); the summer of the living corresponds to the winter in the land of the dead; a scarcity of game or fish on earth means that it is plentiful in the otherworld; and so forth. (Eliade 1964: 205).

As this suggests, there is are tantalizing correspondences among the cosmologies of the various mythological systems of the world. For example, in Dante Alighieri's

Inferno, the poet and the psychopomp Virgil leave Judecca by scaling down the massive bulk of Lucifer, who is frozen to the waist in a field of ice at the very center of the pit of Hell. When they emerge, they surface into the daylight of the opposite hemisphere at the foot of Mount Purgatory—twelve hours later! The presence of certain shared topographical and mythic features (the infernal rivers with their origins in the upper world, the figure of the infernal dog, the razor bridge which the hero must traverse) in mythological systems as distinct and separate as the pan-Eskimoan and Greco-Roman systems is striking.

12. According to Ann Fienup-Riordan, the ceremony of *Aaniq* introduced the Bladder Festival. Men, termed "mothers," went about the village, leading a group of boys whom they termed their "dogs," returning last year's bowls to the houses and bringing back to the *qasgiq* newly made bowls filled with *akutaq* (Fienup-Riordan 1994: 275-279). This was one of the few times when the children were allowed to be rowdy in the presence of elders. They grabbed at the food in the bowls without permission, like dogs. It was one of those crucial moments that she speaks of in her provocative analysis of Yup'ik ceremonials, a time of reversals, when acceptable roles and behaviors were flip-flopped, when boundaries were dissolved and passages were opened, and the spirits entered and mingled with humankind. Throngs of rowdy children portended the approach of the spirits.

13. *Arnaucuaq* was born in 1917 and raised in *Kayalivik*, a small community, now abandoned, just north of *Qaluyaaq*. He has mentioned elsewhere that he witnessed the *Nakaciuryaraq* twice. In his recounting of the events of the festival, he mentions that he was one of the "dogs" in the ceremony of *Aaniq*. This would indicate that he was a young boy at the time.

Many of his references, like the one above, are cryptic, as is the case with many other elders who have recounted their experiences of now defunct traditional ceremonials. Often we, the translators, are at a loss as to what they are talking about. Our audience and readers have had little experience of the events the narrators are relating, since few of the Yupiit living today have ever observed the events they are describing. In some cases we suspect the narrators themselves were too young to have been able to fully appreciate the significance of the ceremonies they witnessed. Most certainly the generation of elders alive today who observed the traditional ceremonies like *Nakaciuryaraq* did so not as organizers, celebrants and tradition bearers, but as youthful onlookers and occasional participants. In this and the following two stanzas, we believe that he is referring to particular dances associated with the ceremony.

14. They hold the hems of their *qaspeq*s, forming a cup in the skirt. They sway slowly and rhythmically from side to side, bending at the knees with the feet stationary and the upper body rocking. The symbolism of this movement is not understood. We know that in the act of creation, both on *Qaluyaaq* and on *Nunivaar*, a woman, who is either Raven's daughter or the sky woman, holds soil in the cup of her skirt, which she casts forth and which forms itself into land.

15. See the note on *Aaniq* above.

16. In late March, April and early May the pack ice breaks up, allowing the hunters to venture out into the ocean to hunt for seal. Seals congregate in the

shelter of the pack ice and, particularly *tungunquq* 'bearded seals,' are most plentiful at this time; by mid-May the broken ice pack is receding northward and seals are scarcer, although the large herring runs in late May or early June attract the species of smaller seals, which become temporarily abundant.

Tan'gurraam Anguyavkanrilla — The Boy Who Made Peace
Pages 354-383

a. Una aũg'allruarput ellminek kitugcan:
Pikna-llu kangra
mingunaku
una-llu acia uitermek.
Aa!
b. Taillruuq qaneryaramek uumek 'cali'. 'I'-aaq aũg'allruuq 'l'-aaq-llu erinaunani.

1. When using demonstrative pronouns and adverbs, which are systematically complex in Yup'ik, the *Kuigpagmiut* 'Yukon dwellers,' the *Qissunamiut* 'Chevak dwellers' and the *Naparyaarmiut* 'Hooper Bay dwellers' are *Qagkumiut* (<*qagku-* and -*miu* 'dweller of') or *qagaa-i* (<*qagaa* and -*i* 'deictic') from the perspective of the *Qaluyaarmiut* 'Nelson Island dwellers'; that is, they are the 'ones outside (extended)' or 'outside.' The *Caninermiut*, the coastal dwellers on the plain south of *Qaluyaaq* 'Nelson Island' and north of the mouth of the *Kusquqvak* 'Kuskokwim River' are (again from the perspective of the *Qaluyaarmiut*) *unegkumiut* 'the ones downriver, toward the sea, or toward the exit (extended),' or *unkumiut* the ones down toward the river, down below (extended).' The *Kusquqvagmiut* 'Kuskokwim dwellers' are *Qaũgkumiut* 'the ones inside, inland, or upriver (extended),' or *qamkumiut* 'the ones inside, inland, or upriver (obscured).' This latter, *Qamkumiut*, is usually in reference to the bounded area of *Mamterilleq* 'Bethel.' The *Nunivaarmiut* 'Nunivak Island dwellers' are *camkumiut* 'the ones down toward the river (or ocean), or down below (obscured).' This, of course, all changes with a shift in perspective; the *Mamterillermiut* 'Bethel dwellers' refer to the *Qaluyaarmiut* as *unegkumiut* 'the ones downriver, toward the sea, or toward the exit (obscured),' and the *Nunivaarmiut* refer to the *Qaluyaarmiut* as *paũgkumiut* 'the ones up, back away from the river, or behind (extended).' For the most part, when using the extended demonstrative term (that is, something which is long or of large extent), people are referring to a very generalized area; when using the obscured demonstrative term (that is, something which is stationary, indistinct, or out of sight), they are referring to something which is bounded but out of sight, for instance, *Mamterilleq* 'Bethel' or *Nunivaaq* 'Nunivak Island.' Although it is grammatically permissible, for instance, to refer to the *Nunivaarmiut* as *kankumiut* 'the ones down toward the river (or ocean), or down below (restricted),' or to the *Caninermiut* as *camkumiut* 'the ones down toward the river, or down below (obscured),' terms of these sort are rare. When using the demonstratives to refer to people or regions, there is a tendency to use these terms only in reference to entities that are somewhat unbounded in area, or to entities that, when bounded, are obscured. The use

of the restricted term, for instance *kankumiut* for the island or a village of *Nunivaarmiut*, would imply that it was visible.

2. They felt and pinched his flesh to see if he were hale and hearty.

3. The reaction of Yup'ik readers and audience is one of shock and horror that anyone could be so cruel.

4. In narration, a character's state of awareness is sometimes mentioned. *Ellangelleq* 'awareness' is awareness of existence, consciousness of a world process going on about one. It refers to a child's first conscious memories, perhaps somewhere between the ages of three and five. *Usvinglleq* 'sense, understanding' seems to indicate a later stage of development, a consciousness of one's self existing in an intelligible world of meanings and relationships. Eliza Orr believes this corresponds to a later stage, perhaps five or older.

5. He means that they don't learn things right away, that it takes time for them to learn how to do things.

6. He refers to the Tununak Catholic Church. At the front of the church, to the left of the sanctuary, is a small shelf set at about eye level. On permanent display on the shelf is a small ceremonial drum and a wooden staff with feathers set around it. The drum is about half the size of a standard drum but other than that is typical of Yup'ik drums, that is it is a shallow hooped rim with a nylon head stretched over the hoop. The staff, which is set beside it, is cylindrical, roughly two and a half inches in diameter, and it is 19 inches long. About a third of it is colored a rust orange from the local red ochre dye. It has nine small tapped holes into which white owl feathers have been set in clusters of three, like branches coming off an evergreen. It is referred to locally as the "peace drum." According to Mike Angaiak, the feathers symbolize animals and flesh which are shared in feasting, and as the story makes clear, the red is blood spilled in war, and the white symbolizes winter.

It was placed there in the mid 1980s in an effort on the part of the Yup'ik deacons and the Jesuit Fathers to enculturate the church liturgy and theology. It initially occasioned some mild controversy among local parishioners, who after a hundred years of being admonished to abandon traditional beliefs, now viewed a symbol of their formerly tabooed tradition being displayed as a prominent icon in the church. Not long after the "peace drum" was put on display, during a funeral in the church, one of the relatives of the deceased requested the priest to take it down during the funeral mass because it was a symbol of shamanism and "devil worship." Nowadays the "peace drum" occasions little comment and has evidently been accepted by some as part of the church decor.

Evidently some form of this story was told in the church as an explanation for the "peace drum," although we have no knowledge of the occasion.

7. This is an idiomatic expression, meaning, "What kind of person are you, that you're not scared?" An internal organ metonymically represents moral and personal qualities, as in the English expressions, "You've got some kind of nerve!" or "He's got a lot of heart!"

8. The lower two-thirds of the staff in the "peace drum" set is the color of the natural wood, a very light spruce.

9. See Note 7 above.

Apanuugpak Anguyagmi — Apanuugpak During The War
Pages 384-403

a. Qanemcista qanaallruuq imirissuun tunulluku carraq-llu ilii tegumas-ciiganani.

b. "W", uum qaneryaram ayagnera, apertuumauq kass'allatun w-tun pivkenaku "wh". Cali igaucugngauq 'ũgayassaagaucestekaqa.'

1. *Qulvarkaq*, Bob Hooper, who is known for his sense of humor, is making a joke, playing on bases and suffixes. *Anguyagta* is a warrior or soldier (<*anguyag-* 'to wage war' and *-te-* 'one who Vs'; *anyguyaggsuun* is a weapon (<*anguyag-* and *-ssuun-* 'device for V-ing.' He implies that the three warriors are so lethal that they themselves are weapons.

2. Sharp hunting implements which might pierce the skin covering of the kayak, like arrowheads and harpoons, were stored in wooden containers. These containers were carefully carved and constructed in the *qasgiq* by the men and frequently were made to resemble game animals, like seals, or skillful predators, like wolves, which the hunter wished to emulate, and were decorated with mythological, symbolic and personal icons and scenes (Fitzhugh and Kaplan 1982: 73. 81, 172-179). They are an excellent example of traditional Yup'ik art, evidencing the painstaking craftsmanship and creativity that went into the making of even the simplest and most utilitarian items. With respect to tools, weapons, hunting implements and gear, the greatest diligence and effort must be expended to assure success in the hunt, since animals could not be expected to give themselves to a careless and indifferent hunter with poor gear and implements.

3. Despite the odds, he is confident that he will survive.

4. The narrator was confused and referred to *Panik*, but he obviously means *Apanuugpak*, so we made a substitution.

5. Yupiit have a tendency to avoid using given names. The most common naming tactic is to refer to one another by kinship terms, i.e., *ilungaqa* 'my female cross cousin,' *uyuraqa* 'my younger sibling,' *alqaqa* 'my older sister.' One may refer to another in terms of the relationship one bore to the namesake, that is, the former but now deceased bearer of the name; thus, a small child, perhaps a non-relative, may be called, for example, *maurluqa* 'my grandmother,' or *cakiqa* 'my mother-in-law,' regardless of the gender of the child, since Yup'ik names are given without respect to sex. Another tactic involves relationships in a family being generalized throughout the community; thus, it is not unusual to refer to an individual in terms of his oldest child, for example, *Cakayiim Atii* 'Cakayak's Father.' Other instances of this sort, where a family relationship name becomes a name throughout the community, are: *Ciuliq* 'foremost one,' a name given to the oldest brother by younger siblings; or *Qull'iq* 'the one on top,' given to a brother who is not the oldest, but is still the older of several brothers, or *Panik* 'daughter,' given to the first daughter. Finally, there are cases where one acquires a sobriquet or *inqun* 'baby or pet name' which simply sticks. Stress is placed on knowing and valuing one's relations, group solidarity and camaraderie being considered very important. One way to highlight and teach this value is by assuring that members of the

group know the relationship they bear to one another and use these terms in everyday address.

Where *Pangalgalria* calls *Apanuugpak* '*Tugulullraa,*' we are unable to discover any meaning of kinship relation in the name. We surmise that it is simply an *inqun*, a sobriquet of affection. Although Yup'ik names can often be analyzed, the traits of the name are not necessarily associated with the individual who was given the name. Individuals do not acquire names on the basis of deed or particular character traits. Even when names have a meaning, for example, *Atrilnguuq* 'one with no name,' or *Cingarkaq* 'one to be kissed,' it is the reference, and not the meaning of the name, that counts. In the above, *Apanuugpak*'s is purely idiosyncratic, with no other meaning; *Panik* means 'daughter,' although it is not used here as a kinship term. *Pangalgalria*, which can mean 'one who gallops or runs like a quadruped,' has a remote significance, since as the story will reveal, he is able to run in great strides. Further on in the text we will encounter a character named *Ukinqucugpalek* 'one with a great hole (in the prow of his kayak)'; this name as well has significance. But these correspondences between name and deed and character are the exception in everyday life.

6. See Note 4 above.

7. As the translators understand it, *Apanuugpak* and his two companions are actually further upriver, having gone past the enemy village on the riverbanks. We conjecture that they may have gone around a bend of the river and therefore are shielded from the current of the incoming tide. When the tide is rising, the current of coastal rivers flows upstream with the incoming tide. Thus, *Apanuugpak* and his companions, although upriver from their enemies, have the tidal current coming against them, although they may be in the lee of the current because of the projecting land at the bend of the river. The enemy, on the other hand, are downriver and have the current at their backs, carrying them closer and closer to *Apanuugpak* and his companions, whom they avoid encountering by periodically paddling backward against the current.

8. Compare this with the account of the same character in *Paningayak*'s, Medina Flynn's *Apanuugpak*. Both *Paningayak* and *Qulvarkaq* are recounting essentially the same episode in the adventures of *Apanuugpak*, namely the time when he is blockaded by an overwhelmingly superior enemy force and uses his great voice to scatter them. Yet the two versions differ, not only in perspective and in the relative weight given to certain details of the respective narratives, but also in regard to the events themselves, for example, with respect to the character *Ukinqucugpalek*.

9. *Ukinqucugpalek* means 'the one having a large hole (in the prow of his kayak).' See Note 5 above on naming. The style of kayak used by the Central Yup'ik south of Norton Sound had a hole fashioned in the prow for handling and hauling it onto the ice. Kayaks were custom-fitted, using the owner's body measurements. According to Curtis, the size of a kayak on *Nunivaaq* 'Nunivak Island' was determined by some of the following measurements: little finger to elbow, first finger of right hand to thumb of left when arms are outstretched, the width of first and second fingers held together. He states that the measurement of a typical *Nunivaar* kayak showed a length of fifteen feet, a beam of three, and a manhole

thirty inches in diameter (Curtis 1930: 13). Thus, the fact that an entire young bearded seal skin was used to cover the prow section of his kayak would indicate that he was a very big man.

10. Dog fur had the reputation of being very warm and functional and was used in making traditional clothing. Nowadays nobody uses dog fur and it would be considered gauche to wear dog fur clothing.

11. 'one who gallops or runs like a quadruped.' See Note 5.

12. A pale, almost whitish, tan without spots or discoloration would be the color of a newly bleached and dried *amirkaq* 'young bearded seal' skin, which is generally used to cover kayak frames.

13. He feigns modesty. As a legendary warrior, he had done many things that were worthy of note.

Apanuugpak — Apanuugpak
Pages 404-425

a. Ciumek qanellruuq:
Aling cunawa-gguq tua tamakut
yuum ataucim
anguyiit nang'arkaa
taukuk yuug' malruk.

1. Some people drink saltwater to settle their stomachs, for example, when they are seasick. Perhaps he is nauseous from fear and drinks saltwater to settle his stomach.

2. 'one who is never obstructed or hindered'

3. Literally she says 'since he perhaps was an evil spirit.' She really means 'since he was a shaman,' or one with a familiar spirit. She is talking to high school students, and since she probably assumes they know little about shamanism and traditional religious practices, she refers to shamans in terms of a contemporary stereotype that the students would understand, that shamans, who trafficked with the devil, were devils themselves.

4. Shamans had the ability to cause a person to go underneath the ground or to go up into the air, placing them in unfamiliar surroundings. Thus, someone might go off into the wilderness, in familiar surroundings, and then suddenly become disoriented and in a highly unusual situation, such as traveling beneath the ground or being carried into the atmosphere. This was the action of a shaman who was vexing them. The implication is that *Apanuugpak* caused him to travel beneath the ground. Thus *Apanuugpak* knows all about it.

5. This is a smart rejoinder. He means that their efforts are futile, that they can't be harmed. Perhaps he is referring to a dumpsite, where the *Eqtarmiut* deposit the shells of consumed mussels. The arrows land there instead of lodging in the bodies of *Apanuugpak* and *Pangalgalria*, as intended by his enemies.

6. This exclamation actually begins with a glottal and ends with a glottal: !I!. It is a shushing utterance, meant to temporarily startle the child into silence. Many parents and adults are loathe to scold a child (perhaps because of the traditional

belief that to do so would offend the ancestral spirit of the child's namesake and thus bring sickness, misfortune or death to the name-bearer), so it is not unusual to threaten a misbehaving child with being gotten by scary outlanders, for instance: *Kaaka! Kass'at (carayiit, pulissat, etc.) piciqaatgen!* Be quiet! The white people (ghosts, the police, etc.) will get you! No one really expects that this will happen! The irony in the situation above is that *Apanuugpak* is indeed about to get them.

7. See Note 1 of "The Boy Who Made Peace" describing warfare among the Yupiit. The sneak attack described above, blocking the entrance and then raining down arrows and fire from above, was a favorite tactic. Victor Kanrilak, Jr. remembers also hearing his grandfather, Oscar Usugan, and Peter Asuluk of Toksook tell about the aftermath of an attack: the victors would leave one man alive to tell the tale of their exploits; and to be sure that there was no misunderstanding about what they could have done to the lone survivor, they would leave a mark on him, for instance, by cutting off his ear. Oswalt describes a similar occurrence in his account of the battle of Bloody Creek in the War of the Eye. The Aglurmiut planned a surprise attack on their enemies not far from the village of Old Kalskag. The enemies, however, discovered the Aglurmiut plan and cleverly ambushed them, killing all but one man, an old man of very poor eyesight who was trailing behind the main body of kayakers. When the old man asked for the way back to his village, they sliced off his ear and, throwing it in the river, told him to follow it and the current downstream (Oswalt 1990: 41).

In the context of the above, *Apanuugpak* is probably addressing the one male survivor, whom he is sparing, as well as the women and children.

8. The translators are at a loss to reconcile this account of *Ukinqucugpalek*'s demise with the account given by *Qulvarkaq*, Bob Hooper, in "*Apanuugpak* in War." According to *Qulvarkaq*, *Ukinqucugpalek* was in a swarm of kayaks which surrounded *Apanuugpak* and *Pangalgalria*. When *Ukinqucugpalek* charged, his kayak capsized and he was speared and killed under the water by *Apanuugpak*. Perhaps *Paningayak* means to say here that *Ukinqucugpalek* was killed in a previous incident.

9. 'one without a shoulder blade'

10. an old village situated between two prominent hills on the plain between *Cevvarnermiut* 'Chefornak' and *Negtemiut* 'Nightmute'

Tuqumarraarluni Utertelleq —
One Who Came Back From The Land Of The Dead
Pages 432-453

a. Ciumek qanellruuq 'aturarkain' taũgaam uumek cimillruarput 'aturarkait.'

b. Uumek line-amek ayagniumayaaquq taũgaam nugtartellruaput naaqellra asqigcarluku.

c. Ciumek: 'maavet tua-i ilaitnun.'

d. Aũg'allruarput ayagnicurlallra: 'Ellii-llu-gguq waniw' qanta...'

e. Aũg'allruarput ayagnicurlallra: 'Anngami.'

f. Aũg'allruarput ayagnicurlallra: 'iliita angalkum.'

g. Ciumek: "aatameng."

1. *Cakataar*'s story resembles in some respects a story collected by E.W. Nelson from *Negiqliq* 'Andreivsky or St. Mary's' on the Yukon. A young woman became ill and died, waking to a new presence and a strange land. She travels to the abode of the dead, where she finds her deceased grandparents. Their food and water consists of libations and offerings from their native village. When the time had come for the celebration of the Feast for the Dead, messengers were sent out from the host village to the neighboring communities with invitations. The grandparents and their granddaughter were sitting on the bench of the *qasgiq*, invisible to the living inhabitants. They follow the messengers back to the host village to participate in the feast.

From "The Land of the Dead"

As the shades of the girl and her grandparents went out of the kashim the old man gave the girl a push, which caused her to fall and lose her senses in the passageway. When she recovered she looked about and found herself alone. She arose and stood in the corner of the entrance way under a lamp burning there, and waited for the other shades to come out that she might join her companions. There she waited until all of the living people came out dressed in fine new clothing, but she saw none of her companion shades.

Soon after this an old man with a stick came hobbling into the entrance, and as he looked up he saw the shade standing in the corners with her feet raised more than a span above the floor. He asked her if she was a live person or a shade, but she did not reply, and he went hurriedly to the kashim. There he told the men to hasten out and look at the strange being standing in the passageway, whose feet did not rest on the earth and who did not belong to their village. All the men hurried out, and seeing her, some of them took down the lamp and by its light she was recognized and hurried into the house of her parents.

When the men first saw her she appeared in form and color exactly as when alive, but the moment she sat down in her father's house her color faded and she shrank away until she became nothing but skin and bone, and was too weak to speak.

Early the next morning her namesake, a woman in the same village, died, and her shade went away to the land of the dead in the girl's place, and the latter gradually became strong and again lived for many years. (Nelson 1899: 489-490)

2. In the lower village of *Tununeq* is a large wood frame building which is used as a community hall. Eskimo dances are held there and on occasion feasts for the entire community are given there as well. Sometimes a family will prepare a large feast for the community to commemorate a deceased relative. Feast foods are typically as follows: reindeer stew, fish soup, boiled seal, boiled walrus, steamed blackfish, baked and fried salmon, various kinds of dried fish, fried bread, different kinds of *akutaq* as well as soda pop and candy. The family or organization that gives the feast is responsible for supplying, cooking and serving the food. At some feasts large amounts of food, dried fish and even clothing are distributed to the

guests at the end of the feast. Many feasts are followed by an Eskimo dance.

3. This line actually begins the group, but we have changed the order to make it easier to understand.

4. We deleted the preceding phrase: 'And here was her bowl...'.

5. Seal blubber is cut into strips, then cross-cut with an *uluaq* 'curved woman's knife,' after which it is placed in a seal poke or a plastic bucket and placed in a cool place. Eventually the oil runs out and this is the oil which is used as a dip and a condiment for food, especially dried fish and jerked meat. The strips of blubber, or rinds, which are left behind have an aged, sharp taste and can be eaten as a condiment.

6. We deleted the preceding line: 'When she left.'

7. The Yupiit regularly take *maqiq*s 'saunas' to clean. Each extended family has an outlying house which is partitioned into two rooms; an inner room contains a semi-submerged 55-gallon drum stove covered with volcanic rocks, and an outer room is used for dressing and undressing and for cooling off. The stove room is often quite small and confined, with room for only two to four people, and is heated with a roaring wood fire. It is a dry heat, like a Finnish sauna, and the heat is often quite intense, causing the bathers to sweat profusely. When the heat becomes suffocating, they go into the dressing room, which is separated by a small door, and cool off, returning later to the stove room to sweat some more. Upon the conclusion of the sweatbath, when the fire in the stove is dying down, the bathers wash their hair and bodies in individual basins, using soap and water.

Sweatbaths are not taken just for hygienic purposes, but are occasions for socialization. Men bathe with other men and women with other women. A man and wife bathe together. On *Qaluyaaq* at least, men and women who are not married do not take sweatbaths together.

In times past, sweatbaths were communal. A great fire was started and the men and boys stripped and started to sweat. When the fire died down, the sky window was covered to keep in the heat. According to *Cuniq*, Jents Flynn, the men never bathed in urine and the women did not take steambaths but washed in urine.

8. The Yupiit, like other Eskimo people, recycle names. When someone dies, his or her name is given to a child born afterwards. Yup'ik names have no inherent gender: the name of the deceased can be passed on to either a female or a male child, regardless of the gender of the namesake. In many respects, the child is considered a reincarnation of the person who originally bore the name. For instance, he or she acquires the same kinship relations as the original name bearer (although natural kinship relations remain the same also). Thus, a male child who is named after a paternal grandmother may be called 'mother' by his father and 'younger sibling' by his grandmother's older brother. There is also a tendency to discover the traits of the original name bearer in the namesake and spiritual offspring. If the original name bearer was particularly fond of a certain food, then it is no surprise if the one named after him likes the same food.

Tengesqauktaraam Atii — The Father Of Tengesqauktar
Pages 454-467

a. Ciumek qanellruuq: Tuaten-ggem tua-i qanquatellrukiitnga, /aũg'um angutem iliini...

1. It was believed that if one spoke to the dead, one would lose the power of speech. See "*Apaqassugaq*" in *Qanemcikarluni Tekitnarqelartuq* (Orr and Orr 1995). In this episode, *Apaqassugaq* returns from the dead and appears to two men in a remote and uninhabited fishing camp; they are loathe to speak to him because of the belief that they will become mute. It is only after he reassures them, that they venture to speak with him.

2. Those who return from the dead, as well as *alangrut* 'ghosts,' are portrayed just so. Their faces are concealed or invisible, often hidden by a veil of hair or concealed in a hood and ruff. In the case of the daughter above, her eyes, the organs of sight, are removed. She is immobile, silent, and withdrawn from social contact. This metaphor of social invisibility is frequently encountered in Yup'ik ritual observance. The rules for a girl's first menstruation prescribe seclusion and social invisibility. She lives apart from the family, goes about silent, hooded and belted, avoids all eye contact with others, and eats only certain foods. This lasts for five days. The rites of mourning are similar. The family avoids social contact for five days, refrains from work, and eats only certain foods. They too go about hooded and belted, as though they were invisible. As Ann Fienup-Riordan writes, these are crucial moments, when the passages between the worlds are opened, and the traditional boundaries and passages must be observed, not only to preserve the distinction of separate realms but also to clear desirable pathways of contact and communication between the realms (Fienup-Riordan 1994).

3. It was believed that contact with ghosts could cause sickness and even death unless certain precautions were observed.

Arnaq Irniani-llu — Mother And Her Child
Pages 474-503

1. He means a story frame of the sort that often introduces a *quliraq* (e.g., Once upon a time there was this village which was situated along the banks of a river, and on the other side there was a great hunter...)

2. She was buried in the traditional manner, in a grave box above ground.

3. A *qamigaun*, which is a small sled carried on a kayak, used to transport the kayak when one reaches stretches of ice on the water.

4. A ghost cannot cross a line which was drawn in the snow with a steel knife. See "*Saaniigem Alangrua* 'The Teakettle Ghost'" (Tennant and Bitar 1981: 6-13).

5. That is, cutting a line in the snow.

6. He is indicating that her upper torso was showing.

7. The shamans are seated back toward the wall. The people would choose them one at a time and drag them down towards the center. But being afraid of the ghost, they would just run back to their seats. This motif in which the humble and despised man surpasses the proud and powerful is recurrent in Yup'ik stories.

8. She is emerging out of the underground entrance into the *qasgiq*. Only her upper torso is above floor level. When she raises her foot to step onto the floor, her foot passes through the planking as though either she or the material is insubstantial.

9. She is up flush against the door frame or floor planking, unable to find solid matter to step up onto the flooring of the *qasgiq*. He is attempting to wiggle and squeeze himself between her and the frame of the underground entrance, all the while making polite requests of her to make room for him. The fit is tight on both sides. However, he must squeeze in there in order to face her directly.

10. He is referring to his familiar spirits.

11. The base is *qame-* 'to die down, be extinguished,' but the sense is to descend slowly into the ground, which is the way ghosts are traditionally exorcised.

12. The narrator is making a drumming noise against the microphone.

13. This, as well as other stories, is told with a group of elders present. He is inviting *Macian*, Mathias James, to come to the microphone.

14. He is either a son-in-law or a brother-in-law.

15. He is referring to the two young men who were fleeing from the ghost.

16. He is trying to imitate the Chevak-Hooper Bay dialect since the in-law is from *Qissunaq*. On *Qaluyaaq* they would say *ayautnaamken* 'let me take you away,' but in *Qissunaq*, although they would say *ayautnaumken,* they have "compression." So *Macian* applies compression to the *Qaluyaaq* form and says '*ayautnamken.*'

17. Finding an idiomatic English equivalent of *pellugyartuutelliniluku* is difficult. Literally, it means 'he brought her to pass or disappear.' The notion here is that he and his familiar spirits are casting her back to the nether region of ghosts, forcibly bringing her through the solid ground into this region.

Tengesqauktar — Tengesqauktar
Pages 504-525

a. Ciumek qanelllruuq 'pingacugataqa' tau͡gaam uumek cimillruaput 'piciqngataqa'.

b. Ciumek qanelllruuq 'alingcetaartellregni' tau͡ggaam uumek cimillruaput 'alingcetaartellerka'.

c. Ciumek qanelllruuq 'tautnalliniaqekegket' tau͡gaam uumek cimillruaput 'tuatnalliniaqekek'.

1. He is speaking of Pauline Tom, a high school student in his audience.

2. This is an idiom. Literally, it means "his mind got better." The *Yupiit* believe that thoughts are powerful and can affect other people and our relationships with them. People are advised to think well of others and that in so doing they will be able to improve the actual situation. Avoidance is the preferred method of dealing with interpersonal conflict. Confrontation, frankness and openness in conflict resolution are discouraged. People are advised to overlook situations that may lead to conflict. When asked for an explanation, people refer to the New Testament in which Christians are urged to love and pray for their enemies. In a small, close-knit community it is dangerous to succumb to negative and venomous relationships.

3. Literally: "That's what we people do."

Illugngali — Illugngali
Pages 526-545

1. *Asrir-* can mean variously 'naughty, mischievous.' In regard to a child, it refers to someone who does bad things such as breaking things or tormenting other children. It can also mean an adult who is not afraid of anything, who is not loathe to hurt people or engage in daring, heedless actions. The implication is that the person who is *asrir-* shows a disregard for rules, conventions and the sensibilities of others. The range of connotations goes beyond just 'naughty' or 'mischievous.' In some cases we use 'naughty' or 'mischievous,' but in others we use 'reckless,' 'bold' or 'audacious.'

2. Storytellers have markedly different styles. Some, like *Tumailnguq*, Dick Lincoln, or *Arnaucauq*, Mike Angaiak, rely on verbal depiction, using words and descriptions to contextualize the action. Others, like *Cakataar*, Jack Angaiak, and *Ussugan*, Oscar Usugan, depend on gesture and non-verbal expression to depict the narrative. In the latter case, although the narrator's intentions are clear to the participating audience, it is often difficult to make participant reference and authorial intentions evident in the printed text alone. Therefore, explanatory notes become necessary. The reader should try to visualize body language, voice, and facial expression in the telling of this story. It is helpful to note that this story was perceived by the audience as being highly amusing; both the narrator and the audience laughed throughout the narration. In this passage, the wife of *Illugngali* is warning her two children not to tell their father about the haunting. She is aware of his impulsive nature and wants to avoid a commotion.

3. He is indicating the present cemetery in *Tununeq*, where the dead are interred in the ground, usually with white wooden crosses and brass name plates to identify the deceased.

4. Participant reference here is confusing. It would seem that the parents are scolding the tale-telling child for having told *Illugngali* about the haunting. It must be remembered that in the context of this story ghosts and spirits are extremely dangerous and *Illugngali*'s behavior is viewed as recklessness.

5. A consequence of contact with the dead is ritual pollution, which is made manifest in physical sickness or death.

6. He is indicating *Illugngali*, that is, his place of burial.

7. In the Yup'ik cosmography, the spirit or ghost who is exorcised by the shaman is confined to a dark, gloomy place beneath the ground, an underworld with hardly any head space. The wind blows fiercely and big chunks of flat rock are flying in the wind. Therefore, *iivkar-* 'to conceal' connotes exorcism, of casting the spirit into the limbo of ghosts and spirits. The exorcist does this by placing the palm of his hand on the crown of the ghost's head and resting it there. Gradually the spirit descends through the swirling eddy of matter that engulfs his feet. Should the exorcist press too hard, the spirit, like a hydraulic, will spring up again.

8. The Bering Sea coast of Nelson Island features a line of low-lying mountains which form rocky cliffs along the shore. In many places tidal action has formed very shallow cave-like indentations. They are pursuing an enemy who places himself in one of these indentations.

Callartellria Angun — The Scabby Man
Pages 546-573
  a. wall'u: elatii

1. This story was transcribed from a cassette tape which was stored in the library of the Paul T. Albert Memorial School. The original narrative performance occurred sometime between 1979 and 1982. Jack Angaiak was telling the story to an audience of high school students. The recording begins with group 3; the short introductory section was unfortunately missing from the original recording. When we transcribed the recording in February, 1994, we asked Jack Angaiak about the introduction and he supplied us with groups 1 and 2, which according to Jack is the proper introduction. It should therefore be noted that the introductory section, groups 1 and 2, and the rest of the story, beginning with group 3, constitute two separate narrative performances.

2. There is a change of subject and scene here. The principal actor in groups 1 and 2 is a man who intends to curse and kill his opponent, *Callartellria*. The family refers to his wife and daughter. The subject of group 3 is *Callartellria*, the scabby shaman, who is the intended victim. He is sitting overlooking a river, watching unsuspectingly the approach of his antagonist. There is a great deal of narrative compression in the first three groups and the reader must understand that much has occurred in leading up to the main narrative events, which begin in group 3.

3. Three-hole kayaks are unusual; *Yupiit* ordinarily had kayaks with one hole. However, larger kayaks were known to be used in the Aleutians and southward.

4. Being a shaman, he separates his soul substance or inner essence from his diseased exterior, and leaving the latter outside, he enters the *qasgiq*. The word *qantarkuq* has no direct equivalent in English; it seems to correspond roughly with the physical dimension of life (in contrast to *ella-* 'consciousness'). Thus, as it was explained to the translators, when at the moment of death the consciousness departs the physical body, it is able to observe the *qantarkuq* from an external vantage point. People explained it using the synonym *yuuciq* 'life' or *ayuquciq* 'appearance.' However, viewing the matter in terms of the mind-body dichotomy may be somewhat inappropriate since we do not pretend to fully understand the Yup'ik cosmological and anthropological system. Our translation, 'bodily raiment' is highly tentative. Eliza Orr, the Yup'ik translator, believes that in the story he means by *qantarkuq* his outer shell, his skin, the sore-infested exterior of his body.

5. Going by the text alone, this passage is difficult to comprehend since he is depending on gesture and context to convey the action. Eliza Orr, who was present during one of the dramatic recitals of this story, describes it thus: The grave boxes containing the dead are filing into the *qasgiq*, filling up the space along the walls, from the back to the front, first one semi-circle of the *qasgiq* and then the other.

6. The scabby shaman is being licked by one of the dead, who is the materialization of the voice.

7. When asked for an explanation by the translators, Jack Angaiak said that these existed before his time.

8. She removed the skin of a young bearded seal whole, without splitting or

cutting it, and soaked it to make it soft and pliable. Then she sewed up all the apertures, constructing an airtight poke, and stuffed it with beluga *mangtaq*, that is, slices of layered whale fat and skin. The *mangtaq* is preserved in its own oil, although a slow aging process occurs, thus preparing a special delicacy.

9. He is going back to the village where he obtained his clothes.

10. That is, his beluga *mangtaq* in the seal polk.

Angutet Pingayun — Three Men
Pages 574-593

a. Ciumek qanellruuq 'yuk imna/ angun' taŋgaam uumek cimillruaput 'yuut imkut/ angutet'.

1. He is peering in from the sky window, which is dead center and directly above the fire pit and underground tunnel entrance. It was usually covered with a membrane of translucent seal gut. In this instance, the window structure was there, but there was no seal gut covering. A series of beings with different colored faces, who in this version of the story, are identified as being primarily human, peer down from the sky window. In another version we have collected from the same narrator, these beings are identified as being primarily geese, a different color for each species: the white-faced one is a *nacaullek*, an emperor goose (*Philacte canagica*); the blue-faced one is a *tuutangayak*, a Canada goose (*Branta canadensis*); and the black-faced one is a *neqlernaq*, a black brant goose (Branta nigricans).

2. The words in the brackets were added later by *Cuniq* and were not part of his original narration. Perhaps this is its *yua* 'its person,' its presiding spirit. Yup'ik masks often portrayed a face contained within a larger figure. For example, a well-known mask in the Edward William Nelson Bering Sea Eskimo ethnology collection of the National Museum of Natural History shows the upper half of a sea parrot's (*Mormon arctica*) body as it would appear when swimming on the water. The mask is surrounded by an aura of symbolic appendages, i.e., paddle-like bird wings; extended thumbless hands, palms pierced with a hole; halo-like reindeer neck fur; all of which have iconographic significance (i.e., the impaired grasp of the numinous spirit, permitting the passage of game; the *ella*, or universe, in which all beings are embedded). In the center of the mask is an art nouveau face of the *yua*, or what Nelson calls its *inua*, that numinous aspect of the visible being which is revealed to the spiritually discerning.

Another illustration is found in the domain of myth. Raven, for instance, has the unique ability to appear under different forms. At times he appears as a bird; but if he chooses to, he may simply lift back his beak, like the visor of a cap, in which case the *yua* of a man is dominant, and he takes on a human form. When an animal character which by its unusual behavior is clearly not a mere animal appears to a person in a story, it calls to him on his departure, *"Yuuyuksuarpenga, kingyaqia!* Lest you think I'm a person, as you go, glance back at me!" thereby calling to him to verify that although it talks and has supernatural abilities, it has indeed the form of an animal.

3. Probably because the water is salty and not potable.

References

Albert, Mike. 1981. *"Assilria Angalkuq Anngamaciq:* The Good Shaman, Angamachik." In *Yup'ik Lore: Oral Traditions of an Eskimo People*, edited by Edward A. Tennant and Joseph N. Bitar. Bethel: Lower Kuskokwim School District.

Attla, Catherine. 1983. *As My Grandfather Told It: Traditional Stories from the Koyukuk*. Fairbanks: Yukon-Koyukuk School District and Alaska Native Language Center.

Balikci, Asen. 1970. *The Netsilik Eskimo*. Garden City, N.Y.: Natural History Press.

Barnum, Francis, S.J.. 1901. *Grammatical Fundamentals of the Innuit Language as Spoken by the Eskimos of the Western Coast of Alaska*. Boston: Athenaeum Press.

Bascom, William. 1984. "The Forms of Folklore." In *Sacred Narrative: readings in the theory of myth*, edited by Alan Dundes. Berkeley: University of California Press.

Bettelheim, Bruno. 1975. *The Uses of Enchantment*. New York: Random House.

Bierhorst, John, ed. 1970. *The Ring in the Prairie: A Shawnee Legend*. New York: Dial Press.

Black, Mary. 1981. *"Piciuvkenani Uingulleq:* The Unfaithful Husband." In *Yup'ik Lore: Oral Traditions of an Eskimo People*, edited by Edward A. Tennant and Joseph N. Bitar. Bethel: Lower Kuskokwim School District.

Boas, Franz. 1888. "The Central Eskimo." *Sixth Annual Report of the Bureau of Ethnology to the Secretary of the Smithsonian Institution 1884-85*. Washington, D.C. Reprint, Lincoln: University of Nebraska Press.

———. 1901-7. *The Eskimo of Baffin Land and Hudson Bay, I-II*. Bulletin of the American Museum of Natural History 15.

Carter, Minnie. 1981. *"Saaniigem Alangrua:* The Teakettle Ghost." In *Yup'ik Lore: Oral Traditions of an Eskimo People*, edited by Edward A. Tennant and Joseph N. Bitar. Bethel: Lower Kuskokwim School District.

Curtis, Edward S. [1930] 1970. *The North American Indian, Being a Series of Volumes Picturing and Describing the Indians of the United States, the Dominion of Canada, and Alaska*, vol. 20. Reprint, New York: Johnson Reprint.

Degh, Linda, and Andrew Vazsonyi. 1976. "Legend and Belief." In *Folklore Genres*, edited by Dan Ben-Amos. Austin and London: University of Texas Press.

Dundes, Alan, 1984. Introduction to *Sacred Narrative: readings in the theory of myth*. Edited by Alan Dundes. Berkeley: University of California Press.

Eliade, Mircea. 1964. *Shamanism: Archaic Techniques of Ecstasy*. Translated by Williard R. Trask. Bollingen Series LXXVI. Princeton: Princeton University Press.

———. 1967. *From Primitives to Zen*. New York: Harper and Row

Fienup-Riordan, Ann. 1983. *The Nelson Island Eskimo: Social Structure and Ritual Distribution*. Anchorage: Alaska Pacific University Press.

———. 1994. *Boundaries and Passages: Rule and Ritual in Yup'ik Eskimo Oral Tradition*. Norman and London: University of Oklahoma Press.

———. 1996. *The Living Tradition of Yup'ik Masks: Agayuliyararput Our Way of Making Prayer.* Translations by Marie Meade. Seattle and London: University of Washington Press.

Fitzhugh, William W., and Aron Crowell, eds. 1988. *Crossroads of Continents: Cultures of Siberia and Alaska*. Washington, D.C.: Smithsonian Institution Press.

Fitzhugh, William W., and Susan A. Kaplan. 1982. *Inua: Spirit World of the Bering Sea Eskimo*. Washington, D.C.: Smithsonian Institution Press.

Fortescue, Michael, Steven Jacobson, and Lawrence Kaplan, comps. 1994. *Comparative Eskimo Dictionary*. Fairbanks: Alaska Native Language Center.

Frazer, James George. 1922. *The Golden Bough: a Study in Magic and Religion*. New York: Macmillan.

Freuchen, Peter. 1931. *Eskimo*. New York: Grosset and Dunlap.

Goble, Paul. 1984. *Buffalo Woman*. Scarsdale, N.Y.: Bradbury Press.

Hawkes, Ernest William. 1916. *The Labrador Eskimo*. Washington, D.C.: U.S. Government Printing Office.

Hymes, Dell. 1981. *"In vain I tried to tell you": Essays in Native American Ethnopoetics*. Philadelphia: University of Pennsylvania Press.

Jacobson, Steven A., comp. 1984. *Yup'ik Eskimo Dictionary*. Fairbanks: Alaska Native Language Center.

———. 1995. *A Practical Grammar of the Central Alaskan Yup'ik Eskimo Language*. Fairbanks: Alaska Native Language Center.

John, Michael. 1981. *"Inerquusngalria Ingriq:* The Forbidden Mountain." In *Yup'ik Lore: Oral Traditions of an Eskimo People,* edited by Edward A. Tennant and Joseph N. Bitar. Bethel: Lower Kuskokwim School District.

Krauss, Michael E., ed. 1982. *In Honor of Eyak: The Art of Anna Nelson Harry.* Fairbanks: Alaska Native Language Center.

Lantis, Margaret. 1946. "The Social Culture of the Nunivak Eskimo." *Transactions of the American Philosophical Society* (Philadelphia) 35:153-323.

———. 1947. *Alaskan Eskimo Ceremonialism.* American Ethnological Society, Monograph 11. Seattle: University of Washington Press.

———. 1950. "The Religion of the Eskimos." In *Forgotten Religions,* edited by Vergilius Ferm. Philadelphia: Philosophical Library.

———. 1960. *Eskimo Childhood and Interpersonal Relations: Nunivak Biographies and Geneologies.* American Ethnological Society, Monograph 53. Seattle: University of Washington Press.

Lévi-Strauss, Claude. 1969. *The Raw and the Cooked.* Translated by John and Doreen Weightman. Chicago: University of Chicago Press.

Lüthi, Max. 1976. "Aspects of the *Märchen* and the Legend." In *Folklore Genres,* edited by Dan Ben-Amos. Austin and London: University of Texas Press.

Meade, Marie, trans., and Ann Fienup-Riordan, ed. 1996. *Agayuliyararput: Kegginaqut, Kangiit-llu Our Way of Making Prayer: Yup'ik Masks and the Stories They Tell.* Seattle and London: Anchorage Museum of History and Art and University of Washington Press.

Michael, Henry N., ed. 1967. *Lieutenant Zogoskin's Travels in Russian America, 1842-1844.* Arctic Institute of North America. Anthropology of the North, Translations from Russian Sources, No. 7. Toronto, Ontario: University of Toronto Press.

Nelson, Edward William. [1899] 1983. *The Eskimo about Bering Strait.* Bureau of American Ethnology Annual Report for 1896-97, vol. 18, pt. 1. Washington, D.C.: Smithsonian Institution Press. Reprint.

Nichols, Marie. 1981. *"Yupiit Nallunrilutait:* Yup'ik Homespun Wisdom." In *Yup'ik Lore: Oral Traditions of an Eskimo People,* edited by Edward A. Tennant and Joseph N. Bitar. Bethel: Lower Kuskokwim School.

Nungak, Zebedee and Eugene Arima. 1969. *Unikkaatuat sanaugarngnik atyingualiit Puvirngniturngmit: Eskimo stories from Povungnituk, Quebec, illustrated in soapstone carvings.* The National Museums of Canada, bulletin no. 235, anthropological series no. 90. Ottawa: Naval Archive Research Laboratory.

Orr, Eliza Cingarkaq, and Ben Orr. 1995. *Qanemcikarluni Tekitnarqelartuq: One Must Arrive with a Story To Tell.* Fairbanks: Alaska Native Language Center and Lower Kuskokwim School District.

Oswalt, Wendell H. 1979. *Eskimos and Explorers.* Novato, Calif.: Chandler & Sharp.

———. 1990. *Bashful No Longer. An Alaskan Eskimo Ethnohistory, 1778-1988.* Norman: University of Oklahoma Press.

Pleasant, Charlie. 1981a. *"Ciuqliq Yupiit Anguyallrat:* The First Eskimo War." In *Yup'ik Lore: Oral Traditions of an Eskimo People*, edited by Edward A. Tennant and Joseph N. Bitar. Bethel: Lower Kuskokwim School District.

———. 1981b. *"Kusquqvagmi Callullrat:* Ambush on the Kuskokwim." In *Yup'ik Lore: Oral Traditions of an Eskimo People*, edited by Edward A. Tennant and Joseph N. Bitar. Bethel: Lower Kuskokwim School District.

Rank, Otto, Lord Raglan, and Alan Dundes. 1960. *In Quest of the Hero.* Princeton: Princeton University Press.

Rasmussen, Knud. 1929. "Intellectual Culture of the Iglulik Eskimos." *Report of the Fifth Thule Expedition 1921-24*, vol. 7, no. 1. Copenhagen: Gyldendalske Boghandel, Nordisk Forlog. Reprint, New York: AMS Press.

Reed, Irene, Osahito Miyaoka, Steven Jacobson, Pascal Afcan, and Michael Krauss. 1977. *Yup'ik Eskimo Grammar.* Fairbanks: Alaska Native Language Center.

Rink, Henrik. 1875. *Tales and Traditions of the Eskimo.* Montreal: McGill-Queen's University Press.

Serov, Sergei Ia. 1988. "Guardians and Spirit-Masters of Siberia." In *Crossroads of Continents: Cultures of Siberia and Alaska*, edited by William W. Fitzhugh and Aron Crowell. Washington, D.C.: Smithsonian Institution Press.

Tedlock, Dennis. 1983. *The Spoken Word and the Work of Interpretation.* Philadelphia: University of Pennsylvania Press.

Tennant, Edward A., and Joseph N. Bitar, eds. 1981. *Yuut Qanemciit: Yupik Lore.* Bethel: Lower Kuskokwim School District.

Woodbury, Anthony C. 1984. *Cev'armiut Qanemciit Qulirait-llu: Eskimo Narratives and Tales from Chevak, Alaska.* Fairbanks: Alaska Native Language Center.

———. 1987. "Rhetorical Structure in a Central Alaskan Yup'ik Eskimo Traditional Narrative." In *Native American discourse: poetics and rhetoric*, edited by Joel Sherzer and Anthony Woodbury. Cambridge: Cambridge University Press.

Appendix

Glossary of Italicized Exclamations in the Stories

ai-i! — what? hey! (used to question or when something said is not heard).

aa! — oh! (used when the narrator interjects informations into the story which he forgot to include).

aling! — oh my! (used when one is afraid or surprised).

aren! — *alingnaqvaa!* how very frightening or surprising! oh dear! oh my! (used to express exasperation or surprise).

arenqia! — oops! oh! oh no! *(aren* is the short form of this).

atam! —notice! look!

arenqiapaa! — too bad! (with the implication that it is too bad that things are that way, but there is nothing that can be done about it).

aullut'ar! — be careful! watch out! (an expression of exasperation when something unpleasant is occurring).

eqnarivakar! — how infuriating!

i! — shush! (a shushing utterance meant to temporarily startle the child into silence; the vowel is preceded and ended with a glottal stop, which cannot be written in the Yup'ik orthography).

kitaki! — please! well then!

waqaa! — hello! what's this? (a greeting upon encounter, often inviting a response, that is, one's reason for coming).

Some Character Types in the Framed *Qulirat*

angulvakayall'er — an extremely huge man (in reference to an adversary).

anuurluq — grandmother.

elliraaraurluq — a poor orphan (usually the protagonist in the stories).

maurluq — grandmother.

nasaurluq — young, unmarried girl.

nukalpiaq — an accomplished hunter.

nukalpiartaq — a great hunter.

nukalpiartayagaq — a young hunter (usually the son of the great hunter).

nukasegauciq — a less proficient hunter (said in reference to a hunter who does not excel to the same extent as the great hunter).

tutgara'urluq — grandchild.

uilingiataq — woman without a husband.